STUDIES IN IMPERIALISM

general editors John M. MacKenzie and Andrew S. Thompson

When the 'Studies in Imperialism' series was founded more than twenty-five years ago, emphasis was laid upon the conviction that 'imperialism as a cultural phenomenon had as significant an effect on the dominant as on the subordinate societies'. With more than ninety books published, this remains the prime concern of the series. Cross-disciplinary work has indeed appeared covering the full spectrum of cultural phenomena, as well as examining aspects of gender and sex, frontiers and law, science and the environment, language and literature, migration and patriotic societies, and much else. Moreover, the series has always wished to present comparative work on European and American imperialism, and particularly welcomes the submission of books in these areas. The fascination with imperialism, in all its aspects, shows no sign of abating, and this series will continue to lead the way in encouraging the widest possible range of studies in the field. 'Studies in Imperialism' is fully organic in its development, always seeking to be at the cutting edge, responding to the latest interests of scholars and the needs of this ever-expanding area of scholarship.

We are no longer in France

Manchester University Press

SELECTED TITLES AVAILABLE IN THE SERIES

THE FRENCH EMPIRE AT WAR, 1940–1945
Martin Thomas

THE FRENCH EMPIRE BETWEEN THE WARS:
Imperialism, politics and society
Martin Thomas

EUROPEAN EMPIRES AND THE PEOPLE:
Popular responses to imperialism in France, Britain, the Netherlands, Belgium, Germany and Italy
Ed. John M. MacKenzie

HEROIC IMPERIALISTS IN AFRICA:
The promotion of British and French colonial heroes, 1870–1939
Berny Sèbe

LABOUR AND POLITICS OF EMPIRE:
Britain and Australia 1900 to the present
Neville Kirk

We are no longer in France
COMMUNISTS IN COLONIAL ALGERIA

Allison Drew

MANCHESTER UNIVERSITY PRESS

Copyright © Allison Drew 2014

The right of Allison Drew to be identified as the author of this work has been asserted by her in accordance with the Copyright, Designs and Patents Act 1988.

Published by Manchester University Press
Altrincham Street, Manchester M1 7JA, UK
www.manchesteruniversitypress.co.uk

British Library Cataloguing-in-Publication Data is available

Library of Congress Cataloging-in-Publication Data is available

ISBN 978 1 5261 0675 9 *paperback*

First published by Manchester University Press in hardback 2014

This edition first published 2017

The publisher has no responsibility for the persistence or accuracy of URLs for any external or third-party internet websites referred to in this book, and does not guarantee that any content on such websites is, or will remain, accurate or appropriate.

Printed by Lightning Source

In memory of two remarkable men—

My beloved Neville Alexander
who learned about the Algerian struggle
as a student at the University of Tübingen

&

Henri Alleg
for his encouragement of this project

CONTENTS

List of tables—viii
General editor's introduction—ix
Acknowledgements—xi
List of abbreviations—xiii
Map—xv

	Introduction—Imagining socialism and communism in Algeria	1
1	The land and its conquest	11
2	Grappling for a communist foothold	26
3	'The mountain "was going communist"': peasant struggles on the Mitidja	56
4	'This land is not for sale': communists, nationalists and the popular front	81
5	The nation in formation: communists and nationalists during the Second World War	110
6	For an Algerian national front: unity and division in the liberation struggle	145
7	Sparking an insurrection: pressure from the countryside	180
8	'Our people will overcome': to the cities and the prisons	217
9	'We need a country that talks': imagining the future Algeria	252
	Conclusion—Algerian communists and the new Algeria	267

Bibliography—281
Index—298

LIST OF TABLES

1	Algerian landholdings in hectares, 1930	page 19
2	European landholdings in hectares, 1930	20
3	Departmental elections, third district (Blida): Algerian voters, 1st round, 13 August 1933	74
4	Departmental elections, third district (Blida): Algerian voters, 2nd round, 20 August 1933	74
5	European landholdings in hectares, 1950	154
6	Algerian landholdings in hectares, 1950	154
7	Ethnic profile of PCA leadership: Algerians and Europeans	158
8	Generational profile of PCA leadership: old (pre-1942) and new (post-1942) members	158
9	Comparative industrialisation, India and China	261
10	Comparative electrification, North and South Vietnam	261

GENERAL EDITOR'S INTRODUCTION

Allison Drew has produced a fine study of the communist party in Algeria that is important not only for the historiography of French decolonisation but more broadly for its contribution to our understanding of the global dynamics of decolonisation. Socialism, like humanitarianism, wrestled with the 'national' and the 'international'. Its aspiration may have been to forge a cosmopolitan community that rose above national politics and state interest. But to build a viable political organisation socialists could ill afford to ignore the local specificities and particular exigencies of the society to which they appealed. Socialism in Algeria thus developed at the intersection of three shifting forces: social class, religion and geopolitics. The predominance of the rural in Algeria operated as a major constraint on the development of communism. Religious cleavages served to reinforce divisions between settler and indigenous society. And geopolitics produced a fundamental inborn tension between those who placed greater emphasis on anti-colonialism (and communist parties championing the cause of the nationally oppressed) and those who were more concerned about the advent and spread of European fascism (and willing to moderate their anti-colonialism as a result).

Drew skilfully draws out the alternative political conceptions of Algerian communists through her analysis of the interaction between the Parti communiste français (PCF) and the Parti communiste algérien (PCA). If the PCF was predominantly European, the PCA, which prioritised the struggle against French imperialism, increasingly attracted young radicalised Algerians by its opposition to ruthless repression from the French state and by addressing the problems of poverty and social injustice. The PCA's relationship with the Front de libération nationale (FLN) is also instructive. While the former exercised some influence over the latter, the antipathy of many of the FLN's leaders towards communism, and the FLN's equation of national unity with a one-party state, drove the PCA underground in post-colonial Algeria. Its legacy, however, was to fix in the political imagination of the left the possibility of a plurality, democratic and socialist Algeria, in which civic society, as much or more than state bureaucracy, would repair the damage inflicted by years of colonial rule.

Although Drew says that she wished to write a comparative study of Algerian and South African communism, only to realise that there was a prior need for a book on Algerian communism itself, this manuscript is constantly enriched by comparisons with one of the African continent's major bastions of communism. South Africa likewise experienced tensions – racial tensions – between the 'national' and the 'international'. These were exemplified by the slogan of the 1922 Rand strike, "Workers of the world fight and unite for a white South Africa!", the white mine workers' struggle against wage cuts and retrenchments – though not their call for a colour bar – supported by the Communist Party of South Africa. It took more than two decades before the CPSA and the African National Congress jointly supported the August 1946 African mine workers' strike, the CPSA's black membership having grown considerably in the intervening years.

This book makes a considerable contribution to the ambition of the *Studies in Imperialism* series to publish work on a wider range of European empires, to rethink decolonisation by exploring its global resonances and repercussions, and to trace the historical legacies of colonialism into the post-colonial era. It is deeply researched in the archives and will be a standard work of reference on the Algerian communist movement for many years to come.

Andrew Thompson
University of Exeter, March 2014

ACKNOWLEDGEMENTS

I began this project with the intention of writing a comparative study of communism in Algeria and South Africa. But I realised the need for a book on Algeria's communist movement itself. This was due both to the absence of an English-language study and because I could find very few French-language books on the subject. Algerian communism needs to be examined on its own terms before it can be compared with other communist experiences. I wish to thank the British Academy for funding my archival research and the Arts and Humanities Research Council for a research leave award allowing me time to reflect and write. I am very grateful for their support.

My work was slowed down by an ongoing personal trauma: the disappearance of my elderly father Thomas Drew under bizarre circumstances on 21 July 2007. Frail, suffering from severe cardio-pulmonary disease, needing oxygen and reportedly only able to walk 250 yards before becoming seriously out of breath, he nonetheless vanished from his home without a trace. Since then I have become all too familiar with the world of missing persons and with police investigations into such disappearances.

I wish to thank the archivists, librarians and other staff at the following archives and libraries for their gracious assistance: Archives nationales d'Outre-Mer, Aix-en-Provence; Bibliothèque François Mitterrand, Paris; Bibliothèque Marxiste, Paris; British Library and British Newspaper Library, London; Centre des archives contemporaines, Fontainebleau; Comintern Archives, Russian State Archive of Socio-Political History, Moscow; Borthwick Institute for Archives, University of York; International Institute of Social History, Amsterdam; Institut d'histoire sociale, Nanterre; Archives of the Parti communiste français, Archives départementales de la Seine-Saint-Denis, Bobigny; Institute of Commonwealth Studies, London; The National Archives, London; and the Nelson Mandela Centre of Memory, Johannesburg.

Many people have generously helped me with this project, first and foremost those whom I interviewed in Algeria and France, who shared their experiences and ideas with me. The late Henri Alleg, Sadek Hadjerès, Boussad Ouadi and Slimane Tounsi were enormously helpful in facilitating contacts. My sincere thanks to Slimane Tounsi and his family in Ghardaïa for their kind and generous hospitality; A. Bakelli of the Forum algérien citoyenneté modernité, Ghardaïa, for fascinating discussions; the Abou Ishak Ibrahim Tefayech Association for the Service of Heritage, Ghardaïa; Boussad Ouadi and the wonderful staff at the Librairie El Idjtihad in Algiers; Saïd Yacine Hannachi of Librairie Média-Plus in Constantine; and Dr Robert Parks and staff at the Centre d'études maghrébines en Algérie in Oran. Jim House and Jean-Louis Planche read draft chapters; David Howell and Jill Lovecy read the entire manuscript; James McDougall and Didier Monciaud advised on Arabic terms. All of their comments have greatly improved this book. I am also very grateful to the staff at Manchester University Press and to two anonymous readers for their help, to Corinne Orde for copy-editing and typesetting, to Don Shewan for the map, to Abdul Samed Bemath for the index, to Geoff Wall and Margaret Ferguson for discussions on Camus, and to the Algerianist community in Britain, which is refreshingly receptive to newcomers. My special thanks to Jill Lovecy for help with French translations. The mistakes are, of course, mine.

LIST OF ABBREVIATIONS

Organisations

AEMAN	Association des étudiants musulmans d'Afrique du Nord
ALN	Armée de libération nationale
AML	Amis du manifeste et de la liberté
ANC	African National Congress
AUMA	Association des 'ulama musulmans algériens
CCE	Comité de coordination et d'exécution
CDL	Combattants de la libération
CFLN	Comité français de libération nationale
CGT	Confédération générale du travail
CGTU	Confédération générale du travail unitaire
CNF	Comité national français
CNRA	Conseil national de la révolution algérienne
Cominform	Communist Information Bureau
Comintern	Communist International
CRUA	Comité révolutionnaire pour l'unité et l'action
ECCI	Executive Committee of the Communist International
ENA	Étoile nord-africaine
FEI	Fédération des élus indigènes
FFFLN	Fédération de France du FLN
FFPCA	Fédération de France du PCA
FLN	Front de libération nationale
GGA	Gouverneur général de l'Algérie
GPRA	Gouvernement provisoire de la République algérienne
ICFTU	International Confederation of Free Trade Unions
JC	Jeunesse communiste
KUTV	Communist University of Toilers of the East
LDD	Ligue française pour la défense des droits de l'homme et du citoyen
MNA	Mouvement national algérien
MTLD	Mouvement pour le triomphe des libertés démocratiques
OAS	Organisation armée secrète
OS	Organisation spéciale
PCA	Parti communiste algérien
PCF	Parti communiste français

LIST OF ABBREVIATIONS

PNR	Parti national révolutionnaire
PPA	Parti du peuple algérien
PUPOM	Parti de l'union populaire de l'oued-M'zab
RILU	Red International of Labour Unions
SAS	Section administrative spécialisée
SFIC	Section française de l'internationale communiste
SFIO	Section française de l'internationale ouvrière
UDMA	Union démocratique du manifeste algérien
UFA	Union des femmes d'Algérie
UGEMA	Union générale des étudiants musulmans algériens
UGSA	Union générale des syndicats algériens
UGTA	Union générale des travailleurs algériens
UJDA	Union des jeunesses démocratiques d'Algérie
USTA	Union syndicale des travailleurs algériens
WFTU	World Federation of Trade Unions

Archives

ANOM	Archives nationales d'Outre-Mer (Aix-en-Provence)
CAC	Centre des archives contemporaines (Fontainebleau)
CSAS DU	Duncan Papers, Southern African Archives, Borthwick Institute for Archives (York)
LAI	League Against Imperialism Archives (Amsterdam)
NMCM	Nelson Mandela Centre of Memory (Johannesburg)
PRO	Public Record Office (London)
RF	Ruth First Papers, Institute of Commonwealth Studies (London)
RGASPI	Russian State Archive of Socio-Political History (Moscow)
TNA	The National Archives (London)

COLONIAL ALGERIA

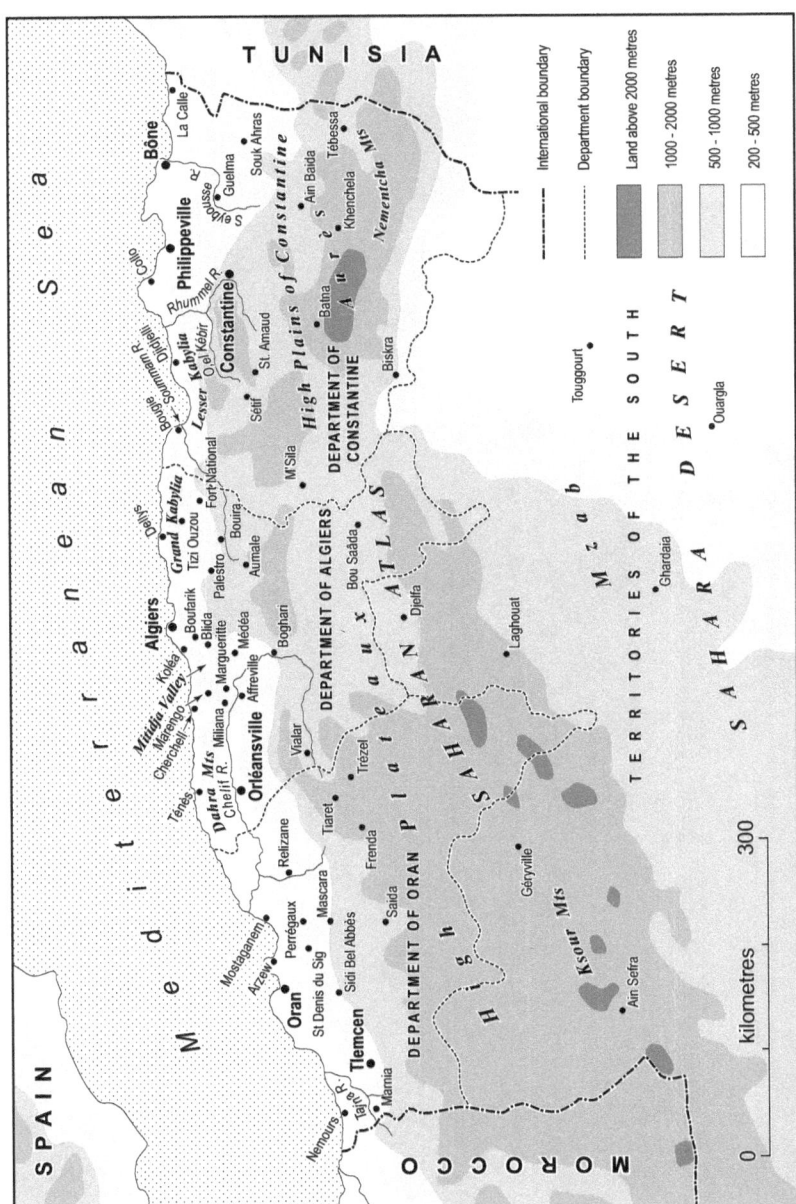

Source: John Ruedy, *Modern Algeria: The Origins and Development of a Nation*, 2nd edn (Bloomington, IN: Indiana University Press, 1992, 2005), p. 82. Reproduced and adapted by permission of Indiana University Press. All rights reserved.

INTRODUCTION

Imagining socialism and communism in Algeria

Today, the very idea of an international socialist community seems utopian. Like nationalism, socialism is an imagined community based on 'deep, horizontal comradeship'. But if nations are typically imagined within territorial boundaries 'as both inherently limited and sovereign', socialism's imagined community spans the globe.[1] Two years after the 1917 Russian Revolution, the launch of the Communist International (Comintern) offered a revolutionary alternative to the Socialist International that had been devastated by the outbreak of war in 1914. Through participation in communist organisations, individuals across the world became part of an imagined community that aspired to be nationally and territorially boundless. The Comintern became an increasingly hierarchical and gendered instrument of Soviet foreign policy. Nonetheless, communism's ambition was to make socialism coterminous with humankind – in contrast to nationalist aspirations of coexistence with other nations.[2]

Communists necessarily proclaimed internationalism, but first and foremost they had to come to terms with the societies in which they lived and worked. Assessing their national conditions and proposing solutions to national problems were prerequisites for building a socialist movement. They faced a fundamental tension, however, between the Comintern's declared project of applying uniform policies across all of its national sections and the specificity of their own national conditions, which necessitated the application and adaptation of Marxist ideas to very diverse environments. While at times the Comintern played a constructive role within its national sections, all too often its efforts to impose uniformity conflicted with local conditions, impeding the efforts of communists to address their own national problems.

Algeria is a case in point. This book examines the efforts of communists in French colonial Algeria to imagine the Algerian nation.

It has become commonplace in the historiography of communism in Algeria to attribute its difficulties in attracting Algerians to the paternalistic attitudes of the local communists of European heritage.[3] Thus, Emmanuel Sivan, author of the only comprehensive history of communists in Algeria, argues that they aspired, but ultimately failed, to develop their party into the nucleus of a counter-society, one which sought to reform and eventually overthrow and replace the colonial order. For decades the party's membership remained predominantly European, imbued with a colonial mentality and easily swayed by the Parti communiste français (French Communist Party, PCF). When Algerians eventually joined the Parti communiste algérien (Algerian Communist Party, PCA) in significant numbers, Sivan contends, they were imbued with nationalist aspirations. These two opposing world views, each with its own discourse, could not be reconciled within the same organisation and explain the PCA's ultimate demise, so Sivan concludes.[4]

Yet individual attitudes are too complex and variable to be explained by reference solely or even primarily to ethnic or national background. Moreover, attitudes alone cannot explain the history and fate of communism in Algeria. Indeed, envisioning a post-capitalist socialism requires an imaginative leap far beyond the world as we know it. The very idea of socialism in Algeria was daunting, both in comparison with industrialised France, which claimed Algeria as its own and had its own influential communist party, and even with the settler society at the southern end of the African continent that so closely mirrored Algeria – South Africa. From the outset the land and its embittered history confounded communists in Algeria.

State power is central in situating communist experience in Algeria. The French state operated in a broadly democratic manner in France, but not in Algeria. Not only were Algerians forcibly deprived of their livelihood through the conquest of land and denied the democratic rights available under the French republican constitutions, the French state repeatedly closed down political space in Algeria. Political space refers to the environment available to individuals and groups for political activity and, by extension, to their freedom of action to engage in politics and thus expand their political influence.[5] Elastic and malleable, political space can extend both horizontally and vertically. Its horizontal dimension refers to its geographic spread, whether across a public square, a market, a village or a railway network, the construction of which promises the growth of political space on a national scale. Its vertical dimension refers either to the public legal sphere or to illegal underground space, where political activists have far less room to manoeuvre and correspondingly less ability to expand their influence. State power and political space coexist in a relationship; the vibrancy of political space and its potential to grow reflect the ability of popular forces within civil society to keep state power in check. Political space is gendered; typically Algerian women did not interact openly in public space, especially public political space. It is also shaped by language, literacy and other forms of communication. Most Algerians were illiterate, especially in rural areas, while most European communists did not speak Arabic or Berber, which limited their abilities to cross cultural, religious and national barriers. Yet despite state and social constraints on political space, communists entered and expanded it whenever possible. During electoral campaigns or trade union actions, they competed for political space with other parties. Sometimes they opened up political space through their own initiatives – for example, campaigning in rural areas where other political groups had not yet penetrated. There is no question that communists in Algeria worked consistently and resourcefully for change.

Structural factors were enormous impediments. A key problem concerned Algeria's complex class structure, which limited the political space for democratic reform movements and in turn hindered the possibilities for political alliances between communists and others groups. Historical sociologists offer hypotheses based on comparative analysis that may illuminate Algeria's specificities. Thus, Barrington Moore, Jr, argued that the possibility of democracy depends on a class balance that allows the development of commercial agriculture but prevents the emergence of a strong landed elite or a conservative landed elite–bourgeois coalition against peasants and workers. In other words, a precondition for democratisation is the political strength of urban classes relative to rural classes. But European settler landowners and Algerian landed elites were significant forces in Algeria, as were the impoverished rural peasantry. Despite a small Algerian urban commercial bourgeoisie, industrial development was limited and dominated by French capital. Algeria was characterised by conditions that, according to Moore's schema, acted as blockages to democratic development. The comparative research of Dietrich Rueschemeyer, Evelyne Huber Stephens and John Stephens supports and extends that of Moore. Indeed, they conclude that large landlords dependent on cheap labour were consistently anti-democratic, while the working class was a key factor in democratisation, its influence dependent on its organised strength.[6]

South Africa, by contrast, possessed the preconditions for democratisation suggested by these writers. The possibilities for a black peasantry and landowning class had been eliminated by mass expropriation – roughly 87 per cent of the land was reserved for whites.

The white landed elite – large-scale white farmers – was particularly influential during the 1940s–1960s. However, a white South African bourgeoisie developed over the twentieth century, accelerated by state-led industrialisation, and by the 1980s the influence of white farmers was declining relative to mining and manufacturing capital. Urban classes – the black working class, black middle class and sections of the white bourgeoisie – were the prime forces in South Africa's democratic transition. While structural factors do not dictate political outcomes, the relative weight of rural classes in Algeria by comparison with South Africa suggests that communists in Algeria faced more structural constraints than their South African counterparts – constraints all the more significant given Marxism's historic orientation towards the urban working class.[7]

Another problem concerned Algeria's deep religious cleavages. As Moore notes, religion *per se* cannot explain social unrest; rather, the problem concerns how religion is linked to social conditions. Islam and Christianity were both imagined international communities and aspirant global religions. In Algeria religious divisions reinforced the great social and political divisions between the settler and indigenous populations: Europeans were overwhelmingly Christian, while the Algerian majority was overwhelmingly Muslim. While the secular French state and its European settlers imposed an anti-Islamic secularisation that attacked local identity, Islam's centuries-old penetration of North African society provided a discourse for anti-colonialism, which Christianity as the religion of the coloniser could not provide. Islamic institutions could tap into the social malaise of different social strata and classes. Defending Islam became an expression and means of anti-colonial resistance. Thus, Algerian politics often took a cultural nationalist form. There was little common ground allowing contact and communication across these religious divisions, aside from the occasional convergence of communist and Algerian nationalist activities.

The pattern of Algeria's religious cleavages contrasted markedly with South Africa's. The latter's localised indigenous religious beliefs were inherently more vulnerable to Christianity's globalising mission. Despite the pernicious racial divisions, leading black South African political activists had been educated in Christian mission schools, receiving religious instruction and education that was similar to that of liberal English-speaking whites. This common framework provided a basis for communication between black political activists and the tiny number of democratic whites. South Africa's political and religious cleavages were cross-cutting; Algeria's cleavages reinforced each other.

Geopolitics is also crucial for understanding the distinctive conditions that communists faced in Algeria. From their first days, as

INTRODUCTION

Chapter 2 discusses, they were torn between the international and the national. While this ambivalence mirrored the tension within socialism itself, it also reflected communism's launch in Algeria as a region of the PCF, with an overwhelmingly European membership that saw socialist revolution in France as the precondition for socialism in Algeria. By December 1920, when the PCF was formed, optimism about a wider socialist revolution was dimming, and the Comintern placed greater emphasis on national and anti-colonial struggles as a means to weaken imperialism. It insisted that communist parties in colonised regions build an affinity with the nationally oppressed. Thus, in 1922 Leon Trotsky censured a motion put forward by communists at Sidi bel Abbès as indicative of slave-holding attitudes. This criticism caused much dissension within the Algerian region, but local communists began calling for independence.

Three years later, in 1925, a PCF representative from Paris reported that the intense repression in Algeria made work extremely difficult. His words – 'We are no longer in France' – underscored the contradictory and politically dangerous nature of the Algerian situation.[8] This was not a warning about cultural differences between secularised Christian Europeans and Muslim Algerians, but about the sharply differing political conditions. While deemed to be part of democratic France rather than a colony, Algeria was effectively occupied by France and ruled by force. Yet the question of national identity was implicit in his statement – if they were not in France, what country was this?

Addressing that question – imagining the Algerian nation – overwhelmed local communists. The international–national dynamic that framed their thinking was far from static. During periods of international upheaval such as war, geopolitical priorities became exaggerated and impacted heavily on domestic politics, including communist politics. Crucially, Algeria's geographic proximity to Europe and its colonial relationship with France, which in turn shaped the PCF's perspective, meant that it felt the impacts of European events very intensely.

Likewise, the Comintern's geopolitical priorities – Europe and Asia – shaped its policies, and France was central to the Comintern's interests in Europe. In the 1920s the Comintern had pressured communists in Algeria to call for Algerian independence. But by the mid-1930s, with the PCF worried about fascism in France and its spread across Europe, communists in Algeria once again viewed their national question through the lens of a Eurocentric internationalism. In marked contrast, South Africa's political autonomy and distance from the Comintern's geographic priorities meant that the national question weighed more heavily in South African communist thinking than the international.

Indeed, while South African communists claimed at mid-century that their movement had merged with the national movement, tensions between communists and nationalists in Algeria remained fraught, despite their periodic efforts at united fronts.[9]

The oscillating international–national pattern characteristic of communism in Algeria was manifested in several phases, beginning with the First World War, which accelerated the country's proletarianisation, as Algerian workers were drawn to France. This distinctive pattern of proletarianisation had profound implications for political organisation: the first Algerian worker-based national organisation – the Etoile nord-africaine (North African Star, ENA) – was launched in Paris, reflecting Algeria's displaced proletariat. In comparison, South Africa's first black worker-based national organisation – the Industrial and Commercial Workers' Union – was formed in Cape Town.

In the Russian Revolution's wake, with popular movements on the upsurge, the French state was concerned with containing post-war radicalism. A key dynamic in this period concerned the possibilities for communist alliances with other movements. However, the Comintern's geopolitical priorities meant that its policies were not simultaneously introduced in its national sections; the attempts of communists in different countries to forge local alliances were thus differentially impacted. This was evident in the new line of class against class, which led to purges of first-generation communists around the world and the collapse of communist alliances with other groups. In Algeria the new line was implemented in late 1927–28. This coincided with the closing down of political space as the French state prepared to celebrate the centennial of its colonial conquest. Yet by the early 1930s, as Chapter 3 shows, the local communist movement had recovered from the new line purges and the fierce repression and made alliances, albeit short-lived, with peasant movements and with the growing Islamic reform movement.

The expansion of fascism and the Comintern's Popular Front policy marked a transitional phase in which international politics became increasingly important. Rural Algerians poured into the cities, opening urban political space. While it was possible to combine the anti-fascist and anti-colonial struggles, this did not happen in Algeria. Instead, Chapter 4 argues, the PCF's critical support for France's Popular Front government led it to moderate its anti-colonial stance, so that for many Algerians anti-fascism and anti-colonialism were seen in oppositional terms. Although an autonomous PCA was launched in October 1936, it followed the PCF's political leadership, which backtracked on the demand for independence. Ironically, despite its formal organisational autonomy, the Popular Front period tied Algeria's communist movement even more firmly to the PCF.

The Second World War reinforced the Comintern's concern with Europe and the PCF's fear of fascism in France. For most communists in Algeria, as Chapter 5 illustrates, the relationship with France became paramount. In February 1939, the PCF general secretary Maurice Thorez proclaimed the thesis that Algeria was a nation in formation composed of some twenty 'races'. Since communists in Algeria had initially seen the national question as a subset of revolution in France, the nation-in-formation thesis had the merit of focusing attention more directly on the development of the Algerian nation itself. Nonetheless, in underestimating the weight of the Arabo-Berber majority, the thesis was highly problematic. Despite its controversial nature, the PCA nonetheless adopted the thesis as its own.

Germany and the Soviet Union signed their Non-Aggression Pact in August 1939. The PCF and PCA were banned the next month; public political space for communists was closed. The underground PCA briefly called for independence as a means to weaken French imperialism. But from June 1941, when the Soviet Union entered the war and its national sections around the world followed suit, the PCA dropped the call for Algerian independence in the name of uniting against fascism. In May 1945, the liberation was proclaimed in France, reopening public political space. Yet at that very moment, as Chapter 6 discusses, European settlers in eastern Algeria were massacring many thousands of Muslims. Viewing the events through the lens of the anti-fascist struggle, the PCA and PCF were slow to recognise and condemn the massacre. Thus, while the PCF's role in the anti-fascist resistance gave it a heroic status in the eyes of some sections of French society, Algerians were at best ambivalent towards communists and more often cynical.

In the aftermath of the 1945 massacre, the PCA campaigned exhaustively against the state's repression. By the late 1940s, young radicalised Algerians were gravitating to the PCA, both because of intolerance within the nationalist movement – an intolerance that ultimately led to its destructive fragmentation – and because nationalist organisations did not address the problems of poverty, inequality and social justice. Reflecting this demographic change, alongside the pull of a burgeoning national liberation movement, the PCA's politics became increasingly autonomous *vis-à-vis* the PCF. As the PCA contested France's claim that Algeria consisted of three French departments and reinterpreted the nation-in-formation thesis to give primacy to the colonised Arabo-Berber majority, it began reimagining the Algerian nation. Crucially, the PCA came to its understanding of the national question through its campaign against state repression. As a result – and in contrast to the

Soviet one-party model – its imagined Algerian nation was premised on the necessity of a vibrant civil society and pluralist democracy.

The post-war years were marked by two global dynamics: firstly, the Cold War rivalry between the United States and the Soviet Union, and secondly, imperialism and anti-imperial movements. These dynamics reinforced each other to pull the PCF and PCA in different directions. Following the Soviet two-camp policy, the PCF saw the United States as the leading imperialist force whose influence was to be resisted at all costs, and it prioritised French and European concerns.[10] The PCA, by contrast, gave primacy to the struggle against French imperialism, its eyes on Vietnam and Africa. One consequence of anti-colonial agitation was an increase in the international flow of ideas about emancipation from colonial rule, as liberation movements sought to learn from other experiences. Armed struggles in Tunisia, Morocco and Vietnam – and not least the Vietminh's historic 1954 victory at Dien Bien Phu – brought communists and nationalists face to face with the possibilities of guerrilla struggle in Algeria.

The PCA's publications on the Vietnamese guerrilla war fostered a climate for thinking about armed struggle; in this sense, the PCA was considering armed struggle before it began in Algeria. Nonetheless, when the Front de libération nationale (National Liberation Front, FLN) launched its war of independence in the rural hinterland in November 1954, the PCA was unprepared. But pressured by its rural members, it supported the armed struggle, albeit from a position of catching up, and the war's intensity compelled it to focus its attention squarely on the national question. The war led to escalating repression, the closure of public political space and a vicious circle of violence; the PCA was banned for a second time in September 1955. For the French state, the PCA represented the extension of Soviet-backed international communism into North Africa. Fearing communist–nationalist collusion, the state subjected PCA activists to ruthless repression, as will be seen in Chapters 7, 8 and 9. The FLN's emphasis on military struggle hampered urban political organisation and accentuated the urban–rural disjuncture. Yet, the tiny underground PCA leadership contended that, however restricted, there was still public space for urban civil society protest, even though it lacked the forces to organise this. Indeed, in December 1960 seemingly spontaneous popular protests swept through city streets across the country, temporarily opening up public political space.

Many communists fought and died in the war. Nonetheless, the relationship between communists and nationalists remained characterised by mistrust and violence. During the rapidly evolving war-time conditions, the PCA envisioned an Algerian nation that was democratic and multicultural, yet predominantly Arabo-Berber, and called for an opening of political space to be filled by Algerian voices. The PCA's ideas on agrarian development and socialism influenced FLN thinking. Yet independence saw the PCA banned for a third time, once again confounded by the international–national dilemma, its visions of a democratic Algeria swept aside.

The PCA's tentative and tardy efforts to imagine the Algerian nation – albeit a reflection of the country's complex class, national and geopolitical circumstances – inevitably impeded its ability to attract Algerians. Thus, Algerians did not join the party in significant numbers until its campaign against repression unfolded in the late 1940s and early 1950s. This had implications for the development and character of Algerian nationalism, epitomised by its cultural orientation and neglect of socioeconomic inequalities and, during the war of independence, by its intolerance of political difference. Indeed, communism's ambivalent stance on Algerian nationalism meant that a nationalist ideology emphasising binary oppositions could occupy the available political space, eclipsing other political and ideological tendencies. This received graphic confirmation shortly after independence when the FLN banned the PCA and declared Algeria a one-party state.

Notes

1 Benedict Anderson, *Imagined Communities: Reflections on the Origin and Spread of Nationalism* (London: Verso, 1983), pp. 15–16.
2 On the Comintern see, *inter alia*, Fernando Claudin, *The Communist Movement: From Comintern to Cominform*, Part One (New York and London: Monthly Review, 1975); E. H. Carr, *The Twilight of Comintern, 1930–1935* (London and Basingstoke: Macmillan, 1982); Kevin McDermott and Jeremy Agnew, *The Comintern: A History of International Communism from Lenin to Stalin* (Basingstoke and London: Macmillan, 1996); Mikhail Narinsky and Jürgen Rojahn (eds), *Centre and Periphery: The History of the Comintern in the Light of New Documents* (Amsterdam: Internationaal Instituut voor Sociale Geschiedenis, 1996); Tim Rees and Andrew Thorpe (eds), *International Communism and the Communist International, 1919–43* (Manchester: Manchester University, 1998); Tauno Saarela and Kimmo Rentola (eds), *Communism: National and International* (Helsinki: Suomen Historiallinen Seura, 1998); Mark Sandle, *Communism* (Harlow: Pearson, 2012); Allison Drew, 'Communism in Africa', in Stephen A. Smith (ed.), *Oxford Handbook of the History of Communism* (Oxford: Oxford University Press, 2013), pp. 285–302.
3 The terminology used to refer to ethnic and national groups in colonial Algeria is contentious. Here, I use 'European' to refer to people of European heritage living in Algeria, 'French' for those born in and normally residing in France and 'Algerian' for the indigenous Muslim majority. Compare Jonathan K. Gosnell, *The Politics of Frenchness in Colonial Algeria, 1930–1954* (Rochester, NY: University of Rochester, 2002).
4 Emmanuel Sivan, *Communisme et nationalisme en Algérie, 1920–1962* (Paris: Fondation Nationale des Sciences Politiques, 1976), pp. 9–10, 206, 242, 261. Hafid Khatib's *Le 1er juillet 1956: L'Accord FLN–PCA et l'intégration des « combattants de la libération » dans l'armée de libération nationale en Algérie* (Algiers: Office des Publications Universitaires, 1991) examines the PCA during the war of independence.

For an indispensable biographical dictionary see René Gallissot (ed.), *Algérie: Engagements sociaux et question nationale de la colonisation à l'indépendance, de 1830 à 1962 – Dictionnaire biographique du mouvement ouvrier: Maghreb* (Ivry-sur-Seine and Paris: Editions de l'Atelier/Editions ouvrières, 2006). For a biographical approach see the work of Jean-Luc Einaudi, *Un rêve algérien: Histoire de Lisette, une femme d'Algérie* (Paris: Presses Universitaires de France, 2001); *Un Algérien: Maurice Laban* (Paris: Cherche midi, 1999); *Pour l'exemple: L'Affaire Fernand Iveton, enquête* (Paris: Harmattan, 1986). For a communist perspective see Henri Alleg (ed.), *La Guerre d'Algérie*, 3 vols. (Paris: Editions Messidor, 1981); For a Maoist approach, Jacques Jurquet, *La Révolution nationale algérienne et le Parti communiste français*, 4 vols. (Marseille: Monde en marche, and Paris: Editions du Centenaire, 1973–84).

5 Political space is distinguished from the more general concept of public space or the public sphere. David Howell, *British Workers and the Independent Labour Party, 1886–1906* (Manchester: Manchester University Press, 1983), pp. 129–32, 277–82, discusses expanding political space in a democratising society. I am very grateful to David for emphasising this concept in our many discussions.

6 Barrington Moore, Jr, *Social Origins of Dictatorship and Democracy: Lord and Peasant in the Making of the Modern World* (Boston, MA: Beacon, 1966); Dietrich Rueschemeyer, Evelyne Huber Stephens and John D. Stephens, *Capitalist Development and Democracy* (Cambridge: Polity, 1992), p. 270.

7 Allison Drew, *Discordant Comrades: Identities and Loyalties on the South African Left* (Aldershot: Ashgate, 2000; Pretoria: Unisa, 2002).

8 'Nous ne sommes plus en France'. Archives of the Parti communiste français (hereafter PCF), Paris, PCF file 120, *Rapport de Henriet*, 1 September 1925, p. 2.

9 H. J. and R. E. Simons, *Class and Colour in South Africa 1850–1950* (Harmondsworth: Penguin, 1969), pp. 10, 261.

10 Danièle Joly, *The French Communist Party and the Algerian War* (Basingstoke and London: Macmillan, 1991), pp. xvi, 42–3; Matthew Connelly, *A Diplomatic Revolution: Algeria's Fight for Independence and the Origins of the Post-Cold War Era* (Oxford and New York: Oxford, 2002), p. 42.

CHAPTER ONE

The land and its conquest

The Frenchmen who conquered the land now called Algeria were ruthless. Before they arrived, the indigenous Berber people had survived many invasions, from the Phoenicians to the Vandals, the Byzantine and the Arabs, who came in the seventh century bringing Islam. The Berbers adopted Islam but maintained their own language and customs. From the eleventh through to the thirteenth centuries the Almoravids and Almohads, Berber dynasties from Morocco, extended their influence from the west. Sunni became the dominant school of Islam. With the overthrow of Islamic Spain in 1492, North African Muslims turned to Ottoman Turks to help fight off Spanish expansion into Africa. Although Spain conquered the west in the sixteenth century, the Ottomans gained control of the east and the area around Algiers, extending their reach until they established the land between Morocco and Tunisia as a geopolitical territory. The Ottoman Regency brought stability, but direct rule lapsed in 1580, after war with Spain. From then on, the region was indirectly ruled by the Turkish military, led by the *dey*, who extracted surplus from the local population under threat of force. The land was divided into regions, each governed by a *bey*, assisted by *calipha* or lieutenants. Under the *bey* were *cadis*, or judges, and *caïds*, tax collectors or local government administrators. Below these were local tribal leaders. The urban authorities lived in what Arabic speakers called the *bled el makhzen* (lands of government) along the coast and coastal plains, in contrast to the *montagnards* or mountain dwellers of the *bled es siba* (lands of dissidence) whom the Turkish military controlled with difficulty. By 1830 the Ottoman regency in Algiers was wracked with infighting, and European financiers dominated the local economy. The French state, in the final days of the Bourbon restoration monarchy, took full advantage.[1]

The fall of Algiers in 1830 was heralded by the looting of its properties. The transfer of land to French *colons* or settlers soon followed, as the French state extended its reach across the Mediterranean. Over the next four decades the French army marched across the Algerian landscape. Governor-General Thomas-Robert Bugeaud, who led the conquest, was utterly frank about his aims: 'There is only one interest one can seize in Africa, the interest vested in agriculture ... I have found no other means of subjugating the country than to seize that vested interest.'[2]

When Algiers fell, only 5 or 6 per cent of the population resided in cities.[3] The perennial risk of invasion necessitated protection, and cities were walled. Each city or town had at least one mosque, whose minaret facilitated the call to prayers and served as a lookout. Close by was the market. Urban Islam was scripture-based, placing a premium on literacy to read the Koran. The cities had *kuttabs*, or Koranic schools, *medersas*, or institutions of higher learning and the *Shari'a* courts. Arabic had a special status as the language of the Koran, as well as the language of administration, trade and commerce.

The cities were home to the *grandes familles*, the notables who traced their lineage back centuries across generations and often owned rural estates. The urbanites were cosmopolitan. In addition to the Arabo-Berbers, many were of Turkish origin, and there were also Andalusians, influential in commerce and culture, Jewish traders from France and Italy, indigenous Jews, generally of modest means, who had lived in North Africa for centuries, Christian slaves and slaves from other parts of Africa. Labour and leisure were divided by gender. Men engaged in trade and commerce; women prepared food and cosmetics, processed sheepskins and wove blankets. Men gathered in cafés to exchange news, and women, who wore a veil outside the home, in *hammams*, or Turkish baths. Despite their small size, the cities' influence extended across the countryside.[4]

The landscape stretched from the coast across the *Tell* (the north) – a hilly and mountainous strip running inland some 150 miles and, with the Mitidja and Chelif plains, the country's most fertile area – to the Atlas mountains, the southern plains and the desert. The overwhelming majority of people lived in these diverse rural environments. In 1830, some 50 per cent of the rural population were sedentary cultivators, either freeholders or landless peasants. Most freehold lands were in the mountainous areas; urban elites and well armed nomads had access to the fertile lowlands. Sedentary cultivators, predominantly Berbers, lived in the Grand Kabylia, the Aurès and Atlas Mountains, the western mountains and the Dahra and Ouarsenis massifs around the Chelif river valley. In Grand Kabylia, for example, villages were self-contained and inward-facing at or near mountain tops, with cultivated land below. As elsewhere in Africa, cultivation reflected a sexual division of labour. Rural women, who generally did not wear veils, prepared food, engaged in weaving and trading and tended the vegetable gardens, which were close to their homes. Further down the slopes men grew wheat, barley and other crops. At the bottom were fig and olive orchards. Landless peasants often lived near cities in the Mitidja valley, the Algiers Sahel and the plain of Constantine, typically on land belonging to the *bey*. Frequently indebted, these landless peasants worked as *khamamisa* or sharecroppers on large estates and resembled feudal serfs. The remaining 45 per cent of the population were nomads or semi-nomads who lived in the *Tell*, the high plains and the Sahara.[5]

Rural society was organised outwards from the family to the lineage, clan, tribe and, sometimes, confederations of tribes. In contrast to urban Islam, rural Islam was organised around cults celebrating the lives of *marabouts*, or holy men and, occasionally, holy women, and in which women were active participants. Sufism, based on cults of these saints and their tombs, emerged in the twelfth century. Sometimes these cults were localised; in other cases, the saintly personages were widely known. Women generally visited local tombs on a daily basis, while Saharan oasis shrines attracted both settled and nomadic communities. Related to maraboutism, but geographically more dispersed, were the *tariqas*, or brotherhoods, mystical sufi orders led by shaykhs. Reflecting the less literate rural culture, Sufism and maraboutism emphasised signs and symbols rather than writing. These two strands of Islam, Sufism and maraboutism, coexisted in tension over the centuries. When the French invaded, the Sufi orders led the resistance.[6]

Ottoman rule left a highly stratified society. Land allocation was based on a complex system of use rights and obligations, with land taxed at 2 per cent of total yield. The major distinction was between the *bey*'s land and that held by tribes. The *bey* controlled *melk*, *beylik* and *mokhzen* land. *Melk* land, individual freehold over which the *bey* retained ultimate control, was widespread. *Melk* land ranged from small peasant-cultivated parcels to large estates worked by sharecroppers while the landlords lived in towns. *Beylik* land was that allocated to local rulers and administered for their own benefit; upon the local ruler's death, the land reverted to the state. *Mokhzen* or *azel* land consisted of land confiscated or purchased by the *bey* and used to reward loyal officials or tribes. Tribal land or *bled el'arsh* was allocated to individual members based on use right; working the land guaranteed security of tenure. Religious institutions also owned land known as *habus* that had been donated by individuals or groups with the provision that they retained rights of use. Irrespective of the type of land tenure, all rural Algerians had access to land.[7]

This changed dramatically as the French state tightened its grip on the territory and its people. Terror was integral to the French conquest. Thus, one lieutenant colonel instructed his troops to 'annihilate all who will not grovel at our feet like dogs'. French forces burned, pillaged and ravaged the tribes between Blida, the Chelif and Cherchell. Yet despite inspiring great terror, confessed Maréchal François Certain-Canrobert, 'the principal aim of pacification is far from being reached'.[8] The bloody 1840s – when French troops used a scorched earth policy and engaged in mass murder of peasants – was accompanied by rapid French settlement. French troops received a share of land as compensation for their efforts. This conquest was a prelude to surveying the land and transferring it into what became known as *le domaine publique* – the state-controlled public domain. *Beylik* and *habus* land was seized outright, and taxation, which tripled during 1839–40, was used to pressure landowners and cultivators. Much of the land seized in the name of the public domain was transferred to the growing number of *colons*. For Muslim women colonisation meant the loss of their Islamic inheritance rights and increased use of the veil.[9]

Algerian responses varied. Some communities migrated – often to Morocco, Tunisia or Syria. Others fought. The Emir Abdelkader forged rural and urban alliances and combined diplomacy and armed struggle to stave off French incursion into the Sahara, attempting to consolidate an independent Algerian state. His efforts continued from 1832 to 1847, when his forces were crushed with help from the Turkish government. Still others negotiated. These included the Mozabites – dubbed the 'Puritans of the desert' because of their ascetic and industrious lifestyle – who practised Ibadi Islam. Constructing dams, reservoirs and unusually deep wells through their own labour and that of slaves imported from further south, they established oases of date palms in the northern Sahara's Mzab Valley. In 1853 they signed a convention with France allowing them autonomy in exchange for an annual payment.[10]

The French rapidly imposed their administrative stamp. On 22 July 1834 King Louis-Philippe had created the post of *gouverneur général* charged with military control and overall administration. The post entailed the fusion of various types of power – symbolised by the clenched fist that Mahmood Mamdani argues characterised colonial rule in Africa.[11] Under the governor-general, the French adapted existing administrative structures into their own system of indirect rule. Thus, the French sent *caïds* to areas where they were outsiders to prevent them from forging local links and to ensure their dependence; *caïds* became hated by the local people for their authoritarian behaviour. The Royal Ordinance of 15 April 1845 divided the land into three provinces, creating three types of local administration to reflect the varied proportions of settlers and indigenous people across the land. Civil territories (later called *communes de plein exercise*), had a substantial proportion of European settlers and were governed by

French common law. Mixed territories or communes had small European settlements and were governed by a combination of military rule and limited self-government for settlers. Arabo-Berber territories were under full military rule.

In France the February 1848 Revolution brought the short-lived Second Republic to power. The *colons*, aspiring to their full democratic rights as French citizens, supported the republic, which declared Algeria to be an integral part of France. The three provinces became the departments of Algiers, Constantine and Oran or Algérois, Constantinois and Oranie. In Paris that June a popular uprising was quashed; the Second Republic was only too pleased to help the rebels and potential trouble-makers settle in Algeria. Others followed, often from southern France. It was an arduous life for those trekking to outlying areas, and many died from malaria, cholera and other ailments; Albert Camus would be one of their descendants on his father's side. In December 1848 Louis-Napoléon Bonaparte became President of the Second Republic. Three years later, he declared himself emperor and launched the Second French Empire. The emperor tightened military rule in Algeria to control the *colons*, whom he thought too greedy for land.[12]

The *Sénatus-consulte* of 12 April 1863 and 14 July 1865 laid the basis for future French land policy in Algeria. The 1863 law – ostensibly to protect Algerian property from the settlers – stipulated that Algerian tribes owned the lands that they had historically and permanently occupied, and that such tribal lands could only eventually become legally transferable if they were subdivided into individual property. The law essentially abolished the use rights on which small cultivators had depended and made Algerian-owned land available on the market. But many *colons* resented the 1863 law, and the civil authorities, siding with them, allowed significant amounts of Algerian land to be transferred into the public domain. The 1865 *Sénatus-consulte* codified differences in the personal status of French and Algerians, relegating Algerians to political inferiority: although France claimed Algeria as French, its indigenous inhabitants were to be subjects, not citizens. However, the 1865 law also established the category of French subjects who could apply for citizenship if they gave up their *statut personnel* (personal status) – i.e. accepted French civil authority over religious authority in such matters as marriage, divorce and other customs.[13]

The Second Empire collapsed in 1870 as a result of the Franco-Prussian War. The popular uprising that same year – the Paris Commune – was quickly suppressed with the massacre of some 14,000 people by French troops. With the establishment of the Third Republic French policy in Algeria aimed to unite European settlers, whether French, Spanish, Italian or Maltese, under the rubric of French citizenship – although in practice the French-born were highest in the social pecking order. Since the 1865 *Sénatus-consulte* Muslims and Jews had been able to apply for French naturalisation on an individual basis, although relatively few took this up. However, in October 1870 the Crémieux decree gave French citizenship and equal rights to Jews in Algeria, although they lost their personal status. Their new legal status accentuated the prejudice they faced from Muslims and the smouldering anti-Semitism that European settlers had carried with them from their home countries.[14]

In January 1871 Mohamed El-Mokrani launched an insurrection in Kabylia. With the insurrection's quashing in June 1872, the balance of power swung back towards the *colons*, whose parliamentary representatives in Paris worked adroitly on their behalf. The Kabylia insurrection was the last major armed revolt against the French in that century. The rural masses were devastated. As a peasant song lamented, '1871 was the year of our ruin. It broke our backs. We were smashed like a plate.'[15] Nonetheless, settler fears of further revolts led to the implementation of the *côde de l'indigénat* (native code), while Arabs and Berbers were divided through differential education and socialisation. The *indigénat*, which codified the de facto treatment of Algerians, was applied in Kabylia from 1874, in the southern territories from 1878 and across the rest of the country from 1881. It compelled Algerians to strict obedience to the colonial regime, imposing harsh punishments on them for infractions that were not illegal in France but were unlawful in Algeria when committed by Algerians. These infractions included travelling without a permit, failure to pay special 'native' taxes, defaming the French Republic and speaking disrespectfully to or about a French official. Crucially, overlapping national and religious differences – reflecting the centuries-old geopolitical and cultural tensions between Catholicism and Islam – were reinforced by absolute legal distinctions.[16]

New land laws were passed. Under the Warnier law of 26 July 1873 all transactions between Europeans and Algerians and amongst Algerians concerning land inventoried under the *sénatus-consultes* came under French law. The 1873 law abrogated key elements of its 1863 predecessor meant to slow the subdivision of communal land. Thus, the new law aimed to dismember Algerian property. From 22 April 1887 the rest of Algerian land fell under French law, much of it expropriated in the name of *l'utilité publique* (public utility). The 1873 and 1887 laws sped up land commercialisation, breaking up jointly and communally owned property and fragmenting Algerian landholdings. Colonisation continued apace; by now most new settlers came from Spain, driven by hunger to a new land, as was the case with Camus' maternal family.[17]

Alongside the laws, railway construction tied the *Tell* into the French economy by facilitating export production. In the 1860s four railway lines connected the ports at Algiers, Bône, Philippeville and Oran to areas some 25 to 50 miles inland; the Bône line ran to an iron mine, the others to farming areas or market towns. By 1880 six companies operated six railway lines running inland from ports and two east–west lines, one around Constantine and one from Algiers to Oran – some 700 miles. As export production expanded, so did the railways. Longer lines crossed the Tellian Atlas, running south to the high plains. In the east, the Biskra line stretched to the date-producing desert oases, and a branch line at Tebessa allowed iron and phosphate transport. In the west, the railway passed through areas of esparto grass cultivation, continuing south into the desert to allow military transport to the troublesome Algerian–Moroccan border. The railways provided jobs; communities along rail lines expanded.[18]

Between 1873 and 1892, the state incorporated 309,891 hectares of land into the public domain. Once in the public domain, land could be placed under military authority or put on the market, which became the primary means of its redistribution from Algerians to European settlers. As fertile low-lying land was expropriated, Algerians were inevitably forced from lowlands to hillsides and up the mountains. Thus, most of the fertile land belonged to Europeans and most of the mountainous rocky areas and infertile land belonged to the Algerians. At times the colonial administration granted land to pro-French Algerians, as happened in the village of Guerrouaou, established in 1845. But generally, the stipulations that Algerians adopt European farming practices and life styles made such initiatives untenable.

Reforestation, implemented by the Service des eaux et forêts (Forest Service), and one of the rationales for expropriation, was especially stressful for Algerians. The French forest code had inspired peasant protests in France, and its effects in Algeria were pernicious. The Forest Service planted shrubs on Algerian-owned land, from the mountain tops downward. Animals were prohibited from grazing on this vegetation; infractions were subject to fines and confiscation of animals. Sometimes entire tribes were expropriated in the name of reforestation for the public good.[19]

This massive land transfer undercut the pre-existing tribal system. Tribes in Algeria were historically based not on kinship but on alliances to a dominant lineage – what Eric Wolf called 'coalitions, organised around a group of power holders'. By eliminating tribal land ownership, the French undercut the power of the dominant lineages while promoting private property. To shatter tribal cohesion, people from different tribes were resettled together into clusters or villages called *douars* – literally, a circle of tents – with land rights through the *douar* instead of the tribe. As cultivators were pushed to the margins of arable land, pastoral activities became more difficult and costly. This eroded the long-standing relationships between cultivators and pastoralists, leading to a shift from a nomadic or semi-nomadic existence to intensive agricultural production, often on estates.[20]

By the turn of the century, many Algerians had lost their access to land, and rural poverty was widespread. Such dire circumstances aroused enormous rage. Peasants burned forests to protest the French reforestation policy that masked expropriation and drew up pamphlets and petitions to promote their cause. Sometimes they attacked French settlements, as in April 1901 when one hundred men from the *douar* of Adelia attacked Europeans in the town of Margueritte, named after the conquering general. In 1868 the people of Adelia *douar* numbered 2,194 and possessed 9,286 hectares of freehold land, 3,000 hectares of communal grazing and forest land, 2,000 cattle and 10,934 sheep. Following the 1863 *Sénatus-consulte*, they lost much of their land to the town's Europeans and to the Forest Service. By 1900 the Adelia numbered 3,206, but they had access to only 4,068 hectares of land, 2,343 of which were used for farming. The loss of grazing land meant fewer animals, which by then included 1,122 cattle and 1,537 sheep. On the day of the revolt the rebels killed the *caïd* and a forest ranger, took over the town and executed five inhabitants for refusing to recite a Muslim statement of faith. The French regained the town later that day, killing sixteen rebels, but the incident shook the French psyche and led to the implementation of trial without jury for Algerians charged with serious legal infractions.[21] This did not stop anti-expropriation protests.

Most Algerians were starved of land. Almost half the rural population farmed their own land, but in most cases, the plots were too small or poor in quality to provide full subsistence. Colonial authorities estimated that a minimum of ten hectares was needed to support one peasant family, yet in 1914, 60 per cent of the landholdings were smaller than that. This meant that many freeholders and their families supplemented their income by working on larger farms; wage labour was by then a characteristic feature of agricultural production. In 1919 the state was still the biggest landholder with between five and six million hectares, despite having granted more than nine million hectares to the *colons* since 1870.

Moreover, agricultural production was geared ever more to the French market. Until 1870 wheat had been the most significant crop, but by the 1880s this had shifted to viticulture, which was predominantly in European hands. By 1914 vineyards constituted 44 per cent by value of European-held property, and wine accounted for one-third by value of Algerian exports. Shifts in demand and a series of bad harvests created severe problems for rural Algerians. In 1919 surplus unsold grain caused financial difficulties for many. This was exacerbated the next year by failed harvests, which led to famine. The year 1922 saw another very bad harvest, and 1924 marked the worst harvest ever. The late 1920s saw some recovery, but mainly in European sectors; Europeans controlled 90 per cent of viticulture, 70 per cent of vegetable and citrus production and 40 per cent of grain production. The economy's reliance on primary production made it particularly vulnerable to the world depression, which hit Algeria in 1930, causing rising unemployment and underemployment in rural and urban areas. The crisis accelerated expropriations, as the *petits colons* – the small European landowners – claimed that they needed more land.[22]

Crucially, there was an Algerian landed elite, however tiny. By 1890 most Ottoman-era notables were financially ruined. In 1900 large landowners fell into two groups: traditional landowners using sharecroppers whose estates were not profitable, and modernising landowners using new techniques who made a profit. The latter in particular benefited from the collapse of the tribal system and the commercialisation of public-domain land, accumulating property from Algerians and Europeans as massive numbers of smallholders lost theirs. At the top end, by 1930 there were 7,035 properties – just over 1 per cent of all properties – that comprised one hundred or more hectares, occupying just over 21 per cent of Algerian-owned land. At the bottom, 434,537 properties – just over 70 per cent of Algerian-owned properties – consisted of less than ten hectares of land each, almost 23 per cent of all Algerian-owned land (see Table 1). Between the large landowners and the very poor peasants was a middle stratum of *fellahin* or *paysans aisés*, literally comfortable peasants, but Wolf's idea of 'peasants who could make ends meet' is probably more accurate. French administrators pointed with pride to these *paysans aisés* as the product of colonial land policy, believing that they would form the backbone of rural development.[23]

Table 1 Algerian landholdings in hectares, 1930

	No. of properties	Per cent of all properties	Area of land	Per cent of all land
Less than 10 ha	434,537	70.36	1,738,806	22.99
10–49 ha	140,010	22.67	2,635,275	34.84
50–99 ha	35,962	5.82	1,595,398	21.09
100+ ha	7,035	1.14	1,593,498	21.06
Total	617,544	99.99	7,562,977	99.98

Source: Adapted from Ageron, *Histoire de l'Algérie contemporaine*, vol 2 (1979), p. 495.

The administrative criterion for defining these *fellahin* was the ability to cultivate 10–20 hectares a year. Assuming that they used the traditional method of letting half their land lie fallow each year, this meant that a *fellah* would own between 20 and 40 hectares. However, the average size of landholdings within the 10–49 hectare category could barely have met the criteria for a comfortable peasant; only those with cultivated holdings greater than 19 hectares could really be considered to be comfortable. Another estimate suggests that in 1930 there were 7,565,967 hectares for 615,544 *fellahin*, or slightly over 12 hectares per *fellah*. By the 1930s, as the size of the rural proletariat peaked, approximately 65–75 per cent of the rural Algerian population could be classified as 'poor' or 'very poor'.[24]

This meant they were hungry. Hunger, the theme of Mohamed Dib's novel *La Grande Maison* (*The Big House*), set near Tlemcen in Oranie, became the constant companion of most rural Algerians. There could not have been a starker contrast between the villages of upper Bni Boublen, where the peasants were '*à leur aise*' (at their ease), and lower Bni Boublen, whose inhabitants – men, women, children and animals – nested in mountain pockets below a cemetery, the living beneath the dead.[25]

There was certainly class stratification amongst rural Europeans, but the distribution was notably different. The Algerian landed elite notwithstanding, landholdings were concentrated disproportionately amongst a small proportion of European owners. The 5,411 properties at the top constituted one-fifth of European-owned properties and occupied more than 73 per cent of European-owned land. By contrast, the 8,777 properties of less than ten hectares comprised one-third of European-owned properties and less than 2 per cent of European-owned land (see Table 2).

The concentration and fragmentation of landholdings at each end, the precarious nature of agriculture and the resultant rural poverty pushed people – both Algerians and Europeans – into the towns. Alge-

Table 2 European landholdings in hectares, 1930

	No. of properties	Per cent of all properties	Area of land	Per cent of all land
Less than 10 ha	8,777	33.56	42,534	1.81
10–49 ha	7,140	27.30	216,787	9.24
50–99 ha	4,725	18.06	364,366	15.53
100+ ha	5,411	20.68	1,721,979	73.41
Total	26,153	99.60	2,345,666	99.99

Source: Adapted from Ageron, *Histoire de l'Algérie contemporaine*, vol 2 (1979), p. 495.

rians had been moving to cities in increasing numbers since the turn of the century, finding work in small factories, workshops and businesses, on docks and in semi-skilled and unskilled public sector jobs. By 1905 some 50,000 Algerians were working in towns, and by the start of the 1914–18 war – then known as the Great War – 8.5 per cent of the population had been urbanised. Alongside the movement to Algerian towns, migration to France began in the early twentieth century in response to French industrialisation. Between 1907 and 1913 some 10,000 Kabyles responded to a call from French industries, in spite of protests from large landowners concerned about the difficulties of recruiting agricultural labourers. The emigrants, young men whose families remained in Algeria, settled in ethnic communities within French cities and sent money back home. Their numbers increased during the war, as Frenchmen left to fight. By the end of 1918, official census counts estimated that some 57,000 Algerians were living in France – probably an underestimation.[26] France demanded more Algerian products as well. During the war railway construction virtually ceased, with the exception of a southward line in the west to reach the Kenadza coal fields. The post-war years saw the consolidation of rail lines under government control and new construction: a southward line from Algiers to Djelfa for grain and sheep, and an extension from Biskra to Touggourt for dates.[27]

Algerian urbanisation proceeded apace. Estimates vary; according to one source, by 1926 one-fifth of the overall population was urban. The three departments had very different demographic patterns, which shaped local attitudes. In 1926 Constantinois was the least urbanised, with 13.7 per cent of the population living in towns. It also had the lowest European density. Not surprisingly, this was the region where Algerian nationalism would be strongest. In Algérois, the figure was 22.2 per cent, and in the most urbanised department, Oranie, it was 28.3 per cent. Reflecting two centuries of Spanish occupation, Oran had a strong concentration of Spanish immigrants; particularly in working-class areas. It also had the largest proportion of Europeans, although Algiers surpassed it a decade later. By one estimate, for every European in the population, Constantinois had 17 Algerians; Algérois, 6 Algerians; and Oranie, 4.3 Algerians.[28]

Whatever the regional variations, in all cities a stark social and spatial divide separated Europeans and Algerians. By the early twentieth century urban Europeans had fused into a Catholic, albeit often secularised, *pied-noir* (black-foot) community of manual and white-collar workers, artisans and shopkeepers with its own distinctive French dialect incorporating Spanish, Italian, Maltese and Arabic words. Racist contempt for the indigenous Muslim majority and Jewish minority was intrinsic to *pied-noir* identity. Just as anti-Semitism was part of *pied-noir* culture, so settlers used the term Arab derisively for objects of material culture – dress, food, markets – but rarely for people. They routinely described Arabo-Berber people as objects. The terms 'tree trunks' and *bicot* (slang derived from the word for goat) were commonly used in the early twentieth century. During the interwar years these were replaced by 'rats', 'melons' and 'bastards'. Europeans typically called Algerian men and women Ahmed and Fatma.[29]

This social segregation was reinforced by spatial segregation. 'The settler's town is a strongly built town, all made of stone and steel', wrote Frantz Fanon. It 'is a well-fed town, an easygoing town; its belly is always full of good things.' Not so the Algerian town. Algerians who moved to the cities to escape rural poverty were squeezed into old and crowded medinas or *casbahs* in city centres or into the *bidonvilles* (shantytowns) that began mushrooming on the outskirts in the 1920s. The Algerian town, continued Fanon, 'is a hungry town, starved of bread, of meat, of shoes, of coal, of light. The native town is a crouching village, a town on its knees, a town wallowing in the mire'.[30] Indeed, for the occasional European visitor, the Algiers *casbah* was 'a parallel universe' whose human density was intolerable. In 1926 each inhabitant had four square metres of ground; by 1931 this had shrunk to three square metres. The population levelled out two years later, as the *bidonvilles* sucked in new arrivals from the countryside.[31]

Yet Fanon's graphic words – true as they were – underestimated Algerian class stratification. Algerian landed elites often lived in towns. Despite the economic decline of the Ottoman-era bourgeoisie, their descendants clung to their status. Very religious and socially conservative, these *vieux turbans* (old turbans) nonetheless had a political influence exceeding their small numbers. Those of their sons who attended French schools became part of and aligned their interests with the French administrative system. *Caïds* and other hated officials were recruited from this group. Alongside this group was a rising economic elite composed of factory owners, managers, high-level civil servants and professionals. French educated and acculturated, they were generally conservative or moderate in their politics. Some had apartments in European neighbourhoods, but their close physical proximity to their European neighbours was mediated by myriad ways of ensuring day-to-day avoidance; segregation was psychologically internalised rather than legislated in law. The larger middle class included small and middle businessmen, civil servants, professionals, technicians, white-collar workers and certain skilled workers.[32] The European population was likewise divided by class; sections of its working class were very poor. They, too, often lived alongside Algerians, their dealings with them similarly circumscribed. Those seen as too neighbourly toward Algerians were warned they were becoming 'a real *bicot*'. Cultural ignorance was inevitable. Thus Camus recalled 'the working-class people of the neighbourhood, who knew nothing of Islam and ... saw only the surface'.[33]

But Algerians were still largely rural. Europeans referred to the countryside as *'le pays arabe'* (Arab country) and used Arabic terms to describe the terrain.[34] Despite the tiny class of large landowners, most rural dwellers lived precariously. The loss of land meant not only hunger but also the loss of their way of life. As a result, they felt colonialism more directly than did the townspeople, argued Mostefa Lacheraf in March 1955. Fanon agreed. 'For a colonised people the most essential value, because the most concrete, is first and foremost the land: the land which will bring them bread and, above all, dignity', he insisted. And dignity in its most concrete form meant freedom from hunger and violence.[35]

Indeed, the theft of the land was at the root of the problem. But the land's theft set off class dynamics. The return of the land might satisfy peasants and rural poor, but it could not address the needs and aspirations of an urban proletariat and an urbanising society linked to France through labour migration. This urban proletariat reflected colonial dynamics – rigidly divided between European and Algerian, Christian, Jew and Muslim, living in proximity to and even alongside each other, yet never together. It was this class – as part of a French nation – that Algeria's early socialists saw as their imagined community.

Notes

1 John Ruedy, *Modern Algeria: The Origins and Development of a Nation*, 2nd edn (Bloomington and Indianapolis, IN: Indiana University, 2005), pp. 1–2, 10–12; Martin Evans and John Phillips, *Algeria: Anger of the Dispossessed* (New Haven, CT, and London: Yale, 2007), pp. 3, 13, 22–4, 230.

2 Eric R. Wolf, *Peasant Wars of the Twentieth Century* [1969] (Norman, OK: University of Oklahoma, 1999), p. 211; Benjamin Claude Brower, *A Desert Named Peace: The Violence of France's Empire in the Algerian Sahara, 1844–1902* (New York: Columbia, 2009), pp. 1–26, 34–6.

3 Population estimates for this period are problematic. Ruedy, *Modern Algeria*, pp. 21, 122, n. 4, estimates three million, with half in the Constantine area, one million around Algiers and 500,000 in the Oran region.

4 Ruedy, *Modern Algeria*, pp. 21–2; Evans and Phillips, *Algeria*, pp. 19, 21–3; Marnia Lazreg, *The Eloquence of Silence: Algerian Women in Question* (New York and London: Routledge, 1994), p. 25.

5 Ruedy, *Modern Algeria*, pp. 24–7; Lazreg, *Eloquence*, p. 28; Evans and Phillips, *Algeria*, pp. 18–20; Benjamin E. Thomas, 'The Railways of French North Africa', *Economic Geography*, 29:2 (April 1953), 95–106, 95.

6 Ruedy, *Modern Algeria*, pp. 21, 28; Evans and Phillips, *Algeria*, p. 21; Brower, *Desert*, pp. 119–21; Lazreg, *Eloquence*, pp. 28–35; Julia A. Clancy-Smith, *Rebel and Saint: Muslim Notables, Populist Protests, Colonial Encounters (Algeria and Tunisia,*

1800–1904) (Berkeley, Los Angeles, CA, and London: University of California, 1994), pp. 36–7, 280–1, n. 14. Saints' tombs topped by white cupolas are dotted across the countryside, and the numbers of women visiting them are notable.

7 Mahfoud Bennoune, 'Socioeconomic Changes in Rural Algeria 1830–1954: A Diachronic Analysis of a Peasantry under Colonialism', *Peasant Studies Newsletter*, 11:2 (1973), 11–18, pp. 12–13; Wolf, *Peasant Wars*, pp. 211–12.

8 Brower, *Desert*, p. 22; « le but principal qui est la pacification est loin d'être atteint », Mostefa Lacheraf, *L'Algérie: Nation et société* (Algiers: Casbah, 2006), p. 63.

9 Ruedy, *Modern Algeria*, pp. 68, 73; Evans and Phillips, *Algeria*, p. 29; Lazreg, *Eloquence*, pp. 45–6, 53; Pierre Vallaud, *La Guerre d'Algérie: De la conquête à l'indépendance, 1830–1962* (Paris: Acropole, 2006), p. 26.

10 Ruedy, *Modern Algeria*, pp. 60–6; Brower, *Desert*, pp. 32–3, 181–3; Wolf, *Peasant Wars*, pp. 217–19; Vallaud, *Guerre*, pp. 31–2.

11 Mahmood Mamdani, 'Political Identity, Citizenship and Ethnicity in Post-colonial Africa', keynote address, Arusha Conference, 'New Frontiers of Social Policy' (12–15 December 2005), http://goo.gl/i1eWZU (accessed 16 December 2013); Mahmood Mamdani, *Citizen and Subject: Contemporary Africa and the Legacy of Late Colonialism* (Princeton, NJ: Princeton University, 1996).

12 Ruedy, *Modern Algeria*, pp. 52, 73–4; Brower, *Desert*, p. 115; Wolf, *Peasant Wars*, pp. 212–13; Vallaud, *Guerre*, pp. 31, 37–8; Olivier Todd, *Albert Camus: Une vie* (Paris: Gallimard, 1996), pp. 19, 1057; Albert Camus, *The First Man* (London: Penguin, 1996), pp. 146–7.

13 Ruedy, *Modern Algeria*, pp. 75–6; Vallaud, *Guerre*, pp. 39–40; Mamdani, *Citizen*, pp. 16–18.

14 Charles-Robert Ageron, *Modern Algeria: A History from 1830 to the Present* (London: Hurst, 1991), pp. 1–12; Charles-André Julien, *Histoire de l'Algérie contemporaine*, vol. 1, 3rd edn (Paris: Presses universitaires de France, 1986), pp. 2–105, 464–7; Nancy Wood, 'Remembering the Jews of Algeria', in Tyler Stovall and Georges van den Abbeele (eds), *French Civilization and its Discontents: Nationalism, Colonialism, Race* (Lanham, MD, etc: Lexington, 2003), 251–70, pp. 254–5; Jean-Louis Planche, 'Alger: Urbanisation et contrôle ethnique, 1930–1962', *Alger: Lumières sur la ville, Actes du colloque* (Algiers, 4–6 May 2002), vol. 1, pp. 231–45; Vallaud, *Guerre*, pp. 47–8, 54–5.

15 Mahfoud Bennoune, 'Algerian Peasants and National Politics', *MERIP Reports*, 48 (June 1976), 3–24, p. 14.

16 Charles-Robert Ageron, *Histoire de l'Algérie contemporaine*, vol. 2 (Paris: Presses Universitaires de France, 1979), p. 24; Ruedy, *Modern Algeria*, p. 88; Janet Dorsch Zagoria, 'The Rise and Fall of the Movement of Messali Hadj in Algeria, 1924–1954' (PhD, Columbia University, 1973), p. 45; Vallaud, *Guerre*, pp. 50–1; Mamdani, *Citizen*, pp. 126–7.

17 Ruedy, *Modern Algeria*, p. 82; Vallaud, *Guerre*, pp. 48–9, 50; Todd, *Camus: Une vie*, p. 1057; Camus, *First Man*, p. 53.

18 Thomas, 'Railways', p. 96; David Prochaska, *Making Algeria French: Colonialism in Bône, 1870–1920* (Cambridge: Cambridge University Press, and Paris: Editions de la Maison des sciences de l'homme, 1990), pp. 105–7, 109–11, 125–6, 197–8 on Bône.

19 Ruedy, *Modern Algeria*, pp. 83, 90, 95; Michel Launay, *Paysans Algériens: La Terre, la vigne, et les hommes* (Paris: Editions du Seuil, 1963), p. 64; David Prochaska, 'Fire on the Mountain: Resisting Colonialism in Algeria', in Donald Crummey (ed.), *Banditry, Rebellion and Social Protest in Africa* (London: James Currey, and Portsmouth, NH: Heinemann, 1986), 229–52, pp. 234–5; Paul Radiquet, 'Les paysans d'Algérie en lutte contre les expropriations', *Cahiers du Bolchevisme*, 8 (15 April 1933), 576–82, p. 576.

20 Launay, *Paysans*, p. 426; Wolf, *Peasant Wars*, pp. 214–15.

21 Henri Alleg, 'Le torrent souterrain', in Henri Alleg (ed.) *La Guerre d'Algérie*, vol. 1 (Paris: Editions Messidor, 1981), 13–283; p. 162; Ruedy, *Modern Algeria*, pp. 95–6; Wolf, *Peasant Wars*, p. 217; Prochaska, 'Fire', pp. 241, 249.

22 Ruedy, *Modern Algeria*, pp. 85, 98–9, 123, 115–17; Radiquet, 'Paysans', pp. 576–7.

23 Wolf, *Peasant Wars*, p. 229, suggests that peasants making ends meet had 50–100

hectares in wheat or 1–20 hectares in vines and comprised one-third of the Muslim population; Ageron, *Histoire*, vol. 2, pp. 221, 495; Ruedy, *Modern Algeria*, pp. 90, 100, 122–3, uses Ageron's table, but notes problems with the figures.
24 Ageron, *Histoire*, vol. 2, pp. 507–8; Ruedy, *Modern Algeria*, pp. 122–3.
25 Mohammed Dib, *La Grande Maison* (Paris: Editions du Seuil, 1952, 1996), p. 118.
26 Ruedy, *Modern Algeria*, pp. 99, 125; Ageron, *Histoire*, vol. 2, p. 530; Rabah Aissaoui, 'From colonial dispossession to exile: Algerian migration to France from the early twentieth century to the eve of the Second World War', *Socialist History*, 39 (2011), 1–23.
27 Thomas, 'Railways', pp. 96–7.
28 Ageron, *Histoire*, vol. 2, pp. 470–1, 474, 476.
29 Emmanuel Sivan, 'Colonialism and Popular Culture in Algeria', *Journal of Contemporary History*, 14:1 (January 1979), 21–53, pp. 21–6; Gosnell, *Politics*, pp. 140–86; Prochaska, *Making*, pp. 202–7; on the imbedded anti-Semitism see *Le Franc-parleur oranais: Organe du Parti républicain antijuif* (1899), *L'Avenir de l'Oranie: Journal républicain radical antijuif* (1905).
30 Frantz Fanon, *The Wretched of the Earth* (New York: Grove, 1968), p. 39; Ruedy, *Modern Algeria*, p. 125; Prochaska, *Making*, pp. 11–25.
31 « un univers parallèle », Jean-Louis Planche, 'Les Lieux de l'Algérianité', in Jean-Jacques Jordi and Jean-Louis Planche (eds), *Alger, 1860–1939: Le Modèle ambigu du triomphe colonial* (Paris: Editions Autrement, 1999), 180–203, pp. 183–5.
32 Planche, 'Lieux', pp. 186–7; communication from Jean-Louis Planche, 20 February 2009; Ageron, *Histoire*, vol. 2, pp. 222–3; Ruedy, *Modern Algeria*, p. 125.
33 Sivan, 'Colonialism', pp. 29, 38; Camus, *First Man*, p. 91.
34 Sivan, 'Colonialism', pp. 30–1.
35 Lacheraf, *L'Algérie*, p. 58; Fanon, *Wretched*, p. 44.

CHAPTER TWO

Grappling for a communist foothold

The land was hostile indeed to socialists. The vast terrain, limited infrastructure, rigidly divided urban working class and overwhelmingly rural population made the diffusion of socialist ideas extremely difficult. Even language was a barrier: the indigenous majority spoke Arabic or Berber, but socialist ideas were formulated in French. Repression made left-wing activism extremely risky, while the *indigénat* made it illegal for Algerians to join political parties. Yet Algeria's socialists were optimistic. They could claim that Marx himself had spent a few months in Algeria in 1882 – for health reasons – and that Marx and Engels had written about the French conquest of Algeria. Marx and Engels readily recognised colonialism's violence and economic devastation, but they did not mention its political or cultural implications.[1]

Nor did Algeria's socialists. Their movement originated in France and reflected the well established intellectual socialist tradition. French socialists could point to France's secular and anti-clerical revolutionary tradition – incorporating the French Revolution and the Paris commune. From 1905 this movement found organisational expression in the Section française de l'internationale ouvrière (Socialist Party, SFIO), alongside a weaker anarchist tradition.[2] An Algerian section reflecting the interests of organised European workers was launched in 1906. Its members lived in coastal cities and railway towns, and railway workers disseminated socialist literature. Its organ *Lutte sociale (Social Struggle)* was launched in late 1907 in Oran – a trade union and local-government-oriented French-language publication with occasional Spanish articles reflecting Spanish immigrant influence. In January 1908 *Lutte sociale* announced the first congress of the Fédération socialiste algérienne, to be presided over by philosophy professor Marcel Cachin, on tour in Algeria. Cachin stressed the need to alleviate the misery of Algerian workers, and *Lutte sociale* began calling for working-class unity across national lines.[3] Socialists were prominent in the Ligue française pour la défense des droits de l'homme et du citoyen (League for the Rights of Man and Citizen, LDD), which advocated the greatest possible extension of Algerian representation in local assemblies, the Chamber of Deputies and the Senate. Generally, though, the SFIO gave scant attention to Algeria. Its leader, Jean Jaurès, envisioned the liberation of Algerians through their gradual assimilation into the French polity. Yet the party itself took no steps towards that goal before the 1914–18 war.[4]

Algerian political activists were similarly focused on assimilation. As elsewhere in Africa, the defeat of armed resistance against colonial conquest gave way, by the early twentieth century, to attempts to reform the colonial order to allow greater indigenous representation. The first such reform movement was represented by the Jeunes algériens (Young Algerians). Challenging the *vieux turbans*, the Young Algerians gained momentum in 1907–8. Stressing respect for Arab and Muslim culture, they also idealised French culture and aspired to assimilation. Nonetheless, they were met with settler resistance.

Behind these initiatives lay grinding rural misery. Some 32 per cent of rural people were sharecroppers, and 16 per cent, proletarianised. Although close to half of the rural population still farmed their own land, the size and quality of land was generally insufficient for self-subsistence, and Algerians streamed into towns. By 1921 Algiers' *casbah*, already partly demolished to make room for European settlement, was seriously overcrowded. Typically, three people – but sometimes six or seven – shared a room.[5] Algerian men working in France earned about three to four times what they could in Algeria, enabling them to remit comparatively large sums to their families.[6] The urban working class to which socialists turned was divided between Algerian workers in France – a displaced proletariat – and in Algeria a predominantly European labour force alongside newly urbanised Algerians, generally classed as unskilled.

The Young Algerian movement subsided during the war, but revived thereafter. Charles Jonnart, who served as governor-general in 1900–1 and 1903–11, occupied the position again in 1918–19. The Jonnart Law of 4 February 1919 called for a second college for local elections for qualified Muslim voters. This increased the Muslim electorate to about 425,000 or approximately 43 per cent of the adult male Muslim population. Those with the right to vote in municipal elections included honourably discharged veterans, recipients of French honours, land or business owners, active and retired civil servants, chamber of commerce members, agriculture school graduates and elementary school leavers. In contrast, the number of voters qualified to select departmental council members increased to just over 100,000, and Algerian municipal councillors could participate in mayoral elections. Because the maximum representation of Algerians in municipal councils was limited to one-third, and in departmental councils, to one-fourth, it was effectively impossible for Algerians to be elected to the key post of mayor and to control the departmental councils. Despite these limitations, the reforms stimulated political activity.[7]

The Jonnart law conceded to settler concerns, moreover, by dropping the idea of common representation for Europeans and Algerians. Nonetheless, it reinforced settler resistance to further reforms, while intensifying Algerian political activity and anti-French sentiment. Although the Young Algerians criticised the reforms, they were generally accepted. But not by the charismatic Emir Khaled – the Syrian-born grandson of the anti-colonialist Emir Abdelkader – who, aged eighteen, had declared, 'I am Arab, and I want to remain Arab.' In 1919 Khaled launched the influential French-Arabic newspaper *L'Ikdam* (*Courage*), in which Young Algerians attacked the inadequate reforms and *Beni-oui-oui*, or yes-men, who supported French politicians. Khaled demanded extensive reforms: French citizenship with the retention of Muslim personal status, parliamentary representation, abolition of mixed communes and bilingual French–Arabic education for all. Over the next few years he set the pace for Algerian reformists, proclaiming his loyalty to France while frankly criticising its colonial administration.[8]

International communism

In contrast to socialist and Young Algerian assimilationism, communism was from its outset self-consciously international. The First World War had turned European society upside-down, and the Russian Revolution created a tsunami whose effects reached Europe's colonies. The Comintern aimed to guide the international revolutionary movement. Yet there was an inherent tension between its internationalist aims, its growing insistence on the Russian Revolution as the paradigm for revolutionary success, and the increasing influence of the Soviet Communist Party on its executive.[9] Nonetheless, its vision of world revolution fuelled capitalist fears around the world. In France a 1919 May Day strike organised by the Confédération générale du travail (General Confederation of Labour, CGT) brought out half a million demonstrators. The *Bloc national* coalition fought national elections on an anti-Bolshevik platform, took office in November 1919 and inaugurated 'the most conservative legislature since 1871'.[10]

By the time of its Second Congress in July–August 1920, the Comintern saw anti-colonial and national liberation struggles as means of weakening imperialism. Vladimir Lenin and M. N. Roy debated the significance of national liberation movements for socialism, with

Lenin conceding the politically ambivalent nature of bourgeois democratic movements and advocating support for national revolutionary movements. Reflecting the belief that class struggle in Europe and North America was approaching civil war – an assumption already undermined by the waning of Europe's revolutionary prospects – the Comintern adopted twenty-one points stipulating conditions for affiliation. Social democratic principles were replaced by democratic centralism, enabling the party centre to have full power and authority. Factions were subordinated to the central committee. Parties were to propagandise against the International Federation of Trade Unions – the Amsterdam International – in support of a Red International of Labour Unions (RILU). Intensely debated by socialists around the world, the Comintern's requirements propelled organisational changes in groups seeking affiliation.[11]

The launch of the Section française de l'internationale communiste (SFIC) – the French Communist Party – in December 1920 at Tours was 'a great catch' for the Comintern. Attended by some 370 overwhelmingly male delegates, the Tours congress was a stormy affair. The twenty-one points, published in *L'Humanité* on 8 October 1920, were contentious, and significant numbers opposed their centralising nature. However, a centrist faction led by Marcel Cachin and Ludovic-Oscar Frossard and supported by Boris Souvarine and Fernand Loriot's left faction, successfully pushed their acceptance.[12]

Charles-André Julien represented Algeria's socialists, most of whom supported affiliation. Born 1891 in Caen, he had accompanied his father to Algeria in 1906. A teacher, LDD member and permanent socialist delegate in Algeria, Julien had been elected in 1919 as a Socialist regional councillor in Oran. Socialist Party membership cards issued for the three Algerian departments in October 1920 showed Algiers with 700 members, and Constantine and Oran with 400 members each.[13] At Tours Julien pointed out that the congress motions had been debated in Algeria while Algerians themselves were dying of hunger. These dire conditions would, he believed, push the new communists towards revolution.[14]

The twenty-one points had been published in *Lutte sociale* on 18 November, and Julien had been instructed to seek clarification on points eight and sixteen. Point eight stated that a party seeking affiliation to the Comintern must 'denounce without any reserve all methods of "its own" imperialists in the colonies, supporting, not only in words but practically, all movements of liberation ... It should demand the expulsion of its own imperialists from such colonies.' Point sixteen insisted on centralisation but acknowledged that the Comintern was 'bound ... to consider the variety of conditions under which the different parties have to work and struggle'.[15]

The Tours congress approved affiliation to the Comintern, although discussion of these two key points was curtailed. This did not worry Algeria's new communists: from their perspective, point eight's stipulation for the expulsion of imperialists from colonies was mediated by point sixteen's recognition of local diversity. Their mandated delegates – representing an entirely European membership – overwhelmingly supported affiliation: 94.7 per cent approval from Constantine; 86.7 per cent from Algiers, and 100 per cent from Oran. Like the Socialist Party before it, the new PCF's organisation was mapped onto the French state's administrative organisation, with the Algerian region organised into three federations – Algérois, Oranie and Constantinois – corresponding to the three administrative departments; each in turn was subdivided into sections.[16]

The PCF's members claimed both the French and Russian revolutionary heritages, and the movement was launched in Algeria in seemingly auspicious circumstances.[17] As in France, the First World War had precipitated the growth of an urban Algerian workforce. Postwar inflation pressured workers, and trade union membership increased rapidly, doubling in Algérois and more than tripling in Oranie. The socialist press, which had vanished during the war, revived between 1918 and 1920, with *Lutte sociale* in Oran, *Demain* (*Tomorrow*) in Algiers and *Le droit du people* (*The People's Right*) in Constantine. *Lutte sociale* proposed a joint column called 'Across Algeria's socialist groups' so that socialists in each region would know what the others were doing.[18] Strike waves in 1919–20 – by dock workers, mine workers, cigarette workers, bakery workers and carters – echoed those in France and raised hopes for the unity of Algerian and European workers, although it was clear that forging such unity would not be easy. One 'Tiberius Gracchus' opened his article with 'Algerian proletarians, let us unite!' and ended with 'Native, Spanish and Italian proletarians, let us unite!' – indicating the fragmented working class. The presence of Algerian workers amongst the strikers and demonstrators sparked hysteria within the settler community about a combined Bolshevik and Muslim threat, but Algeria's first communists – with *Lutte sociale* as their organ – were optimistic.[19]

The Sidi bel Abbès thesis

Nonetheless, the issues addressed in points eight and sixteen were to cause problems for the emerging communist movement. Soon after the PCF's formation, communists in Algeria voiced concerns about points eight and sixteen. As early as April 1921 the Constantine-based medical doctor Louis Laurens argued that Revolution in France was a precondition for revolution in the colonies. A socialist France would facilitate Franco-Algerian cooperation and enable French civilisation to guide Algerian development.[20] That same month a similar view was put forward by communists in Sidi bel Abbès – a rural town between Oran and Tlemcen that had been founded as a French military camp and was home to the French Foreign Legion. With an early rail line, Sidi bel Abbès had a high proportion of working-class Spanish immigrants, a strong labour base, especially amongst railway workers, and a socialist tradition – Europeans called it the Red Mecca. Arguing for the primacy of a French Revolution, the Sidi bel Abbès thesis deprecated Muslim landed elites as backward and feudal, insisting that communists should promote trade union organisation but reject point eight's seeming 'abandonment of the colonies'. Critics of the thesis could claim that Russia had experienced revolution despite its social and economic backwardness. Nonetheless, the Bolsheviks believed in the need for revolution in industrialised countries. Internationally, the debates were far from resolved.[21]

At the Comintern's Third Congress in June–July 1921, Julien expressed concern about the conditions of Algerians and, as he put it, the scarcely disguised hostility of European communists towards the indigenous majority. While capitalism in Western countries had transformed social relations and produced an urban working class, Julien contended, elsewhere capitalist development had produced agricultural workers, not urban proletarians, leaving intact the privileged elites, whose interests lay with capitalism. However, the *petite bourgeoisie* and intellectuals were anti-capitalist and so had common interests with workers. Communists must recognise that the anti-imperialist struggle included all these classes, he argued. Since nationalist aspirations had grown since the war's end, the national question would be of first importance in the anti-imperialist struggle. Communists needed to guide national liberation movements, explaining to workers that their interests lay with communists rather than national elites. But Julien's views represented a minority position amongst communists in Algeria. Nor were they endorsed by the other French delegates at the congress, one of whom pointedly dissociated the French delegation from his intervention.[22]

Pushed by the Comintern, in August 1921, the PCF established the Paris-based Comité d'études coloniales (Committee of colonial studies). Aimed at studying conditions in colonised areas and building movements against capitalism, militarism and imperialism, it was headed by Paul Vaillant-Couturier, who supported Lenin's ideas on colonial liberation.[23] In March 1922 Vaillant-Couturier made a propaganda trip to Algeria, with twenty-three meetings in twenty-two days, sweeping through nineteen cities. One was the historic city of Tlemcen, near the Algerian–Moroccan border. Very religious, Tlemcen had four or five large mosques and many small neighbourhood mosques, and women visited the shrines of local saints. Most Tlemcenians had land for cultivation and thus still had 'one foot in the countryside and the other in town'. But it was a class-divided town where 'poverty spoke one language and wealth another', and where even the relatively small numbers of Europeans were divided by class and speech.[24] Class divisions were reflected in political allegiances: the Algerian bourgeoisie, which had grown during the war, supported the colonial administration.

Vaillant-Couturier's speech attracted as many Algerians as Europeans, and his remark that peasants and workers bore the brunt of colonial oppression struck a chord.[25] Algeria was a scandalous land, where imprisonment and political assassination were used against the indigenous masses by those who had stolen the country, claimed Vaillant-Couturier.[26] Yet, on returning to Paris, he seemed swayed by the arguments of the European communists he had met in Algeria and published a series on *'L'Impérialisme français en Algérie'* in *L'Humanité* that assumed the primacy of revolution in Europe. The only security for European settlers, he argued, was the education of Algerians in a North Africa liberated by international revolution; revolution in France would lay the basis for a federated system of republics in North Africa.[27]

On 20 May 1922 the Comintern issued a call for the liberation of Algeria and Tunisia (*Appel de l'Internationale communiste pour la libération de l'Algérie et de la Tunisie*). Noting that repression made communist organisation virtually impossible, the document urged French workers to defend the cause of African workers as their own and French soldiers and sailors not to shoot their North African brothers. In that way the French working class would assist the national revolution while attacking French imperialism.[28] Nevertheless, under Vaillant-Couturier's direction, the Comité d'études coloniales evidently refrained from publishing the document so as to avoid putting undue pressure on comrades in Algeria. It did, however, call for greater work amongst Algerians and for the publication of Arabic political tracts. Nonetheless, the Algerian federations still felt that Paris did not take their perspectives sufficiently into account.[29]

The Algerian federations opposed the Comintern's call for North African independence. The Sidi bel Abbès section argued that diverse colonial conditions negated the viability of a single thesis on the colonial question and that local communists should develop local tactics. It refused to disseminate propaganda that it had not seen and approved. It insisted that revolution in France was a precondition for emancipation in Algeria, that a Muslim revolution would entail a return to feudalism and that propaganda aimed at Algerians would backfire. Similar views were voiced at the second North African interfederal congress on 24 September 1922, which rejected the Comintern's general propositions in the name of local specificities and concluded that it was impossible to build a national liberation movement in Algeria at that time. These attitudes were reflected in *Lutte sociale*, which gave scant coverage to specifically Algerian concerns and, with small print and no photos or illustrations, required a high degree of French literacy.[30]

Yet some Algerians were curious about the PCF. Djerjeraoui – 'a Native Communist' – argued that communism was the only doctrine able to satisfy Algerians' needs for equality.[31] A communist anti-war demonstration on 21 May 1922 attracted several hundred, including many youth, a few women and about fifty Arabs, reported the British consul-general in Algiers.[32] Trade unionist A. Boye urged European workers to 'think of our native comrade as a brother ... more unhappy than us because he carries the marks of long years of oppression' and as 'a victim of our common enemy: international capitalism'.[33] Victor Spielmann, a long-time radical anti-colonialist who defended the cause of the small against the large and belonged both to Emir Khaled's Fraternité algérienne (Algerian Fraternity) and the PCF, launched a series on the 'native question' in *Lutte sociale*, which publicised his brochure on colonisation's impact on Algerians.[34] Such individuals were rare; nonetheless, the need for working-class unity across the national and religious divide was recognised. That was the lesson that *Lutte sociale* drew from South Africa's Rand Revolt – which began in January 1922 as a white mine-workers' strike and culminated in an armed revolt brutally suppressed by state forces in March. The paper attributed the revolt's failure to the white miners' racial prejudice, which had allowed capital to divide and rule. White miners lacked a clear idea of class struggle, it concluded.[35]

The Comintern's Fourth Congress took place in November–December 1922. As revolutionary prospects dimmed, the main issues were 'immediate demands' and 'united fronts'. The Comintern emphasised the national and colonial questions and criticised the PCF's failure to promote point eight. But the PCF was consumed with domestic developments. Raymond Poincaré's January 1922 election as Prime Minister demonstrated the right's strength, while the split between socialists and communists had penetrated the CGT, leading to the expulsion of groups advocating revolution. In February the expelled groups formed the Confédération générale du travail unitaire (CGTU). Despite the socialist–communist split, the Comintern chastised the

PCF for carrying on in the old socialist manner.[36] Leon Trotsky himself castigated the Sidi bel Abbès thesis, 'which employs pseudo-Marxist phraseology in order to cover up a purely slave-holder's point of view, essentially in support of the imperialist rule of French capitalism over its colonial slaves'. Communists in colonised areas should not rely 'on elements so completely infected with capitalist and nationalist prejudices', but on 'the best elements' of the indigenous population, and especially its working-class youth.[37]

The censure shocked communists in Algeria. Maxime Guillon, author of the Sidi bel Abbès thesis and secretary of the Sidi bel Abbès region and the three Algerian federations, resigned immediately. The federations' membership plummeted to 530 as intellectuals and professionals left, including Guillon and Julien, both teachers, and Dr Laurens, amongst others. Some presumably returned to the Socialist Party, which also claimed the French revolutionary tradition.[38] The balance of power amongst the federations shifted: Oranie and intellectuals lost status; Algérois and workers gained. Etienne Mazoyer, a ruined *colon* who had settled in Algiers and become a railway worker and union secretary, became leader of the federations. Following the Comintern, Mazoyer promised greater attention to the colonial question and to Algerian recruitment. New names became prominent in *Lutte sociale*.[39]

The next two years saw greater attention given to North African issues. The PCF's anti-war campaign embraced the French occupation of the Ruhr in Germany and the Rif War in Morocco. In 1923 French troops occupied the Ruhr, following Germany's failure to pay war reparations. The issue polarised French opinion, and the PCF campaigned heavily against the occupation. The PCF also opposed the Rif War, which began in 1919 when Spain attempted to conquer the Riffians. In July 1921 Abd el-Krim defeated the Spanish army in Morocco and in January 1923 declared the Republic of Rif.

Linking the campaigns, the PCF launched the bilingual publication, *La Caserne/El Kazirna*, produced in Paris with the help of Abdelaziz (Ali) Menouer. Born in 1893 into an old bourgeois family in Algiers, Menouer completed primary school and was apprenticed in a ceramics workshop, where he encountered socialist, anarchist and anti-militarist ideas. During the war, he travelled to England and the United States, where he worked at a porcelain factory, organised a trade union and led two successful strikes. Returning to Algeria in 1921, he joined the PCF and was sent to Moscow, where he studied at the Communist University of Toilers of the East (KUTV) in 1922–23. Moving to Paris, he joined the Comité d'études coloniales.[40] *La Caserne* was aimed at soldiers and workers: cartoons with Arabic captions showed European and North African workers and soldiers fighting together against the capitalist boss. Its December 1923 second issue carried appeals to 'Liberate the Ruhr!' and 'Liberate Morocco!' and was immediately banned in Algeria. Its March 1924 fourth issue demanded 'the independence of the colonies'.[41]

Lutte sociale's pages showed more concern with Algerian rights, while remaining ambivalent about nationalism. In 1922 one Mekloub exhorted Algerians to leave their national associations and join workers' organisations, the only places, he contended, where opposition to all forms of exploitation could be found.[42] The paper published more articles on local conditions, notably rural famine and the *indigénat*.[43] From 16 November 1923, its subtitle became *'Journal communiste algérien'*, and it ran the slogan 'workers of all lands unite' in French and Arabic. It advertised initiatives such as the Comité algérien de secours aux indigènes (Algerian committee for aid to natives), launched in February 1923 by Drs Belqacem Benthami and Abdennour Tamzali, both leading Young Algerians, and of which Spielmann was treasurer-general.

January 1924 saw the launch of the Cercle franco-indigène nord-africain (North African French-Native Circle). Organised by Spielmann and Dji Taleb, it promoted the rapprochement of Europeans and Algerians and the gradual extension of Algerian rights – 'while safeguarding and consolidating the development of French influence'.[44] That year also saw the publication of R. A. Crémieux's pamphlet, *A.B.C. du syndicalisme* (*A.B.C. of Trade Unionism*), dedicated to Etienne Mazoyer. Crémieux was scathingly critical of anti-Semitism and anti-Algerian racism amongst European workers. To those European workers who argued that trade unionism was 'good, but not for the natives!' Crémieux retorted: 'Workers of all lands unite ... even and especially, the natives.' Clearly, by 1924 some European communists hoped to organise both European and Algerian workers.[45] The Sidi bel Abbès episode has coloured subsequent interpretations of communism in Algeria, which have attributed the PCF's difficulties in attracting Algerians to European prejudice. Yet even after the thesis was rejected and its proponents marginalised, the party had great difficulties in attracting Algerians.[46]

Bolshevisation and repression

In 1923 the international communist movement had suffered a serious setback with the defeat of an attempted but unfeasible German revolution. The defeat compelled Bolsheviks to reassess their thinking on Europe's revolutionary prospects. The Comintern introduced the Bolshevisation policy at its Fifth Congress in June–July 1924. Amended the next year, Bolshevisation reflected Soviet Communist Party power struggles between the Zinoviev–Kamenev–Stalin triumvirate, on the one side, and Leon Trotsky, on the other. Led by Zinoviev, the Comintern's Executive Committee (ECCI) claimed that the German fiasco was due to so-called right deviationist leadership soft on social democracy. The triumvirate strove to link the fiasco to Trotsky. Bolshevisation was an alleged left turn to counteract the alleged right deviation. The ECCI argued that revolution necessitated that national sections apply the seemingly successful Bolshevik model to their own situation. Ironically, the failure of revolution in Germany, by reinforcing Russian isolation, gave greater credibility to the Soviet experience. Bolshevisation, therefore, reflected the Soviet Communist Party's growing influence within the Comintern.[47]

The Fifth Comintern Congress defined a Bolshevised party as a centralised, mass party 'permitting no fractions, tendencies or groups'.[48] In the ECCI's words, Bolshevisation meant 'the application of the general principles of Leninism to the concrete situation of the given country'. It necessitated 'iron party discipline' and was 'a permanent and continuing process'. The old social-democratic organisation was unacceptable. At the top of the Bolshevik party, the political bureau determined policy, working with the secretariat, which administered policy. The political bureau was elected by the central committee. Beneath the central committee were regional and district committees directing the party's local structures. At the base was the cell, which could be formed in neighbourhoods, workplaces or villages. Communist workers were to form fractions or cells in their workplace to advance party policy and win elections to union posts.[49] The accent on a mass party had particular implications for communists in settler societies where workers were divided along ethnic or national lines. Those communists were to recruit members from the oppressed majority so that the party would be demographically representative of the entire population rather than the privileged workers. In Algeria Bolshevisation entailed greater efforts to recruit Muslims.

The policy had critics, but it also had significant proponents, especially Jeunesse communiste (JC) members – Young Communists who climbed the party hierarchy as a result of their support – and those concerned with the colonial question. The old allegedly social-democratic methods were equated with colonialist attitudes, and some saw Bolshevisation's organisational changes as a means to reorient the PCF towards Algerians. Centralisation was equated with greater efficiency. This was certainly Menouer's view. In France the Ruhr's occupation became the key issue in the May 1924 national elections. A *cartel des gauches*, or left-wing alliance of socialists and radicals, came to power, bringing the troops home and promoting accommodation with Germany. Many communists thought the moment was auspicious for the expansion of left-wing influence.[50]

In June 1924 Menouer wrote to a Comrade Kolaroff in Moscow, complaining of the PCF's lack of interest in the colonial question – 'Until the start of 1924, the party did nothing to organise colonial workers' – and of its foot-dragging on the education of comrades from colonised areas, as well as bemoaning the Comité d'études coloniales' lack of representation at the Fifth Congress of the Comintern.[51] He complained about the decision to send comrade Ferrand of Sidi bel Abbès as the Algerian delegate to the congress, fearing that he would present a one-sidedly European perspective. Those supporting greater emphasis on the colonial question would be pleased if the Comintern's directives and proposed methods of action presented at its Fifth Congress were implemented, Menouer added.[52]

Bolshevisation was introduced to the PCF in September 1924, the month in which the Comité d'études coloniales was reorganised as the Commission coloniale centrale.[53] Jacques Doriot, a Paris-based communist who specialised in anti-colonial agitation and whose loyal support found ready favour in Moscow, signalled the change. Heretofore, the PCF had been remiss in its anti-colonial work. The state of mind that had characterised European communists in Algeria had not entirely disappeared. Diligence was necessary to create federations able to manoeuvre in the complicated North African environment.[54]

The PCF's January 1925 fourth national congress at Clichy streamlined the party's ninety federations into twenty-seven regions. The PCF used the terms *rayon* and *sous-rayon* to denote the levels between the regional committee and local neighbourhood or workplace cells. The three Algerian federations were merged into one region, formalised at a congress in Algiers on 22 March 1925 and accompanied by expulsions. The congress saw the rise of Pierre Biboulet, secretary of the Algiers region, who played a large role in the fusion and in Bolshevisation's implementation; the task did not make him popular amongst his comrades. Along with centralisation came an emphasis on indigenisation. The Algiers congress agreed that the PCF's main task was to awaken the indigenous masses to national and class consciousness.[55]

Communists were discussing running Algerian candidates in the May 1925 municipal elections. Bolshevisation gave new impetus to this. According to sympathetic sources, the campaign generated great enthusiasm amongst Algerians, but also unleashed a wave of government repression. The PCF had received positive feedback from Algerians in France and Algeria following its decision to run Abdelkader Hadj Ali, a Paris-based Algerian and naturalised French citizen, as a candidate for the 'workers and peasants bloc' in the 1924 local Paris elections.[56] The grandson of a ruined landowner, Hadj Ali was born in 1883 at Sidi Saada, near Rélizane in Oranie, and began working in a hardware store at fourteen. Moving to Paris, he worked at various occupations, joined the CGT, became a French citizen in 1911, married a French woman in 1912 and fought in the First World War. After the war he joined the socialists, then the communists, and took up anti-war propaganda. In 1921 he was the first Algerian in the newly launched Union intercoloniale, where he worked with the Vietnamese activist Nguyen Ai Quoc – later known as Ho Chi Minh. By the time Hadj Ali ran for office, he was already a leading member of the Commission coloniale centrale. One of three communist candidates, he was not elected but gained a significant number of votes: the two winning communists gained 41,601 and 40,801 votes to Hadj Ali's 40,781. This strengthened the resolve of Algerian communists in Paris to stress to the Comintern the importance of organising North African workers.[57]

Encouraged, the PCF's Algerian region put forward European and Algerian lists under its 'workers and peasants bloc'. The Algerian list was headed, symbolically, by Emir Khaled, and by Mahmoud Ben Lekhal, who, like Menouer, came from the old Muslim bourgeoisie. Born in Algiers, Ben Lekhal had travelled to Syria and studied in Beirut. Avoiding conscription, in 1921 he joined the PCF in France, becoming celebrated for his work against the occupation of the Ruhr. Sentenced to five years in prison and amnestied after a vigorous PCF campaign, Ben Lekhal went to Paris and joined the Union intercoloniale and the Colonial Commission. His electoral candidacy attracted new Algerian members. Since the fusion conference, *Lutte sociale* had been striving to attract a Francophone Algerian readership through greater coverage of Algerian issues and larger, more readable headlines. But after the elections many new Algerian and European members left, precipitating a feeling of crisis.[58]

Bolshevisation coincided with and was justified by the Rif War, which gave communists an opportunity to implement point eight of the twenty-one points – although their stance was seemingly motivated more by anti-militarism than anti-colonialism. The Spanish withdrew from the Rif in mid-1924, in the aftermath of Miguel Primo de Rivera's September 1923 coup. In May 1924, 12,000 French troops were sent to the Rif, to be attacked by Abd el-Krim the next month. But two years later, in May 1926, faced with a coalition of French and Spanish forces, Abd el-Krim surrendered and was exiled to Réunion. While the Socialist Party was ambiguous, the PCF led a vigorous anti-war campaign against French army actions in Morocco – organising a

24-hour protest in France supported by some 900,000 workers. This anti-war campaign attracted and was sustained by the JC's efforts.[59] In Algeria the leading Young Communists were Europeans, but some Algerians joined around this time. One of these was Ben Ali Boukort. Born in 1904, Boukort was the eldest of ten children of a shopkeeper in a village near Mostaganem in Oranie. An excellent student at teacher-training college, he became attracted to communism after hearing Mazoyer call for an independent Algeria and an end to the Rif War during an electoral campaign. He began reading *Ikdam* and *Lutte sociale*, sending them articles signed 'the young red'. In 1924, he joined the JC, only to be expelled from school for his politics.[60] Another was Sid Ahmed Belarbi, who came from a family of fallen Sunnite notables. He found work as a tramway conductor and joined the CGTU. He became involved with the JC during the Rif War campaign, was sent to Paris for training and climbed the communist hierarchy.[61]

Both in France and Algeria the communist stance on the Rif War brought the PCF into direct confrontation with the French state. The consequences were heavy indeed as anti-war activists were thrown in prison. But the repression provided the rationale for Bolshevisation's more centralised approach. As Ageron noted: 'The bolshevisation of the party in Algeria as in France was facilitated by the Rif war.'[62] A portent of things to come was Pierre Biboulet's arrest in June 1925. The following month, the PCF sent Henri Lozeray, Victor-Noël Arrighi and Jean-Baptiste Aucouterier from Paris to campaign against the war. Arrested on arrival in Algiers, they were sentenced to two years in Barberousse Prison, known to Algerians as Serkadji. In August eleven more comrades – including prominent Young Communists – were detained at Serkadji.

Paul Henriet arrived from Paris that August. Keen to impress PCF headquarters, Henriet reported that he had helped communists in Blida – mainly European artisans – with propaganda to ensure Algerian attendance at an upcoming congress. The tremendous difficulty of communication, given Algeria's size and relatively undeveloped infrastructure, made centralisation an ambitious – if not impossible – goal. Based in Algiers, Henriet informed Paris that letters to Constantine had been unanswered for over one month, and since comrades in Algiers knew very little about conditions in Oran, he was planning a visit.[63]

The country's size and limited infrastructure made national distribution of *Lutte sociale* all the more important. But the paper was hard hit by frequent seizures. It was badly in debt, and its printer Père Targe was angry. He felt that the paper's anti-war propaganda made it a continual target of the regime's wrath and that the paper should focus on legal electoral activity instead. It was vital, Henriet advised Paris, that the party centre subsidise the paper. The repression was so severe that many comrades had withdrawn from politics, and the paper was the only means to reach people in remote areas, he argued. Repressive laws intimidated people from renting meeting space to communists and from attending their meetings. 'The last meetings have proven that natives and Europeans would not come', Henriet observed, necessitating private meetings. They had to be careful to ensure that their most recent friends were not subjected to repression: 'We are no longer in France.'[64] Over the next several years, leading activists were imprisoned for anti-war activities, often for two years. This made it virtually impossible to organise and coordinate activities. Morale plummeted.

Debating independence

Battered by repression, the PCF's Algerian region was internally divided about independence. Many communists still argued that the call for independence was premature, emphasising instead the struggle for equality and working-class unity within the colonial framework. Henriet, particularly impressed by Henri Schiavo, whom he considered an ideal leader, came to share this view. Born 1886 in Algiers, Schiavo had worked in the port of Algiers and helped organise the communist-aligned CGTU. In 1925 he organised commercial workers in Blida. Schiavo did not think a national movement was possible, Henriet reported, but he had created a magnificent trade union movement of Europeans and Algerians, spoke some Arabic and was 'the man of the moment'. Algerians wanted equality with Europeans, Henriet argued. They understood that conditions imposed a class struggle rather than a struggle for independence, which would lead nowhere.[65]

Yet Biboulet, reporting to PCF headquarters in October 1925, insisted that communists promote the national struggle and criticised the party's delay in recruiting Algerians. Even up to the May 1924 legislative elections, he claimed, the party had failed to take a position on the 'native question' for fear of alienating the *petits colons*. In Biboulet's view anti-communist repression was a response as much to its joint European–Algerian electoral campaign as to its anti-war campaign; fraternity between Europeans and Algerians was a greater threat to the state than anti-war agitation. Biboulet believed that Algerians nurtured the hope of independence. 'How can one doubt it,' he wrote, 'when we see the passionate interest with which the Algerian natives follow the events of Rif and of Syria. In the most remote *douars*, in cities and in the countryside, amongst Arabs and amongst Kabyles, amongst the uneducated as well as the intellectuals, everyone is avid for news.' In Blida one Algerian interrupted a communist meeting to call for 'a state that is independent of all European tutelage'.[66]

Tensions deepened the next year. In February 1926 the Algerian region held its annual conference, which stressed an alliance of the working-class and national movements. It urged European communists to surmount their attitude of superiority over Algerians. Even if the national movement led only to a national revolution, that would help to expose class antagonisms; national liberation was one step in the struggle against French imperialism. The conference adopted the slogan of national independence by 14 to 10.[67] Political differences did not necessarily correspond to nationality. One Amar argued that the call for independence did not reflect the actual situation and that the party should launch realistic slogans rather than demands that would be misunderstood by the Algerian and European masses. He urged the party to organise Algerians in trade unions, develop their class consciousness and fight against the *indigénat*. Nonetheless, when the Algiers *rayon* met, it agreed – with 28 for, six against and five abstentions – to call for independence.[68]

In June 1926 the PCF's fifth national congress in Lille reinforced the pro-independence position, deeming the Socialist Party's position on colonialism as counter-revolutionary.[69] Representing the Algerian region, Schiavo underlined the ferocious repression, indicating that the region's PCF membership had fallen, although not as much as Paris headquarters presumed. The region had barely one thousand members before the repressive onslaught began, and in 1926, they distributed 800 membership cards. However, the PCF's Paris representative had addressed thousands of Algerian workers, and communist influence was spreading, especially amongst railway workers, almost 90 per cent of whom had voted for communist CGTU candidates – 31,000 out of 35,000 votes. Yet, like Algerian migrant workers in France, whose travel and trade union contacts allowed them to develop a distinctive world view, the predominantly European railway workers were an exceptional group. Some travelled around the country; others communicated with railway workers in different sites along the track. An imagined occupational community, they developed a wider consciousness and a picture of Algeria that differed markedly from those who stayed in their home villages with limited external contact. This experience, along with their trade union membership and contact with the French trade union movement, enabled them to develop a broader perspective of working conditions and capitalist development. Nonetheless, they represented a tiny minority of workers, especially amongst Algerians. Although Algerians began working in the rail industry on the eve of the 1914–18 war, European railway workers still expressed racist views in their union publication.[70]

Algerians might listen to communists, but few joined the party. The repression was fierce; the risks, too great. Communists reported some twenty-five political prisoners in Algeria. Mahmoud Ben Lekhal and one Hammar were whipped and thrown in the Serkadji dungeon. They went on hunger strike, soon joined by eleven other political prisoners. The Serkadji prisoners were hostages, claimed Pierre Celor, who had campaigned in Morocco against the Rif War and was now a leading figure in the colonial section. The only way to drive French imperialism out of Algeria, he insisted, was to systematically campaign against repression.[71]

In no small part due to repression, communist support for independence remained uneven. The JC, heavily hit by repression, was divided over the issue.[72] Its political secretary, one Ayache, argued that the JC should penetrate popular organisations and call for fraternisation between European and Algerian soldiers without prematurely demanding independence, which would exacerbate repression. *Lutte sociale* had been seized for far less radical slogans, he pointed out. It was regularly suppressed in 1926, despite the efforts of the LDD, which insisted: 'Algeria is French territory like the Alsace. We ask you that the same jurisprudence establishes there the same liberty.'[73]

Indeed, Algerian opposition movements called not for independence but assimilation with equality in all spheres, political, legal and economic. In 1926 the Young Algerians organised the Fédération des élus indigènes (Federation of elected natives, FEI) led by Dr Benthami Ould Hamida and reflecting the sentiments of the small stratum of generally urban middle-class professionals – schoolteachers, pharmacists, lawyers and medical doctors. Its first congress in September 1927 called for Algerian representation in Parliament, equal pay for equal work within the public sector, equal military service, abolition of the *indigénat*, extension of French social legislation to Algeria and revised electoral procedures.[74]

Neither did the Islamic reformist or *salifiyya* movement demand independence. A modernising movement, Islamic reformism grew rapidly in the 1920s, led by Constantine-born Shaykh Abdelhamid Ben Badis, North Africa's leading proponent of reformed Sunni Islam, and other *'ulama* – Muslim scholars who specialised in Islamic law and theology. Islamic reformists saw the marabouts and Muslim brotherhoods as symptomatic of 'anarchy and impiety' and criticised them as upholders of the rural aristocracy. Casting themselves as the bearers of true Islam whose role was to enlighten and educate, particularly the supposedly backwards rural masses, the reformists stressed Muslim unity as their paramount principle. Taking as their slogan, 'Arabic is my language, Algeria is my country, and Islam is my religion', they hoped to unite the diverse Muslim religious strands and sought accommodation with the Ibadists. The movement's discourse was cultural and religious, and Ben Badis preached the equality and cohabitation of French and Algerians. While his movement used concepts such as *umma* (nation), *cha'ab* (people), *watan* (homeland), and *quawmiyya* (nationality), it avoided direct political engagement.[75]

Organising the displaced proletariat

Discussions about independence also preoccupied communists in Paris. By the mid-1920s some 100,000 North African workers – mainly Algerians and overwhelmingly men – lived in France. Seeking a better life, they often found more misery. 'It's hell', reported an Algerian metal worker at Asturies. 'They're killing us.' They worked ten, sometimes twelve hours a day, and then slept ten men in an unhealthy room on straw beds.[76] Some were pulled into the CGTU, which stressed class action: in 1924 it called on Algerian workers in Paris to strike on 1 May for higher wages, an eight-hour day and recognition of factory committees. A few joined the PCF, whose campaign against the Rif War had inspired admiration amongst North African workers.[77]

Soon after, Emir Khaled came to Paris; faced with threats of arrest and expulsion in Algeria, he had moved to Egypt in 1923. Khaled addressed a conference organised by the Fraternité musulmane on 12 July and another organised by the Union intercoloniale a week later. For the communists this second conference was a big success. Taking a strongly anti-colonialist tone, and speaking to a packed crowd, Khaled demanded democratic rights. Impressed, and hoping that Khaled would return, the PCF began campaigning more earnestly for democratic demands. The Union intercoloniale and the CGTU convened a congress of North African workers in Paris on 7 December. It was well advertised and well attended. 'The preparation of this congress allowed us to engage in a great deal of propaganda amongst the many natives [sic] of the Paris region', reported Lozeray. Adopting a tolerant approach to religious beliefs, the PCF benefited from the fact that anarchists always spoke against religion and invariably had to leave such gatherings.[78]

The idea of a North African national movement caught fire. In autumn 1925 Hadj Ali raised this at a PCF Colonial School. 'We told the comrades that we wanted them to get an education in order to form their own organisation', Hadj Ali explained to the PCF's North African subcommission. After the course, 'we reunited the comrades and indicated to them that they should form their organisation, and we decided that it should aim to teach the natives that they would be men the day that they were free and independent.'[79] Planning continued over the next year, and with the active behind-the-scenes involvement of communists, 20 June 1926 saw the Etoile nord-africaine's launch, with Emir Khaled as president of honour.[80] Its demands were based on Emir Khaled's 1924 platform: suppression of the *indigénat*, freedom of travel, press and association, rights to equal work, education and mother-tongue instruction, universal franchise and political amnesty – but not independence. The PCF launched the *Al-Alam-Al-Ahmar* (*The Red Flag*); 12,500 copies were distributed that July, and 14,000 in August.[81]

The ENA got off to a good start, with 450 members after three months, reported the PCF's colonial section.[82] Over the next few months the party's North African subcommission frequently discussed the ENA. Celor reminded the subcommission that the Comintern Executive and the PCF congress at Lille had insisted on recruiting Algerians irrespective of their political understanding. Many Algerians hesitated when they first heard the PCF programme, Celor noted, but the party must try to recruit them. After all, French workers with limited understanding joined the party. Hassan Issad stated that Algerians who did not speak French were not interested in attending meetings. Celor insisted that language should not be a barrier and that non-Francophone Algerians should be placed in cells with at least one other Algerian. Hadj Ali concurred on the open-door policy and the need for at least one Algerian in each cell to put newcomers at ease.

The ENA's identity and legality in Algeria were central issues. Mohamed Djilani and Hadj Ali noted that North African workers were confused about the relationship of the PCF, the CGTU and the ENA; communists had difficulties in explaining the differences between them. Celor stated that the ENA's aim was independence, even though that goal was not in its statutes, and that communists should join the ENA as individuals and steer its members away from assimilation. But Hadj Ali, Mohammed Marouf and one Cherif all felt that independence was too radical a demand: it would alienate prospective petty bourgeois and bourgeois members and frighten workers fearful of repression. Hadj Ali argued that the ENA should not go too far ahead of Emir Khaled's democratic programme and suggested that 'total emancipation' might be less provocative. Issad, however, supported the call for independence, and Celor convinced the others. When the subcommittee voted on 1 October, eight supported independence; Marouf abstained. They recognised that the ENA's message could be carried to Algeria by returning migrant workers, but that it would have to operate underground.[83] French politics had shifted to the right in July 1926 with Poincaré's re-election. Fascist groups were emerging, and the climate for left-wing groups was increasingly difficult. Nonetheless, the ENA's future looked promising. A public meeting in Paris on 30 January attracted a large gathering of North Africans – Hadj Ali estimated 800, and the police spy, 250. Some dozen orators addressed the meeting in Arabic; Hadj Ali spoke in French, demanding independence.[84]

The Comintern's strategy of building a broad anti-colonial coalition culminated in the Congress of Oppressed Nations, convened in Brussels from 10 to 14 February 1927. The congress was attended by 174 delegates from 31 countries and supported by Henri Barbusse, Albert Einstein, Mahatma Gandhi, Romain Rolland, Bertrand Russell and Mrs Sun Yat Sen – the political breadth of these renowned figures indicating that this was the Comintern's ecumenical period.[85] Hadj Ali, Ahmed Messali Hadj and the Tunisian Destour Party's Chedly Khaidallah represented the ENA. After completing his French military service, Tlemcen-born Ahmed Messali had moved to Paris in October 1923, found a factory job and become friendly with Hadj Ali during his June 1924 electoral campaigns. Influenced by Hadj Ali, he joined the PCF in 1925, becoming an adept organiser for the ENA.[86] Messali made an impromptu impassioned appeal for independence, and the ENA put forward its democratic demands, including independence, the withdrawal of French troops and the constitution of an Algerian national army. The congress launched the League against Imperialism, which called for the self-determination of African peoples and whose honorary presidents were Einstein, Labour MP George Lansbury, Jawaharlal Nehru and Mrs Sun Yat Sen.[87]

Back in Paris, the political climate became harsher. The ENA's first organ, *L'Ikdam de Paris*, a bilingual monthly launched in late 1926, had been quickly banned, to reappear briefly in 1927 as *L'Ikdam nordafricain* and then simply as *L'Ikdam*. Khaidallah argued that the ENA should situate itself as a national revolutionary movement rather than follow a particular party or ideology. Notwithstanding this attempt to distance itself from the PCF, the ENA was subjected to heavy repression. The police intimidated owners of cafés frequented by North Africans, making Messali's propaganda work increasingly difficult; the café owners no longer wanted political agitators coming around. Undaunted, *L'Ikdam*'s December 1927 issue called for an Algerian Parliament and criticised the elected Algerian officials who had just submitted demands to the French Parliament – they were not genuinely representative and did not have the right to speak for the Algerian people, it claimed. On 27 December Khaidallah was expelled from France to Tunisia and imprisoned.[88]

The PCF began moving away from alliances with other left-wing groups and national movements.[89] In autumn 1927 the communist

CGTU activist Djilali Chabila replaced Messali as the ENA's secretary-general, and Messali became assistant secretary. If the PCF had any influence in this move, perhaps it felt that Messali could not be counted on to follow the communist lead. It cut back its funds to *L'Ikdam*, which ceased in 1928. Thus, by 1928, when Messali described the ENA as 'a little asleep', the PCF and ENA had already drifted apart, reflecting the Comintern's new line of class against class.[90]

The new line

The late 1920s brought signs of an impending economic slump. The Comintern anticipated a capitalist crisis and argued that class polarisation would result. Comintern officials had been criticising the PCF for its alleged right-wing orientation for some time. With the rise of the French right, from early 1927 the PCF's Jules Humbert-Droz, who worked closely with the Comintern's Nikolai Bukharin and represented the Comintern within the PCF hierarchy, began moving the party to the left. Humbert-Droz pushed for a reorientation of the party's electoral policy, which had heretofore been based on supporting left blocs against the right. This shift, a controversial move away from the united-front policy, became known as the new line of class against class. The idea was to distinguish the PCF as the legitimate working-class party, in contrast to the socialists. The new approach split the left vote and strengthened the right electorally. Nonetheless, from October 1927, communists began running their own candidates in the second ballots, rather than voting for socialists. Just as Young Communists had been key agents in implementing Bolshevisation, so they were in introducing the new line.[91]

A similar shift occurred in the communist-aligned trade union movement. The CGTU's fourth national congress took place in Bordeaux from 19 to 24 September 1927. For the first time North African delegates were present – five out of some 600 delegates from across France. 'The C.G.T.U. showed in this Congress that it had nothing in common with the reformist C.G.T.', reported *Al-Raïat-Al-hamra*. CGTU unions were to highlight their opposition to French imperialism by organising European and Algerian workers to fight for Algerian working-class demands.[92]

In Algeria the new line accentuated divisions. In 1926 Sid Ahmed Belarbi had returned to Algeria, adopting the pseudonym Boualem. He joined the regional political bureau and worked energetically, organising Algerian workers in the CGTU. Nonetheless, frenetic activity could not prevent spiralling dissatisfaction. In 1927 the Blida *rayon* was at the centre of a movement criticising intervention from Paris

– again concerning independence. Schiavo was staunchly 'against the slogan of independence for Algeria, against the National Revolutionary Party, against the slogan "land to the peasants"', it was reported in January 1927. The Blida *rayon* included 54 members, of whom eight were Algerian; all supported Schiavo out of personal respect, even if they did not oppose independence.[93] The call for independence was premature, and universal franchise would give too much weight to the *marabouts*, they argued. They proposed slogans for immediate demands and Algerian rights. The PCF's Colonial Commission swiftly condemned those who refused to support Algerian independence.[94]

As in most national sections during this period, relations amongst communists became hostile. Individuals sought support from PCF headquarters against each other, and disputes were accompanied by expulsions. These disagreements took place when the tiny communist movement was already devastated by repression and in some areas virtually inactive. Thus 1927 was marked by a spate of expulsions and resignations of trade unionists and other activists – so-called oppositionists – who had been in the PCF from the start – a pattern repeated across the communist world. In Algeria some of these – Schiavo, Lemedioni and Constant – became associated with the short-lived *Combat social*, a two- to four-page broadsheet whose masthead bore the slogan, 'The emancipation of workers will be the work of workers themselves.' Bitter in tone, its avowed aim was to undermine *Lutte sociale*. It opposed intervention from Paris and Moscow and political party intervention in the trade union movement – the latter a new-line characteristic. Some former communists moved closer to the socialists. Spielmann continued promoting Algerian–European fraternity.[95]

The new line was formalised at the Comintern's Sixth Congress in July–August 1928. Bukharin argued that post-war Europe had gone through a first stage of revolutionary upheaval and a second stage of capitalist stabilisation during which communists had promoted united fronts. With fascism seemingly secure in Italy and the left in retreat elsewhere in Europe, the capitalist crisis had reached its third period in which the contradictions of capitalism would lead to its collapse. In such conditions the working class would develop revolutionary proletarian class consciousness. With worldwide revolution imminent, social-democratic and reformist policies were seen as counter-revolutionary attempts to divert the working class from the struggle against capitalism – thus, the need for independent working-class leadership.[96]

Hard hit by repression, the PCF's Algerian region was further decimated by the new line purges. Numbers speak for themselves. In late 1925 it had counted 310 Algerian members out of 1540 – around 20 per cent. Shortly before the June 1926 Lille congress, the region reported

80 Algerian members, and by January 1927 fear of arrest had pushed virtually all of them to leave.[97]

By 1929 membership had plunged to 280.[98] A report in February of that year described the regional PCF as non-existent; headquarters must send one delegate to take charge of Algiers and *Lutte sociale* and one to visit the other *rayons*, the report stated. Money was needed for *Lutte sociale*, for trade union publications and for rail travel expenses. The trade union movement was in a state of 'complete disorganisation'. There was serious concern that expelled trade unionists such as Schiavo and Mazoyer would split the CGTU. Unlike South Africa, however, expelled communists never gravitated towards Trotskyism. The regional conference in March 1929 reaffirmed the new line, castigating socialists as imperialist agents and elected Algerian representatives as collaborators, and demanding independence and expropriation of the land.[99]

Reeling from the purges, communists could hardly withstand the repression accompanying the 1930 centennial celebrations of French colonisation. As activists were swept into jails and newspapers seized, European settlers paid homage to French rule. Ten large exhibitions – on commercial, artistic, photographic, medical and other themes – displayed France's accomplishments in Algeria; fifty cars crossed the desert from north to south and back, graphically demonstrating French possession of the land. Only socialists and communists voiced criticism, the latter far more militantly. On May Day 1930, communists in Algiers bravely demonstrated their opposition with flyers proclaiming: 'May 1st, for the independence of your country, for your demands, fraternise with the workers.'[100]

Despite Boualem's accession as the PCF's regional secretary in June 1928 – the first Algerian to hold the position – the CGTU delegate to Algeria reported that the party remained 'composed mainly of Europeans without contact with the natives'. The trade union movement generally represented the privileged railway and tramway workers, 'whose living standards were notably superior to the average living standard of native proletarians'. The party was reasonably organised in Algiers, Oran and Bône, where cells, committees and trade union locals met, but very weak in Sidi bel Abbès, Blida, Constantine and Philippeville, towns where only the railway workers were well organised.[101] Nonetheless, the Arab workers' congress of 15 June 1930 organised by Boualem – part of RILU's efforts to organise workers across the Arab world – was a success. Convened secretly in the working-class community of Bab el Oued, Algiers – nicknamed Bab el Oued the Red, but where Muslims and Christians lived in close proximity without mixing – it was attended by 69 Arab and six European delegates from fourteen towns and cities representing some fifteen occupations. An important step in building links around the country, it demonstrated labour's diversity: tramway and railway workers had the strongest representation, but Tlemcen delegates reported on the deplorable conditions of agricultural workers and women and children carpet weavers.[102]

Local communists were of two minds about PCF headquarters. While some resented its interference, others bemoaned its lack of support. A letter to the PCF's political bureau complained of political differences between the regional party and the colonial section, indicating that it had received no political guidance since August 1929 and that the material they received – when it came – could not be used due to its lack of relevance to local conditions. The colonial section duly acknowledged the problem, explaining that it had been preoccupied with other matters since August 1929, but that it had since been reorganised and would commence regular contact. No doubt some of those matters concerned the ENA. With communists harassed and jailed, the PCF voiced little protest when the ENA was banned on 29 November 1929.[103]

By late 1930, the tiny movement had fragmented further. When Charles Bourneton arrived from France, the tension between Algiers and Oran was palpable. Algiers was concerned with 'high politics' to the neglect of Oran, where the PCF had deteriorated and the trade union movement was dead, he reported. The Sidi bel Abbès *rayon* was moribund and the situation in Tlemcen only slightly better. There was virtually no contact between Algiers and the other *rayons*. Discontent was rife.[104] Some demanded an Algerian Communist Party, arguing that the PCF had proved itself incapable of directing political work in the colonies: 'we need to take the struggle for the P.C.A. all the way, put the question before the CI and demand its rapid intervention.'[105]

Boualem had called for an independent party at the Comintern's Sixth Congress – along with the organisation of peasants and agricultural workers and the indigenisation of the trade union movement.[106] Nonetheless, for some the idea of an autonomous party reflected frustration with Paris rather than the belief that such a party was needed or viable. Despite recognising the need to work amongst and recruit Algerians, the lack of resources coupled with the severe repression seemingly made this aim almost impossible. There was, moreover, no uniformity amongst Algerians as to the nature of the changes they sought. While the Young Algerians imagined an Algerian community within a France spanning the Mediterranean, the ENA imagined an independent Algeria. Although the PCF called for independence, communists were uneven in their support and divided about how to achieve this. Some imagined a working class united across national and religious lines; others envisioned a national struggle for democratic rights. As 1930 closed, the PCF's Algerian region was effectively destroyed. Yet from these harsh experiences two traditions emerged: campaigns against repression and prison strikes became recurring features of Algeria's communist movement.

Notes

1. René Gallissot, 'Marx et l'Algérie', *Mouvement social*, 71 (April–June 1970), 39–63; René Gallissot with Gilbert Badia (eds), *Marx, Marxisme et Algérie* (Paris: Union générales d'éditions, 1976), pp. 383–94; René Gallissot, *La République française et les indigènes: Algérie colonisée, Algérie algérienne (1870–1962)* (Paris: Editions de l'Atelier/Editions ouvrières, 2006), pp. 44–7; Mohamed Lakhdar Benhassine, 'Le Séjour de Karl Marx à Alger … du 20 février au 2 mai 1882', in *Alger: Lumières sur la ville*, Actes du Colloque (Algiers, 4–6 May 2002), pp. 713–29.
2. Charles-Robert Ageron, 'Jaurès et les socialistes français devant la question algérienne (de 1895 à 1914)', *Mouvement social*, 42 (January–March 1963), 3–27; Ahmed Koulakssis, *Le Parti socialiste et l'Afrique du Nord de Jaurès à Blum* (Paris: Armand Colin, 1991).
3. 'Fédération Socialiste Algérienne', *Lutte sociale* (January 1908); Marcel Cachin, 'Questions algériennes', *Lutte sociale* (7–12 January 1912); Tiberius Gracchus, 'Prolétaires algériens unissons-nous!' *Lutte sociale* (20 April 1919); Koulakssis, *Parti socialiste*, p. 124, cf. p. 311, n. 61.
4. Ageron, 'Jaurès', pp. 27–9.
5. Ruedy, *Modern Algeria*, pp. 98–9, 123, 125; Mahfoud Kaddache, *La Vie politique à Alger de 1919 à 1939* (Algiers: ENAG, 2009), pp. 12–13.
6. Ageron, *Histoire*, vol. 2, p. 530.
7. Ruedy, *Modern Algeria*, pp. 112, 91–2; Ageron, *Histoire*, vol. 2, pp. 227–53; Martin Thomas, *The French Empire between the Wars: Imperialism, Politics and Society* (Manchester: Manchester University Press, 2005), pp. 246–9.
8. « Je suis arabe et je veux rester arabe », Ageron, *Histoire*, vol. 2, p. 240; Ruedy, *Modern Algeria*, pp. 109–10, 112–13, 129; James McDougall, *History and the Culture of Nationalism in Algeria* (Cambridge: Cambridge University Press, 2006), p. 74.
9. Taumo Saarela, 'International and National in the Communist movement', in Saarela and Rentola (eds), *Communism*, pp. 15–40, 19–20.
10. Charles Sowerwine, *France since 1870: Culture, Society and the Making of the Republic*, 2nd edn (Basingstoke: Palgrave Macmillan, 2009), pp. 118–19.
11. 'The Twenty-one Points – Conditions of Admission to the Communist International', in Brian Bunting (ed.), *South African Communists Speak, 1915–1980* (London: Inkuleko, 1981), pp. 58–62; 'Les 21 conditions d'adhésion à la IIIe Internationale', in Jean Charles, Jacques Girault, Jean-Louis Robert, Danielle Tartakowskyé and Claude Willard (eds), *Le Congrès de Tours: 18e Congrès national du Parti socialiste* (Paris: Editions Sociales, 1980), pp. 123–7; McDermott and Agnew, *Comintern*, pp. 225–6.
12. Sowerwine, *France*, p. 125; Philip M. Williams, *Crisis and Compromise: Politics in the Fourth Republic*, 3rd edn (London: Longman, 1964), p. 71.
13. In 1919–20, membership rose from 565 to 700 in Algiers and 316 to 400 in Oran, but fell from 450 to 400 in Constantine. *Congrès de Tours*, pp. 77, 181–3, 193–4, 796–8; Gallissot (ed.), *Algérie*, pp. 361–6.
14. *Congrès de Tours*, p. 276.
15. 'Twenty-one Points', pp. 60–1.
16. *Congrès de Tours*, map showing mandates by region. The Socialist Party's membership in Algeria was decimated, especially in Constantine; in 1924 the Algiers section had 375 members; see Koulakssis, *Parti socialiste*, pp. 126–8, 139, 312, nn. 71,

72; Charles-Robert Ageron, 'Les Communistes français devant la question algérienne de 1921 à 1924', *Mouvement social* (January–March 1972), 7–37; Ahmed Koulakssis and Gilbert Meynier, 'Sur le mouvement ouvrier et les communistes d'Algérie au lendemain de la première guerre mondiale', *Mouvement social*, 130 (January–March 1985), 3–32, pp. 5–6; Jacques Choukroun, 'L'Internationale Communiste, le P. C. français et l'Algérie (1920–1925)', *Cahiers d'histoire de l'Institut Maurice Thorez*, 25:26 (1978), 133–59, p. 136; Annie Kriegel, 'Structures d'organisation et mouvement des effectifs du Parti communiste français entre les deux guerres', *International Review of Social History*, 11:2 (December 1966), 335–61, p. 335.

17 Alexandre Juving, *Le Socialisme en Algérie* (Algiers: Jules Carbonel, 1924), esp. pp. 258–77; Ageron, 'Communistes français', p. 11; Gilbert Meynier, *L'Algérie révélée: La Guerre de 1914–1918 et le premier quart du XXe siècle* (Geneva: Librarie Droz, 1981), pp. 690–709; Koulakssis and Meynier, 'Mouvement ouvrier', pp. 4–5.

18 'A travers les groupes socialistes d'Algérie', *Lutte sociale* (31 August 1919); Sowerwine, *France*, pp. 124–5.

19 « Prolétaires Algériens unissons-nous ! ... Prolétaires indigènes, espagnols, italiens, unissons-nous », *Lutte sociale* (20 April, 11 May 1919, 1–7, 22–28 May 1920); Jean-Louis Planche, 'L'Internationalisme au feu des nationalismes: Les Communistes en Algérie (1920–1945)', in Abdeljelil Temimi (ed.), *Mélanges Charles-Robert Ageron*, vol. 2 (Zaghouan: Fondation Temimi pour la recherche scientifique et l'information, 1996), 661–88, p. 663; Gallissot, *République*, pp. 67–8.

20 Louis Laurens, 'Les aspects du socialisme en Algérie' [IV], *Lutte sociale* (30 April 1921); Gallissot (ed.), *Algérie*, p. 418.

21 'Ordre du jour voté par la Section socialiste (S.F.I.C.) de Sidi-Bel-Abbès dans sa réunion du 22 Avril 1921', *Lutte sociale* (7 May 1921); Sivan, *Communisme*, pp. 25–6; Koulakssis and Meynier, 'Mouvement ouvrier', pp. 7–8; Ageron, 'Communistes français', p. 17; Gallissot, *République*, pp. 70–2.

22 Charles-André Julien, H. Carrère d'Encausse and M. Rebérioux, 'Les Communistes et l'Orient en 1921', *Mouvement Social*, 82 (January–March 1973), 106–13.

23 Comité d'études coloniales, 'Projet de résolution sur le communisme et les colonies', *Lutte sociale* (4 February 1922), p. 4. The committee was formally approved at the PCF's December congress in Marseilles.

24 « un pied à la campagne et l'autre en ville ... La pauvreté parle un langage et la richesse en parle un autre », Messali Hadj, *Les Mémoires de Messali Hadj* (Paris: Jean-Claude Lattès, 1982), pp. 22–3, 33.

25 Messali, *Mémoires*, pp. 19, 22–3, 79, 121–2, 124.

26 P. Vaillant-Couturier, 'Vive l'Algérie révolutionnaire', *Lutte sociale* (1 April 1922); Ageron, 'Communistes français', pp. 23–4, 29–30; Choukron, 'L'Internationale', p. 146.

27 P. Vaillant-Couturier, 'Le problème indigène', *Lutte sociale* (4 March 1922); *L'Humanité* (14, 15, 17, 20, 25 April; 13, 15, 16, 24 May 1922).

28 Russian State Archive of Socio-Political History, Moscow (hereafter RGASPI), 495.18.102, *Appel de l'Internationale communiste pour la libération de l'Algérie et de la Tunisie*; Alleg, 'Torrent', p. 195, n. 66.

29 Ageron, 'Communistes français', pp. 26–8, 27.

30 Ageron, 'Communistes français', pp. 29–30; Koulakssis and Meynier, 'Mouvement ouvrier', p. 6; Choukron, 'L'Internationale', p. 137.

31 Djerjeraoui, 'Le Communisme et l'indigène', *Lutte sociale* (7 Janvier 1922).

32 The National Archives, London (hereafter TNA): Public Record Office (hereafter PRO) FO 371/8271, Report from Consul-General Cave, Algiers, 22 May 1922.

33 « Considérons notre camarade indigène comme un frère ... plus malheureux que nous puisqu'il porte les marques de longues années d'oppression ... C'est une victime de notre ennemi commun: le capitalisme international », A. Boye, 'Vie syndicale: L'ouvrier indigène', *Lutte sociale* (15 September 1922).

34 J. Maitron (ed.), *Dictionnaire biographique du mouvement ouvrier français, 1914–1939* (Paris: Editions ouvrières, 1992), vol. 41, pp. 403–4; 'Etudes algériennes', *Lutte sociale* (11 March 1922); Victor Spielmann, *Colonisation et question indigène en Algérie en 1922* (Algiers: Imprimerie du prolétariat, [1922]). Spielmann's life and

work merit a biography.
35 Z., 'La Guerre du Rand', *Lutte sociale* (1 November 1922); Drew, *Discordant Comrades*, pp. 58–64.
36 Sowerwine, *France*, pp. 126–7. The CGTU affiliated to the RILU in 1923.
37 Leon Trotsky, 'Resolution of the Fourth World Congress on the French Question', in *The First Five Years of the Communist International*, 2nd edn, vol. 2 (New York: Monad, 1972), 275–284, p. 284.
38 Ageron, *Modern Algeria*, 380; Sivan, *Communisme*, pp. 28–30; Koulakssis and Meynier, 'Mouvement ouvrier', p. 16; Gallissot (ed.), *Algérie*, pp. 318–21; According to Choukron, 'L'Internationale', p. 146, Algiers had 350 members of whom 250 had 8 stamps on their card; Oran had 100 members with 8 stamps, and Constantine, 80 with 8 stamps. Thus there were about 430 members in all who paid dues regularly, indicating a serious loss of members.
39 Koulakssis and Meynier, 'Mouvement ouvrier', pp. 21–3, suggest that as workers replaced intellectual leaders, their concern to rebuild working-class unity coincided with the desire to impress the Comintern; Gallissot (ed.), *Algérie*, pp. 468–9.
40 Gallissot (ed.), *Algérie*, pp. 469–71. Benjamin Stora, *Dictionnaire biographique des militants nationalistes Algériens, 1926–1954* (Paris: Harmattan, 1985), pp. 59–60, states that he joined the PCF in Paris. Abdelaziz Menouer (sometimes Menouar) used the pseudonyms Aby Hamamou and *El Djazairi* (the Algerian). His unusual life merits a biography.
41 'Le Parti communiste réclame l'indépendance des colonies', Centre des Archives Contemporaines, Fontainebleau (hereafter CAC), 19940494, art. 59, 4370, *La Caserne/El Kazirna* (1923–4); Sowerwine, *France*, p. 129; William A. Hoisington, Jr., *Lyautey and the French Conquest of Morocco* (New York: St Martin's, 1995), pp. 185–204.
42 Mekloub, 'Pour développer le communisme en Algérie', *Lutte sociale* (21 April 1922).
43 Ali Abdulhak, 'Aux travailleurs d'Algérie', *Lutte sociale* (6 April 1923). Joseph Castagne, 'La condition de la femme dans les républiques soviétiques musulmanes', *Lutte sociale* (13 April 1923) indicated interest in Muslim societies. But Lucie Colliard, 'Le votes des femmes', *Lutte sociale* (26 October 1923), argued for votes on the same basis as men without considering the implications for Algeriens.
44 « tout en sauvegardant et en consolidant le développement de l'influence française », 'Un cercle franco-indigène nord-africain', *Lutte sociale* (11 January 1924); Sivan, *Communisme*, pp. 32–4.
45 « Le syndicalisme est bon, mais pas pour les indigènes ! ... Travailleurs de tous pays, unissez-vous ... Même et surtout, les indigènes ! », R. A. Crémieux, *A.B.C. du syndicalisme* (Algiers: Imprimerie du prolétariat, 1924), 24–30, p. 30.
46 Sivan, *Communisme*, pp. 13–36. Koulakssis and Meynier, 'Mouvement ouvrier', pp. 26–7, 32, and Planche, 'L'Internationalisme', p. 664, are more nuanced. They situate the Sidi bel Abbès theses against the backdrop of the 1921 famine, which was particularly severe in Oran, forcing peasants into overcrowded urban camps that became fertile zones for a typhus epidemic. The ensuing panic presumably intensified racism. They argue that Communist attitudes varied, that support for the Sidi bel Abbès thesis was not unanimous and that the rise of a new leadership promoting working-class unity across national lines preceded the Comintern's intervention.
47 Drew, *Discordant Comrades*, p. 76.
48 McDermott and Agnew, *Comintern*, pp. 44–6, 46; Henry Pelling, *The British Communist Party: A Historical Profile* (London: Adam and Charles Black, 1958), pp. 21–2
49 'Theses on the Bolshevisation of Communist Parties, adopted by the Fifth ECCI Plenum, April 1925', in McDermott and Agnew, *Comintern*, pp. 232–3; Kriegel, 'Structures', pp. 336–8.
50 Sowerwine, *France*, p. 129.
51 « Jusqu'au commencement 1924, le parti n'avait rien fait pour organiser les travailleurs coloniaux », RGASPI 517.1.185, Aziz [Ali Menouer], *Rapport sur le travail*

parmi les coloniaux en France, n.d. [1924].
52 PCF file 70, Aziz to Kolaroff, 17 June 1924, p. 1; El-Djazairi, 'Plus d'attention à la question coloniale', *Bulletin communiste*, no. 24 (13 June 1924), 597–8.
53 Pierre Durand, *Cette mystérieuse section coloniale: le PCF et les colonies (1920–1962)* (Paris: Messidor, 1986), p. 48.
54 PCF file 70, Doriot to comrades, 18 December 1924.
55 PCF file 120, P. Biboulet, *Rapport sur la situation politique en Algérie*, 17 October 1925, p. 4; 'Congrès de fusion', *Lutte sociale* (13 February 1925); Gallissot (ed.), *Algérie*, p. 138.
56 Aziz to Kolaroff, p. 2; RGASPI 517.1.185, « 40.000 ouvriers parisiens ont voté pour le Communiste Hadjali Abdelkader », *La Caserne* (May–June 1924), pp. 6–7.
57 Gallissot (ed.), *Algérie*, pp. 326–9; Abdellah Righi, *Hadj-Ali Abdelkader: Pionnier du mouvement révolutionnaire Algérien* (Algiers: Casbah, 2006), pp. 69, 99–111.
58 'Election municipales du 3 Mai 1925', *Lutte sociale* (17, 24 April 1925); *Lutte sociale*, Edition spéciale (May 1925); 'Aux électeurs indigènes', *Lutte sociale* (8 May 1925); 'L'Emir KHALED est ELU', *Lutte sociale* (15 May 1925); Abderrahim Taleb Bendiab, 'La pénétration des idées et l'implantation communiste en Algérie dans les années 1920', in René Gallissot (ed.), *Mouvement ouvrier, communisme et nationalisme dans le monde Arabe* (Paris: Editions ouvrières, 1978), pp. 127–46, esp. 135; Alleg, 'Torrent', p. 201; Gallissot (ed.), *Algérie*, pp. 118–19; Stora, *Dictionnaire*, pp. 47–9.
59 Nicole Le Guennec, 'Le Parti communiste français et la guerre du Rif', *Mouvement Social*, 78 (January–March 1972), 39–64, pp. 47–53, 64–5; Hoisington, Jr., *Lyautey*, pp. 185–204; Koulakssis, *Parti socialiste*, pp. 189–93; Sowerwine, *France*, p. 130; Zakya Daoud, *Abdelkrim: une épopée d'or et de sang* (Paris: Séguier, 1999), pp. 207–35. Arturo Barea's novel *The Track* (London: Flamingo, n.d.) discusses the Rif War.
60 Gallissot (ed.), *Algérie*, pp. 159–61; Benali Boukort, *Le Souffle du Dahra* (Alger: Entreprise nationale du livre, 1986), p. 30.
61 Gallissot (ed.), *Algérie*, pp. 92–6.
62 « La bolchévisation du parti s'accomplit en Algérie comme en France à la faveur de la guerre du Rif », Ageron, *Histoire*, vol. 2, p. 380; Le Guennec, 'Parti communiste', pp. 39–40; Sowerwine, *France*, p. 130.
63 PCF file 120, *Rapport de Henriet*, 1 Septembre 1925, p. 3; Gallissot (ed.), *Algérie*, pp. 68–9, 138–9, 435.
64 « les derniers meeetings [sic] ont prouvé qu'indigènes et européens n'y viendraient pas », *Rapport de Henriet*, pp. 1–2.
65 'l'homme du moment', *Rapport de Henriet*, p. 2; Gallissot (ed.), *Algérie*, p. 549.
66 Biboulet, *Rapport*, pp. 3, 6–7.
67 Delegates from Blida, Algiers, Bordj Bou Arredidj, Constantine, Mascara, Oran and Sétif attended the conference. Choukroun, 'L'Internationale', 145; 'En vue de la conférence', *Lutte sociale* (19 February 1926).
68 « Le rayon d'Alger adopte à une forte majorité les thèses présentées par le Comité central », *Lutte sociale* (26 February 1926).
69 RGASPI 517.1.409, *Sous-commission nord-africaine*, 28 July 1926, p. 1.
70 *Ve Congrès national du Parti communiste français*, Lille, 20–26 June 1926 (Paris: Bureau d'Editions, 1927), pp. 252–4, 622, 695–7; Sivan, 'Colonialism', pp. 29, 44. My thanks to Boussad Ouadi and David Howell for their insights on railway workers.
71 *Al-Lioua-Al-Ahmar*, 1 (October 1926).
72 RGASPI 517.1.456, Aux camarades, Sétif, 4 October [1926].
73 « l'Algérie est terre française comme l'Alsace. Nous vous demandons que la même jurisprudence y établisse la même liberté », CAC 19940500, art. 108, 1966, Ligue française pour la défense des droits de l'homme et du citoyen au ministre de l'intérieur, 18 April 1928; RGASPI 517.1.456, Ayache aux camarades, 20 October 1926.
74 Ruedy, *Modern Algeria*, p. 132.
75 McDougall, *History*, pp. 108–16, 12–13; Ruedy, *Modern Algeria*, pp. 134–5; Alleg, 'Torrent', p. 183; Omar Carlier, *Entre nation et Jihad: Histoire sociale des radicalismes algériens* (Paris: Presse de la Fondation nationale des sciences politiques, 1995), p. 17; Benjamin Stora, *Histoire de l'Algérie coloniale (1830–1954)* (Paris:

La Découverte, 1991), p. 74; Charles-André Julien, *L'Afrique du Nord en marche: Algérie–Tunisie–Maroc, 1880–1952* (Omnibus, 2002), p. 102; Abdelhamid Ben Badis, *Textes choisis* (Editions ANEP, 2006).

76 « C'est l'enfer ... On nous tue », Ameziane, 'La Vie des Nord-Africains', *Al-Lioua-Al-Ahmar*, 1 (October 1926).

77 RGASPI 517.1.185, Confédération générale du travail unitaire, travailleur algérien en ce 1er Mai 1924; Sowerwine, *France*, p. 130.

78 « La préparation de ce congrès nous permit de faire une grande agitation parmi les nombreux indigènes de la région parisienne », PCF file 70 and RGASPI 517.1.185, Henri Lozeray, *Rapport sur le travail colonial du P.C.F.*, p. 4; PCF file 70 and RGASPI 517.1.185, Doriot to camarades, 18 December 1924; Gallissot (ed.), *Algérie*, pp. 387–8; Gallissot, *République*, p. 75; Messali, *Mémoires*, p. 137, n. 1; 'Conférence prononcée à Paris par l'émir Khaled en juillet 1924', in Jurquet, *Révolution nationale*, vol. 2, pp. 474–77.

79 RGASPI 517.1.409, *Sous-commission nord-africaine*, 1 October 1926, p. 6.

80 *L'Humanité* (25 August 1926), p. 2; *Lutte sociale* (4 September 1926); Righi, *Hadj-Ali Abdelkader*, pp. 137, 145–6 notes discrepancies about the date of the ENA's formation. Compare Messali, *Mémoires*, p. 153, and Charles-Robert Ageron, 'Emigration et politique: L'Etoile nord-africaine et le parti du peuple algérien', in Messali, *Mémoires*, 273–97, pp. 284–5.

81 RGASPI 517.1.409, 'Le Journal *Al-Alam-Al-Ahmar*', and 'Le programme de revendications tel qu'il suit a été adopté', in *Sous-commission nord-africaine*, 26 July 1926, pp. 2–3. The paper was repeatedly banned and changed its name: Archives nationales d'Outre-Mer, Aix-en-Provence (hereafter ANOM) 93/20324, *Al-Beirak-al-Ahmar* replaced *Al-Alam-Al-Ahmar* and *Al-Lioua-Al-Ahmar*, 1 (October 1926); ANOM ALG Oran // 3076, no. 6, September–October 1927, was called *Al-Raïat-Al-hamra*; PCF file 172, P. Celor, *Rapport au secrétariat du Parti sur l'activité de la commission coloniale centrale, 25 août au 25 septembre 1926*, 23 September 1926; PCF file 172, *Rapport au secrétariat du Parti sur l'activité de la section coloniale centrale depuis le Congrès de Lille*, 22 August 1926.

82 PCF file 172, *Rapport au secrétariat du Parti*, p. 4.

83 RGASPI 517.1.409, *Sous-commission nord-africaine*, 9 September 1926, pp. 7–8, 2–7; 23 September 1926, pp. 1–2, 4–5; 1 October 1926, pp. 4, 8.

84 CAC 19940494, art. 58, 4346, 'Meeting organisé par L'Etoile nord-africaine', 31 January 1927; Ageron, 'Emigration', p. 285.

85 Bakar Ali Mirza, 'The Congress Against Imperialism', *Modern Review* (1927), 555–66, states 9–16 February; Messali, *Mémoires*, p. 156, misdates his departure for Brussels as 26 February. 'Report on the Development of the League against Imperialism', *Anti-Imperialist Review*, 1:1 (July 1928), 83–96; Jonathan Derrick, *Africa's 'Agitators': Militant Anti-Colonialism in Africa and the West, 1918–1939* (New York: Columbia University, 2008), pp. 173–5.

86 Messali, *Mémoires*, pp. 127, 136–8, 144–5; 153, 284–5; Benjamin Stora, *Messali Hadj (1898–1974): Pionnier du nationalisme algérien* (Paris: Harmattan, 1982), pp. 45–64; League Against Imperialism Archives (hereafter LAI), International Institute of Social History, Amsterdam, *Liste des organisations et déléguées apportant leur concours au Congrès international contre l'oppression coloniale et l'impérialisme*, Palais d'Egmont, Brussels, 10–14 February 1927, does not name the North African delegates.

87 *Déclaration de la Délégation de 'L'Etoile nord-africaine'*, p. 2; *Résolution des Pays de L'Afrique du Nord*, p. 3, LAI, International Congress against Colonial Oppression and Imperialism, Brussels, 1927; Messali, *Mémoires*, pp. 156–8; Stora, *Messali*, pp. 67–71; Gallissot (ed.), *Algérie*, p. 328; 'L'Etoile nord-africaine rend compte des travaux du Congrès de Bruxelles', *l'Humanité* (7 March 1927), p. 3.

88 Messali, *Mémoires*, pp. 159–60; Ageron, 'Emigration', pp. 285–7; CAC 19940494, art. 58, 4346, *L'Ikdam*, 1 (December 1927).

89 '"L'Etoile nord-africaine" proteste contre la suppression de son journal', *l'Humanité* (10 March 1927), p. 6; Stora, *Dictionnaire*, p. 56; Gallissot, *République*, pp. 76–7; Sowerine, *France*, p. 132.

90 « un peu en sommeil », Messali, *Mémoires*, p. 162; Stora, *Messali*, pp. 71–8; Ageron, 'Emigration', pp. 285–6; Gallissot (ed.), *Algérie*, p. 197.
91 McDermott and Agnew, *Comintern*, pp. 72–3; Williams, *Crisis*, p. 71.
92 *Al-Raïat-Al-hamra*, 6 (September–October 1927); Gallissot, *République*, pp. 86–7.
93 « contre le mot d'ordre d'indépendance de l'Algérie, contre le Parti national révolutionnaire, contre le mot d'ordre "la terre aux paysans" ». PCF file 241, Procès-verbal de la réunion de la Commission coloniale centrale, 17 Janvier 1927, pp. 9–10; ANOM ALG Oran 3076, Section du rayon de Blida, 25 January 1927.
94 « la politique de sommeil ». PCF file 241, Procès-verbal de la réunion de la Commission coloniale centrale du 21 Février [1927], p. 1; ANOM ALG Oran 3076, « Section du Rayon de Blida, adopté à l'unanimité moins une abtention [sic] dans sa séance du 25 Janvier ».
95 « L'émancipation des travailleurs sera l'œuvre des travailleurs eux-mêmes », *Combat social* (31 March, 14, 29 April, 19 May, 16 June 1927); Gallissot (ed.), *Algérie*, p. 559; Gallissot, *République*, pp. 87
96 McDermott and Agnew, *Comintern*, pp. 42–54, 68–71, 81–90; Drew, *Discordant Comrades*, pp. 95, 112.
97 PCF file 172, P. Biboulet, *Région communiste d'Algérie*, 17 Octobre 1925; Procès-verbal de la réunion de la Commission coloniale centrale, 17 January 1927; Gallissot (ed.), *Algérie*, p. 549.
98 Stephen Hopkins, 'French Communism, the Comintern and Class Against Class: Interpretations and Rationales', in Matthew Worley (ed.), *In Search of Revolution: In Search of Revolution: International Communist Parties in the Third Period* (London and New York: I.B. Tauris, 2004), pp. 106–28; Sivan, *Communisme*, pp. 36–7, 52–5; Allison Drew, 'Bolshevizing Communist Parties – the Algerian and South African Experiences,' *International Review of Social History*, 48 (2003), 167–202, pp. 197–8, 202.
99 *Rapport sur le redressement de la région Algérienne*, n.d. [stamped 9, 12 February 1929], pp. 1–2; El Maghreb, 'Le Centenaire de l'occupation de l'Algérie', *Cahiers du Bolchévisme*, 4 (April 1930), 363–9, p. 367; Gallissot, *République*, pp. 88–90; Drew, *Discordant*, pp. 137–65. Sylvain Pattieu, *Les Camarades des frères: Trotskistes et libertaires dans la guerre d'Algérie* (Paris: Syllepse, 2002), pp. 41–2, argues that French Trotskyism's weakness reflected, in part, the PCF's hegemony on the left.
100 « Le premier mai, pour l'indépendance de ton pays, pour tes revendications, fraternise avec les ouvriers », Kaddache, *Vie politique*, pp. 191–3; El Maghreb, 'Centenaire', pp. 363–4; Benjamin E. Thomas, 'Motoring in the Sahara: The French raids of 1951–1953', *Economic Geography*, 29:4 (October 1953), 327–39, pp. 328–9.
101 « reste composé dans une majorité d'éléments européens sans liaison avec les indigènes dont le niveau de vie est très sensiblement supérieur au niveau de vie moyen des prolétaires indigènes », RGASPI 517.1.984, *Rapport de Jean Théveny, délégué de la CGTU en Algérie du 1er Décembre 1929 au 1er juillet 1930*, 10 July 1930, p. 4; Albert Ayache, 'Essai sur la vie syndicale en Algérie, l'année du centenaire (1930)', *Mouvement Social*, 78 (January–March, 1972), 95–114.
102 RGASPI 517.1.984, Charles Bourneton, *Rapport sur la tournée en Algérie*, 4/13–30 [sic], Documents annexes. Bourneton visited in November–December 1930; Ayache, 'Vie syndicale', pp. 110–13; Gallissot (ed.), *Algérie*, p. 94; Gallissot, *République*, pp. 91–3.
103 Hopkins, 'French Communism', pp. 117–18; Ruedy, *Modern Algeria*, p. 138; Stora, *Histoire de l'Algérie*, p. 77; Rabah Aissaoui, 'Algerian Nationalists in the French Political Arena and Beyond: The *Etoile nord-africaine* and the *Parti du peuple algérien* in Interwar France, *Journal of North African Studies*, 15:1 (March 2010), 1–12, p. 3.
104 RGASPI 517.1.984, Bureau régional to Bureau politique, PCF, 19 July 1930; PCF Colonial Section to Algerian region [stamped 14 December 1930]; Bourneton, *Rapport*, pp. 3–4, 12–15.
105 « il nous faut mener la lutte jusqu'au bout pour le P.C.A., poser la question devant l'I.C. et réclamer son intervention rapide », Documents annexes, Bourneton, *Rapport*, pp. 20–21.
106 *Correspondance Internationale*, 128 (25 October 1928), 1392–3. Sid Ahmed Belarbi (Boualem) used the name Aberderramé.

CHAPTER THREE

'The mountain "was going communist"': peasant struggles on the Mitidja

For the PCF's Algerian region, 1930 represented the pinnacle of repression. Public political space contracted sharply. Communists and trade unionists were subjected to a state of siege – hounded, imprisoned and deported south. This continued into 1931. *Lutte sociale* was repeatedly seized. When it appeared, Boualem's name figured prominently, promoting the decisions of the Comintern's Sixth Congress. Trade union and neighbourhood cells produced small mimeographed papers such as *L'Esclave du rail* (railway workers), *Le Disque rouge* (postal workers) and *La Cantara rouge* (Bab el Oued).[1] But national coordination was impossible without a national paper. Indeed, the PCF's Algerian region remained so fragmented that an October 1931 report could point only to a 'little Bône and Oran party, and a little Algiers party'. Although Algiers and Blida were only 50 kilometres apart, they had no links.[2] This disastrous situation forced a strategic rethink. A key issue concerned whether the party should operate legally and publicly – pushing the bounds of political space – or clandestinely and underground. Boualem advocated an underground party. Disgruntled individuals and groups wrote directly to the Comintern in Moscow, blaming the PCF's central committee and, especially, the colonial commission for the regional party's deterioration. Finding the complaints justified, the Comintern informed the Algerian region that the Sixth Congress's decision to form an independent party must be implemented. This would hopefully dispel the tensions that had plagued relations between Paris and Algiers almost from the PCF's foundation.[3]

The Comintern's Sixth Congress had emphasised the importance of peasant-based anti-imperialist struggles. Historically, communism's urban orientation reflected European socialist thinking that had privileged the urban proletariat as the leading force in social change, a view reinforced by the Bolsheviks' interpretation of the 1917 Russian Revolution. As the 1920s progressed, however, the increasingly

Russian-dominated Comintern placed greater emphasis on organising the rural populations of colonised and non-industrial countries – although its understanding of peasant-based anti-imperial struggles owed more to the Chinese and Indian than to the African and Arab experiences. The Comintern maintained that peasant struggles could weaken imperialism until capitalism's contradictions led to its collapse. Nonetheless, rural protests in interwar Algeria were generally neglected by urban-based nationalists and communists.[4] Apart from the risks of repression, the urban orientation, minute numbers and disproportionately European composition of the communists precluded serious organisational work from being undertaken amongst rural Algerians.[5] Following the Sixth Congress the ECCI criticised the PCF for neglecting its colonial work, and communists in Algeria for neglecting the peasantry. Comintern pressure on the PCF continued over the next few years, and at the PCF's seventh congress in March 1932 it acknowledged its inadequate colonial work.[6]

That year the Comintern sent its delegate Seraphima Goloubieva to Paris to oversee the PCF's colonial work. Goloubieva, known as 'Suzanne', was concerned primarily with Indochina and left Algeria to André Morel – known as André Ferrat – head of the PCF's colonial section and *L'Humanité*'s editor. Goloubieva and Ferrat met with Ben Ali Boukort, who had gone to France after completing his military service in 1927, joining the PCF, the CGTU and the ENA and organising North African workers in Lyons. A deft organiser, he represented the CGTU and the ENA at the second League against Imperialism conference in Frankfurt in July 1929. He returned to Algeria in 1930, was back in France in 1931 and joined the PCF's central colonial committee in 1932. In that September, the ECCI's twelfth plenum reinforced the idea of a colonial agrarian revolution. Goloubieva and Ferrat evidently gave Boukort responsibility for the PCF's Algerian region. He returned to Algeria to organise the October regional conference.[7]

Boukort found the region demoralised; virtually all cells and *rayons* reported a lack of contact with and scorn for the Algiers leadership. *Lutte sociale* appeared sporadically, although the September 1932 issue pledged regular publication and, unusually, contained a half-page article in Arabic. The Mozabite Sliman Boudjenah was the PCF's Arabic writer and translator. The Mozabites were a close-knit community with collective and redistributive practices, such as the *twiza*, collective labour by the entire community on behalf of one member. In one sense voluntary, self-interest was built in: an individual who failed to participate could not call a *twiza*.[8] Redistribution was coupled with ethnic solidarity. Typically, Mozabite men left their community to earn money to send to their families, who remained behind to ensure the men's support and eventual return.

Born in Ghardaïa, Boudjenah attended school in Médéa, where his father had a shop. His father and uncle followed politics closely; Emir Khaled had tea in his father's shop, and he heard the emir address meetings in both French and Arabic, which impressed him deeply. After studying six years in Tunis, where he became friends with fellow-Mozabite Moufdi Zakaria, he went to Paris and, by his account, attended the 1927 Congress of Oppressed Nations in Brussels. Returning to Algeria, he finished part of his baccalaureate at the *Lycée Bugeaud* in Algiers. However, his anti-colonialist views caused problems with the school administration, and he did not complete his baccalaureate. Instead, he obtained a diploma in translation at the University of Algiers, wrote for Arabic and French-language newspapers, including Victor's Spielmann's, published political tracts under the pen-name *El-Ferkad* and attended leftist political meetings with the aim of promoting the national question in those circles. However, his anti-colonialist views got him in serious trouble; around 1930 he was exiled under special surveillance to the desert community of Beni Abbès. After his return, he worked for *Lutte sociale*.[9]

Much planning went into the party's regional conference, held on 22–23 October 1932. Boukort and Gaston Cornavin, PCF delegate from Paris, already knew about disagreements over the role of Europeans and Algerians in the regional branch and the PCF–Comintern relationship. They promoted Arabisation, a policy adopted at the conference. Arabisation did not reflect a well thought-out conception of the Algerian nation, but it meant both the recruitment of Algerian members and an orientation towards Algerian workers, peasants, artisans and small traders with the aim of establishing close contact with the national movement – in other words, mass work. But if numbers count, the tiny regional party remained virtually moribund, reporting some 130 members in 1932 – hardly sufficient for such ambitious aims.[10]

Back in Paris, Ferrat, a firm proponent of anti-colonial agrarian revolution, delegated Paul Radiquet to travel to Algeria. The idea was to impress upon local communists the need to train cadres and organise peasants and rural workers.[11] Born in 1906 near Paris, Radiquet worked in the chemical industry, joined the JC in 1923, the CGTU's executive committee in 1927 and worked his way up to the PCF's central committee. He organised textile- and mine-workers' strikes in northern and southern France, and Ferrat thought his diverse experience suitable for Algeria. There was no shortage of anti-expropriation struggles in the early 1930s, and Blida, on the nearby Mitidja plain, with a reasonable communist cell and active JC circle, provided an attractive location for communist work.[12]

Colonialism, nationalism and communism in Blida

The early 1930s were years of enormous stress for rural Algerians. Some 65–75 per cent of the rural population was categorised as 'poor' or 'very poor', and the rural proletariat had reached its peak.[13] Peasant anti-expropriation struggles and agricultural workers' strikes were erupting around the country. Attempts to unionise agricultural workers began from around 1930, as communists began organising agricultural workers around Tlemcen. In light of the Comintern's pressure, and encouraged by Ferrat and Boualem, a few Algerian JC members turned their attention to the struggles taking place at the foot of the Atlas Mountains on the Mitidja, a fertile plain where grain, fruit, tobacco and grapes flourished. Reflecting in microcosm the social, political and class dynamics of colonial Algeria, those struggles were fundamental to the development of what Omar Carlier calls the 'political triangle' of city – countryside – mountain that became central to the war of independence.[14]

Algerian peasants had been protesting against the theft of their land since the arrival of the French. The Mitidja was no exception. In 1830 it had consisted of many small *melk* parcels or *haouch* situated amongst larger *beylik* properties. The *haouch* were divided into three sections: firstly, the house, gardens, orchards and corrals; secondly, cultivated lands split into plots worked by individual families; and thirdly, commonly held pasture and brush land for livestock. The average family cultivated slightly less than one *zuwija* of land – an amount that a pair of cattle could plough in a year. This was equivalent to eight to ten hectares, sufficient at that time for subsistence. This fragmented landholding pattern had impeded French acquisition of land. War had disrupted the landholding patterns; once hostilities ended, land was confiscated and allocated for French colonisation. As elsewhere, Mitidja peasants were pushed ever higher up the mountains or expected to labour on European farms.[15]

As part of the Mitidja's colonisation, the French built small towns divided into a European section reminiscent of southern France and a pre-existing Muslim quarter with tightly packed whitewashed houses along maze-like passages. Blida, founded by Andalusians in the mid-sixteenth century and conquered by the French in 1838, developed in similar style.[16] The 1936 census listed 209,427 inhabitants – 41,507 Europeans and 167,920 Algerians – in Blida and its surrounding district. The district had 260,974 hectares of land, with a population density of 80.24 inhabitants per square kilometre.[17] It was a *commune de plein exercise*, a civil territory with a significant European population governed by French law.[18] Local politics was very much a microcosm of Algeria's class relations. Blida's mayor, Gaston Ricci, was from an extremely wealthy Italian family that owned entire mountains around Blida. His brothers Maurice and Henri were successful flour millers and manufacturers of pasta that carried the family name; many of the family firm's workers were Italian women with little formal education. The town had European artisan and trade union traditions and active railway and building workers' unions.[19]

Despite the severe repression accompanying the centenary celebrations, Algerian nationalism developed rapidly in the early 1930s, marked by two main tendencies. One was represented by the FEI. But rent by divisions over tactics, personality, ideology and geography, by 1930 it had split into three sections reflecting the three departments. In the early 1930s Constantine-born Dr Mohamed-Salah Bendjelloul became the federation's most prominent leader.[20] The other was represented by the Islamic reform movement, which had spread from east to west across the country. Michel Launay has documented Islamic reformist influence in Oranie. There, he argues, reformist *'ulama* spread their ideas amongst children of the middle peasants through the *medersas*, leading to a 'new type of young peasant'.[21] The egalitarian sermons of these reformist *'ulama*, Launay contends, 'reflected the ideal of the small peasant and corresponded to the first undifferentiated phase of the national revolution'. Islamic reformism competed with the *marabouts* and their followers; virtually every community had its local saint. Nonetheless, despite its avowedly non-political stance, in the absence of any Algerian working-class political movement – aside from the minute communist party – the culturally oriented Islamic reform movement spread across the political landscape. To French authorities the movement represented a subversive anti-colonialism.[22]

The launch of the Association des 'ulama musulmans algériens (Association of Algerian Muslim *'Ulama*, AUMA) signalled the movement's rapid growth. This took place on 5 May 1931 at the Cercle du progrès (Circle of Progress), a meeting hall organised by the Islamic reformists and symbolically located between the *casbah* and Bab el Oued.[23] The following March an organisation known as El Hidaia (*Le Don*, or Gift) was formed in Blida. It aimed to 'aid France's civilising action' by promoting the intellectual, moral and social recovery of Muslim Algerians through education and the promotion of strict religious principles and by fighting against alcoholism and all forms of public immorality. While promoting a Muslim Algerian identity, it was not anti-French.[24]

El Hidaia's work had three main areas: religious, social and cultural, which sought to revive Arab theatre, letters and history. Its religious work was led by Shaykh Taïeb el-Okbi, a reformist *'alim* who worked closely with Ben Badis. Born in Biskra, el-Okbi had spent twenty-five years in Hedjaz, Saudi Arabia and was much respected for his long stay in Mecca. By early April 1932 El Hidaia had about 160 members, and by June it was claiming some 460 – chiefly bourgeois and petty bourgeois, according to local communist reports. The organisation clearly had a popular resonance.[25]

The PCF had a decade-long, if feeble, presence at Blida. The second *Congrès interfédéral communiste de l'Afrique du Nord* had been held there on 2 September 1922, at which time a commission was formed to formulate an Algerian perspective on communism and the colonial question.[26] Schiavo, Blida's leading trade unionist, organised Algerians into trade unions, but did not support the idea of a national liberation movement. Nonetheless, small numbers of Algerians were attracted to communist ideas. Thus Ali Mira, a solicitor's clerk who learned about peasant expropriation through cases handled in his office and, unusually, an atheist, joined Blida's communist cell at its formation. In the 1920s Mira organised agricultural workers, even picking grapes himself, and he was later selected to study at the KUTV in Moscow. Politics ran in the family: his brother Mohamed Mira was secretary of the Blida rail workers' union. Of a younger generation, born in 1912, Ahmed Mahmoudi worked at Blida's well-known psychiatric hospital and became active in the JC around 1928. During a strike of tobacco shop workers Mahmoudi became friends with Abderrahmane Bouchama, a *caïd*'s son who supported the strike. Bouchama studied in France, where he joined the PCF in 1930, and became an architect. In Paris the Blidéen communist Djilali Chabila had been the ENA's treasurer and secretary-general. In short, whether through local communists or migrant workers, communist ideas seeped into the area.[27]

By 1932, when the PCF increased pressure on its Algerian region to turn to the countryside, the Blida branch was recovering from the expulsions that had depleted its membership a few years earlier. With a turnover in membership, attitudes changed. In no small part this was due to the JC's growth and recruitment of Algerians. In July of that year, the Blida JC cell had six members, all Algerians, one of whom was Mahmoudi; in Algérois there were 55 Young Communists, 26 of whom were Algerian.[28]

The JC's influence was soon felt in Blida. The local PCF was hoping to promote communist ideas within *El Hidaia*. Indeed, Blida's communist cell was very important insofar as the nationalist movement was concerned, reported Dupont in early April 1932.[29] Two Young Communists were *El Hidaia* members, one each in the social and cultural sections, although they were unsure how to promote communist influence inside the organisation. The latter gave weekly lectures on Arab history to audiences of about fifty. He covered French conquest and occupation; the comrades hoped that this would arouse hatred against French imperialism. There was certainly interest in historical approaches that challenged the French orthodoxy and that did not depend on literacy. Lithograph prints depicting heroic episodes and figures in Algerian history found their way across the country, despite censorship, to rural towns like Blida.[30]

Organising peasant protests

When Paul Radiquet arrived in Algiers in late 1932 he planned a trip to Oran, and he designated Maurice Benaïch to go to Blida to mobilise local communists and initiate contact with peasants fighting expropriation. From a Jewish family in Oran, Benaïch was a cabinet-maker by profession. Although a leading figure in Oran's JC and CGTU, he reportedly had difficulties because of Arab anti-Semitism. Coinciding with Radiquet's mission, he left Oran to act as the party's regional secretary in Algiers and then proceeded to Blida.[31]

However, Benaïch evidently resisted travelling to outlying rural areas, and Radiquet felt that he was not making sufficient progress. He sent Boualem to replace Benaïch, who went to Sidi bel Abbès. Boualem was by then a leading communist. Not only the first Algerian secretary of the regional party, he had attended the Sixth Congress of the Comintern, studied at the KUTV in 1929–30 and been elected to the PCF's central committee in March 1932. At Blida, Boualem was to work with a Young Communist named Rafa Naceur, who was initially a member of the Philippeville branch before he moved to Algiers in August 1932. Boualem became particularly well known for his organisational work at Boufarik, where he formed a small circle.[32]

Peasant protests against expropriation had already been going on for some months. About 600 to 800 peasants from the villages of Sidi el Kébir and Ghellaï, comprising roughly 494 hectares of land, were faced with expropriation orders on the grounds that the land was needed for reforestation, ostensibly to prevent flooding during the rainy season. The land in question had quarries that were exploited by two local entrepreneurs; in Ghellaï where peasants made charcoal, the government wished to rent part of the land and sell some of it to the colons. Mayor Ricci himself was an interested party in the affair: his land bordered the *deschra* or hamlet at Sidi el Kébir, and expropriation would give him the chance to extend his property – he evidently enlisted the aid of the local *caïd*, one Zraibi Ali, to convince people that expropriation was necessary for the public utility.[33]

But the peasants were not prepared to lose their land. They consulted the local municipal councillors, who advised them to appeal to the government with a compromise, namely, agreeing to give up part of their land for reforestation. This they refused to do. They could point to the expropriations seven years ago at Oued Abarar, for which no adequate compensation had yet been made, as well as to the expropriation eight years ago at Dellys, where the expropriated peasant was still obliged to pay taxes on land that was no longer his! The region was in a state of ferment, and in nearby Menerville, peasants were refusing to pay taxes.[34] The local communist cell circulated a petition against expropriations, and several communists met with local peasants. Not surprisingly, they were initially greeted with suspicion. But this suspicion did not reflect Fanon's belief of 'the old antagonism between town and country', nor that 'between the native who is excluded from the advantages of colonialism and his counterpart'. These peasants had good reason to be suspicious: in the past, some of them had lost money to individuals offering help. Their attitude softened due to the efforts of Hamed Boukémiat, a municipal councillor in whom they had much confidence and who advised them to listen to the communists.[35]

Radiquet arrived in the Mitidja in early December 1932. He and Naceur travelled by bus, contacting peasants threatened with expropriation. 'For several days we went to see the peasants of various *deschras* to explain what we wanted to do', Radiquet wrote to Paris headquarters; 'it was only after several attempts that we were able to make them understand.' Persistence paid off. The peasants designated nine delegates from the villages around Blida to liaise with the communists. With those delegates, reported Radiquet, 'we continued the propaganda work across the douars to prepare a meeting of the deschras of Sidi-El-Kébir'.[36] They agreed to: first, link the predicament of those facing expropriation with the 1925 Oued Abarar expropriation, for which no adequate compensation had been made; second, ask Algerians in town to support those facing expropriation; third, work with local councillors in whom they had confidence to build a united front; and fourth, prepare an Arabic-language flyer for distribution in all the villages.

The plan worked. The flyer asked peasants to meet in their villages and form anti-expropriation committees. Each village was to designate delegates, and they were to organise an open-air demonstration.[37] The communists set up a meeting with some sixty peasants, with discussions in Arabic and French. A defence committee consisting of eight peasants was elected.[38] Later that month, one Durand from the central colonial section wrote that they were pleased with the work at Blida, but he warned against forming a permanent peasant organisation. The PCF opposed launching a peasant party, instead encouraging the formation of action and defence committees guided by communists and geared towards specific demands, warning that these should not become centralised, either regionally or across Algeria. The party's first priority was to defend the struggles of small peasants, Durand explained. The expropriations at Batna and Menerville – where peasants refused to pay taxes – indicated the potential for a vast peasant-based resistance movement. He hoped that the work at Blida could serve as a model for other areas in Algérois and Oranie, where expropriations were planned in the commune of Renault. Durand suggested organising peasants around tangible demands such as the election of village committees for specific aims.[39]

Communists were also working with the Oued Abarar peasants, who had received a pittance of compensation for land expropriated in 1912. In 1925 about 1,600 more hectares of land was expropriated with promises of compensation, and some of those peasants were now working on rented land. The promised compensation for the 1925 expropriations was so meagre after taxes that the affected peasants refused to take the money. They were understandably bitter. The municipality had approved the Oued Abarar expropriations, and the peasants had little regard for politicians.[40] 'They were very suspicious of us due to the deceptions of which they have often been victims, whether by lawyers or other imperialist agents', Radiquet thought. But councillor Boukémiat encouraged them to cooperate with the communists. Radiquet was sceptical about his motives, speculating that he had his eyes on the upcoming financial delegation elections and needed peasant support. But Boukémiat introduced the communists to three Oued Abarar peasants, who promised to gather peasants from other areas for a meeting on 22 December to organise a defence committee at Ghellaï.[41]

The reference to the meeting of 22 December was to an upcoming anti-expropriation demonstration in Blida being planned by the communists. Lucien Monjauvis, the communist deputy from La Seine who had raised land expropriations with the Minister of the Interior in Paris, was sent to Algeria by the PCF as a gesture of solidarity. He was scheduled to speak at Blida's town hall against expropriations at Sidi el Kébir and Ghellaï. The PCF printed large posters and local peasants spread word of the event across the region.[42] On the day of the demonstration Monjauvis addressed a large crowd of French and Algerian workers in front of the town hall; indicating the level of discontent, peasants from Chréa asked him if they should take up arms. Monjauvis was arrested after his speech but released later that evening after a mass demonstration of some 700. Benaïch was arrested in Algiers.[43]

The efforts to organise peasants continued, bringing the dispute about public or underground work to the fore. Boualem launched a journal called *Le Paysan algérien*. Two or three issues appeared, but to Radiquet's consternation – he stressed public activity – Boualem and

Benaïch preferred a journal without any identifying contact information. The question of public or clandestine activity was a continuing tension between Radiquet and Boualem. Most comrades wanted a party that was 'illegal, clandestine, sectarian', Radiquet felt; indeed, in his words, one that 'would pull the strings' of the revolutionary movement behind the scenes, without obviously participating. Yet Radiquet also claimed that Boualem wanted to recruit 'at all costs' – even bringing back those who had been expelled.[44]

Despite the risk of arrest, total clandestinity was unrealistic. Communists in the Mitidja had shown that public political space could be expanded into villages, markets and town squares; moreover, organised labour had a public profile. A delegation of communist railway workers from the Cheminots Alger PLM went to Blida, meeting with the local union branch and about twenty peasants threatened with expropriation. Railway workers were well placed to disseminate communist ideas. Many of them travelled, and the PCF counted railway workers amongst its members in Algiers, Blida and Menerville, amongst other towns. Likewise, a JC group from Algiers travelled to Sidi Moussa, Larbaâ and Rovigo (now Bougara).[45]

By January 1933 the authorities were worried about communist activity in the Mitidja.[46] At Blida communist activity reportedly declined due to the younger comrades' fear of repression.[47] However, Radiquet and his colleagues turned to the nearby areas of Larbaâ, Rovigo and Tablat where expropriations aimed at reforestation were taking place in l'Oued Djemâa and Sidi Lakrout. 'Interesting results', Radiquet wrote to Paris on 4 February 1933. 'Blida is not alone.'[48] They made contact with older peasants in the markets, telling them about the action at Blida, the PCF and its methods of struggle.[49] Villages held their markets on different days, allowing people to travel from one market to another, contacting individuals from different communities. Markets were thus ideal public political spaces for communists to make new contacts and carry their slogans to wider areas.[50]

It was not easy-going. Neither the comrades nor the peasants were experienced at assessing when to use legal or clandestine methods, Radiquet reported. 'The peasants are so enthusiastic that they come up to us in the city streets, follow us and hassle us to hold delegate meetings. Yesterday, instead of a meeting of a dozen delegates, there were about 80 peasants who had spotted us and gathered around.'[51] And unlike communists, peasants seemed unmoved by the threat of arrest. Thus, as Radiquet was boarding the bus to leave Larbaâ, about a dozen peasants came to greet him. 'Contrary to their custom, even though they had to go back up the mountain, they waited until five in the evening to shake my hand and make an appointment.'[52] Despite harassment, the communists made headway around Larbaâ and Rovigo. At Rovigo peasants from the village of Sidi Hamouda had received a notice on 1 December that 262 hectares were to be expropriated. Peasants from Rovigo had a history of resistance. They had been threatened with expropriation in 1924, but had consulted a lawyer and been able to annul the expropriation order. Now, once again faced with the same threat, they protested to the local chief and the mayor, but to no avail.

Following discussions with the communists, the peasants decided to remain on their land, continue planting their fields and refrain from cashing the ridiculously low compensation sum that they had received for their land. The mayor threatened to send in police and soldiers. The woods at Beni Argat were set alight, evidently in the hope that the peasants would be blamed and fined, and the communists discredited. But the intimidation failed. Peasants acting as lookouts in the mountain made sure that there were no defections, and the communists organised a meeting of 35 peasants, mainly elders. The peasants had selected three delegates each from four sections of Sidi Hamouda, with the understanding that the twelve representatives were to have weekly meetings. Once the peasants started working their land, this intensified their desire to resist the expropriation: they did not want to see their efforts wasted. Eventually the expropriation efforts ceased.[53]

There were several meetings with peasants from Tablat, very near the Atlas mountains, where peasants from the villages of Sidi Lakrout and Beni Lermane were threatened with expropriation. 'One has to be here to understand the anger of these poor people', thought the young French communist Gaston Donnat, travelling around the Tablat region with Radiquet. A teacher, Donnat had arrived in Algeria in late 1931. With a facility for meeting, talking and organising, he and an Algerian student named Ahmed Smaïli formed a communist cell at La Bouzaréah, near Algiers. He realised that the fathers of the peasants he saw had once occupied the fertile land but had been chased up the mountains. Now, they had a few tiny fields, a few trees and small numbers of goats with virtually no grazing land.[54]

One Sunday in January or February 1933, a group of Young Communists went to Beni Lermane. The state had returned Beni Lermane's communal land 84 years earlier. Although there was no official act of expropriation, the Forest Service claimed that reforestation was needed to prevent floods. The peasants did not mince words: 'if one went back to Turkish times one would know that there had never been floods or landslides.'[55] The next Sunday, despite intimidation from the local administration, a large group of peasants, some from Palestro and Berroughia, met with Radiquet and comrades at the Tablat market. The communists addressed a group of 200 or 300 peasants in French and Arabic, using a question and answer format, rather than lecturing.

Thus, the communists evoked a resonance with many local peasants. There were several reasons for this. Firstly, the communists' proposed demands echoed those of the peasants. Secondly, the communists' proposed tactics, such as boycotting compensation, dovetailed with approaches used by the peasants. Thirdly, the type of organisation proposed by the communists made sense in terms of peasants' own *djemâa* system of self-government. Although French policy had fragmented tribes through its resettlement programmes, once Algerians settled in *douars* they formed local councils of tribal elites called *djemâas*. These councils were recognised and given limited functions in the mixed and Arab territories, but not in predominantly European civil territories, where *djemâas-occultes*, or hidden *djemâas*, developed as underground political space to maintain a local government tradition despite the colonial dismantling of tribal structures.[56]

Communists found that collective resistance to expropriations already existed in many areas. By impeding the efforts of Forest Service representatives to gain access to land around Blida and Rovigo, for instance, local peasants had hampered expropriation efforts. As Radiquet noted, 'The peasant movement existed in a latent state.' The communists had simply seized the opportunity of working with that movement, which was growing rapidly. Finally, the communists were able to demonstrate to other peasants their initial success at Blida and Rovigo, where expropriations had been halted as a result of the resistance. In this way they opened up rural political space.[57]

Yet they faced heavy repression. At Tablat, Larbaâ and Rovigo police harassment was routine. On 5 March twenty peasants were arrested at Tablat. On 7 March Radiquet and Naceur were questioned at Tablat. They were arrested at Larbaâ along with several other comrades after enquiring about holding a public meeting in the town hall. They were held for eight days at Serkadji while the authorities unsuccessfully tried to get local peasants to turn on the communists. Nonetheless, Radiquet sensed a lack of support from the regional headquarters. He described this as an attitude of 'boycott' or 'passive resistance' and attributed it to a lack of interest in rural work. Even after the Larbaâ arrests, the regional bureau 'contented itself with work in the form of small discussions with peasants who came to Algeria and with a meeting of a few delegates, which was dignified as a conference.' The day after the arrests was market day, bringing together some 2,000 peasants, about 300 of whom assembled in protest in front of the town hall, despite the absence of communists. So concerned about further protests were the authorities that they withdrew the hunting licences of many peasants and seized their guns.[58]

Communists, Islamic reformists and revolutionary nationalists

In addition to the PCF's work with peasants, Blida's JC members became known through their work in *El Hadiai*. French communism was characterised by an anti-clericalism that was prevalent across much of the southern European left. This anti-clerical stance was even stronger in colonised areas where colonial authorities and settlers derided the indigenous religion as 'primitive'. The Comintern's line of class against class reinforced such anti-clerical views, Henri Alleg argues. *Lutte sociale* castigated 'the Muslim clergy, creation of French imperialism, the big bourgeoisie, the *'ulama*, all those at the head of national reformist organisations' for allegedly being controlled by the French bourgeoisie. European communists were typically imbued with such attitudes and viewed Islamic reformists in this light.[59]

This was not so for Algerian communists, many of whom would have agreed with Hadj Ali Abdelkader that the religious comfort sought by the Algerian proletarian represented 'the expression of his suffering, the rallying cry of an exploited man to all his brothers in misery, to his fellow believers'.[60] Indeed, to Radiquet's chagrin, Boualem 'took religious demands as communist demands'. Not only that, Radiquet discovered: the Algerian comrades on the regional bureau were even more supportive of Shaykh el-Okbi than was Boualem! Like many secularised French communists, Radiquet had difficulty understanding that religion could address social questions in a manner that was not necessarily incompatible with socialism. Nor could he understand why Boualem started talking to a group of peasants about Egypt, not appreciating their interest in events across the Arab and Muslim world. Wasn't Boualem just politicising the anti-expropriation movement, Radiquet wondered?[61]

There was undoubtedly an affinity between Islamic reformism's anti-colonial spirit and the PCF's avowed anti-colonialism, which some French communists understood. Thus, the PCF's general secretary Maurice Thorez, for one, believed that religious movements in Algeria were inspired by the desire to revolt against French imperialism and that popular demands around religion, language and culture could mobilise the Algerian people. Precisely because the Blida JC succeeded in recruiting more Algerian members in the early 1930s, it was able to make links with *El Hadiai*.[62]

By early 1933 the combined activities of Taïeb el-Okbi's followers and the communists were successful enough to worry the French administration. On 16 February 1933 Fernand-Jules Michel, the head of the prefecture of Algiers, issued a circular expressing concern about religious propaganda promoting anti-colonial attitudes, especially the wahabite movement. He instructed that a close eye be kept on meetings led by Ben Badis and Taïeb el-Okbi and on Koranic schools. In parallel with the wahabite movement, the circular added, communists were leading agitation against the forest regime in certain villages and market places. The two movements necessitated an active surveillance.[63]

Although communist activity in the Mitidja had caught the government's eye, the PCF was unable to link effectively with the urban movement. The authorities were cracking down on Muslim activities. Koranic schools were closed and newspapers banned, but Islamic organisations multiplied. Algiers was in ferment. The developments sparked demonstrations on 24 February and 3 March. The British consul-general downplayed the events, noting a 'certain effervescence' amongst 'a small section' of Muslims.[64] By their own account, communists were present at the 24 February demonstration by accident. Even the Algerian communists failed to report preparations for the demonstrations to the regional headquarters. Some of them seemingly considered the religious and nationalist movements to be their private domain, to be kept apart from the party. Yet, once the regional PCF learned of the protest, it produced flyers and tried to get involved. Algerian communists were keen to support el-Okbi's movement; some even saw it as more important than the agitation against expropriation and reforestation, according to one report. European communists, though, seemed unable to explain how the PCF's anti-imperialism differed from nationalist politics. The day after the 3 March demonstration, the party did nothing, according to an internal report, perhaps due to the preference for clandestine work.[65]

Shaykh el-Okbi desired freedom of the Muslim religion from interference by the French state – the separation of religion and state, which existed in France, but not Algeria. On 17 March Governor-General Carde ordered a squadron of fighters and Senegalese troops to prevent el-Okbi from entering the Sidi Okba mosque where he was due to speak. Demonstrations of el-Okbi's supporters 'were dispersed by the police supported by a small number of troops. A well known local communist seized the opportunity to incite the demonstrators to resist the police'.[66] Further demonstrations occurred on 24 April.[67] Nonetheless, the agitation was 'quelled' by early May, reported the British consul-general. The events were to become a political turning point in Algiers.[68]

In March, Thorez had addressed the French Chamber of Deputies on the conditions of Algerian peasants, reiterating the demand for an independent Algeria. He was planning a trip to Algeria to attend the

PCF's regional congress scheduled for 21 May.[69] Shortly before his trip, the PCF's political bureau and central colonial section met. Thorez and Ferrat highlighted the need to develop a 'native policy' and give the PCF in Algeria 'a native orientation'. Thorez argued that 'the next step in the Algerian revolution [was] the anti-imperialist and agrarian revolution'. Radiquet's anti-expropriation work was fundamental to this anti-imperialist struggle, he stressed.[70]

Thorez arrived in Algiers on 10 May 1933. A few days later he addressed a large crowd at Sidi bel Abbès, where workers had been on strike for several months. Close to a thousand Algerian workers squeezed into the Idéal-Palace, claimed the party, where Thorez spoke on anti-racism, anti-imperialism and national liberation. At nearby Perregaux, Thorez and the CGTU delegate Bossus addressed 1,200 workers, including 400 Algerians – for all practical purposes, the CGTU was the only trade union federation open to Algerians.[71] In that same month, Boualem and Mohammed Mestoul founded the ambitiously named Parti national révolutionnaire (PNR) in the Algiers *casbah*. A locksmith, Mestoul had lived in France, where he was impressed by Messali and his newspaper *El Ouma* (*The Nation*), which had been launched in October 1930. On Mestoul's return to Algeria he began meeting with interested individuals in a European café at Soustara, Algiers, using *El Ouma* to discuss nationalism and revolution. Most of the PNR's members were trade unionists, and Boualem, reflecting his studies in Moscow, promoted the PNR to counter the influence of what the Comintern then thought was the overly nationalist ENA. Indeed, by early 1933 Messali was planning to relaunch the ENA in Paris. Thorez thought that the PNR's work was '*pas mauvais*' – not bad – but argued for the creation of broad committees raising democratic demands to mobilise the largest possible numbers of people. The PCF's Algerian region should focus on building a mass movement rather than forming a political party, he stressed.[72]

Through the PNR, the PCF hoped to link revolutionary nationalists and communists. The idea was to form committees around particular demands. Yet the communists were concerned that a new 'Algerian Muslim national party' was a potential rival to the PNR. This new group included both 'ambitious' and 'sincere' types, such as Sliman Boudjenah, who suffered continuous problems with the authorities. He had been released from prison in March 1933 after a vigorous communist campaign. But only after lengthy discussions, claimed one report, did the PCF convince Boudjenah to join one of the PNR's committees.[73]

Mitidja peasants were keen to have more contact with the PCF. The Blida cell now had more than a dozen members as a result of its rural work. The intention was to form new cells in the food, tobacco and railway industries and in peasant communities.[74] Repression at Beni Lermane was particularly intense, and the party acknowledged that it had not been able to give those peasants adequate support. Hearing of Thorez's visit, peasants around Larbaâ and Rovigo asked that he come and speak to them. They planned to assemble at Larbaâ on 23 May. Despite police attempts to keep them from reaching Larbaâ, a large crowd assembled there. Thorez arrived in the afternoon with Radiquet, Bossus, Serrano, Valle and two Algerian comrades. Some 200 Algerians were standing near the town hall. Thorez was swamped by the crowd. Refused entry to the town hall, he spoke outside, his talk translated into Arabic. He told them that he had seen their terrible conditions and that he would defend the rights of expropriated Algerians in the French Parliament. Closing with the words, 'return to your huts, your fields, work them and defend them', he was wildly applauded. Afterwards, one of the peasants – who later expressed a desire to join the party – took Thorez and another comrade around the villages on a mule.[75]

Over the next few months, the PCF's reputation in the area remained strong. By the party's own account, it 'seemed to be the sole defender of peasant interests; moreover, it led their struggles with delegates from the douar, demonstrations, meetings, and knew how to give the movement forms of struggle that had made the government move back'.[76] Its work in the Mitidja, although led by Radiquet and a few interested comrades rather than the regional leadership, represented a significant engagement with rural struggles. More Algerians were joining the party, and at one point pressure from mass demonstrations was significant enough to obtain the release of Radiquet, Bossus and Montjauvis. Nonetheless, Naceur and Taïeb Abdelouahad had been imprisoned since May. In July they were threatened with deportation south, but were eventually released.[77]

Communist electoral activity in the Mitidja

Differences about public versus clandestine activity were resolved in practice. The next significant communist activity in the Mitidja took place during the campaign for the departmental council elections in the third district, scheduled for August 1933. By this time Radiquet had returned to Paris. Following the announcement of elections, communists from Algiers travelled to Blida to meet local peasants. The 1919 Jonnart Law restricted voting to about 43 per cent of adult Muslim men, effectively excluding most peasants. Nonetheless, the elections offered communists the opportunity to engage in propaganda on their behalf, and they suggested that a peasant candidate run on an anti-expropriation programme. The peasants proposed Boukémiat, but the communists argued that he had not been particularly active in the anti-expropriation campaign and suggested Taïeb Abdelouahad, who had been imprisoned because of his work at Larbaâ. The peasants were reportedly enthusiastic with this choice.

The voting district covered some 100 square kilometres. The PCF printed 7,000 copies of an electoral flyer and organised about twenty-five meetings in the mountains and at cafés *maures* (Moorish cafés) in areas targeted with expropriation. This included Blida, Birtouta, Bouinan – where Mahmoudi and the teacher Ali Bouchakdji had been particularly active, Chebli, La Chiffa and Mouzaiaville.[78] The PNR also distributed election material under its name, including a political programme calling for the unity of all anti-imperialist forces in the struggle for an independent Algeria and North Africa. It demanded an end to the *indigénat*, to expropriations, and to police brutality and repression, and for freedom of the Muslim religion and bilingual French–Arabic language instruction for all Algerian children.[79]

Taïeb Abdelouahad was to run against Dr Abdelouahab Bachir, Dr Bentami and Touami el Hadj Brahim. Although the PCF's Algerian region had contested urban municipal elections, this was its first experience of running a rural electoral campaign. It was the first time that peasants and agricultural workers in areas like Birtouta, Bouinan, La Chiffa and Souma had heard of the PCF, and the party hoped to benefit from the electoral fever to popularise its programme and plan of action amongst poor peasants and agricultural workers.[80]

The PCF tried organising peasants around the demand for compensation, but this did not attract them. Nor were they mobilised by the demand for Parliamentary representation. At an electoral meeting in Chebli a communist raised the topic of soviets. One very active peasant who had helped organise the meeting replied that the question of the village soviet was crucial for peasants. Perhaps the concept resonated with that of the peasants' own village councils. In essence they wanted tangible demands and direct political participation, starting in their own communities. Thus, the communists decided that the call for the widest possible participation in assemblies under a government of workers and peasants should be raised alongside basic democratic demands, such as the abolition of the *indigénat* and forest regime, and the right of free press and trade union organisation.[81]

Communists and their supporters faced significant intimidation. At Blida, claimed the PCF's regional bureau, when Bachir's electoral agents saw that 'the mountain "was going communist"',[82] they applied pressure: money, blackmail and arrests of those suspected of having communist bulletins. Many peasants around Blida, Bouinan and Chebli were arrested; in towns those suspected of communist sympathies were summoned to the commissariat and threatened with arrest. Rumours flew that those voting communist would be imprisoned. While the majority of Algerians could not vote, corrupt electoral agents from all clans were buying votes, the communists charged. Yet despite this intimidation, many peasants marched with communist speakers in support of Taïeb, and in towns numbers of radicalised youth supported the party.[83]

On polling day the atmosphere at Blida reportedly felt like civil war. The army was mobilised, and all strategic points guarded. Police and security agents from Algiers maintained a state of siege around the polling station. Dozens of Algerians and Europeans were arrested. With such intimidation, the party felt vindicated by the results. Although it claimed that votes for its candidate had been spoiled in every locality, nonetheless, in the first round Taïeb Abdelouahad received votes in most localities, winning 120 votes out of 3,577 or 3.4 per cent overall, with 183 spoiled ballots. Without any hint of the unrest, the colonialist *Le Tell*, reported the results. They showed significant variations across the area, with appreciable communist influence in Boufarik, where Boualem had organised. Given that most Algerians, and notably the poor peasants and agricultural workers, did not have the right to vote, the party was encouraged by the results (see Table 3).[84]

Le Tell reported that Dr Bachir's election results were annulled. In the second round Dr Bachir remained on the ballot, but Touami el Hadj Brahim withdrew. The PCF maintained its candidate and redoubled its efforts, winning 118 votes out of 3,745, or 3.1 per cent overall, distributed as shown in Table 4.[85]

Having used the Blida elections to popularise its programme, the party turned its hand to Arabic-language publicity. *Lutte sociale* appeared in September 1933 with an Arabic-language page. The police quickly seized the forthcoming text from the printers. Boudjenah was arrested on 8 September and sent to Serkadji, spending three months in solitary confinement. Starved of human contact, he was transferred at his request to the criminal section. Both the PCF and the socialists campaigned for his release. Monjauvis wrote twice to the Minister of Interior, who replied that Boudjenah had been arrested for actions against the French state and that on 27 November 1933 he had been sentenced to two years of special surveillance in the desert community of Adrar in Ain Sefra.[86] He was sent south by train. At an overnight stop at Berigo, Boudjenah was put in a cell without food or water, passing the night standing up to avoid mosquitoes. At Saida he was held at the barracks and fed by local Mozabites. At Bech a French commandant publicly humiliated him until the local *caïd* asked that he be put under his authority until the next caravan for Beni Abbès.[87] After this,

Table 3 Departmental elections, third district (Blida): Algerian voters, 1st round, 13 August 1933

Voting location (commune)	Dr A. Bachir	T. El Hadj Brahim	Dr Bentami	T. Abdelouahad (PCF)	Other	Registered	Voting	Valid votes	% PCF
Blida	1,088	154	356	47	—	3,096	1,771	1,645	2.9
Birtouta	15	22	86	2	?	158	128	125	0.2
Boufarik	54	221	10	51	18	439	370	354	14.4
Bouïnan	110	117	74	—	?	473	303	301	—
Chebli	27	78	34	3	—	167	148	142	0.2
Mouzaïaville	44	138	163	16	—	472	373	361	4.4
La Chiffa	13	39	110	1	—	228	168	163	0.6
Souma	100	310	76	—	—	831	499	486	0.1
Total	1,451	1,079	909	120	18	5,684	3,760	3,577	3.4

Source: Le Tell, 16 August 1933, p. 2.

Table 4 Departmental elections, third district (Blida): Algerian voters, 2nd round, 20 August 1933

Voting location (commune)	Dr Abdelouahab Bachir	Dr Bentami	Taieb Abdelouahad (PCF)	Other	Registered	Voting	Valid votes	% PCF
Blida	1,454	378	43	0	3,096	1,913	1,875	2.0
Birtouta	68	44	0	—	158	118	112	0
Boufarik	205	83	15	7	439	322	310	4.8
Bouïnan	194	119	1	—	473	318	314	0.3
Chebli	56	70	1	—	167	134	127	0.8
Mouzaïaville	117	183	6	1	472	326	307	0.2
La Chiffa	75	68	2	—	228	149	145	0.1
Souma	203	302	50	—	831	569	555	0.9
Total	2,372	1,247	118	8	5,864	3,849	3,745	3.1

Source: Le Tell, 23 August 1933, p. 1, and RGASPI 517.1.1526, *B.R. d'Alger au B.P. du P.C.F.*, 27 September 1933.

no Algerian printer wanted to work for the party. The risks of arrest and banishment were too great. The party had hoped to send the plate to a printer in Marseille, but no Algerian wanted their Arabic script to appear on a plate. Thus, despite the party's best intentions, both production of Arabic-language material and public political activity remained extremely risky.[88]

Communist experiences in the Mitidja illustrate that Algerian peasants were open to alliances with urban activists. Viewed through the eyes of the communists working with them, these rural folk fit neither Fanon's image that the peasant was the 'first ... to discover that only violence pays' nor Sivan's characterisation of a 'limited and deaf resistance'.[89] In the late nineteenth century Algerian peasants had used fire and petitions to protest the French seizure of land.[90] By the 1930s, not seeking to form a peasant party, they were making alliances with lawyers, municipal councillors and communists, employing a range of tactics – petitions, boycotts, demonstrations – to seek redress. Language, religion and ideology – 'Arabic is my language, Algeria my country and Islam my religion' – were critical factors in shaping Algerian nationalism, and the Islamic reformist message had a resonance in rural areas, but the land question – in both its economic and cultural dimensions – was central. By working with and linking up anti-expropriation struggles in various villages, communists opened up rural political space. They expanded it further by demonstrating to rural communities the possibilities inherent in the electoral process.

Yet developments conspired to make links between urban activists and rural movements difficult to sustain. First were demographic factors. Ruedy has suggested that, 'given the physical environment and the level of technical development of the era, the countryside had probably reached saturation shortly before or after 1930'.[91] Peasants lost their land and became agricultural workers. The rapid growth of the rural Algerian population under such conditions led to a rush to towns in the 1930s. This demographic shift inevitably led to an increase in urban-based political activity, although the urban–rural dynamic was maintained through newly arrived impoverished peasants and agricultural workers who settled in the densely populated *casbahs* and squatter camps. Secondly, government authorities, fearing the combined menace of religious-inspired nationalist protest and communist-backed peasant protest – whether real or imagined – unleashed a crackdown on the Islamic reform movement. This in turn catalysed an upsurge in urban protest, particularly in Algiers, although national and cultural factors far outweighed class interests in these protests. In January 1934 the PNR, unable to continue autonomously, affiliated *en masse* to the relaunched ENA, becoming its first Algerian branch.[92]

The Mitidja case signalled the importance of alliances, both for peasants and for communists, who were most successful when they engaged in combination with land, national and religious struggles intersecting with and reinforcing each other. In the Mitidja they briefly did this. But communist interest in the difficult task of rural organising, always weak, was distracted by the mounting political activity in Algiers. Moreover, developments in Algeria were overshadowed by events in Europe. By the time of André Ferrat's February–June 1934 visit to Algeria, Europe's political terrain had shifted. The Comintern had its eyes increasingly on Europe, where fascism and Nazism were spreading. The PCF already feared French fascism and German aggression.

Communists in Blida continued to work with poor peasants and began organising agricultural workers, as did nearby nationalists, such as the brothers Mustapha Sahraoui and Larbi Sahraoui of Larbaâ. When Ferrat arrived he promoted the younger Mahmoudi over Ali Mira. However, Blida's communists were unable to get external support from Algiers. Ferrat's thinking had shifted back to towns. Rural activity needed to be preceded by solid work amongst the urban Algerian working class, whose political consciousness, defined in class terms, was far more advanced than that of the peasantry, he claimed. Because those urban workers were newly arrived from the countryside, they were well placed to offer revolutionary leadership to the peasants.[93] The overwhelmingly European communists, predisposed to prioritise urban workers and with little desire to traverse the rough roads and mountainous terrain by bus or donkey, refocused on the towns. Nonetheless, the political triangle of city – countryside – mountain was in place.

Notes

1 RGASPI 517.1.1525.
2 « petit parti bônois, oranais et petit parti algérois », RGASPI 517.1.1144, Report on Algeria, 23 October 1931, p. 1.
3 On illegality see RGASPI 517.1.1506; RGASPI 495.4.128, RGASI 517.1.1320, 'To our comrades, the comrades of Algeria', 17 August 1932; *Lutte sociale* (February 1931).
4 Launay, *Paysans*, is one of the few books to focus on rural life.
5 Alexandre Juving, *Le Socialisme en Algérie* (Alger: Jules Carbonel, 1924), p. 271, argued that rural Algerians would not understand communism and that rural Europeans and urban Algerians acquainted with rural life should undertake communist propaganda in rural areas.
6 Hopkins, 'French Communism', pp. 117–18; Ruedy, *Modern Algeria*, p. 138; Stora, *Histoire de l'Algérie*, p. 77; Thomas-Adrian Schweitzer, 'Le Parti communiste français, le Comintern et l'Algérie dans les années 1930s', *Mouvement Social*, 78 (January–March 1972), 115–36, pp. 118–21; Sivan, *Communisme*, pp. 72–3.
7 Boukort, *Souffle*, pp. 39–46; Schweitzer, 'Parti communiste', p. 121; ANOM ALG

Alger F407, *Surveillance spéciale: Boukort Benali, Note*, n.d.; Maitron (ed.), *Dictionnaire biographique*, vol. 27, pp. 324–9; Gallissot (ed.), *Algérie*, pp. 159–61, 289–91; Stora, *Dictionnaire*, pp. 340–1.
8 Interview, A. Bakelli, Ghardaïa, September 2011. The *twiza* addresses the free-rider problem.
9 Interview, Mohamed Boudjenah with Slimane Tounsi, Ghardaïa, 3 September 2011; Mohammed ben Saleh Naceur, questions posed to Sliman Boudjenah by the intermediary of Ahmed Fersouce, Ghardaïa, 24 September 1973. My thanks to Slimane Tounsi for translations from Arabic and for insightful discussions.
10 RGASPI 517.1.1320, 'Avant la conférence', 24 October 1932; 'En marge de la conférence du Parti – Que signifie: Arabisation du Parti?', *Lutte sociale* (October, December 1932); Boukort, *Souffle*, p. 46; Schweitzer, 'Parti communiste', pp. 118–19; Sivan, *Communisme*, pp. 70, 74–6.
11 RGASPI 517.1.1506, Durand to Labosse and Radi, 9 January 1933; Sivan, *Communisme*, pp. 74–5.
12 Sivan, *Communisme*, pp. 74–6, is the only scholarly discussion of this episode I have found, but he underestimates the extent and success of Radiquet's work in Blida. B. Marie Perinbam, 'Fanon and the Revolutionary Peasantry – the Algerian Case', *Journal of Modern African Studies*, 11:3 (1973), 427–45, p. 431; Gallissot (ed.), *Algérie*, pp. 516–17.
13 Ruedy, *Modern Algeria*, p. 123.
14 Carlier, *Nation*, p. 121; Launay, *Paysans*, p. 56.
15 John Ruedy, *Land Policy in Colonial Algeria: The Origins of the Rural Public Domain* (Berkeley and Los Angeles, CA: University of California, 1967), pp. 6, 57–8, 67, 88.
16 David Macey, *Frantz Fanon: A Life* (London: Granta, 2000), pp. 212–13.
17 Gouvernement général de l'Algérie, Direction générale des finances, Service de statistique générale, *Annuaire statistique de l'Algérie*, new series, vol. 1, 1939–49 (Algiers), p. 22.
18 Ruedy, *Modern Algeria*, p. 73; Wolf, *Peasant Wars*, p. 216.
19 RGASPI 517.1.1332, Fayet, 'Rapport sur ma délégation en Algérie', December 1932, p. 11; RGASPI 517.1.1506, *Situation du mouvement communiste en Algérie*, April 1933, p. 1; Mohamed Rebah, *Des chemins et des hommes* (Algiers: Mille-Feuilles, 2010), p. 170.
20 McDougall, *History*, pp. 71, 74; Ruedy, *Modern Algeria*, pp. 134–5.
21 « type nouveau de jeune paysan », Launay, *Paysans*, pp. 144, 148.
22 « La prédication égalitaire des Ouléma ... reflétait l'idéal du petit fellah, et ... correspond à la première phase, indifférenciée, de la révolution nationale », Launay, *Paysans*, p. 371; Perinbam, 'Fanon', p. 431; Stora, *Histoire de l'Algérie*, p. 75.
23 McDougall, *History*, pp. 12–13; Alleg, 'Torrent', p. 183; L'Association des Oulémas d'Algérie, in Claude Collot and Jean-Robert Henry (eds), *Le Mouvement national Algérien: Textes, 1912–1954* (Paris: L'Harmattan), pp. 44–7.
24 « aider l'action civilisatrice de la France ». RGASPI 517.1.1320, Statuts de l'Association musulmane blidéenne, El Hidaia, stamped 4 July 1932. Some documents say *Idaia*. PCF documents mistranslated this as *L'Accord*.
25 RGASPI 517.1.1373, Report of Dupont, 2 April 1932; RGASPI 517.1.1332, *Rapport de l'instructeur de la section coloniale centrale en Algérie*, June 1932, p. 15; Alleg, 'Torrent', p. 188.
26 Juving, *Socialisme*, pp. 263–4; Alleg, 'Torrent', p. 200.
27 'Extrait du récit de M. Akli Banoun', in Mahmoud Bouayed, *Histoire par la bande* (Algiers: SNED, 1974), pp. 52–3; Stora, *Dictionnaire*, p. 50; Gallissot (ed.), *Algérie*, p. 484.
28 RGASPI 517.1.1373, Report of Dupont, 2 April 1932; RGASPI 517.1.697, *Rapport sur l'Algérie fait par le camarade Celor*, 11 July 1928; Gallissot (ed.), *Algérie*, p. 440.
29 Report of Dupont, 2 April 1932.
30 *Rapport de l'instructeur*, p. 15; McDougall, *History*, pp. 57–8.
31 RGASPI 517.1.1320, 'A la fraction communiste du MOPR', 13 September 1932, p. 5; RGASPI 517.1.1320, 517.1.1526, Letter to [Radiquet ?], 23 November 1932; RGASPI 517.1.1320, Secrétariat pour la région aux camarades, 12 December 1932.

32 RGASPI 517.1.1506, *Rapport sur la situation en Algérie*, n.d. [date stamped 23 June 1933], p. 3; RGASPI 517.1.1526, Boualem to PCF colonial section, 22 June 1933; Gallissot (ed.), *Algérie*, pp. 95, 105; Sivan, *Communisme*, p. 58; Carlier, *Nation*, p. 60.
33 Letter to [Radiquet?], p. 1; Secrétariat pour la région aux camarades, 12 December 1932; *Situation du mouvement communiste*, pp. 3–6. *L'Humanité* (28 December 1932), p. 3, reported that 800 peasants were threatened with expropriation; other communist accounts state 600. Gallissot (ed.), *Algérie*, pp. 516–17, does not mention Radiquet's Blida activities.
34 Letter to [Radiquet?].
35 Fanon, *Wretched*, p. 112; Perinbam, 'Fanon', p. 427; letter to [Radiquet?].
36 « Pendant plusieurs jours, nous sommes allés voir les paysans des différents *deschras* pour leur expliquer ce que nous voulions faire … ce n'est qu'après de multiples démarches que nous sommes arrivés à leur faire comprendre … nous avons continué le travail de propagande à travers les douars pour la préparation d'une réunion des *deschras* de Sidi-El-Kébir », Secrétariat pour la région.
37 [Radiquet?], letter to comrade, 23 November 1932, pp. 1–2.
38 Secrétariat pour la région.
39 RGASPI 517.1.1320, Au secrétariat de la région algérienne, 16 December 1932, pp. 1, 7–8.
40 Letter to [Radiquet?]; Paul Radiquet, 'Paysans', p. 581; *L'Humanité* (28 December 1932), p. 3, claims that people expropriated in 1912 received only seven *sous* in compensation.
41 « Leur méfiance est grande envers nous, par suite des duperies dont ils furent plusieurs fois victimes, soit par les avocats, ou autres agents de l'impérialisme », Secrétariat pour la région, pp. 2–3.
42 *L'Humanité* (11 December 1932); RGASPI 517.1.1331, *Aux ouvriers et paysans arabes, à la population laborieuse de Blida*, poster; *Situation du mouvement communiste*, p. 3; Sivan, *Communisme*, p. 76.
43 « Monjauvis Député de Paris est arrêté à Blida », *L'Humanité* (22, 23 December 1932); Carlier, *Nation*, p. 121, dates Monjauvis' visit as 1933, but presumably refers to his December 1932 trip.
44 « tirerait les ficelles de tout le mouvement révolutionnaire, quelquefois sans y participer effectivement, et ainsi le parti "fera tout marcher" », RGASPI 517.1.1506, *Rapport sur la situation*, p. 3.
45 *Situation du mouvement communiste*, pp. 1, 3; *Rapport sur la situation*, pp. 6–7.
46 *L'Humanité* (17 April 1933), pp. 1–2.
47 Letter from R[adiquet?], 13 January 1933, RGASPI 517.1.1526; [Radiquet?], *Situation du mouvement communiste*, p. 3.
48 « Résultats intéressants … Blida n'est pas isolé », RGASPI 517.1.1506, Letter from R[adiquet?], 4 February 1933.
49 Radiquet, 'Paysans', p. 578.
50 *Situation du mouvement communiste*, p. 3; Lazreg, *Eloquence*, p. 28.
51 « Les paysans sont tellement enthousiastes qu'ils nous abordent dans les rues des villes, nous suivent et nous gênent pour la tenue de réunions de délégués. Hier, au lieu de cette réunion devant comprendre une dizaine de délégués, les paysans qui nous avaient aperçus sont venus autour de nous à près de 80 », RGASPI 517.1.1506, R[adiquet] to central colonial section, [c. February 1933].
52 « Ils avaient attendu, contrairement à leurs habitudes, jusqu'à 5 heures du soir alors qu'ils doivent remonter en montagne, pour me serrer la main et prendre rendez-vous », R[adiquet] to central colonial section, p. 2.
53 R[adiquet] to central colonial section; Radiquet, 'Paysans', p. 579.
54 « Il faut s'être sur place pour comprendre la colère de ces pauvres gens », Gaston Donnat, *Afin que nul n'oublie: L'Itinéraire d'un anti-colonialiste, Algérie-Cameroun–Afrique* (Paris: Harmattan, n.d.), p. 33; Gallissot (ed.), *Algérie*, pp. 251–5.
55 « si on remonte jusqu'aux temps des Turcs on peut savoir qu'il n'y a jamais eu de crues ou d'éboulements », R[adiquet] to central colonial section, p. 2.
56 Wolf, *Peasant Wars*, p. 217; Launay, *Paysans*, p. 425.
57 « Le mouvement paysan existait l'état latent », *Situation du mouvement commu-*

niste, p. 5; Rapport sur la situation, p. 8.
58 « se contenta de poursuivre le travail sous forme de petites conversations avec les paysans qui venaient à Alger et d'une réunion de quelques délégués, baptisée conférence », Situation du mouvement communiste, p. 6; L'Humanité (14 March 1933), p. 2.
59 « le clergé musulman, création de l'impérialisme français, la grande bourgeoisie, les oulémas, tous ceux qui sont à la tête des organisations nationales réformistes », Alleg, 'Torrent', pp. 193, 191.
60 « l'expression de sa souffrance, le cri de ralliement d'un exploité à tous ses frères de misère, ses coreligionnaires ». Alleg, 'Torrent', p. 191.
61 « prenait les revendications religieuses comme des revendications communistes », Rapport sur la situation, pp. 4–5, 7.
62 RGASPI 517.1.1526, Information pour le comité régional de la Région algérienne du Bureau politique et de la section coloniale centrale sur la situation en Algérie, 4 May 1933, pp. 2–4; Alleg, 'Torrent', p. 193.
63 The Islamic reformist or salifiyya movement was sometimes characterised as wahabite. TNA: PRO FO 371/17294, no 5391, Préfecture d'Alger, Affaires indigènes et Police générale, 16 February 1933, pp. 191–2; Alleg, 'Torrent', p. 190; Julien, L'Afrique du Nord, pp. 104–5.
64 TNA: PRO FO 371/17294, G. P. Churchill, British Consul-General, Algiers Quarterly Report, 31 March 1933, 175–86, p. 183; ANOM Alg: Alger, Sûreté départementale d'Alger, Rapport: Association des 'Ulemas Essouna', 14 March 1933.
65 Situation du mouvement communiste, pp. 6–8; Rapport sur la situation, p. 3.
66 Churchill, Algiers Quarterly Report, 31 March 1933, p. 183; RGASPI 517.1.1525, Région algérienne du Parti communiste, one-page French/Arabic flyer.
67 RGASPI 517.1.1506, 'Aux membres du Bureau politique: Notes sur la situation en Algérie' [September 1933?], p. 2.
68 L'Humanité (25 March 1933), p. 3; TNA: PRO FO 371/17294, no 5391, G. P. Churchill to Lord Tyrrell of Avon, 9 May 1933, pp. 189–90; Jean-Louis Planche, 'Antifascisme et anticolonialisme à Alger à l'époque du Front populaire et Congrès musulman, 1935–1939' (3rd cycle thesis, Université de Paris VII, 1979), p. 49.
69 Joly, French Communist, p. 34; Durand, Mystérieuse, pp. 117–18; McDermott and Agnew, Comintern, pp. 123–4; RGASPI 517.1.1525, Pour la création d'un véritable P.C. en Algérie clarifions la ligne politique du parti vis-à-vis du mouvement national-révolutionnaire.
70 « politique indigène ... une orientation indigène », « la prochaine étape de la révolution en Algérie est la révolution anti-impérialiste et agraire », Information pour le comité régional de la Région Algérienne, 4 May 1933, pp. 2–4; RGASPI 517.1.1526, Projet de résolution du Bureau politique sur les tâches immédiates de la région algérienne; Alleg, 'Torrent', p. 193.
71 ANOM ALG GGA 3CAB/24, Communisme: Thorez; RGASPI 517.1.1525, Bulletin régional édité par la région algérienne du Parti communiste, nouvelle série 1, May 1933; L'Humanité (16 May 1933), p. 2; Donnat, Afin que, pp. 33–4; Durand, Mystérieuse, pp. 116–7; Kaddache, Vie politique, pp. 211–12.
72 Planche, 'Alger', p. 5; Planche, 'Lieux', p. 187; Gallissot (ed.), Algérie, pp. 480–1; Stora, Messali, pp. 80–3; RGASPI 517.1.1506, Parti nationaliste révolutionnaire, Statuts, pp. 142–44; Carlier, Nation, pp. 60–1, 196, 199.
73 'Slimane Boudjenah libéré grâce à notre action', Lutte sociale (March 1933), p. 3; RGASPI 517.1.1526, B.R. d'Alger au B.P. du P.C.F., 27 September 1933, pp. 6–7; Sivan, Communisme, pp. 42, 66–7.
74 RGASPI 517.1.1525, Pour la création d'un véritable P.C.
75 « rentrez dans vos gourbis, dans vos terres, travaillez-les et défendez-les », ANOM Alg: Alger, Sûreté départementale d'Alger, Rapport: Réunion à L'Arba par le Député Communiste Thorez, 23 May 1933; RGASPI 517.1.1506, Le Mouvement paysan, [c. August 1933]; Durand, Mystérieuse, pp. 116–17.
76 « apparaissait comme le seul défenseur des intérêts des fellahs, plus, il dirigeait leurs luttes par les délégués de douar, les manifestations, les conférences, savait donner au mouvement les formes de lutte qui ont fait reculer le gouvernement », RGASPI

517.1.1526, *Algérie*, [c. September 1933?] p. 5.
77 *L'Humanité* (11 July 1933), p. 2. The PCF and Red Aid assisted them, but Naceur's file suggested that he had offered his services as a police spy, and the party later expelled him. See RGASPI 517.1.1525, *Rapport sur le cas Naceur*, 12 September 1933; RGASPI 517.1.1526, letter to Semard, 27 November 1933, p. 3; RGASPI 517.1.1506, S.C.C. to camarades, 29 December 1933.
78 *B.R. d'Alger au B.P.*, p. 8; interview with Sadek Hadjerès, Paris, 24 March 2011.
79 RGASPI 517.1.1506, *Rapport sur le parti national révolutionnaire*, 14 Septembre 1933.
80 *B.R. d'Alger au B.P.*, p. 7. Bachir, a medical doctor and politician, was a charismatic figure in Blida. Touami Hadj M'Hamed was a Boufarik proprietor or landowner. Bentami was possibly the politically moderate assimilationist Dr Ould Hamida Benthami, a French-educated professor of ophthalmology, naturalised French citizen, leading Young Algerian and head of the FEI until 1930.
81 *B.R. d'Alger au B.P.*, pp. 2–4.
82 « la montagne "marchait communiste" », *B.R. d'Alger au B.P.*, p. 8.
83 *B.R. d'Alger au B.P.*, p. 8.
84 *B.R. d'Alger au B.P.*, p. 8, annex; Pierrel to secrétariat, 18 August 1933, RGASPI 517.1.1506. The PCF's electoral results varied slightly; the first reported round was adapted from *Le Tell*, 10 August [sic] and the second from *L'Indépendant*, 20 August 1933.
85 *Le Tell* (19, 20, 23 August 1933).
86 'A bas le code de l'indigénat: Libérez Sliman Boudjnah', *Lutte sociale* (October 1933), p. 1; 'Indigénat toujours en action', *Alger socialiste*, 15 December 1933, p. 2; *Journal officiel de la République française, Débats parlementaires, Chambre de Députés: Réponses des ministres aux questions écrites*, 9 May 1934, pp. 1099–1100; Naceur, questions posed to Sliman Boudjenah.
87 Naceur, questions posed to Sliman Boudjenah; interview, Boudjenah with Tounsi.
88 *B.R. d'Alger au B.P.*, pp. 6–7; Sivan, *Communisme*, pp. 42, 66–7.
89 Fanon, *Wretched*, p. 61; « résistance restreinte et sourde », Sivan, *Communisme*, p. 75; Carlier, *Nation*, p. 107.
90 Prochaska, 'Fire', pp. 249–50; Robert Kuhlken, 'Settin' the Woods on Fire: Rural Incendiarism as Protest', *Geographical Review*, 89 (July 1999), 343–63, p. 349.
91 Ruedy, *Modern Algeria*, p. 120.
92 Planche, 'Lieux', p. 189.
93 Durand, *Mystérieuse*, p. 73; Gallissot (ed.), *Algérie*, p. 440; Sivan, *Communisme*, p. 77; Benjamin Stora, 'Faiblesse paysanne du mouvement nationaliste algérien avant 1954', *Vingtième Siècle: Revue d'histoire*, 12 (October–December 1986), 59–72, p. 68; Stora, *Dictionnaire*, p. 220.

CHAPTER FOUR

'This land is not for sale': communists, nationalists and the popular front

In the 1930s impoverished rural Algerians swarmed into already densely populated urban areas. The traditional medina became both ruralised and Europeanised. The new urbanites maintained tight networks with their rural relatives, linking town and countryside ever more closely. However, urban youth spent more time in the streets by comparison with their parents, congregating at cafés, barbers' shops, shoemakers' stalls, cinemas and meeting halls. While rural women became farm workers, their urban counterparts left their homes for factory and domestic work. Urban public space expanded, noisy with voices speaking in Arabic, Berber, French and sometimes Spanish. In the concentrated medinas, First World War veterans obtained licences to open *cafés maures,* in which an urban plebeian culture developed. *Nawadi* (intellectual circles) offered space for political and cultural debates where both the formally educated and autodidacts mingled. All of this fed into the *Nahda,* the Muslim cultural and political renaissance that was already well underway in Tunisia and further east, and which in Algiers was represented by the Circle of Progress and the Islamic reformist religious schools.

French education promoted the idea of the nation-state and the values of rationality and progress. Trade unions and political organisations convened meetings in large halls, aggregating larger numbers of people and providing space for secular orators alongside religious ones. Trade unions, in particular, were arenas allowing some interaction between Europeans and Algerians. All these conditions facilitated the imagining of a new urban community, yet one tightly tied to rural areas.[1]

But this Algerian renaissance was accompanied by mounting state repression of the Muslim religion and Arabic-language press and by Muslim protests against this. So acute was the repression that it became known as a 'war of religion'. Reformist *'ulama* were forbidden to preach in mosques; Koranic schools were closed; the Arabic language press banned. The Islamic reformist leader Ben Badis led rallies against these attacks on religious freedom. Dr Bendjelloul, leader of the Constantine FEI, whose assimilationist views were outlined in *La Voix indigène*, led protests against the banning of the Arabic press. The period saw various types of political activity: electoral activity, demonstrations, strikes, boycotts and violence.[2]

Such conditions might have provided fertile ground for communists. However, despite its aim of Arabisation, until mid-1934 the PCF's Algerian region continued its class-against-class policy, labelling Muslim nationalist groups as 'national-reformists'.[3] With a few significant exceptions, such as its Mitidja activity, the PCF functioned in a desultory manner. Its tiny numbers meant that it was perpetually short-staffed and ill-equipped to promote any policy, although Paris headquarters sent several emissaries to rectify this. Radiquet returned in 1934, and Ferrat, by then involved in a clandestine Communist opposition group, visited Algeria between February and June. Ferrat firmly supported anti-colonial politics, and the trip allowed him to implement his ideas.[4] *Lutte sociale* had not appeared for about six months. Ferrat re-established publication on a bi-monthly basis, writing under the pseudonym 'Mourad'. He trained Algerian cadre, chief amongst them, Ben Ali Boukort, Amar Ouzegane, and Larbi Bouhali, and organised the PCF's April 1934 regional conference.

Boukort had studied at the KUTV after the 1932 conference, but was called back to Algeria before completing his course. He assumed responsibility for Algiers and for *Lutte sociale*, using the editorial experience gained while working on *El Amel* in Paris. Ouzegane, born 1910 in Algiers, came from a family of Kabyle notables. At fourteen he began working as a telegraph operator, then joined the trade union movement and the JC. Larbi Bouhali, born 1912 at El Kantara in Constantinois was the orphaned son of poor peasants. He attended Koranic and French schools, but he had to interrupt his studies and begin work as an accounts clerk. Attracted to radical ideas – including atheism – he joined the PCF. In June Ferrat sent Bouhali to Paris, where he worked with the Party's colonial section for a month before travelling to Moscow via Brussels to attend the KUTV. His time in Moscow was not easy; he and two other Algerians were isolated under tight security, but were eventually joined by four other Algerians.[5]

Taking its lead from French developments, on 26 June the regional PCF called for a united front with socialists and nationalists. Hoping to engage with Algerian movements activated by the war of religion, the communists proposed a joint campaign. With the notable exception of Messali Hadj, most Algerian leaders were not demanding independence. In France, Messali's ENA was gaining influence amongst Algerian émigrés, despite its repression by French authorities, and by 1934 its newspaper *El Ouma* had a circulation of 43,500.[6] But in Algeria the FEI aspired to closer assimilation with France on the basis of equal rights. Although the PCF had been calling for independence since the 1920s, it began emphasising a minimum programme of democratic rights rather than independence *per se*. Ironically, just as Messali's ENA broached independence, the PCF began to avoid it. Nonetheless, the party's overtures were rejected by both groupings. Most 'national-reformists' were fearful of being labelled anti-French by association with the communists; the ENA categorically rejected the communist label.[7]

Constantine's war of religion

The war of religion reached its apex on 3–5 August 1934 in the traditional city of Constantine, the regional capital. Highly cultured, with a long literary tradition, Constantine had some 101,000 inhabitants in 1931. Muslims constituted 51 per cent of the population, Jews, about 12 per cent, and Europeans, the remaining 36 per cent. Muslims and Jews had coexisted peacefully for centuries; however, as in other Algerian cities, they lived in 'communautés juxtaposées, non mêlées' – juxtaposed, not mixed communities. European culture was steeped in anti-Semitism, stoked by the right-wing anti-Semitic *Croix de feu* (Cross of Fire), and the past few years had seen a rise in Muslim anti-Semitism. Mayor Emile Morinaud had been in office since 1898, oscillating between anti-Semitic policies and pragmatic alliances with Jewish office-holders.[8]

Jews formed an intermediate stratum between Muslims and Christians. Most of Constantine's Jews were poor, but they were often artisans or shopkeepers rather than factory workers, and their income was virtually always higher than their Muslim counterparts. Similarly, there were proportionately more Jewish than Muslim professionals. By contrast, Constantine had a growing floating Arab population of unemployed and homeless people as indebted and expropriated peasants lost their land and moved to the city and into gruelling poverty. An outbreak of typhoid accentuated the misery but could not stamp out the idea of a Muslim renaissance. The year 1934 saw numerous mass demonstrations against poverty and political repression: on 12 February, 1 May and 18 May – the last jointly organised by the FEI and the *'ulama* – and on 31 July, an anti-war demonstration organised by communists and anti-fascists, in which the communist brothers Lucien and Bernard Sportisse, indigenous Arabophone Jews, participated.[9]

The tension exploded on 3 August, after a Jewish soldier urinated on a mosque. Hearing of this, close to 2,000 Muslims invaded one of Constantine's Jewish quarters, attacking shops and cars, before moving to the city centre. Fifteen people were wounded, including three policemen; one Muslim died of his wounds. On 4 August the city authorities convened a meeting of Jewish and Muslim leaders, who counselled calm and tolerance. Despite their appeals, early the following day close to 1,000 Muslims gathered at Mansourah plateau. By 9 a.m. fights erupted in a Jewish-quarter market. In retaliation, Muslims were shot, and Arab shops looted. A rumour that Dr Bendjelloul had been killed precipitated more violence. Jews and Jewish shops were attacked. Crowds controlled the main streets the entire morning. Jews found in isolated spots were killed. At around 6 a.m. on 6 August some 600 to 800 demonstrators came into the city by road and train. By 10 a.m. police reinforcements had arrived to restore calm. The news spread to surrounding towns, where Jews and Jewish shops were attacked on the 5th and 6th. The official account reported 28 dead, including 25 Jews and 3 Muslims, and 81 wounded, comprising 38 Jews, 35 Muslims, 7 soldiers and one fire fighter. In all, 1,777 persons were reported as badly affected, either from physical violence or damage to property.[10]

Lucien Sportisse was a witness. Born in 1905 and raised in the Constantine neighbourhoods of St Jean and Camp des Oliviers, Sportisse joined the socialists in 1925 and the communists in 1927, becoming an energetic trade union organiser. Influenced by the communist teacher Paul Estorges, he was a keen learner, and in addition to Arabic and French, he studied Hebrew, Latin, German and Esperanto. But financially unable to continue to fund his studies at the University of Algiers, he became a teacher, seeing rural poverty at close hand. In 1934 he was teaching at the village of Akbou in Kabylia, but in August he was back in Constantine. The communists called a meeting on the 5th to discuss the situation. En route Sportisse was stopped by a crowd, who realised that he was Jewish, but speaking Arabic, he convinced them to release him. Later, his Muslim and European comrades accompanied him home. That evening the party's office at El Kanta was torched – by European fascists, local communists presumed.[11]

Local reports voiced a common refrain: the initial passivity of the troops who, instead of restraining the crowds, allowed Arabs and Europeans to loot Jewish shops. Indeed, some Arabs reportedly felt they had European approval. The reports also pointed to a common class base: most rioters were young and very poor men, uprooted from their rural communities, often homeless and working as shoeshine boys. Trying to dispel the idea that the events were the inevitable product of religious hate, Ben Badis argued that they were not 'a Muslim uprising but a riot of Muslims'. Most Muslims in Constantine, he maintained, were as sickened by the atrocities as Europeans – perhaps more so. Yet even as Muslim and Jewish leaders stressed brotherhood and tolerance in the riot's aftermath, cynical Europeans stoked up anti-Semitism. Ben Badis countered that there was 'only one race – the human race'.[12]

French communists such as Ferrat and Monjauvis saw the events through orthodox ideological lenses, stressing Constantine's extraordinary economic misery and arguing that the events should be seen as a peasant-based anti-imperialist uprising sidetracked by French imperialist agents. A demonstration of 15,000 Algerian agricultural workers in late May – just days after a demonstration of 10,000 urban Algerian workers – indicated rural class consciousness, argued Ferrat. Muslims constituted the rural poor, and while Jews were part of the urban poor, Constantine also had its share of successful Jewish businessmen, commercial entrepreneurs and intellectuals. These constituted a Jewish comprador bourgeoisie, Ferrat contended. Most of the anti-Semitic attacks took place in well-to-do Jewish areas; anti-Semitic attitudes were thus masking class interests, he concluded.[13]

Constantine communists saw the events as the outcome of colonial divide and rule of the working class. The large colons, fearing a Muslim revolt, had diverted class consciousness by fomenting animosity between Jews and Muslims, local communists argued. Certain bourgeois Jewish leaders, such as the departmental councillor Henri Lellouche, were themselves anti-Muslim. When Dr Bendjelloul presented a motion for Muslim equality, Jewish leaders refused to support it, playing into the divide and rule through their own prejudice. Lucien Sportisse met with PCF's colonial section in Paris on 17 August, presenting the riots as an anti-Semitic pogrom inspired not by Muslims but by imperialist divide and rule. The French communists countered that the anti-Semitism was secondary to the riot's anti-imperialist aspect – but Sportisse felt a certain anti-Semitism within the PCF. The PCF printed about 15,000 flyers entitled *Fellahs, khemmas, ouvriers agricoles!*, hoping to channel the anger evident in the Constantine events towards communism – with no evident result.[14]

By late 1934 the PCF's Algerian region was even tinier and more isolated from Algerian organisations than earlier in the year. It faced severe repression: of perhaps two hundred members, some forty were in prison. But its problems reflected not only the heavy repression but also the confusion and demoralisation following the Constantine riots. Boukort, its leading activist, was imprisoned at Serkadji around September–October 1934, while Boualem resigned as regional secretary shortly after the Constantine events, citing leadership battles. His resignation caused much bitterness, and on 30 December the Algerian region's enlarged central committee met and resolved that he be expelled. Morale plummeted further in February 1935 when Boukort was deported to Beni Abbès and kept under surveillance.[15]

Fascism and the popular front

Ben Badis' belief in one human race went directly against the fascist beliefs gaining ground in Europe. Hitler's accession to the German chancellorship in January 1933 and the repression of German labour signalled the failure of the Comintern's isolationist class-against-class policy to stop fascism's march across Europe. By late 1933 most of the Comintern's national sections in Europe were either banned or underground. The Comintern's popular-front strategy, which evolved to fight fascism as the threat of war in Europe loomed, has often been seen as a positive step away from class against class. It offered new prospects for engaging constructively in public arenas with other social and political organisations, and many communists in Algeria saw the new strategy in this light. Far from being Moscow-driven, the catalyst for the new approach began with the joint anti-fascist activity of socialist and communist workers in France in February 1934 – culminating in a general strike on 12 February, parallelled the same day in Algiers with a demonstration of 10,000, close to half of whom were Algerians. Perhaps foreseeing the need for broader alliances, in June Moscow advised the PCF Politburo to soften its stance towards social-democrats. In neighbouring Spain, the smashing of the Asturian miners' strike in October 1934 led to a fragile anti-fascist coalition. Thorez elaborated the popular-front concept in that same month, and the Comintern's political secretariat ratified it in January 1935.[16]

The year 1935 saw further attacks on Algerian rights. Most notorious was the Régnier Decree of 30 March 1935, which extended the *indigénat*, stipulating prison sentences of up to two years and fines of up to 5,000 French francs for demonstrating against French rule and inciting to civil disorder. Together with the 1933 Michels circular, the Régnier Decree became the focal point of Algerian protest.[17] Algerians were politically divided between the assimilationist FEI, the Islamic reformists' religious nationalism and the secular nationalism of the ENA, which was in the process of launching itself inside the country through the dissemination of its organ, *El Ouma*. The idea of forging a broad Muslim opposition movement had been around since Emir Khaled's proposal. In 1934 discussions amongst Algerian leaders stepped up, and *La Voix des humbles* (*Voice of the Humble*) and *La Défense* began promoting the idea. The Régnier Decree accelerated this movement.[18]

The PCF's Algerian region still had more success amongst Europeans than Algerians. Its candidates ran on a Popular Front ticket during the May 1935 municipal elections, but these electoral coalitions were shaky affairs. In Bône, Philippeville, Sidi bel Abbès, Oran and Algiers, the PCF ran its own candidates. Although many of the local campaigns were hastily and inadequately organised and lacked materials or guidance from the regional headquarters, generally, the party reported, its candidates did better than the previous year. In July 1935 alone the number of its European members rose from 150 to 600. Sales of *Lutte sociale*, about 3,000 in August, rapidly increased over the next months.

The period was one in which communists used cultural media to promote their ideas – the didactic use of culture in this period characterised the left in many countries. Albert Camus paved the way in these cultural endeavours; young and idealistic, he believed ardently in the persuasive possibilities of literature and theatre. Camus was one of the few Europeans to engage with Algerian intellectuals – perhaps reflecting his childhood experience – although his writing and cultural work was based within a European cultural tradition. Born in 1913, Camus grew up in Belcourt, a working-class quarter of Algiers bordering an Algerian neighbourhood. His father had died at the Battle of the Marne, and he and his brother lived with their mother – timid, deaf, illiterate – their uncle and their domineering grandmother. Home was a three-room flat without running water and electricity, 'where there were only objects of immediate utility'. A student at the less prestigious of Algiers' two high schools – nicknamed the 'lycée "juif"' – Camus was acutely conscious of the poverty – 'a fortress without drawbridges' – that isolated him from even working-class boys in his area. Yet he also observed that 'the boundaries between classes were less clear-cut than between races'. As a child he had befriended a local Arab boy, and he had Algerian classmates at school, although 'there were few in the *lycée*, and they were always sons of wealthy notables'.[19]

The young Camus was well aware of the difference between France and Algeria. Taught at school that he was French, he became friends with a boy from France who made it clear that Camus was not really French. Thus, for Camus France remained 'an abstraction that people called upon and that sometimes laid claim to you'.[20] Nonetheless, believing in the French republican notion of equality for all, as a young man Camus joined the student journal *Ikdam*, which appealed to France to live up to its republican ideals and extend full citizenship rights to Arabs and Berbers.[21] His close friend Claude de la Poix de Fréminville had already joined the PCF in Paris; another friend, Robert Namia, who came from a Jewish settler family near Blida, was in the party's Bab el Oued cell – the intellectual cell. After travelling in

Europe, where he saw Italian fascism, Camus joined the PCF in August 1935. 'It's necessary to live communism's difficulties and victories ... I am at an important turning point,' he confided to de Fréminville. He would work loyally to help the party's cultural endeavours. Indeed, his name became widely known, although his party membership was not.[22]

In July 1935, a mass anti-fascist demonstration in Paris laid the foundations for a left-wing electoral coalition; the CGT and CGTU pledged trade union unity. The new strategy was formally announced at the Seventh Congress of the Comintern in Moscow that July–August. The strategy was accompanied by a policy of decentralisation, the idea being that national sections would promote the popular front with tactics appropriate to their own national conditions – a tacit recognition that diverse conditions demanded diverse responses. The practice of sending Comintern representatives to intervene in the work of national sections declined, with notable exceptions, including Belgium, France, South Africa and Spain.[23]

The PCF remained on the margins of Algerian politics. Without a functioning regional leadership, it was unable to hold meetings and communicate with its branches. It ran candidates on a clearly communist programme at Orléansville and Tlemcen, but in other areas it could not even offer a distinct position *vis-à-vis* ENA candidates. Hoping to rectify this and capture the movement for Muslim unity, in early August the party called for an expansion of the popular front to include an anti-imperialist bloc to which all Muslim groups should be invited to join.[24]

The PCF also began discussing the establishment of an autonomous Algerian Communist Party. During the 1920s indigenisation had been seen as a precondition for an autonomous party. But activists now argued that an autonomous Algerian party would facilitate indigenisation in this period of intense political ferment. Ferrat supported the idea, as did the Algerian communists. At the conference of the Algiers *rayon* on 5 January 1935, Ouzegane – who had taken over some of Boukort's responsibilities – had argued that the party should present itself as a party of the Algerian people and as an Arab party which the most politically conscious Europeans could join rather than what it was then – a European party that accepted Arabs. After all, he explained, it would be absurd to think of the PCF as a party of immigrants that French workers could join. However, he sensed that some European communists were resistant to that idea.[25]

Ouzegane found Camus to be different, however. Camus was one of the few European leftists to take Algerian intellectuals seriously. Emile Padula, secretary of the communist group at Belcourt, had introduced

Camus to Algerians who sympathised with the reformist *'ulama*, and he hung out with some of them at the Circle of Progress. Camus was impressed by Ouzegane; the sentiment was evidently reciprocated. Unlike most European communists, Ouzegane found, Camus was not patronising towards Algerians. And whereas most European communists were hostile to religion, whether Catholicism or Islam, Ouzegane found Camus 'plus souple' – more flexible – able to bridge the cultural and political worlds.[26]

There was a growing agreement about the need for an autonomous party. Despite the weakness of Communist forces on the ground, it was hoped that political autonomy would allow the movement more latitude in relating to local conditions. The matter was discussed at the Comintern's Seventh Congress, at which Ouzegane and Mohamed Badsi were delegates. Born 1904 in Tlemcen, Mohamed Badsi completed his military service in France, remained in Paris, met Hadj Ali Abdelkader and in the mid-1920s joined the PCF. In 1926 he was sent to Moscow to study at the KUTV. He returned to Paris in 1928, and the following year went to Tunisia to rebuild its trade union movement. Back in Algeria in 1933, Badsi set up a PCF branch in Tlemcen, where Abderrahmane Bouchama, the communist architect from Blida, was also based. Multilingual – Badsi spoke Arabic, French, Turkish and Russian – he was certainly one of Tlemcen's leading communists. His brother Sid Ahmed Badsi was also a Communist; their other brother followed the *'ulama*. Mohamed Badsi and Ouzegane took different approaches towards the communist orthodoxy, and at the Seventh Congress of the Comintern Badsi stood out for his differences with the PCF delegation on the colonial question.[27] The congress discussed Algeria's communist movement, acknowledging that the decapitation of its Algerian leadership had left it disoriented. The region had 'vegetated', and its activities were mainly limited to urban work amongst Europeans. The congress proposed the formation of an Algerian Communist Party guided by the Comintern while maintaining fraternal relations with the PCF.[28] When the new PCF delegate Jean Chaintron arrived in Algeria, the idea of an autonomous party was already accepted.[29]

Anti-fascism and anti-colonialism

Using the pseudonym 'Jean Barthel', Chaintron spent over a year in Algeria from September 1935 to January 1937. Before leaving France, he had liaised with Ferrat who, increasingly critical of the Comintern, felt that the PCF was putting too much stress on anti-fascism to the neglect of the anti-colonial struggle. In Ferrat's view the popular front in Algeria should take anti-colonialism rather than anti-fascism as the point of departure and create a Muslim united front that parallelled the European popular front.[30]

Shortly after Barthel's arrival, a letter dated 17 September bearing his name and addressed to all cells and branches was intercepted by the police. It was passed on to *La Dépêche algérienne*, which published it on 16 October 1935 under the scaremongering headline 'A plot against state security in Algeria' and a subtitle highlighting the party's 'criminal activities' aimed at rousing the Algerian population against France. Known as the Barthel circular, its thesis – that the principal question for Algerians was not fascism or anti-fascism, but imperialism or anti-imperialism – bore Ferrat's influence. It contended that the main political task was the formation of an anti-imperialist front alongside the European popular front. This anti-imperialist front would include the communist party and national reformist and national revolutionary organisations. Significantly, it accepted that France and Algeria were two separate nations, describing France as 'the oppressor nation ... the nation of imperialism', a view that enraged Europeans.[31]

The circular made a profound impact amongst politicised Algerians, more of whom began joining the party. While communists were delighted with the wide dissemination of their views, the free publicity came with the costs, as Barthel warned, of further repression. Despite support from local socialists and lawyers from the Socialist and Radical Parties, Barthel was sentenced on 10 December under the Régnier decree to a year's imprisonment and 500 francs, although he was subsequently granted provisional freedom.[32] He worked closely with a small number of activists, emphasising the selection and training of Algerian cadres to penetrate Muslim communities, hardly noticing Camus.[33]

Boukort, still in Beni Abbès and in poor health, nonetheless kept himself intellectually stimulated, writing long letters discussing historical figures such as Galileo and Thomas Müntzer and asking comrades to send him copies of the satirical *Le Canard enchaîné*, as well as *Al Ahram*, so that he could practice his Arabic. Around November 1935 he published *Peuple d'Algérie, quels sont tes amis?* (*People of Algeria, who are your friends?*) under the pseudonym El Mounadi, with a preface by Barthel. A passionate attempt to argue Islam's compatibility with communism, it was widely distributed and caused quite a stir: 'If the prophet Mohammed lived today, in this period where Muslims are subjugated and chained in the majority of countries, he would call them to the liberation struggle.' Communists wanted to replace imperialist domination with a workers' and peasants' government that would confiscate the land of the feudal elites and settlers. The revolutionary struggle was the only means of saving Muslims from barbarism and ensuring bread, land, liberty and peace, argued Boukort.[34]

In key respects Barthel continued Ferrat's agenda, namely to indigenise the Party and build a popular front and an anti-imperialist front. Thus, he promoted a core of Algerians who had joined the PCF in the late 1920s and early 1930s – Belkhaim, Bouhali, Debabèche, Mahmoudi and Marouf – insisted on parity of European and Algerians at the leadership level and argued that an autonomous party would help indigenisation. Barthel was an effective orator and organiser: by January 1936 European membership had doubled, and Algerian membership had risen appreciably. Nonetheless, PCF headquarters pressured the Algerian region to tone down its anti-colonialism.[35]

The PCF's eighth congress took place on 22–25 January 1936 at Villeurbanne, near Lyon. Its programme for a *Rassemblement populaire* called for a popular front of communists, socialists, radicals and smaller leftist parties on the basis of a common electoral platform: 'for bread, peace and freedom'. Personnel changes signalled subtle shifts in policy emphasis. Ferrat was marginalised – to be expelled in July of that year. Henri Lozeray became head of the colonial section, assisted by Robert Deloche. Ouzegane spoke to repeated applause, noting that while the Algerian communist movement had in the past followed the French, it was now focusing on Algerian specificities: since European workers were anti-Muslim, they hoped to form Algerian trade unions. They also needed to build a united anti-imperialist front of reformist and revolutionary forces. The congress highlighted the union of exploited French workers and oppressed Algerians, and Abyssinia's resistance to Italy's October 1935 invasion was emphasised as an example of the convergence of the anti-fascist and anti-imperialist struggles. A resolution supporting the establishment of an autonomous Algerian party was adopted.[36] The PCF's Algerian region endorsed the shift. As *Lutte sociale* explained, 'We do not preach narrow nationalism, but the union of the colonial oppressed and the metropolitan exploited. We claim the right of people to self-determination and to their freely chosen union.'[37]

In January 1936 Camus and his friends launched the *Théâtre du travail* (Labour Theatre) in Bab el Oued. Along with his work at the adult education *Collège du travail* (Labour College), Camus saw this as an expression of political engagement. The French writers André Malraux and André Gide were the rage amongst left-wing European youth, and the theatre's repertoire included works by Malraux, Gorky, Machiavelli, Balzac and de Rojas. Its first play, a benefit for unemployed workers, was Camus's adaptation of Malraux's novella, *Le Temps du mépris* (*Days of Contempt*), the timely tale of a German communist who escaped from the Nazis thanks to a comrade who took over his identity. A dramatic success, the overwhelmingly European audiences were enthusiastic, and on one occasion Namia gave such an impassioned speech that the audience burst into 'The International'.[38]

In Europe the popular front agenda was on the upswing. In February, the Spanish Popular Front won a narrow electoral victory. In Algeria the political ferment provided propitious conditions for Barthel's work. Independence was not directly broached, but there was significant discussion of the national question. In the same month, Ferhat Abbas claimed that from a historical perspective there was no Algerian nation and thus that Algeria's future lay in assimilation with France – with the expectation that Algerians be treated equally. Two months later Ben Badis insisted that there was indeed an Algerian nation, which was 'not France, [could] not be France, and d[id] not wish to be France'. Across the country the explosion of circles, clubs and societies where politics was endlessly discussed opened political space and fuelled the development of national consciousness.[39] On 1 May 1936 the reunited CGT organised a mass meeting attended by some 11,000 workers, mostly Algerian, in the Algiers stadium, while 5,000 workers demonstrated in Oran. That year saw agricultural strikes at Soummam, Philippeville and the Mitidja, and strikes at the Bougie and Jilelli cork factories, Constantine quarries, Oran and Algiers building sites and the Timezrit mines.[40]

May 1936 saw the Popular Front's electoral victory in France, led by the socialist Léon Blum. The PCF vote rose from 8.4 per cent of the total in 1932 to 15.3 per cent in 1936, with a corresponding increase in parliamentary seats from 12 to 72. While sympathetic to the new government, the PCF followed the ECCI's advice and refused Blum's invitation to join the government, hoping instead to influence it from outside – a decision that angered many PCF leaders and members.[41]

Public political space expanded in France and Algeria. The appointment of the liberal Maurice Viollette as Minister of State was a positive signal for many Algerians: as governor-general in the mid-1920s, Viollette had tried, unsuccessfully, to push through reforms enabling Algerians to obtain French citizenship without renouncing their personal status. The Algerian masses were hopeful and relieved, commented *La Voix des humbles.* But large land holders made clear their concerns with Viollette's reformist agenda.[42]

Strike waves erupted in France and Algeria: on 12 June 1936 a general strike in Algiers led to the occupation of the Shell refinery and the port; on 14 June 20,000 demonstrated in Oran in support of the Popular Front. Muslim unity efforts leapt forward. Seeing the possibility of government reforms, Islamic reformists moved closer to the

FEI, proposing an Algerian Muslim Congress. To bring the federation on board, the presidency was offered to Dr Bendjelloul, who on 16 May had called for meetings across the country so that local groups could select delegates to attend the national congress.[43] In an auspicious sign, Boukort's exile down south ended. Boukort credited the Popular Front government with reducing his sentence. International Red Aid representatives visited him in April; on 20 May he was freed. He immediately resumed his political work, travelling to Tlemcen, where Mohamed Badsi introduced him to local Muslims and took him to meetings of the Friends of the Soviet Union.[44]

The Muslim unity movement took organisational form with the launch of the Algerian Muslim Congress in Algiers on 7 June 1936. The congress included 19 representatives from Oran, 10 from Constantine, 31 from Alger and six well-known personalities, including Boukort. Its unity was far from perfect. The PCF joined as part of the Popular Front. ENA members joined as individuals but were kept off the board of directors out of concern about their party's radical stance on independence. The president of the Oran FEI did not attend. Nonetheless, in July the Muslim Congress adopted a Charter of Demands of the Muslim Algerian People that included a broad range of democratic demands premised on assimilation with France. The charter was presented to the French government later that month; Dr Bendjelloul and his colleagues received an 'open-ended commitment' from Blum and Viollette to address their concerns.[45]

Boukort, widely admired as a victim of French imperialism, ran as a communist candidate in Algiers' second district departmental councillor elections on 5 July. It was a time of unprecedented social upheaval, with urban demonstrations and strikes of farm workers and sharecroppers in rural areas. The party went all out on propaganda, distributing 13,000 posters and 200,000 flyers; *Lutte sociale* sold out at 35,000 copies. Abbas, Sétif's departmental councillor, endorsed Boukort in *La Défense*. Boukort won 2,181 votes on the first round to the 2,162 votes of the moderate Mebarek Ben Allel. On the second round, Boukort won 4,050 to Mebarek's 2,739 votes. But the authorities deemed Boukort ineligible, and Mebarek was proclaimed the winner. Despite the assimilationist aspirations of most Algerian leaders, colonial authorities nonetheless believed that the nationalist movement was 'essentially anti-French' and dominated by communists, whose goal, they believed, was Algerian liberation.[46]

On 18 July 1936 General Francisco Franco attempted to seize power in Spain; civil war erupted, inspired by a popular revolt from below. The war in Spain produced a solidarity movement in Algeria, particularly in Oran. The city was home to many Spanish immigrants, some bringing socialist and anarchist ideas, and Spanish was widely spoken by Europeans and Algerians. It was Algeria's most working-class city, with a long socialist tradition. But it was also marked by a deep anti-Semitic tradition that had penetrated daily life and culture, and a growing fascist movement supported by the large landowners. Larbi Bouhali returned from Moscow that month. Unable to find work in Constantine, he was appointed to International Red Aid, and actively supported the Spanish republican movement.[47]

At that time the only left-wing newspapers were political party organs. The local press was overwhelmingly pro-colonial and European-centred. Not surprisingly, the first popular front newspaper was launched in Oran, supported by socialists and radical-socialists and funded by four or five thousand shareholders from diverse social backgrounds. Charles-André Julien proposed the Paris-based journalist and socialist Michel Rouzé as the first editor-in-chief, and *Oran républicain*'s first issue appeared on 21 February 1937, proclaiming that it would 'tell the truth each morning'. The Spanish Civil War featured prominently; the Algerian socialist Mohammed el Aziz Kessous wrote a column on Muslim political representation; and a 'Muslim page' featured news on Arab countries. It was envisioned as the first of three autonomous newspapers linked by the themes of republicanism and opposition to anti-Semitism and Muslim oppression. Planning began for *Alger républicain*, but its launch was delayed due to financial difficulties; *Constantine républicain* never appeared.[48]

Despite prioritising anti-fascism over anti-colonialism, the PCF was nonetheless increasingly attractive to radicalised Muslims. Algerian communists organised in rural areas around demands for bread, peace and freedom. As the prefect of Algiers explained to Governor-General Georges Le Beau, 'as soon as the first strikes broke out in France, propaganda agents, European and native, travelled across the Mitidja and the Sahel'.[49] The communist Mohammed Marouf was particularly effective in the Sahel, organising agricultural strikes which broke out on 10 June and developed 'a considerable force'.[50] In Mostaganem, communists organised vineyard workers. In September there were reports of violence during harvests at Aboukir, Mazagran, and Saint Lucien near Relizane.[51]

Granted amnesty by the Popular Front government, Messali returned from exile in Switzerland to Paris. On behalf of the ENA he presented a Plan of Immediate Demands to the government before journeying to Algeria. The Muslim Congress convened a rally at the Algiers stadium on 2 August to receive the report-back from their delegation to Paris. Messali arrived unexpectedly, carrying a green, white and red flag reportedly designed and sewn by his wife, Emilie Busquant. Stooping to pick up some soil, he declared: 'This land is not for sale'.⁵² Although agreeing with the Charter's immediate demands, he told his listeners, 'we say frankly and categorically that we disapprove the Charter of Demands on the question of the attachment of our country to France and of parliamentary representation.' The ENA 'will never accept our country's being attached to another against its will; we do not wish, under any pretext, to jeopardize ... the hope for national freedom of the Algerian people.' The crowd was electrified. People ran up to him, raised him on their shoulders and carried him across the stadium. From the stadium he led a procession to the Grande Poste.⁵³

Messali traversed the country organising ENA branches. On 10 August he went to his home town of Tlemcen, making a brief trip to Sidi bel Abbès, where he lectured to two audiences of about 200. He spent over a month in Tlemcen, returning to Algiers on 26 September. An ENA meeting on 29 September attracted about a thousand. While Messali's ideas resonated with many Algerians – he claimed to have set up 36 branches with some 11,000 members – many Algerian leaders, especially those of the FEI, remained as concerned about the call for independence as they had been when the PCF raised it.⁵⁴

Launching the Algerian Communist Party

In the Soviet Union, the Great Terror was unfolding. News of the Moscow trials of alleged traitors and the executions of 'counter-revolutionaries' reached Algeria. Disconcerted by the news, but familiar with bourgeois misrepresentations of the USSR, Barthel reassured himself that intellectuals such as Malraux and Romain Rolland were not questioning the events.⁵⁵ After all, he had reason to feel satisfied. The PCF's Algerian region was reaping the benefits of the politicised atmosphere. Its Algerian members had risen from 10 per cent of its total membership in 1935 to about 16 per cent in 1936. Although *Lutte sociale* claimed that Messali's demand for independence was too advanced, it ran more articles by Algerian writers and more pieces relevant to Algerian readers; its sales had leapt from 3,000 to 13,000 to 15,000 per issue. On 6 September 1936 the paper sponsored a daylong festival, borrowing the idea from *L'Humanité*'s Paris festival. Attended by several thousands, the day included music, sports, a picnic, a meeting and a dance. Barthel and Ouzegane, who was also secretary of the Algiers committee of the Muslim Congress, spoke about the benefits that the Popular Front government had brought to workers.⁵⁶

The JC was growing too, publishing the monthly *Jeunesse* and attracting audiences ranging from 70 to 300 to its events. In Algérois communists organised trade unions at Affreville, Cherchell and Blida.

In Oranie Mohamed and Sid Ahmed Badsi and one Klouche were active at Tlemcen, while communists organised at Relizane and worked with the *'ulama* at Mostaganem. There was less communist activity in Constantinois. But Barthel toured the country during that September, and in Bône, where relations between communists and socialists had cooled, he held a public meeting that attracted some 800 people including 250–300 Algerians. In Souk Ahras on the 29th, he addressed a crowd of 300, of whom about 50 were Algerian.[57]

But there was mounting tension between the communists and the staunchly anti-communist Dr Bendjelloul, who criticised the *'ulama* for their alliance with the communists. At the 23 September Muslim Congress executive committee meeting, the communist municipal councillor Ferchouk Amara criticised Dr Bendjelloul for his hostility towards communists and Islamic reformists. On 6 October the tension between Bendjelloul and the Muslim Congress executive committee came to a head. A committee of ten, most of whom were communists, relieved Bendjelloul of his office. Dr Bachir of the Algérois FEI became the new president.[58]

The spread of communist influence made it a propitious moment to launch the new Algerian Communist Party. This took place on 17–18 October 1936 at Salle Henri Barbusse in Bab el Oued. Much planning went into the launch, attended by close to 200 delegates, including the PCF's secretary Marcel Gitton from Paris. The selection of delegates was based on proportional representation reflecting branch membership. Thus, the largest branches – Belcourt, Bab el Oued and Hussein Dey – were allowed ten delegates each; Oran had six; Blida, Orléansville, Le Sersou, Constantine and Mostaganem, five delegates each; Tlemcen and Sidi bel Abbès, four each. All branches had been advised to keep the commitment to Arabisation in mind when selecting delegates. There were very few women communists, but branches were instructed that delegations of four or more should include one woman.[59]

The stricture on Arabisation was closely followed. In all, there were about 62 Algerian, 67 European and six women delegates, in addition to about sixty invited guests. Claiming 5,000 members, the PCA was divided into three regions, each directed by a regional committee of twenty members, who were to meet at least every two months. These regional committees would liaise regularly with the central committee, which was based in Algiers and had 35 members who would meet every three months. In turn the central committee would select from its members a political bureau of ten members and a three-person secretariat, which was responsible for *Lutte sociale* and other day-to-day matters. The rapid membership recruitment had meant a decline in the general political understanding of new members. Thus the congress agreed to set up a party school and introduce basic education in each region. Yet despite the stress on Arabisation, French communists in Algeria still had much influence.[60]

Barthel opened the congress, introducing Gitton. Both accented the need for a united fight against fascism. This was reinforced by Boukort, who had recently published a 63-page booklet on the Popular Front entitled *Quand le peuple d'Algérie parle* (*When the People of Algeria Speak*). Ouzegane presented the report on communist activities. The socialist Ben Hadj, secretary of the Muslim Congress, extended fraternal greetings along with the hope that communists would cease to criticise Dr Bendjelloul and that the doctor would return to the Muslim Congress. Barthel rejected any possibility of reconciliation.[61]

There were significant differences about the prioritisation of the anti-fascist struggle. One of the Badsi brothers argued that the PCA would have more success amongst Algerians if it were led by Algerians, assisted by a few Europeans, and if it prioritised the anti-colonial rather than the anti-fascist struggle. Given the rapid growth of the anti-colonial ENA, his argument made sense, and he had supporters. But Lucien Sportisse disagreed. After the 1934 Constantine riots, Sportisse had been arrested, imprisoned and removed from his teaching post because of his communist beliefs. Expelled from Constantinois, he moved to Oran and, working with Communist CGT leader Nicolas Zannettacci – who had been politicised as a child by the extreme cruelty meted out to Arabs – organised workers and unemployed people across Oranie. In Oran he married fellow-communist Alice Cremadès, daughter of a railway worker of Spanish descent. On 26 July 1935 he was arrested for organising agricultural workers at Aïn-Témouchent, between Oran and Tlemcen. Imprisoned, he was released after a three-month campaign – his mother started learning French after this arrest so that she could understand what was happening to her son. A persuasive orator, Sportisse argued that fascism was the greatest danger and that fascist countries would never allow an independent Algeria. A Tlemcen delegate asked for a vote. Barthel replied that all resolutions would be voted on the next day. However, Constantine delegate Paul Estorges asked the PCF to take a firm anti-colonial stance and criticised the Popular Front for not doing so.[62]

The next day a Batna delegate deplored the fact that the Popular Front government had not improved the position of Algerians in mixed communes. A Madame Cremade stated that communist women in Oran had joined the World Congress of Women against War and Fascism, hoping to recruit more women. She spoke of the difficulty of recruiting Algerian women, suggesting that sewing lessons might be an inducement. An Arab delegate from Perregaux asked for an Arab-language paper, and a Sidi bel Abbès delegate spoke of fascist attacks on local communists. Another Tlemcen delegate asked that the congress take a decision on Badsi's position. Gitton replied that the priority in Algeria was fascism, not colonialism – prioritising the anti-colonial struggle was Trotskyism, he claimed. Because the Popular Front included colonialist organisations, he explained, it was not possible to raise all the demands of the Algerian people. The congress must be realistic.[63]

At the closing of the congress, Barthel approved the organisational resolution and manifesto – evidently without discussion. The central committee was unanimously elected; Badsi was not included. When several people asked for his inclusion, Gitton stated that Badsi's political views precluded his membership on the central committee. Pragmatically, Badsi replied that he understood his error and would follow the party's line. He was added to the central committee – although his Tlemcen cell was later criticised for nationalist tendencies. The political bureau was selected by unanimous decision – Boukort, Ouzegane, Barthel, Debabèche and Henri Domenech – as was the secretariat – Boukort as first secretary, Ouzegane and Barthel. That same month, ironically, Messali backed down on the demand for independence, pragmatically placing more emphasis on immediate democratic demands.[64]

The PCA's manifesto elaborated its views on the relationship of the anti-fascist and anti-colonial struggles. Fascism, the most savage form of colonialism, was the most ferocious enemy of colonised people, it contended, pointing to Italian fascism's destructive impact in Libya and Abyssinia. All those aspiring to the programme of peace, bread and liberty should join the Popular Front and the Muslim Congress, and those two bodies should unite in progressive action, it argued. The new PCA would combine 'the great republican and revolutionary traditions of the French people' with 'the Algerian people's noble and glorious traditions of culture and freedom', continuing in the line of Algeria's national heroes, Abdelkader, Mokrani and Khaled. The manifesto included a list of immediate democratic demands, ending on the vision of a 'free and happy France alongside a free and happy Algeria'. Independence was not mentioned. But the reference to a free Algeria was ambiguous enough to satisfy the PCF and PCA leadership and most of the Algerian cadres, and Barthel returned to France in November.[65] It was increasingly dangerous to speak publicly of independence. Messali's efforts to tone down his radicalism came too late. The ENA was subjected to increasing criticism from the FEI, the PCA and finally the Islamic reformists. That autumn 1936 the FEI began withdrawing from the Muslim Congress, which was unable to hold together the divergent political tendencies grouped within it.

Unity efforts collapse

In December 1936 the Popular Front government unveiled its Blum-Viollette bill to increase the number of Algerian voters in French elections. It represented a significant reform. Heretofore Algerians seeking French citizenship had to renounce their personal status under Muslim law. The bill allowed Algerians meeting the criteria for the qualified franchise to become French voters without renouncing their Muslim personal status, increasing the number of Algerian voters by 12 to 14 per cent. This would allow the number of deputies elected by Algerian voters to increase from nine to twelve. The bill could have been passed through decree, as most other bills relating to Algeria were. Instead, the government tabled it in Parliament.[66]

The proposal created shock waves amongst Europeans. The Algerian response was mixed. In January 1937 FEI and Muslim Congress leaders responded enthusiastically. Although Ben Badis had criticised reforms that separated the elite from the masses, he nonetheless saw the Blum-Viollette project as a tentative step towards equality; if it were rejected, there would be no hope of gaining any reforms through the French Parliament. Many Islamic reformists supported the bill on the principle that Muslim Algerians should have citizenship rights without renouncing their personal status as Muslims. Yet they soon questioned the Blum-Viollette bill and the Charter of Demands. As for Messali, he condemned the proposal for giving the right to vote to some 25,000 bourgeois Algerians while leaving six million *fellahs* in misery.[67]

Concerned with Messali's popularity, the French government dissolved the ENA that January 1937. The PCA was silent; its failure to condemn the government's action increased the gulf between the communists and the Messalistes. Two months later Messali launched the Parti du peuple algérien (Algerian People's Party, PPA) with the ambiguous slogan of 'Neither assimilation nor separation, but emancipation' – by now he accepted the need for caution on the demand for independence. The PPA's rapid development was facilitated by the growing and concentrated urban population, as well as the appeal of its ideas. It attracted a plebeian and *petit-bourgeois* but culturally sophisticated audience; those who read El Ouma might read French classics like Victor Hugo's Les Misérables and were in touch with Algerian nationalists in France.[68]

But the PCA saw the PPA, like its predecessor, as a rival competing for the same social base. Thus, it continued to malign Messali and his followers as fascist agents. As general secretary of the *Maison de la culture* (House of Culture), Camus became embroiled in this enmity, which deepened under the shadow of the Spanish Civil War.[69] Launched on 8 February 1937, the House of Culture was part of a network of

French cultural centres initiated by the Popular Front government; the Communist writer René Blech directed the Paris centre. In Algiers, the House of Culture acted as an umbrella organisation for a range of bodies – Camus' Labour Theatre, Friends of the Soviet Union, the French-Muslim Union, Esperanto speakers, and local artistic groups. It offered Camus the ideal forum for developing his idea of a Mediterranean culture – which presumably reflected his own displacement from French identity. Thus, it aspired to promote Mediterranean and Algerian culture and to make Algiers a cultural and intellectual centre of the Mediterranean world. To this end it hosted lectures and debates, published brochures on Algerian political rights – its activists supported the Blum-Viollette bill – and monthly bulletins written in an intellectual style inaccessible to most working-class people. It attracted students, teachers and intellectuals, but few Algerians attended its events. When Camus' friend Jeanne Sicard organised an evening of Arab music and dance, only forty people showed up. Such events did not draw European crowds; but neither did they attract Algerians.[70] It was not that Algerians were uninterested. In Constantine, for instance, *medersa* students performed an Arabic play stressing equal education for girls and the value of travel for expanding cultural horizons to an audience of some 800. Clearly, Algerians were more inclined to attend Algerian than European performances, especially those organised under the auspices of a French network.[71]

Indeed, Camus' cultural framework, if not entirely Eurocentric, could be criticised as abstract. This was seen in his vision of a hybrid Mediterranean culture – a culture that looked to Spain, not fascist Italy, a culture that linked Mediterranean Europe and North Africa, itself a crossroads of East and West. Mediterranean culture aspired not to a Mediterranean nationalism, he explained, but to 'a nationalism of the sun' – nature was accessible to all. It aspired not to state collectivism, as in Russia, but to a Mediterranean collectivism; indeed, the Spanish Civil War was being fought over collectivist values. The left must support this Mediterranean culture, Camus argued, rather than allow it to be monopolised by right-wing intellectuals. The oblique critique of state-led collectivism would hardly have set well with the Communist establishment. While the notion of a Mediterranean culture was intriguing, Algerians needed to develop their own culture – so stifled by the French – before they could participate equally with other nations in building a Mediterranean culture.[72]

Camus' fall from grace began with the case of André Gide. In the late 1920s, Gide had been critically acclaimed by the left for his anti-colonial works, *Voyage au Congo* and *Retour du Tchad*. In 1936 he visited the Soviet Union. He expressed his disillusionment in *Retour de l'U.R.S.S.*, published in November 1936. This drew a picture that conflicted sharply with the Soviet films shown at the Ciné-travail (Labour Cinema). Criticising the Soviet Union was not acceptable as far as the PCF was concerned, and it made its position clear in Algeria. But Camus and his friends were concerned about Gide's reports and wanted an open discussion. Against Blech's advice, they went ahead. The communists boycotted it, and fewer than forty people showed up. The communists presented their view of Gide on 25 February 1937.[73]

Camus sympathised with the PPA although he was not well acquainted with its activists. He conveyed his views to Ouzegane who, as a staunch communist, tried to convince him otherwise. But Camus felt that the PCA had lost sight of Algerian rights in the course of the anti-fascist struggle. On 2 May his 'Manifesto of Algerian Intellectuals' was published in *Jeune Méditerranée*, the House of Culture bulletin. While supporting the Blum-Viollette bill, the tone was anti-colonial. Culture cannot live when dignity dies, he argued. His life as a communist became increasingly difficult. In June he became embroiled in legal battles, accused by a Young Communist of misappropriating funds from the House of Culture. Criticism of his leadership of the Labour Theatre and other allegations soon followed. He was cautioned by Ouzegane and Padula about deviating from the official position.[74]

As the war in Spain gathered force, the PCF and PCA hardened their stance: anti-fascism was the priority. When war in Spain began, the French government had planned to support the Spanish Republic. But hoping to appease Germany and maintain his alliance with the radicals, Blum reversed this decision; France and Britain pursued a policy of non-intervention. In late September 1937 the USSR decided to give military support to the Spanish Republic, and the International Brigade was launched the next month. Some five or six hundred Algerians fought with the Republicans. These included communists such as Camus' friend Robert Namia; Maurice Laban and Georges Raffini from Constantine; Ahmed Smaïli from Kabylia; Abdelhamid Guessoum; Rabah Oussidhoum, a metal-worker who became captain and head of the Paris Commune Batallion and died at the Battle of Caspe in March 1938; the former communist René Cazala, who died in battle several weeks later, and the anarchist Mohamed Saïl. Blum's policy of neutrality strained his relationship with the communists, and he resigned as Prime Minister in June 1937.[75]

In August of that year Messali and his associates were arrested under the Régnier decree and sentenced to two years' imprisonment. *L'Humanité* labelled them Trotskyists; the communists castigated Messali's supporters as *agents provocateurs*.[76] Camus and his friend Maurice Girard continued stressing their support for Algerian rights within communist circles, although some of Camus' friends left the party. Boukort, Ouzegane and Elie Mignot called Camus and Girard to a meeting. Girard resigned – but not Camus. That autumn Robert Deloche arrived from Paris, charged Camus and Girard with Trotskyism and reported to the Comintern. Camus was expelled from the PCA and left the Labour Theatre, which collapsed soon after.[77]

The PCA's second congress took place 18-19 December 1937 at Cervantès Hall in Belcourt. It had hardened its anti-nationalist line. 'Against fascism! For peace! Union of the French and Algerian peoples', proclaimed *Lutte Sociale*. Fascism's shadow loomed over North Africa; thousands of copies of Hitler's *Mein Kampf* were flooding the country. Urging support for the Popular Front and Muslim Congress, it denounced Messali as an enemy of the Popular Front and castigated certain PPA leaders as traitors of the Algerian people. The PCA's new secretariat included two PCF members, Robert Deloche and Elie Mignot, and two Algerians, Boukort and Kaddour Belkaïm, who had been secretary of the Oran region. The political bureau included Ali Debabèche, Nicolas Zannettacci, Amar Ouzegane and Maurice Martin, with Mahmoudi and Marouf as substitutes. Larbi Bouhali joined the central committee.[78]

The PCF's ninth congress took place from 25 to 29 December, in Arles. Indicating a firmer approach to the national and colonial questions, Thorez signalled a shift in the national question: while the PCF upheld the right of colonies to independence, the right of divorce did not signify the obligation to divorce. If the anti-fascist struggle was the priority, then the interest of colonised peoples lay in a union with the French people – and not in a stance that favoured fascist forces. Belkaïm underlined Thorez's point: the union of the Algerian and French people was and would always be necessary. Fascist propaganda was being diffused across North Africa by Spanish and Italian radio. In January 1938 *Lutte sociale* declared that faced with fascist aggression, any consideration of Algerian independence without a French–Algerian alliance was 'mad and criminal'.[79]

The PCA claimed 5,000 members, although Deloche thought that 3,000–3,500 was more realistic. Its contacts with Algerians were generally limited to political leaders and personalities. It faced stiff competition from the PPA, and as Messali's party grew, so the PCA's influence waned. During the June 1937 Algiers local elections, the PCA had performed creditably amongst Algerian voters. From then on, they switched to the PPA, which began winning with big majorities. Although the PCA seemed to be growing in Oranie, it declined in Algérois, where it was susceptible to the PPA's competition, and in Constantinois, where Algerians left due to Bendjelloul's campaign.

Although Deloche doubted that the communist movement in Algeria could regain its former influence, by the time he left Algeria in late May 1938, he optimistically estimated that the party numbered some 4,500 – an appreciable gain over his earlier estimate.[80]

The Blum-Viollette bill, on which the Popular Front had pinned its hopes for Parliamentary reform of Algerian rights, was buried in a Chamber committee. The Federation of Mayors, representing the settler vote, had campaigned hard against it. At the 1938 Senate vote it was defeated. The other side of communist strategy, the Muslim Congress, which had met once more in July 1937, likewise collapsed in 1938. The divergent movements that it had tried to unite went their separate ways. Bendjelloul attempted to form an electoral coalition. But Abbas parted company with him and, hoping to gain support for assimilation, founded the Union populaire algérienne in July 1938. The PPA continued to spread across the country, most successful amongst the urban working and lower middle classes that the PCA itself hoped to win.[81]

Over the past decade communist policy on Algerian independence had flipped. For many communists the class-against-class policy had been a failure resulting in a communist sect of 150 members. The demand for independence promoted by the PCF in the late 1920s resulted in severe repression of communists, with prison sentences of up to two years. However, as public political space expanded in the mid-1930s, the Party attracted Algerian members precisely because of its call for independence. Barthel's stress on the anti-colonial struggle was inspirational. Although most Algerian leaders were not then calling for independence, appeals to fight colonialism and demand independence struck an emotional chord with politicised Algerians.

International developments, namely fascism's march across Europe, propelled changes in communist strategy worldwide. Yet the Comintern's popular-front strategy, developed in France, had an inherently European bias. This bias was seen both in the focus on an anti-fascist struggle based primarily in a Europe dependent on colonial resources and in the damping down of the demand for Algerian independence to avoid alienating European settlers concerned with fighting fascism. Moreover, in the Algerian context, crucial aspects of the strategy – a new tolerance for the socialist and radical parties – spoke far more to Europeans than to Algerians. Indeed, some European communists saw anti-fascism as a justification for forgetting the vexed issue of anti-colonialism. Yet, as the PCF itself had acknowledged, the Abyssinian fight against Italian fascism suggested that the two movements might have been combined.

In this international context, the launch of an autonomous Algerian

Communist Party did not mean a decrease in French influence within the new party. To the contrary, fascism's spread across Europe and into North Africa meant that the PCF saw control of the PCA as important. Thus, the popular-front years witnessed a continuous flow of PCF emissaries to Algeria. The historian Charles-Robert Ageron described the PCA's politics during these years as 'the French policy of assimilation', wondering whether such a policy could ever have convinced the Algerian masses. In a complementary manner, Sivan argued that communists in Algeria showed an 'excess of zeal' in applying the PCF's anti-fascist strategy, attributing this to their psychological dependence on their French comrades. However, in focusing on the official PCA stance, both writers underestimated its internal contestations over this issue.[82]

Whatever the limitations of the popular-front strategy, the Popular Front government brought some amelioration for some Algerians and promised more through the Blum-Violette bill. Thus, certain Algerian communists were convinced that this was the best route, especially as fascist influence spread to North Africa. But this view was far from hegemonic within the PCA, amongst either European or Algerians, some of whom left to join the PPA. By the late 1930s politicised Algerian overwhelmingly saw the PPA rather than the PCA as their political home.

Generally, Algerian leaders were concerned about association with the PCA precisely because, irrespective of communism's shifting policies, colonial authorities saw communists as anti-French. Thus, the PCA's desire to build a broad alliance with Muslim organisations offered a pragmatic justification of its decision to place independence on the back burner, despite its internal contestations over the issue. In other words, while the communist decision to downplay anti-colonialism reflected a European bias, it also coincided with the wishes of many Muslim leaders.

With the collapse of the Popular Front government in France, many Europeans drifted away from the PCA. Despite the expansion of public space in the 1930s, this space nonetheless remained sharply divided across national and religious lines. In this respect, there was a close parallel with South Africa, where white workers refused to support the call for black democratic rights. There, the strategy produced two movements: a white anti-fascist movement to protect existing white rights, and a black movement to gain democratic rights. As George Orwell pointed out, anti-fascism could mask the desire to maintain imperial and colonial privileges over the colonially oppressed.[83]

Camus' brief career as a communist marked the peak of communist efforts to form a cultural bridge between Europeans and Algerians. The profound inequalities dividing Europeans and Algerians meant that neither group could imagine a Mediterranean community at that time. Camus soon found another outlet for his passion. Since May 1938 he had been working on the manuscript that became L'Etranger (The Outsider), and later that year the newspaper editor Pascal Pia recruited him as a journalist for Alger républicain, launched on 6 October 1938 in Bab el Oued. Operating on a shoestring budget in the Popular Front's gloomy aftermath, Alger républicain promised its largely European readership the dream of republican egalitarianism. Its first issue rejected the idea of 'two sorts of French', demanding the immediate social equality of all French, irrespective of origin, religion or ideology, and 'progress for indigenous Algerians towards political equality'. Camus believed in the republican ideal. Yet while the ideal continued to attract certain Algerian leaders, it did not move the masses. Instead, it was Messali's words – that the land of their birth was not for sale – that inspired them to imagine an Algerian nation.[84]

Notes

1 Kaddache, Vie politique, pp. 237–8; Carlier, Nation, pp. 16, 22, 43, 49, 51–3, 113, 125–6, 137–62, 188–90; Jim House, 'The Displacements of Colonialism: Migration, Re-Housing and Nationalism in Algiers, 1945–1962' (unpublished paper, 2012), pp. 2, 5.
2 Ruedy, Modern Algeria, pp. 135, 139.
3 Lutte sociale (October, December 1932).
4 Gallissot (ed.), Algérie, pp. 289–91; Donnat, Afin que, pp. 45–6.
5 RGASPI 517.1.1710, Rapport sur l'Algérie, 9 September 1935, p. 15; ANOM ALG Alger F407, Surveillance spéciale: Boukort Benali, Note, n.d.; Sivan, Communisme, pp. 77–8; Jean Chaintron, Le Vent soufflait devant ma porte, Patrick Rotman (ed.) (Paris: Editions du Seuil, 1993), pp. 132–3; Amar Ouzegane, Le Meilleur Combat (Paris: Julliard, 1962); Gallissot (ed.), Algérie, pp. 156–8, 159–61, 499–503.
6 Ruedy, Modern Algeria, p. 138; Rabah Aissaoui, 'Algerian Nationalists in the French Political Arena and Beyond: the Etoile nord-africaine and the Parti du peuple algérien in Interwar France', Journal of North African Studies, 15:1 (2010), 1–12, pp. 3–4; Stora, Messali, pp. 95–138.
7 RGASPI 517.1.1710, Rapport sur L'Algérie, 9 September 1935, p. 7, 30 July 1935, p. 9; Ageron, Histoire, vol. 2, pp. 382–3; 'Pour le front unique d'action', Lutte sociale (15–31 August 1934), p. 1.
8 Joshua Cole, 'Anti-Semitism and the Colonial Situation in Interwar Algeria: The Anti-Jewish Riots in Constantine, August 1934', 77–111, pp. 79, 81, 104, and Samuel Kalman, 'Fascism and Algérianité: The Croix de Feu and the Indigenous Question in 1930s Algeria', 112–39, pp. 114–15, both Martin Thomas (ed.), The French Colonial Mind: Violence, Military Encounters and Colonialism, vol. 2 (Lincoln, NE, and London, 2011); Charles-Robert Ageron, 'Une émeute anti-juive à Constantine: (août 1934)', Revue de l'Occident musulman et de la Méditerranée, 13–14 (1973), 23–40, pp. 23–5, 34–6. The population figures vary slightly; I have used Cole's.
9 Interviews with Riad Benchikh-el-Fougoun, Constantine, 23 September 2011, William Sportisse, Paris, 18 June 2001, 24 June 2012; Nedjma Benachour-Tebbouche, Constantine et ses romanciers: Essai (Constantine: Media-Plus, 2008); William Sportisse, Entretiens avec Pierre-Jean le Foll-Luciani, Le Camp des Oliviers: Parcours d'un communiste algérien (Rennes: Presses Universitaires de Rennes, 2012), p. 37.

10 Cole, 'Anti-Semitism', pp. 77, 91–4, 99; Ageron, 'Emeute', pp. 24–7; Ruedy, *Modern Algeria*, p. 140; Stora, *Histoire de l'Algérie*, p. 73; 'Tragédie de Constantine', *Lutte sociale* (15–31 August 1934), p. 1. The figures vary; I have used Cole's and Ageron's.
11 Sportisse, *Camp*, pp. 35, 47–51.
12 Ageron, 'Emeute', pp. 28–33; Kaddache, *Vie Politique*, pp. 213–14.
13 Ageron, 'Emeute', pp. 31–3; André Ferrat, 'Que signifient les évènements de Constantine?', *Cahiers du Bolchévisme*, 16 (15 August 1934), 940–7, pp. 943–6; Sportisse, *Camp*, pp. 39–40.
14 Interviews with William Sportisse; Sportisse, *Camp*, pp. 38–40, nn. 16–18; ANOM ALG Alger 2i/33.
15 RGASPI 517.1.1735, Report of enlarged central committee, n.d.; ANOM ALG GG 9h-49-2, Gouvernement général de l'Algérie, Territoire militaire d'Aïn-Sefra: Affaires indigènes, Carnet 'B', Boukort Ben Ali; 'Libérez Benali Boukort!' *Lutte sociale* (16–31 October 1934, 1–15 November 1934); Boukort, *Souffle*, pp. 661–4; Chaintron, *Vent*, p. 133. Ouzegane used the pseudonym Arthur Doden at the Congress; Sivan, *Communisme*, pp. 79–81; Todd, *Camus: Une vie*, p. 119.
16 McDermott and Agnew, *Comintern*, pp. 121–4, 139; cf. Williams, *Crisis*, p. 72. On the popular front in Algeria see Planche, 'Antifascisme'; Benjamin Stora, *Nationalistes algériens et révolutionnaires français au temps du Front populaire* (Paris: L'Harmattan, 1987).
17 Ruedy, *Modern Algeria*, p. 140; Einaudi, *Rêve*, p. 85.
18 Ageron, *Histoire*, vol. 2, pp. 433–4; Gosnell, *Politics*, pp. 109–10, 123.
19 Camus, *First Man*, pp. 158, 113; Herbert R. Lottman, *Albert Camus: A Biography* (London Axis, 1997), p. 96; McDermott and Agnew, *Comintern*, p. 121.
20 Camus, *First Man*, p. 162.
21 Todd, *Camus: Une vie*, pp. 48–57; José Lenzini, *Albert Camus* (Toulouse: Editions Milan, n.d.), pp. 6–9, 11; Robert Zaretsky, *Albert Camus: Elements of a Life* (Ithaca, NY, and London: Cornell University, 2010), pp. 8, 10–11, 27.
22 « Il faut vivre les difficultés et les victoires du communisme ... je suis à un tournant important », Todd, *Camus: Une vie*, pp. 121, 91, 107, 112; Lottman, *Camus*, pp. 162–3; Lenzini, *Camus*, p. 13; Zaretsky, *Camus*, p. 26; Boualem Khalfa, Henri Alleg and Abdelhamid Benzine, *La Grande Aventure d'« Alger républicain »* (Paris: Messidor, 1987), p. 16.
23 McDermott and Agnew, *Comintern*, pp. 121–3, 126–7, 134–5, 139; Guillaume Bourgeois, 'French Communism and the Communist International, in Rees and Thorpe (eds), *International Communism*, pp. 95–102, 96–7; Alleg, 'Torrent', p. 220.
24 RGASPI 517.1.1735, Mignot and Lenoir, *Rapport de la région algérienne à l'occasion du 7e Congrès de l'I.C. - Elections municipales*, n.d., pp. 4, 1–3 [stamped 17 October 1935]. On other Popular Front efforts see CAC 19940500, art 183, 3167, GGA, Rapport mensuel September 1935, p. 2; Ageron, *Histoire*, vol. 2, pp. 383, 434.
25 Maitron (ed.), *Dictionnaire biographique*, vol. 27, p. 327; Todd, *Camus: Une vie*, p. 94; RGASPI 517.1.1735, Amar to comrades, 6 January 1935.
26 Todd, *Camus: Une vie*, pp. 125, 194; Lottman, *Camus*, p. 98; Zaretsky, *Camus*, pp. 19, 23, 120–1.
27 Maitron (ed.), *Dictionnaire biographique*, vol 18, p. 31; Gallissot (ed.), *Algérie*, p. 78; Henri Alleg, *Mémoire algérienne: Souvenirs de luttes et d'espérances* (Paris: Stock, 2005), pp. 116–17; interview with Abdelkader Guerroudj, Alger, 28 September 2011; Gallissot pp. 148–9.
28 *Rapport sur l'Algérie*, 30 July 1935, p. 12; 9 September 1935, p. 15; RGASPI 517.1.1735, *Rapport sur l'Algérie*, 8 August 1935, p. 17.
29 Chaintron, *Vent*, p. 135, states he arrived on 1 September; police reports state mid-September: CAC 19940500, art 183, 3167, GGA, *Rapport mensuel*, September 1935, p. 2.
30 Sivan, *Communisme*, pp. 83–4; Todd, *Camus: Une vie*, pp. 126–7.
31 « Un complot contre la sûreté de l'Etat en Algérie », Alleg, 'Torrent', pp. 203–4; « la nation oppresseuse ... la nation de l'impérialisme », in 'La « Circulaire Barthel », Alleg (ed.), *Guerre*, vol. 3, pp. 478–80, 479; Chaintron, *Vent*, pp. 137–8.
32 ANOM ALG/GGA/9H/49-3, Préfet d'Alger to GGA, no. 1714, 20 January 1936,

p. 1; Ageron, *Histoire*, vol. 2, p. 383; Sivan, *Communisme*, pp. 84, 89; Durand, *Mystérieuse*, p. 126; Chaintron, *Vent*, pp. 138–40.
33 Chaintron, *Vent*, p. 141; Sivan, *Communisme*, pp. 87–8; Todd, *Camus: Une vie*, pp. 110–13, 131, 126, 1066, n. 10; Lottman, *Camus*, pp. 162–3; Jean Lacouture, *André Malraux* (London: André Deutsch, 1975).
34 « Si le prophète Mohammed existait aujourd'hui, en cette période où les peuples musulmans sont asservis et enchaînés dans la plupart des pays, il les appellerait à la lutte libératrice », ANOM ALG GGA 3CAB/24, 'L'action du Komintern en Afrique du Nord', *Bulletin de renseignement du 14 Aout 1936*, pp. 7–8; ANOM ALG GG 9h-49-2, Boukort to GGA, 4 September 1935, and Boukort to Louise Fayet, 1 Septembre 1935; Boukort, *Souffle*, p. 63; Durand, *Mystérieuse*, 126; Chaintron, *Vent*, p. 147.
35 Sivan, *Communisme*, p. 89; Todd, *Camus: Une vie*, p. 119.
36 'Intervention d'Amar Ouzegane au congrès de Villeurbanne du PCF (Janvier 1936)', in Jurquet, *Révolution nationale*, vol. 2, pp. 546–51; Sivan, *Communisme*, pp. 89, 92; 'The Abyssinia Crisis – Seventy Years On', *Socialist History*, 28 (Autumn 2005).
37 « Nous prêchons non le nationalisme étroit, mais l'union des opprimés des colonies et des exploités des métropoles. Nous réclamons le libre droit des peuples à disposer d'eux-mêmes ... et à leur union librement consentie », Ageron, *Histoire*, vol. 2, p. 384; Ageron highlights the changing stance on independence between January and April 1936. See also Durand, *Mystérieuse*, p. 128; Sivan, *Communisme*, p. 93.
38 Todd, *Camus: Une vie*, pp. 161–6; Lottman, *Camus*, pp. 96, 102–3, 128–33; Lacouture, *Malraux*, pp. 183–4, 380; Zaretsky, *Camus*, pp. 20, 28.
39 Ruedy, *Modern Algeria*, p. 136, nn. 17–18; Raymond F. Betts, *France and Decolonisation, 1900–1960* (Basingstoke and London: Macmillan, 1991), p. 47; Carlier, *Nation*, pp. 43–4.
40 'For a Free Algerian Republic: the 25th anniversary of the Algerian Communist Party', *African Communist* (April–May 1962), 26–40, p. 32.
41 McDermott and Agnew, *Comintern*, pp. 137–9; Todd, *Camus: Une vie*, p. 117; Chaintron, *Vent*, p. 144; Lacouture, *Malraux*, p. 235.
42 Ageron, *Histoire*, vol. 2, pp. 437, 449–50; Ruedy, *Modern Algeria*, p. 140; 'For a Free Algerian Republic', p. 32.
43 Stora, *Histoire de l'Algérie*, p. 81; Einaudi, *Rêve*, p. 101; Ruedy, *Modern Algeria*, pp. 140–1; Alleg, 'Torrent', p. 233.
44 ANOM ALG/GGA/9H/49, Colonel Trinquet au GGA, 24 April 1936, and Commissaire Central to Directeur, Sécurité Générale, 3 June 1936; ANOM ALG GG 9h-49-2, Boukort to Louise Fayet, 1 September 1935; *Rapport mensuel*, September 1935, p. 2.
45 Ruedy, *Modern Algeria*, pp. 140–1; Ageron, *Histoire*, vol. 2, pp. 437–8; Sivan, *Communisme*, p. 94.
46 ANOM ALG/GGA 3CAB/24, Communisme, 'La vogue du Parti communiste', p. 5, n.d. [c. July 1936]; ALG/GGA/9H/49.
47 McDermott and Agnew, *Comintern*, p. 139; Einaudi, *Rêve*, pp. 11–19; 50, 91–3; Chaintron, *Vent*, pp. 145–6; Lacouture, *Malraux*, pp. 235–55; Sivan, *Communisme*, p. 95; Gallissot (ed.), *Algérie*, p. 156.
48 « Oran républicain dira chaque matin la vérité », *Oran républicain* (21 February 1937), p. 1; Mohammed el Aziz Kessous, 'La représentation au Parlement des musulmans algériens, *Oran républicain* (22, 24, 26 February 1937), p. 2; 'La page musulmane', *Oran républicain* (5 March 1937), p. 4; Alleg, Benzine and Khalfa, *Aventure*, pp. 17–18; Guillaume Laisne, 'Engagements d'un Quotidien en Société Coloniale: Le cas d'Alger Républicain (1938–1955)', Mémoire présenté pour le Master recherche, Institut d'études politiques de Paris (2007), pp. 21–4.
49 « dès que les premières grèves ont éclaté en France les agents de propagande, européens ou indigènes[,] ont parcouru la Mitidja et le Sahel », ANOM ALG/GGA/9H/49, Préfet d'Alger to GGA, 8 July 1936.
50 « une ampleur considérable », 'Vogue du Parti communiste', p. 5; Alleg, 'Torrent', pp. 226–7.
51 CAC 19940500, art 183, 3153, GGA, *Propagande communiste: Rapport mensuel – Septembre 1936*, 4 November 1936, p. 8.

52 « Cette terre n'est pas à vendre », Carlier, *Nation*, p. 132. According to Stora, *Messali*, p. 148, Messali recounted: « Je me suis alors baissé, et j'ai dit que cette terre ne se vendait pas ... On ne vend pas son pays ».
53 Quoted Ruedy, *Modern Algeria*, p. 142; Alleg, 'Torrent', p. 237; Planche, 'Lieux', pp. 195–7. On Messali's arrival with a new Algerian flag, interview with Dr Chawki Mostefaï, El Mouradja, Algiers, 19 September 2011.
54 GGA, *Propagande communiste*, p. 10; Ruedy, *Modern Algeria*, p. 143.
55 Chaintron, *Vent*, p. 155; Lacouture, *Malraux*, pp. 227–8.
56 Sivan, *Communisme*, p. 87; GGA, *Propagande communiste*, pp. 1–2; Alleg, 'Torrent', p. 238; Chaintron, *Vent*, p. 146. Chaintron estimated a weekly print run of 15,000 copies. CAC 19940500, art 183, 3167, GGA, *Propagande communiste: Rapport mensuel – Octobre 1936*, 30 November 1936, p. 2, states 13,000 sales in October.
57 *Propagande communiste – Septembre 1936*, pp. 4, 8, 10–12; *Propagande communiste – Octobre 1936*, p. 2.
58 *Propagande communiste – Septembre 1936*, pp. 6–7; Alleg, 'Torrent', p. 239; Ageron, *Histoire*, vol. 2, pp. 441–2; Planche, 'Lieux', p. 197.
59 ANOM ALG GGA/9h/49-3, *Directives aux comités de rayons pour la préparation du Congrès*, 18 September 1936; Alleg, 'Torrent', p. 226. The *Directives* anticipated 120 delegates; according to 'For a Free Algerian Republic', p. 26, about 200 delegates were present.
60 *Propagande communiste – Octobre 1936*, p. 1; ANOM ALG GGA/9h-49-3, *Congrès du Parti communiste d'Algérie*, n.d.; CAC 19940500, art 183, 3167, A.S. du Congrès du Parti communiste d'Algérie, 26 November 1936; Sivan, *Communisme*, p. 100. At the time of the launch, Elie Mignot assisted Barthel, and Pierre Fayet led the trade union movement.
61 Sûreté départementale d'Alger, *Congrès du Parti communiste: Rapport*, 20 October 1936, p. 1; ANOM ALG GGA/9h/49-3; *Propagande communiste – Octobre 1936*, p. 2; RGASPI 517.1.2016; PCF 261 J7/, *Algérie! La France te parle!* Speech by Marcel Gitton to PCA Congress, October 1936 (Algiers: Franco-Italienne, [1936]).
62 Sûreté départementale d'Alger, *Congrès du Parti communiste*; Interviews with William Sportisse; Planche, 'Antifascisme', p. 7; Einaudi, *Rêve*, p. 94; Todd, *Camus: Une vie*, pp. 127–8; Sportisse, *Camp*, pp. 53–60.
63 Madame Cremade was possibly Alice Cremadès or a relative. Sûreté départementale d'Alger, *Congrès du Parti communiste*, Todd, *Camus: Une vie*, pp. 127–8; Jennifer Anne Boittin, *Colonial Metropolis: The Urban Grounds of Anti-Imperialism and Feminism in Interwar Paris* (Lincoln, NE: University of Nebraska, 2010), p. 206.
64 Sûreté départementale d'Alger, *Congrès du Parti communiste*, pp. 2–6; *Propagande communiste – Octobre 1936*, p. 2; Gallissot (ed.), *Algérie*, pp. 78–9; Ruedy, *Modern Algeria*, p. 143.
65 « des grandes traditions républicaines et révolutionnaires du peuple français ... les nobles et glorieuses traditions de culture et de liberté du peuple d'Algérie ... aux côtés d'une France libre et heureuse, UNE ALGERIE LIBRE ET HEUREUSE », *Pour le salut du peuple d'Algérie: Manifeste adopté par le Congrès du Parti communiste d'Algérie, 1936* (Algiers: Bureau d'Editions, 1936), pp. 2–8, quotes 4, 8; ANOM ALG GGA 3CAB/24; Chaintron, *Vent*, p. 153.
66 Ageron, *Histoire*, vol. 2, pp. 450–1.
67 *Propagande communiste – Septembre 1936*, p. 10; Ruedy, *Modern Algeria*, p. 143; Ageron, *Histoire*, vol. 2, pp. 450, 454–5, 458.
68 Ruedy, *Modern Algeria*, p. 143; Carlier, *Nation*, pp. 38, 93; Stora, *Messali*, pp. 155–63.
69 Mahfoud Kaddache, *Histoire du nationalisme algérien: Question nationale et politique algérienne, 1919–1951*, 2nd edn, vol. 1 (Algiers: Société nationale d'édition et de diffusion, 1981), pp. 479–80; Stora, *Messali*, pp. 169–74.
70 Todd, *Camus: Une vie*, pp. 185–8, 190, 194; Lottman, *Camus*, pp. 128, 135–42.
71 McDougall, *History*, p. 56.
72 Albert Camus, 'The New Mediterranean Culture', in Philip Thody (ed.), *Albert Camus, Lyrical and Critical Essays* (New York: Alfred A Knopf, 1969), pp. 189–98, 190; Zaretsky, *Camus*, p. 39.

73 Todd, *Camus: Une vie*, pp. 195–7; Lottman, *Camus*, pp. 141–2; Lacouture, *Malraux*, pp. 271–2.
74 Todd, *Camus: Une vie*, pp. 199–200, 203; Lottman, *Camus*, pp. 167–9; Zaretsky, *Camus*, p. 28.
75 Todd, *Camus: Une vie*, pp. 197–9; Lottman, *Camus*, pp. 215, 251; Lacouture, *Malraux*, p. 252; McDermott and Agnew, *Comintern*, pp. 139–42; Einaudi, *Algérien*, pp. 27–38; Gallissot (ed.), *Algérie*, pp. 196–7, 397–403, 518–20, 545, 555–6; 'For a Free Algerian Republic', p. 31; 'Mohamed, Sail, 1894–1953', Libcom.org, http://goo.gl/LNfktb (accessed 31 October 2012); PCA 261 J7/ box 1, folder 5, 'Un combattant exemplaire des B. I.: L'Algérien Oussidoum', *Amis d'Espagne* (October 1961), p. 5; interviews with William Sportisse.
76 Ruedy, *Modern Algeria*, p. 143; Stora, *Messali*, pp. 179–82.
77 Todd, *Camus: Une vie*, pp. 200–4, 1072–3, n. 32; Lottman, *Camus*, p. 169; R. Deloche, RGASPI 517.1.1888, *Rapport sur la situation en Algérie fin mai 1938*, 20 June 1938, p. 6, cf. Lenzini, *Camus*, 22; Zaretsky, *Camus*, p. 31.
78 ANOM ALG/GGA/9h/49, part 2 , 'Contre le fascisme! Pour la Paix! Union des peuples de France et de l'Algérie', *Lutte sociale* (25 December 1937); Gallissot (ed.), *Algérie*, pp. 100, 156.
79 « fou et criminel », Sivan, *Communisme*, pp. 97–8.
80 Sivan, *Communisme*, p. 106; Deloche, *Rapport*, pp. 2, 12; Stora, *Messali*, pp. 182–4
81 *Propagande communiste – Septembre 1936*, p. 10; Ruedy, *Modern Algeria*, pp. 143–4; Ageron, *Histoire*, vol. 2, p. 450.
82 « la politique française d'assimilation », Ageron, *Histoire*, vol. 2, p. 386; Sivan, *Communisme*, pp. 97, 100.
83 George Orwell, 'Not Counting Niggers', in Sonia Orwell and Ian Angus (eds), *The Collected Essays, Journalism and Letters of George Orwell*, vol. 1 (Harmondsworth, Middlesex: Penguin, 1970), pp. 434–8.
84 Lottman, *Camus*, pp. 184–5; Laisne, 'Engagements', pp. 25–6, 31–6; Zaretsky, *Camus*, p. 40; Jacqueline Lévi-Valensi (ed.), *Camus at Combat: Writing 1944–1947* (Princeton, NJ, and Oxford: Princeton University, 2006), p. 204, n. 494; Paul Viallaneix, 'The First Camus', in Albert Camus, *Cahiers II: Youthful Writings* (New York, Alfred A. Knopf, 1976), 3–104, p. 4; Alleg, Benzine and Khalfa, *Aventure*, pp. 18–26.

CHAPTER FIVE

The nation in formation: communists and nationalists during the Second World War

Europe's precarious peace deteriorated. When Germany entered Austria on 12 March 1938, Britain accepted the event as a *fait accompli*. Radical socialist Edouard Daladier became French Prime Minister in April, signalling that France's foreign policy would be motivated by fear of war and communism. The signing of the Munich Pact on 1 October 1938 represented British and French attempts to maintain peace through concessions to Hitler. The USSR had been excluded: when the Great Terror swept through the Soviet Union from 1936 to 1938, the country's international reputation plummeted amidst calls for its diplomatic isolation. In the French Parliament communist deputies voted against the government on the Munich Pact. The Popular Front collapsed, to be killed by government decree. When organised labour protested, government defeated the unions. Business celebrated. The public political space available to communists contracted.[1]

Isolated, the Soviet Union preached peace but planned for war. The Comintern and its national sections continued to prioritise anti-fascism over anti-colonialism. For the PCF, Franco-Algerian unity was crucial for fighting fascism. To justify this, PCF general secretary Maurice Thorez proposed the thesis that Algeria was a 'nation in formation',[2] an idea of cultural *mélange* strikingly similar to Camus' notion of a Mediterranean culture. With much fanfare Thorez visited Algeria to introduce the new thesis – a 35 mm documentary film of 13 minutes was produced in both French and Arabic![3] On 11 February 1939 he addressed 10,000 people at a PCA rally in Algiers. 'We, communists, we do not know races', he asserted. 'We only want to know peoples.' But just as in France twenty races had fused into one nation through the French Revolution, so, he continued, 'an Algerian nation is ... being formed through the mixing of twenty races'.[4] These included the Numids, Romans, Berbers, Arabs, Jews, Turks, Greeks, Maltese,

Spanish, Italian and French. While the PCF supported the right to self-determination, Thorez explained, this right did not mandate separation – the right to divorce did not necessitate divorce. Instead, reported a police agent, Thorez promoted the union of the Algerian and French peoples in defence of a common French revolutionary heritage. The French nation could guide the Algerian 'nation in formation', and the PCA was the organisation best-suited to lead it, precisely because it was open to all, irrespective of religion, race, ethnicity or gender. But the nationalists were not swayed. Most of them rejected the view the Algerian nation was not yet fully formed, even if in 1936 Abbas had questioned the Algerian nation's existence. Some of the audience proclaimed their support for Messali Hadj, but, noted the police spy, neither their presence nor their protests attracted attention.[5]

Most European communists still assumed that Algeria's liberation depended on socialist revolution in France. Although sceptical of Thorez's thesis, they observed that at least he spoke of an Algerian nation, albeit one in the process of development. The PCA had sent Alidin Debabèche and Omar Bendib to France for training in the expectation that they would recruit other Algerians after their return.[6] However, the central committee's Zannettacci wondered whether Algerians would accept the thesis, which presented the supposed races as qualitatively and quantitatively equal in their demographic and cultural weight. Indeed, indicating its uncertainty about the thesis, the PCA delayed publicising it for three weeks.[7] But in March Laurent Casanova proposed 'one Algerian nation one and indivisible alongside the French nation', and Kaddour Belkaïm agreed that the Algerian nation's development could only be realised through union with France. Other Algerians agreed: the *Voix indigène* called for a 'Sacred union' of France and Algeria.[8]

Camus published a series on the Kabyle famine in *Alger républicain* in June of that year. Traversing Kabylia he found people starving, children fighting with dogs for scraps. Condemning the *caïd*'s fusion of police, administrative and judicial power, he proposed education, agricultural training and job creation through public works. The Kabyles called for schools as they called for bread, he wrote. The artificial barrier separating European and Algerian schooling must end. Assimilation was possible only when 'peoples made to understand each other could get to know each other on benches at the same school', he insisted. Colonialism could only be justified, if it could 'help the conquered peoples to keep their personality', he argued; Kabyles should have the right to be French while maintaining their personality.[9] The communist vision of national identity had seemingly moved closer to that of Camus. Following the 'nation in formation' thesis, the PCA denounced nationalist calls for a Muslim front. Instead, on 28 July it took up the idea of a *Rassemblement franco-musulman* proposed by Dr Bendjelloul the year before. But Algerian receptivity to this idea had diminished.[10]

Meanwhile, European politics deteriorated. In February 1939 France and Britain had recognised Franco's government in Spain. In March Spanish Republican forces surrendered. Spanish refugees poured into France. Amidst rising xenophobia, that spring France built its first internment camps to hold them. Following Czechoslovakia's final dismemberment on 15 March, Britain reversed its appeasement policy, promising to protect Poland from a German invasion. The Soviet Union and Germany signed the Molotov–Ribbentrop Non-aggression Pact of 23 August 1939, agreeing to Poland's partition. This created shock waves across the communist world – not least in the PCF. Yet, one by one communist parties endorsed the shift. Despite heated controversy, the PCA's political bureau endorsed the pact on 26 August.[11]

On that same evening the PCA held a private meeting attended by some one hundred people at Bab el Oued's Salle Barbusse – hastily rearranged as the manager of the originally scheduled venue had changed his mind. The PCA's general secretary Ben Ali Boukort presided, along with Kaddour Belkaïm and Marcel Planes, secretary of the Algiers region. The PCA maintained that the USSR was just as eager to negotiate a 'peace pact' with Britain and France. In Planes' view, an Anglo-Franco-Soviet pact was the best hope for peace. Boukort criticised the fascists and socialists, but also the *Alger républicain*, which, he contended, had abruptly changed the political line. Despite controversy, the meeting voted in support of the Non-aggression Pact.[12]

On 1 September German troops invaded Poland. Two days later, Britain and France declared war. French leaders used the empire to show strength: a poster depicting the French and British empires in red and Germany in black optimistically proclaimed, 'We will win because we are the strongest.'[13] With the Soviet Union neutral, the Comintern shifted course. Until then it had distinguished between peaceful bourgeois democracies and aggressive fascist states. On 9 September the ECCI claimed that the imperialist powers were competing for world domination and characterised the war as 'an imperialist and unjust war for which the bourgeoisie of all the belligerent states bear equal responsibility'. Pointing the finger at British and French imperialism, it called on the working classes to organise from below to defeat their national bourgeoisies.[14]

War and clandestinity

Public political space closed down. Confronted with the risk of internment, communists and nationalists retreated to underground political space. In France the government began a concerted attack on the PCF, which on 19 September declared its commitment to France. By the 21st, however, pressured by the Comintern, the PCF's central committee declared that the war could no longer be seen as anti-fascist – a statement that confused its own members. When the Comintern declared the war to be an imperialist conflict in which communists should not take sides, communist deputies in the French Parliament took the cue and called for peace. But for the French government, the PCF was now aligned with France's enemy. On 26 September the government banned the PCF, PCA and PPA and suspended communist local councils. Thorez, drafted into the army, deserted on 4 October and fled to Moscow. That month several communist municipalities were suspended and 34 communist deputies arrested. In November any individual seen as a threat to national security was deemed subject to internment. Thousands of PCF members were arrested. More than 500 French communists and trade unionists were deported to detention camps in southern Algeria, such as Djenien Bou Rezg, Mecheria, Bossuet and Géryville; Djenien Bou Rezg, the best-known camp, was an old military fortress some 800 km south of Oran. In February 1940 Thorez was stripped of his French nationality. In March, 35 French communist deputies were put on trial, most receiving sentences of up to five years; the 27 seen as the most dangerous were separated from their other comrades.[15]

The repression hit Algeria immediately. Messali, released in August 1939, was rearrested. *Lutte sociale* and *Alger républicain* were banned; Pascal Pia and Camus promptly launched *Soir républicain* on 15 September. Marshal Philippe Pétain set up a permanent military tribunal to crush opposition in Algeria. In Algérois police swooped down on the homes of activists in communist and communist-aligned organisations: the PCA, JC, Friends of the Soviet Union, Secours populaire (Red Aid) and Union des jeunes filles d'Algérie (Union of Young Women of Algeria). One of these was Gilberte Chemouilli. The daughter of an Arabic-speaking Jewish father and a Christian mother, Chemouilli grew up in Bab el Oued. She joined the PCA on 1 October 1938 and in late 1939 was arrested and tortured along with three other comrades, including Paulette Lenoir. Similar raids took place in Oran and Constantine. The regime rounded up more than 10,000 alleged opponents across the country and threw them in prison, work camps or detention camps. PCA and PCF activists were interned in separate locations. 'It is not martyrs we need to make', Camus wrote, 'but free and respected citizens.'[16]

The PCA lost its general secretary – Boukort resigned in late 1939, citing disagreement with the Non-aggression Pact, and was soundly criticised by his former comrades. In January 1940 the PCA set up an underground central committee headed by Ouzegane that included Bouhali and the exiled Spanish communist, Ramón Via Fernandez.[17] PCA members with experience in the Spanish Civil War, such as Laban, Raffini and Smaïli, played an important role in this period – Laban and Raffini had been in the International Brigade, and Smaïli, a political commissar in the Spanish Republican Army.[18] They were assisted by Spanish communist refugees. They published several roneotype issues of *Lutte sociale*, but distribution was extremely difficult. Ouzegane developed links with French communist Roland Lenoir, eventually becoming closer to the French communists than to his PCA comrades who, having fought in Spain, developed ties with the Spanish communists. In April–May 1940 the entire central committee – except Via Fernandez – was arrested and interned. Bouhali and Ouzegane were sent to Djenien Bou Rezg. Gilberte Chemouilli and her three comrades were finally sentenced – Chemouilli to two years for acting as PCA liaison and working on the clandestine *Lutte sociale*.[19]

German troops invaded France in early June 1940, marching into Paris on 14 June. Despite the French army's modern tanks, its military ideas were out of date, and France lacked the air power to cover its ground troops. Prime Minister Paul Reynaud resigned, failing to get the support of his Vice-Premier, Philippe Pétain, and the French army commander, General Maxime Weygand, both of whom favoured accommodation with Germany. On 17 June Pétain announced an end to fighting. The next day, from London, General Charles de Gaulle broadcast the launch of the France libre or Free France movement. The French anthropologist Germaine Tillion formed the first of many resistance groups, which used propaganda, demonstrations and terror, accosting the enemy with guns, knives and dynamite.[20]

France's collapse caused shock waves felt across its empire and in Moscow. On 19 June the ECCI's Secretariat announced on behalf of the PCF: 'French communists ... will fight decisively and fiercely against the enslavement of our nation by foreign imperialists.'[21] On the 22nd France signed an armistice with Germany ceding northern France and the Atlantic seaboard. Pétain became head of state in unoccupied France, headquartered at Vichy, where he led a conservative, repressive regime that collaborated with the Nazis. The French republican slogan 'Liberty, Equality, Fraternity' was replaced by a 'national revolution' proclaiming the values of 'Work, Family, Fatherland'. Camus, who had moved to Paris after losing his newspaper post, described 'pro-German policies, a totalitarian-like constitution, an overwhelming fear of an impossible revolution: all of this to soothe an enemy who will crush us nevertheless and to save privileges which will not be threatened.'[22]

Vichy Algeria

The French began their great trek to escape the Nazis. Six million joined what became known as the Exodus, fleeing in cars, in carts, on bicycles and on foot. Workers left their jobs, and peasants their farms, their animals dying along the roadside, all moving east or south towards the Mediterranean.[23] Algiers teamed with Spanish Republicans and International Brigade veterans who had fled Spain after Franco's victory and with new arrivals fleeing the Nazis. Spanish refugees flooded into Oran. On one occasion Oran's mayor prevented a boatload of Spanish refugees from disembarking for so long that they ran out of food; local communists brought them food and water. But despite such humanitarian efforts, a huge portion of the local European population sympathised with the new regime – this included Jews until Pétain's anti-Semitic legislation came into force. Conservative settlers saw the Third Republic's defeat as a defeat for the left, while the *gros colons* who dominated the upper administrative echelons saw Vichy as a golden opportunity to profit through exports to the Nazis. Before the war Jacques Doriot's right-wing Parti populaire français was popular among recent European immigrants, but now far-right and fascist groups mushroomed. Right-wing youth groups caused mayhem in the streets and helped to purge Jews and other undesirables from the universities.[24]

The theme of empire figured prominently in the struggle over France's future. Both the Vichy regime and de Gaulle's Free French Forces laid claim to the empire. For Pétain's supporters the empire offered the possibility of post-war collaboration with Germany. For de Gaulle the empire held the hope of restoring a post-war France to its former glory.[25] Vichy's laws were applied more forcefully in North Africa than in the other French territories. His regime attacked those deemed to be enemies of France: Jews, communists, Freemasons and Algerian nationalists. In July Jean-Marie Charles Abrial became governor-general. In October the government abolished the Crémieux decree that had given French citizenship to Algerian Jews, who numbered some 3 per cent of the population; a new *Statut des juifs* denied Jews the right to engage in certain professions. So intense was anti-Semitism among European settlers that Algerian authorities exceeded the statute, even banning Jewish primary and secondary students from schools. Jews were denounced and dismissed from their jobs, providing employment opportunities for non-Jews. Anti-Semites rejoiced.[26]

The Vichy regime continued the emergency powers imposed at the war's start, protected settler interests and rejected political reform for Algerians. Internment was intensified with the use of several types of institutions: prisons housing criminal and political prisoners together; *bagnes*, work camps using forced labour; *groupements de travailleurs étrangers* for undesirable foreigners – the one at Aïn Sefra dubbed the French Buchenwald of North Africa – and *centres de séjour surveillé*, surveillance centres for local and foreign activists. Over the next two years some 7,000 to 10,000 people were interned.[27]

Nonetheless, France's unexpected fall signalled an unforeseen vulnerability. Some were jubilant when German troops entered Paris, but most were silent, a silence that authorities mistook for loyalty to the Pétainists. In occupied France Germans released Algerian political prisoners and opened a propaganda office in Paris focusing on the Maghreb. A small PPA group launched an underground wing to organise in the Algiers *casbah* and asked the Germans to help with training. But when Messali heard this, he rejected any collaboration with the Nazis.[28]

France's fall was certainly felt at the University of Algiers. Like the PCA, anyone connected with the PPA risked severe repression, but medical student Chawki Mostefaï nonetheless organised nationalist propaganda and recruited students into a university PPA cell. Mostefaï had attended primary school in Bordj Bou Arréridj and secondary school at the College of Sétif, graduating in 1938. At Sétif he was drawn into politics through a Jewish classmate named Simon Lévy, who invited him to join the Young Socialists. He and his friends attended Young Socialist Sunday meetings for two to three years, where Mostefaï learned about socialist and Marxist ideas. Mostefaï and his university comrades – they numbered about ten – felt that the German occupation signalled France's weakness, providing an opportune moment to take up arms. Aware that earlier insurrections against France had failed, thus strengthening colonialism's grip, they felt that there should be one coordinated insurrection, not many small ones. Thus they joined the PPA; Mostefaï represented the university students on the PPA's leading body.[29] Although the occupation certainly changed Algerian perspectives of French invincibility, nationalists were fragmented amongst themselves, as were opponents of the Vichy regime generally. Algerian notables opposed the banned PPA, which along with the PCA had been decimated by repression, and even those nationalists who had sympathised with the PCA now eschewed it. Indeed, Mostefaï saw the PCA as his 'mortal enemy'.[30]

Isolated, the tiny numbers of communists still at large met secretly.

In the east, Raffini recruited William Sportisse, raised in the low-income housing at Camp des Oliviers in Constantine. As a boy, William had been profoundly influenced by his older brothers Lucien and Bernard, who had organised the Constantine JC. By the time William joined the PCA, motivated by Germany's invasion of France, he was already attending Party meetings, and he distributed papers, engaged in anti-war propaganda and organised workers.[31] In the west, Thomas Ibanez, a teacher in Oran considered by Oranie comrades as 'the soul of the Communist Party', led another attempt to reorganise the PCA, working with Jean Torrecillas of Oran, Dr Jean Cattoir of Constantine, and Lisette Vincent in Algiers. Given the intense repression, it was impossible to hold regular meetings and elections. Ibanez and his comrades constituted themselves as a central committee composed mainly of people of Spanish descent. Thus, Gabrielle Gimenez, born in 1920 to working-class parents of Spanish heritage in Oran, joined the JC when she was 16 and later the underground PCA. Ibanez hoped to recruit Smaïli to the central committee and tried to engineer his escape from Serkadji Prison before he was interned down south.[32]

Once the USSR voiced its opposition to the war, its earlier anti-fascism was overshadowed by an anti-imperialist emphasis. The independence of colonies was once again seen as a means to weaken the imperial powers. The new approach empowered those supporting the call for independence, which had been dropped during the Popular Front era. These included Ibanez and Smaïli, who saw the call for independence as necessary to attract Algerians who had been overjoyed at France's defeat and naively hoped that Hitler could liberate them. But the pro-independence position conflicted with that of the PCF, and Roland Lenoir insisted that the PCA follow the 'nation in formation' thesis. Lenoir argued that the PCA should begin with immediate daily demands, then Algerian unity and finally unity of the Algerian and French peoples. Any discussion of independence should take place within that framework, he stressed.[33]

Ibanez and comrades were deep underground. Although their call for independence may have struck a chord amongst the presumably minute number of Algerians who heard it, the extreme repression meant that the PCA remained isolated and had great difficulties disseminating its few publications.[34] Nonetheless, on 28–29 September 1940, the PCA held a conference demanding independence. Smaïli was present; he criticised the conference preparation and the manner in which the central committee had constituted itself. Arguing that this did not reflect a commitment to Algerianisation, he and others refused to work with it. Laban acknowledged the problem, hoping to convince Smaïli to reconsider.[35]

Despite the discord, the conference agreed on a manifesto published in *Lutte sociale*'s November 1940 issue, a single sheet with a piece by Ibanez justifying the Non-aggression Pact. The PCA's manifesto put independence and a democratic Algerian government at the top of its list. It called for land for those who worked it, including Algerian and European peasants, smallholders and farm workers; industrial development; and schooling, hygiene and clean water for all. The achievement of those goals required unity, it enjoined its readers, both unity of Algerians, including Arabs, Kabyles, Mozabites, Jews and Europeans, and unity with the French nation. Led by both the PCA and the PCF, the Algerian and French peoples could defeat imperialism.[36]

The PCA was hit by another wave of arrests that November. Again, Ibanez avoided arrest. He sought the help of Via Fernandez and began working with Laban, Raffini, Odette Rossignol Dei, Mohamed Kateb, Lisette Vincent and Gimenez, who had fled to Algiers. More arrests followed, but with the help of Spanish communists, the group re-established contacts in Oranie and Constantinois, communicating with numeric codes and invisible ink, independence being their main priority.[37]

Maurice Laban was responsible for propaganda. He had been raised in the rural Constantinois town of Biskra. His parents taught at the 'native school', where he and his sister were the only European children, and where he became friends with the four Debabèche brothers, also future communists. Growing up amongst Algerians, Laban was entirely comfortable with the demands for Algerian unity and independence. He stressed the importance of rural organising in Kabylia and the Aurès and on the Algerian–Tunisian border, while acknowledging that the PCA had virtually no influence in rural areas or amongst the Algerian masses. Its support came mainly from dockers and from railway, tramway and building workers. Many Algerians had hoped for change after France's fall, but their conditions had not improved, and Laban hoped that the PCA could gain their support by demanding independence. *Lutte sociale* underlined this point, warning against PPA 'Hitlerians' whose support for German imperialism was a betrayal of the Algerian people and proclaiming, 'Long live the united and free Algerian people, long live Algerian independence.' The USSR had been vilified since the Non-aggression Pact, it added, yet Muslims in the USSR were happier than anywhere else.[38]

The next year brought more crackdowns. On 12 January 1941, Laban, Rossignol Dei and Kateb were arrested when the police discovered the *Lutte sociale* printing press. Gimenez, picked up *en route* to a meeting, was tortured with water, whippings and electricity. By then, the central committee was almost entirely composed of activists from Oranie. On 25 January Algerian soldiers in the French army mutinied and seized weapons. The authorities tried to keep news of the event out of the press, but rumours circulated, and the episode intensified the repression. 'The battle of Algiers against the Communists', proclaimed *L'Echo d'Alger* on 27 January.

Pétain's military justice continued. In March, 27 PPA leaders were condemned on sedition charges at a military tribunal in Algiers and sentenced to terms ranging from three years to sixteen for Messali – the extremely harsh sentences signalling the regime's desire to smash the PPA. The PCA's Ibanez and Debabèche were arrested in the same month. Via Fernandez again helped Communists in Oran, and Paul Caballero and François Serrano, both sons of Spanish immigrants, took over the leadership. The atmosphere of persecution permeated communist perceptions; they accused each other of being informants. Those seen as unconventional or as outsiders were the victims of such accusations. Ibanez and Smaïli were both accused, notwithstanding that Ibanez was imprisoned and the police were hunting Smaïli, and both were later sentenced to death: Ibanez had been a socialist until he joined the PCA in 1936; Smaïli had rejected the central committee's European dominance.[39]

Communists join the war effort

The international communist movement switched tracks once again in June 1941. The Soviet Union's neutrality had been sorely tested from summer 1940 as tensions with Nazi Germany mounted. When Germany invaded the USSR on 22 June 1941, the Soviets entered the war, which the Comintern now characterised as anti-fascist. Communists around the world were instructed to support the war effort; the French and Algerian Communist Parties followed suit, and the PCF joined the resistance. The Soviet need for allies necessitated a shift away from the earlier anti-imperial and anti-colonial stance.[40]

Somehow, the PCA found another printing press. Its propaganda subtly shifted to allow tactical alliances with the PPA. Distinguishing between PPA members who supported fascism and the PPA's 'sincere nationalists' – 'our brothers' – who remained faithful to the people, it commemorated the June 1936 Muslim Congress and called for another such show of unity around the call for independence. It was more than ever necessary that the Algerian people overcome their divisions to build a united anti-fascist front in North Africa and the Mediterranean, it argued, demanding '*l'union populaire*' for peace and national liberation. Those who continued to maintain divisions amongst the Algerian people were traitors: 'Fighting against them with the same ardour as against imperialism is the first step in constituting an Algerian National Front.'[41]

But the communists' pleas fell on deaf ears. Most Algerians were far too burdened with hardships to consider such appeals The young British-born and French-raised Harry Salem had arrived in Algeria around May–June 1940. Drawn into politics following the Nazi invasion of the USSR, Salem could not initially find the underground PCA. He became friends with José Aboulker, a medical student from a politically progressive bourgeois Jewish family, who described himself as a 'profoundly patriotic Jewish anti-fascist'. Anti-fascist resistance was carried on clandestinely in small groups – one base of operations in Algiers being the youth hostel where Salem lodged. He and other young people distributed anti-fascist flyers and eventually linked up with the JC.[42] Unusually for a European, Salem had Algerian friends. He learned that the war in Europe was not their primary interest, even if they did not want a German victory: 'it wasn't their war.' There was a marked similarity with black South African reactions to the war: while many sympathised with the anti-fascist struggle, they were more concerned with their own lack of democratic rights. Most black South Africans were indifferent to the war in Europe, as were most Algerians.[43]

Despite enormous difficulties, in 1941 the PCA held its fourth conference, paying homage to Kaddour Belkaïm, who on 27 July 1940 had died of typhus due to lack of medical care at the Djenien Bou Rezg camp. The party flagellated itself for its alleged shortcomings: it was demographically unrepresentative, sectarian and suffered from defective leadership; its distribution of documents was irregular, leaving outlying branches without adequate guidance; its finances were chaotic.[44] It softened its call for independence to reflect Thorez's thesis: 'Towards the independence of Algeria ... a nation in formation. Forward to a democratic Algeria alongside France of the Popular Front. Today, liberty of France and also liberty of Algeria.'[45]

National liberation could not simply be a struggle of Muslims against Europeans, the central committee insisted. Thorez's 'nation in formation' thesis remained relevant, it argued, particularly as the abolition of the Crémieux Decree and Vichy's anti-Semitic laws laid the basis for a backlash against Jews – people remembered the 1934 Constantine massacre. It proposed the return of land to peasants, sharecroppers and farm workers alongside calls for an anti-imperialist Algerian front and 'an independent, democratic and popular Algerian republic'. International proletarianism must take priority over pan-Islamic utopianism – hence, the unity of French and Muslim workers against French and Muslim exploiters.[46]

Despite the communists' pro-war stance, 1941 and 1942 saw acute repression. A military tribunal judged 81 Spanish communists on 6 February 1942 in Oran and meted out severe punishments. There were 21 who were condemned *in absentia*. Four of these were sentenced to death, while most of the others received 20-year sentences, the lightest sentence for this group being 15 years of forced labour. Of those who were present at their trial, 17 received sentences of 10–20 years, while five got off with one year and a fine. The remaining 38 were acquitted.[47]

PCA members fared no better. Lisette Vincent, arrested on 16 August 1941, was tortured and held in Serkadji, one of 61 communists accused of reconstituting the banned PCA. The 61 were tried in a military tribunal in Algiers on 9 February 1942. About half of the 55 men and six women were of Spanish descent, and eight were Algerians.[48] Eight of the 61 died in detention before trial. In March 1942, 41 of them, including seven Algerians, were convicted. Of these, six – Vincent, Ibanez, Raffini, Ditmar Danelius, Emile Touati and Smaïli *in absentia* – were sentenced to death; nine, including Gimenez, to indefinite forced labour; 14 to forced labour for 7–20 years; 12 to prison for 1–5 years. Laban, Rossignol Dei, Yvonne Saillen and Isabel Vial – a teacher from Oran who later hung herself in prison – received varying sentences. Another military tribune in Algiers targeted trade union leaders and activists – dockers and building, metal and postal workers, amongst others. Other arrests and trials took place in Oran and Constantine. Via Fernandez avoided arrest, set up a new underground group and established contact with Marseille. The PCF sent Maurice Deloison to assist. The contrast with South Africa, where communist support for the war protected them from internment could not have been starker.[49]

Some were sent in chains to Lambèse, the site of a second-century Roman military base and a French prison built in 1855. One was Jacques Salort, a young CGT activist from a humble background, who worked with Saillen and Ibanez and helped rebuild the underground PCA in Algiers. He was arrested in June 1941, tortured, imprisoned in Serkadji, condemned during the trial of the 61, sent by train in a chained group of four men by four to Batna and then another eleven kilometres to Lambèse. The conditions were brutal – isolation, hunger, cold and snow. Prisoners were kept in separate cells, which they could leave for only 15 minutes a day, and were forbidden to speak to each other. They could read, but were only allowed to write one letter a month. Salort met Messali and other PPA activists, some twenty activists from the Tunisian Neo-Destour Party and Italian communists captured in Tunis. They were eventually able to mingle, but Messali, ever suspicious of communists, warned his followers to keep their distance.[50]

In May 1942 the PCF established the anti-Vichy Front national in France. In Algeria public pressure over the fate of communists condemned to death made itself felt on Governor-General Yves-Charles Châtel, who had taken over in November 1941.[51] Baya Bouhoune Allaouchiche became a liaison for the 27 French deputies imprisoned at Maison Carrée. Born 1920 in Algiers, Allaouchiche had French citizenship due to her father's First World War military service. Her family were nationalists with traditional attitudes about the role of women: she left French school at eleven and entered an arranged marriage at fourteen. But attracted by the PCA's stance on religious and racial equality, she rebelled and found the underground party, even though this caused tensions within her family.

Communists worked in risky conditions, disseminating flyers along with the occasional underground paper from France. *Lutte sociale* appeared sporadically, printed either on two sides of a letter-sized sheet or on one side of an even smaller sheet, and sometimes its distribution led to brawls between communists and nationalists in areas where nationalists were strong. As the Nazi threat against the USSR continued, PCA publications gave more coverage to the fight against Hitler, especially once the Battle of Stalingrad began on 17 July 1942. But the international focus also reflected the lack of cadres available to write on local issues – the repeated waves of arrests had taken their toll, the authorities were pleased to report.[52]

The Anglo-American landing

The United States' entry into the war in December 1941 precipitated debates about how to penetrate Nazi territory. North Africa became a southern front. On 7–8 November 1942 some 76,000 Anglo-American troops landed in Morocco and Algeria in Operation Torch, capturing the ports of Casablanca, Oran and Algiers. There were already about 120,000 French troops in North Africa, 50,000 in Algeria, 55,000 in Morocco and 15,000 in Tunisia. In Algiers, José Aboulker and other resistance partisans helped plan the landing. Gilberte Chemouilli, released from prison on 14 July 1942, resumed her political activities after the Allied landing, working as a secretary for the PCA and *Alger républicain* and marrying Bouali Taleb, the communist leader of the Union des jeunesses démocratiques d'Algérie (Union of Democratic Youth of Algeria, UJDA).[53]

Imprisoned communists might have hoped that the Allies would free them, but political intrigues between the Allied forces and the French predominated. De Gaulle's Comité national français (French National Committee, CNF), formed in September 1941, had been recognised by the Soviet Union, but the Americans were hostile. By the time of the Allied landing, de Gaulle's Free French Forces had proved their fighting ability, and later that month de Gaulle's group signed an agreement with the PCF. Antagonistic to de Gaulle, in December 1942 the Americans ensured that General Henri Giraud took command in North Africa. Giraud cooperated with de Gaulle, although their relationship was never easy.[54]

The Anglo-American operation had two principal repercussions for France and Algeria. Firstly, it propelled the Axis forces to occupy the remainder of free France. From 11 November German and Italian troops occupied southern France and Tunisia. Secondly, it catalysed the resurgence of Algerian nationalism. France's fall had already signalled a weak state. Now it was seen as dependant on the United States and Britain, co-authors of the August 1941 Atlantic Charter that called for the right of all peoples to self-determination. The Allied landing raised Algerian hopes that the United States and Britain might influence France to implement reforms reflecting the Atlantic Charter.[55]

Students at the University of Algiers were energised, and Mostefaï tried to recruit them to his PPA cell. But they also talked to the communists, who asked the students to explain their political doctrine. The students would return to Mostefaï with that question. He replied that the struggle needed the participation of all for a 'national objective' – it was not just the struggle of a few. The Muslim religion also had a political dimension, he argued, while recognising the need to adapt Islam to changing conditions. The communists then asked the students about their views on class. Mostefaï had no answer. He asked the PPA leadership but they also had difficulties: Islamic education did not prepare them for such questions. So Mostefaï replied that to liberate themselves from the French, they had to take a road in common with other sections of society. They needed an overarching strategy that prioritised independence. The question of socialism or capitalism would be decided after independence, when they could organise a pluralist society. The Allied landing sparked renewed interest in such debates.[56]

When Governor-General Châtel announced plans to conscript Algerian men, Ferhat Abbas and other Algerian leaders responded with a 'Message from the Algerian Muslim Representatives to the Responsible Authorities' – which included the French and Allied forces. Written on 20 December 1942, it noted that Algerians were deprived of their rights and liberties, while pointing out the United States' commitment to self-determination. As a precondition for Muslim support for the war effort, it asked that a conference of Muslim leaders be convened to draw up a statute of political, economic and social rights. Only on the basis of such a statute were Abbas and his colleagues prepared to promise Algerian support. The French refused to accept the message, however, until it had been addressed to the French authorities and reworded to ask for 'liberation within an "essentially French framework"'. Even then the French were negative. Undeterred, in February 1943 Abbas and his colleagues began drafting the *Manifeste du peuple algérien* (*Manifesto of the Algerian People*).[57]

The Soviets won the Battle of Stalingrad on 2 February 1943, a massive victory costing more than 1.5 million casualties and a turning point in the war. Prisoners at Lambèse celebrated, and although their hopes for imminent release were dashed, their conditions improved. Through Soviet pressure, political conditions eased enough to allow the PCF and PCA some freedom of action. On 7 February the 27 PCF deputies were released from Maison Carrée, where they had been transferred in 1941; other communists had to wait longer. War conditions prevented the PCF deputies from returning to France. Since the PCA detainees had not yet been released, the PCF deputies dominated PCA affairs over the next several weeks, promoting French and Algerian unity against fascism.[58]

Thus, as Algerian nationalism was on the upswing, with nationalists demanding independence, the PCA stressed the Nazi threat and kept independence on the back burner. *Lutte sociale*'s 21 February issue paid homage to Stalin and the Red Army. *Alger républicain* reappeared three days later with the slogan: 'All for the victory over Hitlerian Germany.' The paper was managed by Paul Schmitt, a socialist from Oran, and Michel Rouzé, a left-wing Paris-born journalist who tricked his way out of German captivity and, at Schmitt's invitation, came to Algeria. The staff included PCA member Joseph Parrès, condemned to death under the Vichy regime but later liberated, and a few Spanish republicans. The Algerians were few but significant: the communist Smaïli, the socialist Mohammed el Aziz Kessous and the journalist Abdelkader Safir.[59] Indeed, Mostefaï thought the PCA's influence was 'fairly big'. It was legal again and could hold meetings, while the PPA was 'outside the law'. Nonetheless, the PPA undoubtedly had an impact, and some Algerian communists joined.[60]

On 31 March 1943 Abbas's manifesto was sent to Governor-General Marcel Peyrouton, who had replaced Châtel after the Allied landing. The manifesto called for the end of colonisation; the right to self-determination; a new democratic constitution; full Algerian participation in government; liberty and absolute equality of all people, without distinction of race or religion; suppression of feudal property; implementation of agrarian reform and recognition of Arabic as an official language alongside French.[61] Accepting the manifesto as a 'basis for future reforms', Peyrouton appointed a commission of conservative and moderate Algerians to draft a set of demands that could be readily implemented. Undeterred, Abbas sponsored an *Additif au manifeste*, a condensed and more radical supplement to the original manifesto. This demanded, at the war's end, the establishment of a sovereign Algerian state on the basis of a constitution drawn up through a constituent assembly based on universal suffrage of all inhabitants of the country.[62]

In the meantime, the resistance in France had coalesced into an underground movement called Combat, which published a clandestine newspaper of the same name. La France combattante (Fighting France), formed in July 1942, signalled the alliance of de Gaulle's external resistance and internal resistance in occupied and free France. Camus, whose novel *L'Etranger* had been published in 1942, joined the resistance in 1943 and began writing for *Combat*.[63] French communists, socialists and Gaullists launched Fighting France in Algeria in late March 1943, when most – but not all – of Pétain's legislation was abolished. The abrogation of the *Statut des juifs* and the restoration of the Crémieux Decree were stalled on the grounds that this might antagonise Muslims when their support was needed for the war. That month the imprisoned PCA members were released. Over the war's course the PCA had lost experienced activists. Belkaïm, Serrano, Torrecillas and others had died in prisons or detention camps.[64] Others, such as the brothers Bernard and William Sportisse, were mobilised into the army after the Allied landing. But because Jews were still subject to the racist Vichy laws, they were mobilised into Jewish sections of the French army to work on specific tasks. In Constantinois Jewish soldiers were charged with rebuilding roads near the Tunisian border and housed in a former Vichy internment camp for Jews. But they rebelled – they wanted to fight, not do construction. General Giraud opposed re-establishing the Crémieux decree; Jewish soldiers, including the Sportisse brothers, were sent to West Africa to obtain troops.[65]

The leading Algerian communists now included Bouhali, Ouzegane, Smaïli, Mohammed Marouf, Ahmed Amara and Djamal Sfindja. Ouzegane was freed in May, and Bouhali in June. Once in Algiers, Ouzegane renewed his links with the PCF, promoting its anti-nationalist position. Thus, he told a group of Algerians in Sétif shortly after his release: 'It is through union with your French comrades that you will obtain your rights. We refuse to collaborate with those who trick the masses and try to commit them to a dangerous path.' Those demanding independence, Ouzegane insisted, were 'false nationalists' promoting the Algerian bourgeoisie's interests. A special May Day 1943 issue of *Lutte sociale* called on Algerians to crush fascism and liberate France. An article entitled 'Produire, produire' urged production for the war effort.⁶⁶ Militaristic discourse became normal. On 24 May *Lutte sociale* heralded the Giraud–de Gaulle accord; only 'a people united, an army united' could go into battle with enthusiasm, it claimed.⁶⁷ The PCA appealed for equal rights: like the French, it urged, Algerians deserved Liberty (from prison), Equality (with all the civic rights given to French citizens) and Fraternity. There was no mention of independence.⁶⁸

Despite American efforts, Fighting France's formation facilitated de Gaulle's installation in Algiers on 30 May, the same month that Tunis was liberated. A provisional government led by de Gaulle and Giraud, the Comité français de libération nationale (French National Liberation Committee, CFLN), was set up on 3 June 1943 at Algiers, which became the capital of Free France. The Ordinance of 1 July 1943 restored the PCA to legality. French Communists resumed open political activity that month, launching the weekly *Liberté*. It focused on France and the war against fascism. The first issue called for Algerian civil rights and French and Algerian union, and Ouzegane expressed communist thanks to the Allies.⁶⁹

The CFLN became the de facto government in exile. It tolerated communists, but had no Algerian commissioners. Socialists and Gaullists rejected the demands for complete equality and self-determination. De Gaulle believed firmly that France's post-war prestige depended on its empire; his government placed Abbas under house arrest and pressured Algerian leaders into dropping the call for independence. On 25 July 1943 a demonstration at Philippeville led to 12 deaths and 50 serious injuries – all of Algerians – a sign of simmering tensions in the region.⁷⁰

The communists rapidly dominated the media. *Alger républicain* reappeared on 2 October, and in December the PCA launched *Algérie nouvelle* to replace *Lutte sociale*. Both *Liberté* and *Algérie nouvelle* achieved considerable success, selling respectively 80,000 and 45,000 copies, the biggest sales of any North African newspapers, even selling to army personnel. Many Europeans, fed up with Vichy, turned an interested ear to the communists.⁷¹ Using the media, communists tried to weaken de Gaulle's power within the CFLN, playing him off against Giraud. But their efforts backfired after Giraud resigned, leaving de Gaulle in control. Despite this setback, communist influence grew. Their rhetoric became more militant and peppered with personalised attacks. Their demand for equality for all alienated European supporters, whom they derided as having a colonialist mentality. Yet they succeeded in becoming part of the CFLN, their first participation in a French government.⁷²

The Comintern's dissolution

The Comintern's dissolution on 22 May 1943 had shocked the communist world. Since 1939 the Comintern had effectively been an appendage of Soviet foreign policy, and the decision, taken as the war was changing course, was clearly Stalin's. Most likely it reflected his desire for post-war concessions from the Western Allies – renunciation of world revolution in exchange for post-war recognition of a Soviet sphere of influence. From then on national sections were to use their own judgement about their particular situations.

Yet the Comintern's disbanding did not mean greater autonomy for the PCA. The war and with it support for France remained the defining features of communist activities. The PCF delegates, led by François Billoux and Etienne Fajon, were represented on the PCA's central committee and on the CFLN. Promoting the idea of a patriotic union around de Gaulle, they sought to make the PCF into 'a big party of State'. Within the PCA they reinforced the primacy of France's liberation and the 'nation in formation' thesis. To this end, the PCA was to call for the unity of all to end the war, while supporting the daily struggles of the oppressed. This was seen at a communist mass meeting on 29 August.[73]

Attended by some 3,000 people – Algerians and Europeans of all classes – the meeting took place at the Majestic cinema in Algiers. Billoux proposed revitalising the Party through a purge and pushing forward with the war in France. It was not a question of whether tomorrow the French republic would be more or less democratic or social, he argued. If they waited, France would only be 'a republic of cadavers'. Ouzegane attacked Abbas and his manifesto: Abbas demanded autonomy but lacked the means to achieve his aim, he told the crowd, whereas the communists had the Red Army. Ouzegane supported independence, but this was not the moment to demand it, he insisted.[74]

This stance ensured the PCA's continued marginalisation from Algerian politics. After the Allied landing Ouzegane and other communists spoke at Larbaâ, where a young Sadek Hadjerès was in the audience. Born 1928 at Larbaâ Nath Irathen (formerly Fort-National), Hadjerès was the son of a teacher who subscribed to the progressive *La Voix des humbles*. Speaking Berber at home, Arabic in the streets and French at school, Hadjerès was raised in urban society and in the rural mountain culture of his family village where he spent the summers. Schooled at Médéa and Blida, where the PPA had a few partisans but was not yet implanted, when the College of Blida was closed to accommodate Allied troops, he returned to Larbaâ. He and his friends were happy with Ouzegane's criticisms of colonialism, the police and the *bachagas*, but they were struck by his virulent anti-nationalism – in fact, this was how Hadjerès learned that there was a nationalist movement. After the meeting Hadjerès and three others visited a sympathetic European communist. They asked him why the PCA did not demand independence. He replied that Algerians could not ask for independence because their women were veiled. Yet Hadjerès's mother was veiled, and he knew that she understood the need for liberation. He felt that European communists were speaking to Algerians without trying to understand their culture or world view. Indeed, the PCA's harsh anti-nationalism angered many Algerians. Despite the PCA's branding of nationalists as pro-Nazi, many nationalists had fought against fascism in France and Italy, and the PCA's words were an insult.[75]

The PCF's attempts to reorient the PCA bore fruit in a conference at Hussein Dey, near Algiers, on 14–15 September 1943. Billoux presided; Bouhali was the first secretary, assisted by Ouzegane. The PCA issued an *Appel au peuple algérien* (Call to the Algerian People) – its reply to Abbas's manifesto – that demanded full democratic rights for Algerians and the abolition of all political inequalities, but not independence. It stressed the primacy of joint struggle with France against the Nazis. Yet Algerians released from camps and coming out from underground could not understand why Algeria should prioritise France's liberation before its own.[76]

The PCA's promotion of a patriotic union between France and Algeria was furthered by the formidable André Marty. Seeking to revive the North African communist parties, Marty arrived in Algiers in October 1943 – when the Crémieux Decree was finally reinstated – bringing with him Stalin's prestigious support. A hero of the 1919 Black Sea mutiny, Marty became a communist deputy in 1924, rising up the PCF and Comintern ranks. From 1936 to 1938 he was in charge of the International Brigade in Spain. In 1937 he headed the Moscow-based investigation into problems in the Communist Party of South Africa. His arrival in Algeria indicated a hardening of the communist position on a united war effort and signalled the importance, both for the Soviet Union and the PCF, of carefully choosing the PCA's leading figures. Billoux felt that both Bouhali and Zannettacci placed too much emphasis on Algerian rights.[77] Marty wasted no time. He set up a party school with Etienne Fajon and Roger Garaudy, where he targeted Laban's 'nationalist deviation', and organised a conference of the three North African communist parties, which took place in Algiers on 30 November. Billoux opened the conference, followed by Ouzegane, who stressed unity with France against fascism, opposed the call for independence and criticised the PPA and Muslim elected officials. Thorez's 'nation in formation' thesis was reaffirmed.[78]

In some respects the PCA looked healthy. The communist press was thriving: *Liberté*'s sales topped 100,000 copies. Notably, the PCA was the only ethnically mixed political party, and its European enrolment, mainly working-class, was growing, attracted by the communist stance on the war. PCA and JC cells were springing up across country. Both Young Communists and young Algerians joined the UJDA, especially in Constantinois. These Algerians were either sympathetic to the PCA or at least not anti-communist. Through their participation in the UJDA, European communists gained insight into Algerian needs and viewpoints.

Communist women formed the Jeunes filles communistes d'Algérie (Communist Girls of Algeria) and the Union des femmes d'Algérie (Union of Women of Algeria, UFA), launched in 1944. Open to women without distinction of national origin, the UFA was initially led by European communist women, notably Alice Sportisse and Lise Oculi. Initially it was assumed that European women would fight fascism, and Algerian women would fight for Algerian rights. Gradually the UFA attracted growing numbers of Algerian women who, avoiding organisations with men, felt able to mix with other women. It responded more directly to their interests, and over the next few years its leadership became more ethnically representative. Addressing meetings with ease in French, Arabic and Berber, Baya Allaouchiche became a leading UFA voice.[79]

Overall, however, the PCA's recruitment of Europeans, reinforced by the presence of PCF cadres, meant continued underestimation of the national question and qualification of independence as provisional. Many of the communists recruited during this period, products of Fajon's party school, thought that Nazism's defeat would lead to a socialist revolution in Europe and that this in turn would lead to Algeria's liberation. The Soviet Union may have been sceptical about post-war socialist prospects – hence its concern with carving out a sphere of influence – but these young people idealistically believed that socialism was imminent. That was certainly Harry Salem's view. Semi-underground, he was very involved in the JC and the UJDA. He had proved himself a very successful editor and administrator at the UJDA's *La Jeune Algérie*, and in 1943 he began translating English news releases for the *Agence France-Afrique*. There he met Lucette Larribère, from the well-known communist family in Oran, and through her, Gilberte Serfaty, who came from an indigenous Jewish family in Mostaganem and who had been forced by the Vichy laws to suspend her English studies at the University of Algiers. The two women joined the PCA cell at *France-Afrique*, and became active in the UFA. Another indigenous Jew, fifteen-year-old Daniel Timsit, became involved in the JC that same year: 'I was an internationalist before being national,' he later recalled. 'No more barriers, no more Jews, Muslims, Christians. We were humanity.'[80]

Salem sensed that communists and nationalists were working from two world views: while the PCF and PCA gave primacy to the USSR and its interests, Algerian nationalists looked towards the USA, which proclaimed the rights of peoples to self-determination. Marty saw Algeria through the prism of Soviet and French interests, supporting Ouzegane's anti-nationalism and confirming him as the PCA's political secretary. Others, such as Estorges, felt Marty's displeasure. The Arabic-speaking secretary of the PCA's Constantine region, Estorges had long felt that the communists neglected anti-colonial work. He had many contacts with the *'ulama*, including Ben Badis, about whom Marty was sceptical. Marty had also been furious to learn that Zannettacci and trade unionist Abdallah, who was close to the *'ulama*, had organised the PCA and CGT at Bône around the call for independence. Had it not been for Billoux's intervention, Zannettacci would have been expelled.[81]

France clearly expected to retain its empire after the war. On 12 December 1943 de Gaulle announced his aims of reasserting French control in Indochina and reforming Algeria, setting up a commission to develop an Algerian reform programme. Representing the PCA, Ouzegane called for French citizenship and political rights for all Algerians and complete administrative reform. Neither education nor language should justify exclusion from French citizenship, he stressed. Through Arabic language radio, newspapers and lectures, Algerians were sufficiently politically sophisticated to participate fully and effectively as French citizens. When Bendjelloul asked Ouzegane for his view on Abbas' idea of Algerian citizenship, Ouzegane replied that communists believed that the Algerian nation was still in formation and that the mixture of the European, Arab and Berber peoples would produce an Algerian race and nation. He underlined the need to avoid opposition between Algerians and Europeans, not all of whom were exploiters.[82]

De Gaulle's response to Abbas' manifesto was crystallised in the Ordinance of 7 March 1944, which Governor-General Catroux, replacing Peyrouton, had taken the lead in formulating. This expanded the Algerian electorate, the first such change since the Jonnart Law, granting French citizenship to 65,000 additional Algerians without mandating a change in their personal status as Muslims and giving all Algerian men the right to vote in a second Muslim college. After France's liberation other Algerians could become French citizens based on terms determined by a national constituent assembly. Overall, the ordinance meant that Algerian representation in all elected bodies increased to 40 per cent. The *indigénat* was abolished, making Algerians juridically equal to Europeans.[83]

But the ordinance only intensified European–Algerian polarisation. Most Europeans, increasingly anxious about their future, saw the ordinance as a sign of de Gaulle's weakness. It was welcomed by Bendjelloul and the conservative *élus*, on the one side, and communists and socialists, on the other. The communist *Liberté* described the increase in suffrage as 'a big step forward', even if not enough.[84] However, for most Algerians – who might have supported such concessions in 1936 – they were too little, too late; this included the Messalites, Abbas and his followers, and most of the reformist *'ulama*.

One week after the ordinance became law, these groups came together and launched the Amis du manifeste et de la liberté (Friends of the Manifesto and Freedom, AML) in Sétif, Abbas' home town and since 1942 the capital of Algerian nationalism. The AML aimed to spread the manifesto's ideas, especially those of Algerian nationhood and federation with a reformed France, to contest ruling-class privileges and expose the reactionary nature of French and Algerian elites. Both Bendjelloul's pro-assimilationist supporters and the communists rejected it. But the reformist *'ulama* gave their support, and Messali advised his followers to join. The PCA was profoundly out of sync with Algeria's nationalists.[85]

PCF–PCA dynamics

The AML grew rapidly. Political ideas spread quickly in the densely populated urban quarters and penetrated the rural areas through teachers. Algerian teachers associated with *La Voix des humbles* preached social justice, ideas that circulated alongside and sometimes intersected with notions of peasant struggle and *jihad*, while communist teachers spread notions of equality. The Arabic word *istiqlal* – independence – became part of the popular vocabulary. Members of the banned PPA flocked to the AML. Colonial authorities vainly hoped that Abbas' idea of federation within a French framework would outstrip Messali's call for independence.[86]

The AML's success pressured the communists. The PCF recovered far faster than did the PCA. The PCF's North African delegation convened a plenary session on 30 March, calling for communist entry into government, the arming of patriots, support for the war effort and national unity.[87] Communists faced harsh conditions, Marty conceded: 'the political climate in Algiers is very different from that in France, and the anti-communist intrigues are too strong.' Algerians were disappointed with the delayed and inadequate reforms, while the *colons* dreamed of making Algeria into a new Versailles against the French people. But Algerians would support aid for France if their legitimate demands were satisfied. Lozeray insisted that the PCA improve its organisational work. Ouzegane acknowledged these criticisms. The delegation agreed on political education for pro-French policy. Marty concluded that 'the question of independence at this moment would only be a slogan of the enemy'. It was critical to ensure communist participation in the CFLN along the lines agreed by the central committee as soon as possible. The resolutions were agreed unanimously.[88]

The PCF's strength and resources *vis-à-vis* the PCA enabled it to shape the smaller party's positions. In May 1944 Jean Cristofol, the PCF deputy for Marseille, became the PCA's political instructor. He criticised communists in Constantinois who were close to the *'ulama* and who thought the PCA line was too French. Laban was given an official warning, Bendib and Younès were criticised as too soft on religion, and Estorges was placed under Bouhali's supervision. Smaïli had died in a road accident on 29 January. The second conference of the communist parties of North Africa took place on 15 May 1944, presided over by Marty, who called for the total union of France and its overseas territories. Marty endorsed Ouzegane as the PCA's leading Algerian. Ouzegane expelled Lisette Vincent in June. When the Belcourt cell demanded an explanation for her expulsion, it was dissolved.[89]

Allied forces landed in Normandy on 6 June 1944, as the Red Army was beating back the Nazis in the east. Just three days earlier the CFLN had prudently declared itself the provisional government of the French Republic with de Gaulle at its head. De Gaulle's forces landed in northern France on 14 June; Allied forces landed in the south on 15 August. The Resistance began fighting in Paris on 19 August; by the 25th Paris was liberated. The euphoria was palpable, the belief that liberation would allow a 'new France', genuine. *Combat*'s slogan, 'From Resistance to Revolution', expressed the optimism, while Jean-Paul Sartre and Simone de Beauvoir planned *Les Temps modernes*, a journal committed to the revolutionary role of writers. De Gaulle arrived in Paris with American troops. Marty and the French communist delegation followed. De Gaulle formed a provisional government in September; Yves Chataigneau became Algeria's new governor-general. France was in turmoil over the punishment of Nazi collaborators. Camus agonised, but despite his horror of capital punishment, he endorsed it for the most extreme war crimes.[90]

The PCA was not left on its own, however. Three leading French communists, Joanny Berlioz, Roger Garaudy and Antoine Demusois became instructors, and Léon Feix, the PCF's North African delegate.

Henriette Neveu became *Liberté*'s editor; her husband Raymond Neveu, secretary of the Algiers region. The French communist André Moine and Caballero and Ouzegane became PCA secretaries. Marty returned briefly for the PCA's next conference on 23–24 September. Not to be outdone by the AML, the PCA had launched the rival Amis de la démocratie (Friends of Democracy), which attacked the PPA's call for an 'impossible independence' and accused the nationalists of being in the pay of the United States and Britain. The Friends of Democracy stressed equal rights and immediate demands. It asked Algerians to continue fighting fascism, to produce more, to approach helpful European workers and to aid the French people. It castigated the *'cent seigneurs'* (one hundred lords) controlling the country's largest landholdings. Ouzegane pointed to the PCA's rising membership as evidence of success. Its membership had doubled from 2,500–3,000 in 1939 to more than 5,000 in 1944. However, the new members were disproportionately European; some were probably attracted by the party's seeming proximity to power through its relationship with the PCF.[91]

The communists did receive overtures from Algerians, however. Ben Ali Boukort had contacted the PCA in 1943 and, arrested in October 1944, he wrote to Berlioz from prison. He had 'kept a communist attitude', he informed Berlioz. It was difficult 'to abandon the fruit of 15 years of activism and Marxist–Leninist education because he had been mistaken in the understanding of an event'. If the party supported Muslim victims of repression, he suggested, he was certain that the disagreements between communists and nationalists would disappear and that a fruitful collaboration would develop, 'if one could overcome a certain sectarianism'. But Boukort's olive branch was ignored.[92]

Whatever the PCF's official stance, in practice communists were compelled to respond to the mounting calls for independence. A confidential report of the US Military Intelligence Service noted: 'many of the communist agitators who are active throughout Algeria are preaching an independent Algeria ... their public statements do not conform with the word-of-mouth propaganda which they spread among the Arabs.' That communists conceded to this pressure, thought the analyst, indicated the strength of nationalist feeling. Thus, just as nationalists were forced to think about doctrine because of communist pressure, so communists were compelled to respond to the rising clamour for independence.[93]

In October 1944 Camus – now *Combat*'s editor – replied to the Minister of Colonies' appeal that France must 'conquer hearts' for a new colonial era. Camus maintained that the European settlers, so many of whom had supported the Vichy regime, were the 'most serious obstacle' to equality in Algeria. 'We will not find real support in our colonies', he wrote, 'until we convince them that their interests coincide with ours and that we do not have two policies: one granting justice to the people of France and the other confirming injustice toward the Empire.'[94]

Algerian nationalism in ferment

Indeed, nationalism was thriving precisely because of this double standard. In September 1944 the AML had launched its weekly *Egalité*, which soon outsold all Algerian and European newspapers. The PPA stepped up its underground work, forming paramilitary cells of six to eight men in Kabylia and Constantine, setting up university and secondary school cells around the country and campaigning against conscription. The PPA's *L'Action algérienne* urged its youthful constituency to organise for total independence; its November issue derided the PCA as a PCF region. The *'ulama* organised youth in schools and scouting clubs.[95] Sadek Hadjerès had joined the scouts at Blida through a Jewish school friend persecuted under the Vichy regime, at Larbaâ he became a scout leader. As the nationalist movement developed, the scouts were drawn under its fold.[96]

Misery provided fertile conditions for the nationalists. Algiers' *casbah* was a case in point. Buildings that had once housed the traditional Muslim bourgeoisie were now rented out room by room to entire families, resulting in extraordinary overcrowding. Three-quarters of the *casbah*'s inhabitants had been born in rural areas; two-thirds of those were from Kabylia. Some retained small plots of land, and most kept their rural ties, living near those from the same region. Rural poverty and unemployment drove them to the city. Yet the *casbah*'s youth faced long-term unemployment.[97]

The situation worsened each year. The 1944–45 winter was abnormally dry, yielding a dismal harvest the following summer that compounded the misery of unemployment and the shortages of manufactured goods. The UFA organised women around social issues, demonstrating against high food prices and discriminatory food rationing. Growing up in Constantine, Noureddine Abdelmoumène recalled that the government gave them ration coupons for food and wheat. But the wheat was very bad; people became sick.[98] Young Algerians were ready for a radical message. The international climate raised their hopes – the approach of the war's end, the discussions for a post-war United Nations, the preparations for the new Arab League, all signalled change.

By early 1945 nationalist aspirations were stronger than ever. 'There can be no doubt that the Nationalist movement ... is substantially stronger at the present time that it was at the outbreak of the war', reported the US Military Intelligence Service. 'It is also beyond question that there is a real discontent ... throughout Algeria and ... an acute food shortage. It seems probable that there will be minor disturbances resulting from this discontent during the course of the next few months'. Nonetheless, it doubted 'that the Nationalist movement [wa]s capable of a successful uprising in the foreseeable future unless a major outside power step[ped] in to assist them.'[99] In February the British consul-general reported European fears of an Arab uprising as soon as the British and American troops left. Small European farmers were allegedly selling their land and moving into towns. There were also signs of 'increased communist activity'. A joint PCF–PCA meeting that month extolled the Red Army's virtues, and on the 26th Fajon held a conference of North African communists in Algiers.[100]

The ferment even reached the Mzab, where the PCA claimed a cell, and *Liberté*, 'along with a little communist leaflet distributed in Ghardaïa and called "Tomorrow's Mzab" continued to attack dishonest caïds and other feudal elements'. After four years of banishment, Sliman Boudjenah published *Kitab el-Ferkad* (*El-Ferkad's Book*), an Arabic-language booklet on politics and morality that stressed the need to turn ideas into action. Returning to Ghardaïa in the early 1940s, he became a notary. With his red fez and his spectacles, he epitomised the modern intellectual, yet his vision of modernity was iconoclastic. He argued that if the Mozabites convinced France to honour its 1853 convention guaranteeing Mozabite autonomy, they could pull all Algeria behind them, and independence would follow. A local barber named Mella, a friend of Boudjenah's and a communist sympathiser, clandestinely distributed communist newspapers. Nonetheless, Mozabite society was very solidaristic, and political parties were considered divisive. While the PPA had individual supporters, it was not implanted in the community. Nor was there a trade union tradition. Most Mozabites were small self-sufficient cultivators, and the men migrated to towns and worked in commerce. Yet there was a strong tradition of redistribution, and conspicuous consumption was frowned upon. Community ties far outweighed class, and new ideas penetrated the society only with great difficulty.[101]

The AML's first congress, on 2–4 March 1945, was attended by representatives from 165 sections from around the country; its membership had swelled, with claims of 350,000 or even 500,000 members. The communists were markedly absent, having accepted de Gaulle's provisional government; they were envisioning joint work with the socialists – the traditional French left alliance. The PPA, however, was there in force sufficient to marginalise Abbas and his supporters, who favoured autonomy and federation to France. The congress voted overwhelmingly for independence. International events strengthened the credibility of the pro-independence movement: the Arab League, launched in Cairo that same month, promoted the sovereignty and independence of Arab nations.[102]

Tensions mounted. The PPA called on Algerians to avenge their martyrs and defend the party that would bring liberation.[103] Within the AML divisions deepened. Plots and rumours of plots abounded, alongside public calls for Algerians to unite behind Messali and Abbas. An AML circular of late March 1945 announced that it expected to move from passive resistance to violence and recommended that Algerians arm themselves. The nationalist movement 'has acquired a certain cohesion and a more definite orientation', reported the British consul-general. The governor-general's military cabinet noted a very high level of meetings; the authorities surmised that Algerians were planning an uprising at the very moment of peace as a means to influence the Allies to pressure France. European fears sky-rocketed.[104]

Organised labour raised its head. The labour movement's traditional May Day commemorations had stopped during the war; even after the Allied landing, conditions were too difficult to hold such events. But with the war's end near, the CGT planned an event. Trade union leader Aissat Idir believed strongly that the CGT and AML/PPA should organise May Day demonstrations. Assuming that the CGT would focus on communist concerns, he wished to stress democratic rights and national liberation. After all, Algerians were fighting overseas to defend rights for Europeans that they did not have in their own country.

The AML/PPA preparations moved quickly. AML organiser Omar Belouchrani distributed flyers and posters. 'Algiers and many Algerian cities were like a cauldron', he recalled. 'The training of the activists necessarily had to lead on to practical actions. One could not remain indefinitely on red alert without risk of losing all effectiveness.' The nationalists decided to demonstrate carrying both Allied flags and their own Algerian flag. It was now or never, explained Mostefaï. They knew that France would celebrate the war's end with French flags. It was vital to show the world that Algerians wanted independence and had their own national flag. Recollections of the flag Messali had carried in 1937 were hazy. Mostefaï was charged with designing a new flag. The flags were sewn and sent to the main cities.[105]

In April the tension was palpable. As the PCA organised Friends of Democracy meetings, *Liberté* warned of 'pro-Hitlerian and anti-French activities'.[106] Two PPA representatives visited the British consul-general hoping to obtain representation at the upcoming United Nations conference in San Francisco, but they were informed that it was for independent states only.[107] The PPA moved deeper underground. Even in seemingly isolated villages, French authorities sensed a difference. Camus was in Algeria for three weeks. Deeply worried about the French purges, in January he had reaffirmed his earlier opposition to the death penalty. But he wanted to keep Algeria before French eyes. On 29 April the AML held a meeting in Sétif attended by some 2,500 people. Abbas's pamphlet, *J'accuse l'Europe* was distributed. Abbas addressed the meeting, applauding Messali, who on 23 April had been deported to Brazzaville. 'Europe should accuse itself', wrote Camus, 'since with all its constant upheavals and contradictions, it has managed to produce the longest, most terrible reign of barbarism the world has ever known.'[108]

Hunger was Camus' recurring theme. 'The basic diet of the Arabs consists of grains ... consumed in the form of couscous or flatbread', he informed his readers. 'For want of grain, millions of Arabs are suffering from hunger.' Drought was compounded by 'deteriorating equipment ... fuel rationing, and labor shortages due to the military mobilizations'. Without external aid Algeria could not feed itself. 'Is it clear that in a country where sky and land are invitations to happiness, this means that millions of people are suffering from hunger?', he appealed. 'On every road one sees haggard people in rags. Travelling around the country one sees fields dug up and raked over in bizarre ways, because an entire *douar* has come to scratch the soil for a bitter but edible root called *talrouda*, which can be made into a porridge that is at least filling if not nourishing.'[109]

Yet European workers were more concerned with fascism than famine. The CGT held its May Day demonstrations. In Algiers the PCF's Pierre Fayet reminded workers that Hitlerism was not yet dead. AML demonstrators waved Algerian flags, demanding 'Free Messali, free the detainees. Independence', keeping their distance from the largely European trade union demonstrations. Three processions headed to the main post office. Mostefaï led a procession of North African students, many of whom had studied at Bordeaux, Lyon and Toulouse, continuing their studies in Algiers after France was occupied. The PCF instructor ordered Bouali Taleb to denounce these so-called 'pseudo-nationalists'; he did so, sick at heart.[110]

Hopes for a peaceful day notwithstanding, violence erupted in Algiers and Oran. 'First of May was celebrated in Algiers in almost a pre-war manner', reported the British consul-general. Estimating 500 to 1,000 people, he remarked on the 'large number of women and Arabs taking part in the processions', as well as 'parties of Spanish Republican workers carrying Spanish flags and placards calling on the United Nations to break off diplomatic relations with the Franco Government'. The demonstration would have been peaceful, 'but for the unfortunate clash which took place between the police and Arab nationalist demonstrators'.[111] The authorities had ordered the police to disperse the demonstrators, he elaborated. 'A procession was formed and moved in an orderly manner towards the Central Post Office. Only one placard bearing the words: "Libérez Messali! Algérie pour les Algériens!" was carried'. But as Algerians shouted nationalist slogans, 'cries of "Vive Pétain" came from the windows overlooking the street'.[112] The police fired. Eleven died, ten of them Algerian; many were wounded. *Alger républicain*'s Boualem Khalfa, an AML activist, witnessed the events.[113]

The authorities had evidently expected trouble. Indeed, reported the British consul, they 'welcome[d] the incident as a salutary showdown, expect[ed] further demonstrations on "V" Day and intend[ed] to use all such force as may be necessary to quell and prevent future disturbances'. The PCA, for its part, left no doubt where it stood: a communist flyer of 3 May denounced provocateurs 'who took its slogans from Hitler's in Berlin'.[114] By the first week of May the division between Algeria's nationalists and leftists looking towards France could not have been starker.

On 7 May German forces surrendered at Reims, France. Military operations ceased the next day. The war over, Europe rejoiced. Janet Flanner, the *New Yorker*'s Paris correspondent, had already predicted that French politics would 'start up again soon'. De Gaulle's slogan was '*rénovation*', but the only group capable of 'construction' were the communists, 'the great heroes of the underground years, the best-organized party in France', and now 'avowedly pro-French' in contrast to its pre-war internationalism.[115] Indeed, the PCF emerged from the Second World War strengthened and, in the eyes of many, heroic. But this was not so for communists in Algeria, where nationalist fires, fanned by France's vulnerabilities, were spreading.

Notes

1. Sowerwine, *France*, pp. 170–2; Julian Jackson, *The Fall of France: The Nazi Invasion of 1940* (Oxford: Oxford University Press, 2003), p. 117; George Vernadsky, *A History of Russia*, [1929] (New Haven, CT: Yale, sixth revised edition, 1969), pp. 389–91.
2. « nation en formation », Alleg, 'Torrent', p. 243.
3. Ciné-archives, Fonds audiovisuel du PCF, Archives françaises du film, Forum des images, Archives départementales de Seine-Saint-Denis, Bobigny (hereafter Ciné-archives), *Le Voyage de Maurice Thorez en Algérie*, http://goo.gl/gL1MBm (accessed 21 September 2013).
4. « Nous, communistes, nous ne connaissons pas les races. Nous ne voulons connaître que les peuples ... Il y a une nation algérienne qui se constitue ... dans le mélange de vingt races », PCF 261 J7/, box 1, file 4, Maurice Thorez, *Le Peuple algérien uni autour de la France*, Speech by Maurice Thorez, 11 February 1939, Algiers, *La*

Brochure populaire, no. 7 (Paris: April 1939); Maurice Thorez, *Fils du peuple* (Paris: Editions Sociales, 1960), p. 170; Alleg, 'Torrent', p. 247, argues that the PCF was responding to Hitler's racist ideas.
5 ANOM ALG Alger-4I-18, Police spéciale d'Alger, Rapport no. 1086, a/s Meeting Thorez, 12 February 1939; Joly, *French Communist*, pp. 75, 77–8; Alleg, 'Torrent', pp. 243–5; Raymond F. Betts, *France and Decolonisation, 1900–1960* (Basingstoke and London: Macmillan, 1991), p. 47; Martin Evans, *The Memory of Resistance: French Opposition to the Algerian War (1954–1962)* (Oxford and New York: Berg, 1997, pp. 214–15; Mohammed Harbi, *Une vie debout: Mémoires politiques*, vol. 1, 1945–1962 (Paris: La Découverte, 2001) p. 157. *Aujourd'hui l'Afrique* (June 2004), p. 92 shows packed halls at Thorez's 1939 speeches, with banners proclaiming 'Acte de Justice, Acte de Sagesse Politique' and 'Front des démocrates contre le fascisme'; courtesy Jean-Pierre Lledo.
6 ANOM ALG Alger-4I-18, Renseignement, a/s organisation de cours à Paris par le Parti communiste, 22 February 1939.
7 Jean-Louis Planche, *Sétif 1945: Histoire d'un massacre annoncé* (Paris: Perrin, 2006), pp. 42, 328, nn. 89–90; Alleg, 'Torrent', p. 247.
8 « Une nation algérienne une et indivisible à côté de la nation française », Charles-Robert Ageron, 'Le Parti communiste algérien de 1939 à 1943', *Vingtième Siècle* (October–December 1986), 39–50, 40; Gosnell, *Politics*, pp. 109–10, 124–8.
9 Albert Camus, 'Misère de la Kabylie', in *Actuelles, III: Chroniques algériennes, 1939–1958* (Paris: Gallimard, 1958), 31–90, pp. 38, 63–4, 76, 89; Edward J. Hughes, 'La prélude d'une sorte de fin de l'histoire: Underpinning Assimilation in Camus's *Chroniques algériennes*', *L'Esprit créateur*, 47, 1 (2007), 7–18, p. 9.
10 ANOM FM 81F/752, PCA, *Pour la formation d'un front de la liberté en Algérie contre la pénétration allemande en Afrique du nord*, n.d.
11 ANOM ALG Alger F407, Commissaire, Chef de la Police spéciale, 25 August 1939; Ageron, 'Parti communiste', p. 42; Williams, *Crisis*, p. 73; David Wingeate Pike, *In the Service of Stalin: The Spanish Communists in Exile, 1939–1945* (Oxford: Clarendon, 1993), pp. 1–3, 21; Jacques Cantier, *L'Algérie sous le régime de Vichy* (Paris: Odile Jacob, 2002), pp. 76–7.
12 ANOM ALG Alger F407, Commissaire, Chef de la Police spéciale, 27 August 1939.
13 « Nous vaincrons parce que nous sommes les plus forts » The phrase is attributed to Paul Reynaud, an appeasement critic and Prime Minister from March to June 1940. Betts, *France*, p. 48; Vernadsky, *History of Russia*, pp. 393, 420–2; B. H. Liddell Hart, *History of the Second World War* (New York: G. P. Putnam's Sons, 1971), pp. 3, 13.
14 ECCI Secretariat 'Short Thesis' on the Second World War, 9 September 1939, in McDermott and Agnew, *Comintern*, pp. 247, 193, 198.
15 ANOM 81F/752, 'Décret du 26 septembre 1939 portant dissolution des organisations communistes', and GGA to Ministre de l'Intérieur, 4 Octobre 1939; McDermott and Agnew, *Comintern*, p. 197; Jackson, *Fall*, pp. 105, 121–3; Cantier, *L'Algérie*, p. 77; Lacouture, *Malraux*, pp. 286–7; Einaudi, *Rêve*, p. 170; Alleg, 'Torrent', pp. 248–9; Alleg, *Mémoire*, pp. 38–9.
16 Interview with Gilberte Sportisse, Paris, 24 June 2012; GGA to Ministre de l'Intérieur, 4 Octobre 1939; *Lutte sociale*, 1 (Novembre 1940); Zaretsky, *Camus*, p. 43; Ruedy, *Modern Algeria*, p. 143; Khalfa, Alleg and Benzine, *Aventure*, pp. 24–5; Planche, *Sétif*, p. 42.
17 Cantier, *L'Algérie*, pp. 336–7.
18 Sivan, *Communisme*, p. 182; André Marty, 'La question algérienne', *Cahiers du communisme*, 8 (August 1946), 3–29, in Jurquet, *Révolution nationale*, vol. 4, 413–34, p. 431; Gallissot (ed.), *Algérie*, pp. 498–9.
19 Ageron, 'Parti communiste', pp. 42–3; Boukort, *Souffle*, p. 118; Gallissot (ed.), *Algérie*, pp. 157, 159–61, 457–60, 499–503, esp. 501; Annie Rey-Goldzeiguer, *Aux origines de la guerre d'Algérie, 1940–1945* (Paris: La Découverte, 2002), pp. 41–2, 54; Khalfa, Alleg and Benzine, *Aventure*, pp. 24–5; Zaretsky, *Camus*, p. 6. On the PCA's response to Boukort's resignation, ANOM FM 81F/752, *Rapport politique presenté à la 4ème conférence du parti communiste d'Algérie* [1941]; interview

with Gilberte Sportisse.
20 Pétain, *Appel du 17 Juin*, Media Larousse, http://goo.gl/NaOP26; Sowerwine, *France*, pp. 205–8.
21 McDermott and Agnew, *Comintern*, p. 201.
22 Zaretsky, *Camus*, p. 56.
23 Jackson, *Fall*, pp. 174–7; Claude Francis and Fernande Gontier, *Simone de Beauvoir: A Life ... a Love Story* (New York: St Martin's, 1987), p. 186.
24 ANOM FM 81F/752 notes the persecution of Spanish refugees; Cantier, *L'Algérie*, p. 77; Alleg, *Mémoire*, pp. 48, 50, 63, 65, 78; Vernadsky, *History of Russia*, p. 423; Rey-Goldzeiguer, *Origines*, pp. 17–18, 31–2, 37–9; Planche, *Sétif*, p. 45; Einaudi, *Rêve*, pp. 165, 170; interviews with Jean-Pierre Lledo, Cambridge, England, 29 October 2008, Paris, 21 June 2010.
25 Martin Thomas, *The French Empire at War, 1940–45* (Manchester: Manchester University, 1998), p. 165; Betts, *France*, pp. 49–51.
26 Thomas, *French Empire at War*, p. 237; Betts, *France*, Sowerwine, *France*, 196–9; Liddell Hart, *Second World War*, pp. 21, 84–6; Jackson, *Fall*, pp. 158–60, 232–3; Lacouture, *Malraux*, pp. 293–4; Einaudi, *Rêve*, p. 180; Rey-Goldzeiguer, *Origines*, pp. 18, 40–1; Wood, 'Remembering', p. 258.
27 Cantier, *L'Algérie*, pp. 346–9.
28 Stora, *Messali*, pp. 184–6.
29 Interview with Mostefaï; Cantier, *L'Algérie*, p. 336.
30 Interview with Mostefaï; Alleg, *Mémoire*, pp. 72–3; Ageron, 'Parti communiste', p. 43; Rey-Goldzeiguer, *Origines*, p. 50.
31 Interview with William Sportisse, 24 June 2012.
32 « l'âme du Parti communiste », Einaudi, *Rêve*, p. 172; Ageron, 'Parti communiste', p. 43; Rey-Goldzeiguer, *Origines*, 46; Andrée Dore-Audibert, *Des Françaises d'Algérie dans la guerre de libération* (Paris: Karthala, 1995), p. 88; Marnia Lazreg, *Torture and the Twilight of Empire: From Algiers to Baghdad* (Princeton, NJ, and Oxford: Princeton University, 2008), p. 163; Sivan, *Communisme*, p. 118, claims Ibanez was Spanish; Gallisot (ed.), *Algérie*, p. 347, states he was born in Oran. Spanish and Spanish-descent communists were important to the PCA during this period. However, Spanish refugees generally worked in Spanish organisations, such as the Spanish Communist Party; Sivan's claim, pp. 118, 126, of Spanish *'tutelle'*, or guardianship, is exaggerated.
33 Ageron, 'Parti communiste', p. 44; Einaudi, *Rêve*, pp. 170–4; Letter from Thomas Ibanez to the central committee of the PCF, September 1940, in Einaudi, *Rêve*, pp. 267–9; Gallissot (ed.), *Algérie*, pp. 347–9, 555–6.
34 Planche, *Sétif*, pp. 48–49, suggests that Algerian PCA membership increased in spring 1940 because of the call for independence but declined once it became clear that the party was not actively promoting this slogan. The PCA then fell back on its core membership of dockers, train and tramway workers, and postal and building workers, as indicated in an extract from the Report of Maurice Laban to the central committee of the PCF, January 1941, in Einaudi, *Rêve*, pp. 271–2. A notable increase in Algerian membership in 1940 is unlikely because the PCA was so far underground. Alleg, *Mémoire*, pp. 67, 72, states that he and other Young Communists lost contact with the PCA in 1941.
35 Cantier, *L'Algérie*, p. 338.
36 *Lutte sociale*, 1 (November 1940); Ageron, 'Parti communiste', p. 44; Einaudi, *Rêve*, pp. 174–7; Gallissot (ed.), *Algérie*, pp. 347–9, 555–6; Cantier, *L'Algérie*, pp. 339–40.
37 Einaudi, *Rêve*, p. 179; Einaudi, *Algérien*, pp. 39–53; Dore-Audibert, *Françaises*, p. 88; Cantier, *L'Algérie*, pp. 339–40.
38 Report of Maurice Laban to central committee of PCF, in Einaudi, *Rêve*, pp. 271–2; Einaudi, *Algérien*, pp. 9–26 'Vive le peuple Algérien uni et libre, vive l'indépendance de l'Algérie', *Lutte sociale*, 2 (January 1941); Gallissot (ed.), *Algérie*, pp. 397–403; Rey-Goldzeiguer, *Origines*, p. 67.
39 « La bataille d'Alger contre les communistes », Thomas, *French Empire at War*, p. 166; Gallissot (ed.), *Algérie*, pp. 347–9, 397–403, 555–6; *Lutte sociale*, 6 (June 1941); Einaudi, *Rêve*, pp. 182, 186–7, 194–5, 21; Einaudi, *Algérien*, pp. 55–62; Dore-

Audibert, *Françaises*, p. 89; Cantier, *L'Algérie*, p. 334; Sivan, *Communisme*, p. 118, states that aside from Smaïli, the entire political bureau was arrested.

40 Vernadsky, *History of Russia*, pp. 426, 429; McDermott and Agnew, *Comintern*, p. 199; Williams, *Crisis*, p. 73; Planche, *Sétif*, p. 49; Ageron, 'Parti communiste', p. 45.

41 « Lutter contre ceux-là avec la même ardeur que contre l'impérialisme, devient la première étape à la constitution du Front Nationale Algérien », *Lutte sociale*, 6 (June 1941), p. 1; PCA, *Pour la formation d'un front de la liberté en Algérie contre la pénétration allemande*; Ageron, 'Parti communiste', p. 46; Rey-Goldzeiguer, *Origines*, p. 54; Cantier, *L'Algérie*, p. 342.

42 Alleg, *Mémoire*, pp. 45, 66–7, 70–1; Gallissot (ed.), *Algérie*, pp. 41–3, 59–64; Rey-Goldzeiguer, *Origines*, p. 7, n. 3.

43 « ce n'était pas leur guerre », Alleg, *Mémoire*, p. 72; Drew, *Discordant Comrades*, p. 225; Baruch Hirson, 'Not Pro-war, and not Anti-war: Just Indifferent. South African Blacks in the Second World War', *Critique*, 20–1 (1987), 39–56.

44 ANOM FM 81F/752, *Rapport politique présenté à la 4ème conférence du parti communiste d'Algérie* [1941]; Gallissot (ed.), *Algérie*, p. 100, dates Belkaïm's death as 30 July 1940.

45 « Vers l'indépendance de l'Algérie ... une nation en formation. Avant Algérie démocratique à côté de la France du Front Populaire. Aujourd'hui, liberté de la France et aussi liberté de l'Algérie », ANOM 81F/752, PCA Comité central, *Plan pour la discussion des tâches de la 4ème conférence du P.C. d'Algérie*; *Lutte sociale*, 1 (November 1940); Cantier, *L'Algérie*, p. 342.

46 ANOM FM 81F/752, PCA Comité central, *Aux Comités régionaux*, n.d. [1941], pp. 2–3, 8.

47 ANOM 81F/752, GGA to Ministre Secrétaire d'Etat à l'Intérieur, Vichy, 19 February 1942 lists the 81 accused; cf. Ageron, 'Parti communiste', p. 43.

48 ANOM 81F/752 GGA to Ministre Secrétaire d'Etat à l'Intérieur, Vichy, 24 March 1942. Spanish communists were particularly hard hit. According to Ageron, 'Parti communiste', pp. 43, 47, of twenty-five communists arrested in November 1941, fifteen were Spanish; nine more Spanish communists were arrested in December 1941.

49 ANOM FM 81F/752, 'Renseignements – a/s de la situation du parti communiste Algérien' [date stamp 6 November 1942]; Planche, *Sétif*, p. 49; Dore-Audibert, *Françaises*, pp. 89–90; Alleg, *Mémoire*, p. 66, n. 1; Gallissot (ed.), *Algérie*, pp. 580–1; Cantier, *L'Algérie*, pp. 340–41; Drew, *Discordant Comrades*, pp. 232, 249.

50 'Un témoignage sur l'année 1942: Extraits des souvenirs de Jacques Salort d'Alger républicain sur la Centrale de Lambèse en 1942', in Abdelhamid Benzine, *Lambèse* (Dar el Idjtihad, 1989), pp. 209–12; Stora, *Messali*, p. 187.

51 ANOM 81F/752, GGA to Chef du Gouvernement Ministre Secrétaire d'Etat à l'Intérieur, 4 July 1942, and Chef du Gouvernement Ministre Secrétaire d'Etat à l'Intérieur to Général de Corps d'Armée, Secrétaire d'Etat à la Guerre, n.d., c. July 1942.

52 Ageron, 'Parti communiste', p. 48; Planche, *Sétif*, p. 49; Cantier, *L'Algérie*, pp. 340–41; 'Renseignements – a/s de la situation du Parti communiste algérien'; *Lutte sociale* (15 September, 11 November 1942); Gallissot (ed.), *Algérie*, pp. 158–9; Jurquet, *Révolution nationale*, vol. 3, pp. 317–18, n. 85.

53 Thomas, *French Empire at War*, pp. 159–90; Betts, *France*, p. 55; Liddell Hart, *Second World War*, pp. 324–8; Alleg, *Mémoire*, pp. 72, 77, 79; '8 novembre 1942 – Des résistants français lors du débarquement allié: Entretien de Jacques Cantier avec José Aboulker, compagnon de la libération', in Jean-Jacques Jordi and Guy Pervillé (eds), *Alger 1940–1962: Une ville en guerres* (Paris: Autrement, 1999), pp. 70–5; Gallissot (ed.), *Algérie*, pp. 41–3; interviews with Henri Alleg, Paliseau, 11 May 2001, 23 June 2010; interview with Gilberte Sportisse.

54 Thomas, *French Empire at War*, pp. 159–63; Sowerine, *France*, 209–10.

55 Ruedy, *Modern Algeria*, p. 145; Planche, *Sétif*, p. 56; Liddell Hart, *Second World War*, pp. 310, 329–30; Betts, *France*, p. 55; Rey-Goldzeiguer, *Origines*, p. 221; *Lutte sociale* (15 September, 11 November 1942).

56 Interview with Mostefaï.
57 Ruedy, *Modern Algeria*, p. 145; Thomas, *French Empire at War*, p. 168; 'Message des représentants des musulmans algériens aux autorités' and 'Message des représentants des musulmans algériens aux autorités françaises', in Collot and Henry (eds), *Mouvement national*, pp. 153–5.
58 Salort, 'Témoignage', pp. 211–12.
59 'Tout pour la victoire sur l'Allemagne hitlérienne', *Lutte sociale* (21 February 1943), in RGASPI 517.1.1966, *Sur le matériel reçu d'Algérie*, n.d. [1943], pp. 4–5; *Lutte sociale* (3 April 1943); Sivan, *Communisme*, 119; Khalfa, Alleg and Benzine, *Aventure*, pp. 31–5; Gallissot (ed.), *Algérie*, pp. 536–8, 549–51.
60 « assez grande ... hors la loi », interview with Mostefaï.
61 'Mémoire remis le 31 mars 1943 à Monsieur le Gouverneur Général par MM. Ferhat Abbas, Bendjelloul, Benkhellal, Docteur Tamzali, Saiah Abdelkader et Zerrouk Mahieddine. L'Algérie dans le conflit colonial', *Manifeste du peuple algérien*, in Collot and Henry (eds), *Mouvement national*, pp. 155–64; Thomas, *French Empire at War*, p. 168.
62 'Document remis au général Catroux le 11 juin 1943 par MM. Ferhat Abbas et le docteur Tamzali. Projet de réformes faisant suite au Manifeste du peuple algérien musulman du 10 février 1943 présenté par les délégués financiers arabes et kabyles le 26 mai 1943', in Collot and Henry (eds), *Mouvement national*, 165–70, p. 168; Ruedy, *Modern Algeria*, pp. 145–6; Ageron, *Modern Algeria*, pp. 99–100; Thomas, *French Empire at War*, pp. 168–9; Evans, *Memory*, p. 26.
63 Sowerwine, *France*, p. 210; Janet Flanner (Genêt), *Paris Journal, 1944–1965*, ed. by William Shawn (New York: Atheneum, 1965), pp. 14, 158–9, 349; Francis and Gontier, *de Beauvoir*, p. 202; Alistair Horne, *Seven Ages of Paris* (New York: Alfred A. Knopf, 2002), p. 363; Zaretsky, *Camus*, p. 59; Viallaneix, 'First Camus', p. 4; David Carroll, 'Foreword', in Lévi-Valensi (ed.), *Camus at Combat*, pp. vii–xxvi, vii.
64 'For a Free Algerian Republic', p. 29; Sivan, *Communisme*, p. 120. Other communists went abroad: Lucien Sportisse joined the French resistance in Lyons; Caballero, Mahmoudi and others joined the Free French in Italy; Wood, 'Remembering', p. 259.
65 Interview with William Sportisse; Gallissot (ed.), *Algérie*, pp. 562–3.
66 « C'est par l'union avec vos camarades français que vous obtiendrez vos droits. Nous refusons de collaborer avec ceux qui trompent la masse et essaient de l'engager sur une voie dangereuse », Ageron, 'Parti communiste', pp. 48–9; ANOM ALG/Alger 4I-18, 'Note succincte sur les principaux leaders musulmans du Parti communiste algérien dans le Département d'Alger', 3 May 1943; *Lutte sociale*, 21 (1 May 1943), quoted in *Sur le matériel reçu d'Algérie*, pp. 5–7. See Alleg's view of Ouzegane, *Mémoire*, pp. 121–2.
67 'un peuple uni, une armée unie,' *Lutte sociale* (24 May 1943), quoted in *Sur le matériel reçu d'Algérie*, p. 8; *Lutte sociale* (3 April 1943); Dore-Audibert, *Françaises*, p. 90.
68 *Sur le matériel reçu d'Algérie*, pp. 1–4, suggests that the Comintern promoted the call for equal rights in November 1942 and that this was broadcast on Radio France and discussed in an article by André [Marty?].
69 Sowerwine, *France*, pp. 210–12; « Une déclaration d'Amar Ouzegane: sans le 8 novembre 1942, il n'y aurait plus, ici en Algérie, qu'un peuple de cadavres décimé par la famine », *Liberté* (1 July 1943); Amar Ouzegane, 'Préparons l'union des peuples d'Algérie et de France par la victoire de la liberté', *Liberté* (22 July 1943); Planche, *Sétif*, pp. 62, 65; Alleg, *Mémoire*, pp. 83, 87; Ruedy, *Modern Algeria*, pp. 146–7; Ageron, *Modern Algeria*, p. 100; Ageron, 'Parti communiste', p. 49; Sivan, *Communisme*, p. 120.
70 Betts, *France*, pp. 58–9; Planche, *Sétif*, p. 64.
71 Planche, *Sétif*, p. 67; Gallissot (ed.), *Algérie*, pp. 59–64, esp. 61; cf. Ageron, 'Parti communiste', pp. 49, n. 6, 50.
72 Planche, *Sétif*, pp. 68–9; Betts, *France*, p. 56.
73 « un grand parti d'Etat », Planche, *Sétif*, p. 66; McDermott and Agnew, *Comintern*, pp. 204–8; Vernadsky, *History of Russia*, pp. 438–9.
74 RGASPI 517.2.2, *Télé Beyrouth* (17 September 1943); Planche, *Sétif*, p. 66.

75 Interview with Sadek Hadjerès, Paris 24 March 2011, interview with Mostefaï.
76 Alleg, *Mémoire*, pp. 89–91; Gallissot (ed.), *Algérie*, p. 501, dates the conference as 14–15 August 1943.
77 « La rencontre émouvante d'André Marty et de ses fidèles compagnons, les 27 députés communistes », *Liberté* (21 October 1943), p. 1; Planche, *Sétif*, p. 66; Alleg, *Mémoire*, p. 117; Wood, 'Remembering', p. 259; Pike, *In the Service*, p. 344, n. 68.
78 'La délégation du Parti communiste Français en Afrique du Nord aux comités centraux des Partis communistes d'Algérie, de Tunisie et du Maroc', *Liberté* (2 December 1943), p. 5; 'Le Régime de Vichy en Afrique du Nord (Ecole élémentaire du Parti communiste algérien, cours n. 3, fin 1943)', 'L'œuvre des communistes Français en Afrique du Nord (Février 1943–Septembre 1944) – Extraits', 'L'Union avec le peuple de France (Ecole élémentaire du Parti communiste algérien, cours n. 3, fin 1943', all Jurquet, *Révolution nationale*, vol. 3, pp. 321–8, 329–44, 344–50; Gallissot (ed.), *Algérie*, pp. 460–3; Einaudi, *Rêve*, p. 237; Planche, *Sétif*, p. 66.
79 Neil MacMaster, *Burning the Veil: The Algerian War and the 'Emancipation' of Muslim Women, 1954–62* (Manchester and New York: Manchester University, 2009), pp. 33–4; Rey-Goldzeiguer, *Origines*, p. 215; Alleg, *Mémoire*, pp. 91, 94; Sivan, *Communisme*, p. 121; Jurquet, *Révolution nationale*, vol. 3, pp. 317–18, n. 85; Dore-Audibert, *Françaises*, pp. 28–33.
80 « J'ai été internationaliste avant d'être national ... Plus de barrières, plus de juifs, de musulmans, de chrétiens. Nous étions l'humanité », Gallissot (ed.), *Algérie*, pp. 60–1, 552–3, 568–70, quote p. 568; Alleg, *Mémoire*, pp. 91–5, 99–100, 105–6; Biographie de Gilberte Serfaty, Mouvement social algérien: Histoire et perspectives, http://goo.gl/oAI0SN (accessed 8 May 2011).
81 Alleg, *Mémoire*, p. 92; Planche, *Sétif*, pp. 66–7, 69; Gallissot (ed.), *Algérie*, pp. 39–40.
82 'La Commission des réformes musulmanes' and 'Audition de M. Omar Ouzegane (23-12-1943) représentant du Parti communiste algérien', in Collot and Henry (eds), *Mouvement national*, pp. 171–5; Ageron, *Modern Algeria*, p. 100.
83 Ruedy, *Modern Algeria*, p. 147; Thomas, *French Empire at War*, pp. 178–9; Betts, *France*, pp. 63–4; MacMaster, *Burning*, p. 33.
84 « un grand pas en avant », Sivan, *Communisme*, p. 131.
85 Rey-Goldzeiguer, *Origines*, pp. 216, 222–3; Ruedy, *Modern Algeria*, pp. 147–8; Ageron, *Modern Algeria*, p. 101.
86 Ruedy, *Modern Algeria*, p. 147; Evans, *Memory*; Rey-Goldzeiguer, *Origines*, pp. 59–61, 65–8, 226–8, 233; Ageron, *Histoire*, vol. 2, p. 568.
87 *Liberté* (13 April 1944), p. 2.
88 « Alger n'est pas à la température française ... les menées anticommunistes ont trop de prise ... la question de l'indépendance en ce moment ne serait qu'un mot d'ordre de l'ennemi », RGASPI 517.2.2, Délégation du Comité Central en Afrique du Nord (Session plénière du 30 Mars 1944), 27 April 1944.
89 Planche, *Sétif*, p. 69; Einaudi, *Rêve*, p. 237; Einaudi, *Algérien*, pp. 90–9; 'La mort de SMAILI Ahmed', *Liberté* (3 February 1944), p. 2.
90 'De la résistance à la révolution', Sowerwine, *France*, pp. 213–15; Williams, *Crisis*, p. 74; Thomas, *French Empire at War*, p. 183; Carroll, 'Foreword', p. xiv; Zaretsky, *Camus*, pp. 60, 66; Francis and Gontier, *de Beauvoir*, pp. 206, 211–12.
91 'Manifeste des Amis de la démocratie', *Liberté* (14 September 1944), p. 3; *Manifeste des Amis de la démocratie*, 14 Septembre 1944, in Collot and Henry (eds), *Mouvement national*, pp. 188–91; Amar Ouzegane, 'Rapport présenté à la Conférence centrale du Parti communiste algérien, le 23 septembre 1944', in Jurquet, *Révolution nationale*, vol. 3, pp. 387–402.
92 « gardé une attitude communiste ... d'abandonner le fruit de 15 ans de militantisme et d'éducation Marxiste-Léniniste parce qu'il s'est trompé dans l'appréciation d'un évènement ... si l'on sait se débarrasser d'un certain sectarisme », PCF 261 J7, box 1, file 3, Boukort to Berlioz, 20 November 1944, pp. 2–3.
93 TNA: PRO FO 371/49275 [United States Military Intelligence Service], 'Notes on the Moslem Nationalist Movement in Algeria' [c. February 1945], p. 6; Ageron, *Histoire*, vol. 2, p. 568; Alleg, *Mémoire*, p. 104; Gallissot (ed.), *Algérie*, p. 462; Sivan, *Communisme*, pp. 121, n. 15, 122; Lévi-Valensi (ed.), *Camus at Combat: Writing*

1944–1947 (Princeton, NJ, and Oxford: Princeton University, 2006), p. 215.
94 Lévi-Valensi (ed.), *Camus at Combat*, pp. 70–1; Zaretsky, *Camus*, p. 59.
95 Sivan, *Communisme*, p. 123; Ageron, *Histoire*, vol. 2, pp. 568–70; Ageron, *Modern Algeria*, p. 101.
96 Interview with Hadjerès; Gallissot (ed.), *Algérie*, pp. 332–6.
97 Jean Lehadouey, 'La Casbah et sa misère', *L'Humanité nouvelle*, 6 (March 1944).
98 Ruedy, *Algeria*, p. 148; MacMaster, *Burning*, pp. 35–6; interview with Noureddine Abdelmoumène, Algiers, 25 September 2011.
99 [United States Military Intelligence Service], 'Notes on the Moslem Nationalist Movement', p. 8.
100 TNA: PRO FO 371/49275, British Consul General, 21 February, 8 March 1945.
101 « le journal "Liberté" continue, de même qu'une petite feuille communiste diffusée à Ghardaïa et intitulée le "Mzab de demain" à attaquer les caïds prévaricateurs et autres féodaux », Exhibit, Museum of the Armed Forces, Algiers (23 September 2011), GGA à Monsieur le ministre des affaires étrangères (Afrique-levant), a/s situation politique en milieu musulman à la date du 1er Avril (3 April 1945), Cabinet du GG de l'Algérie, no. 614, CDP; Ouzegane, 'Rapport présenté', p. 400; *Kitab El-Ferkad* (Algiers, 1937), author's possession; interviews with Mustafa Mella, Aissa Bellalou, Fafa Boudjenah and Mohamed Boudjenah, September 2011, Ghardaïa.
102 Rey-Goldzeiguer, *Origines*, pp. 225–6, 231; Ageron, *Histoire*, vol. 2, p. 570; 'Déclaration commune du Parti socialiste et du Parti communiste algérien', *Liberté* (29 March 1945), p. 2.
103 TNA: PRO FO 371/49275 [Parti populaire algérien], *Bulletin intérieur* no. 3 [c. March 1945].
104 TNA: PRO FO 371/49275, British Consul-General, 16 March 1945; Rey-Goldzeiguer, *Origines*, pp. 216, 222–3, 237–9.
105 « Alger et bien des villes d'Algérie étaient tel un chaudron. Le conditionnement des militants devait nécessairement déboucher sur du concret. On ne peut indéfiniment rester en alerte rouge, sous peine de perdre toute efficacité », Boualem Bourouiba, *Les Syndicalistes algériens: Leur combat de l'éveil à la libération, 1936–1962* (Paris: Harmattan, 1998; Algiers: ENAG/DAHLAB, 2001), pp. 67–8; Stora, *Dictionnaire*, pp. 268–9; Gallissot (ed.), *Algérie*, pp. 103–4; interview with Mostefaï.
106 Joanny Berlioz, 'L'Afrique du nord, foyer d'activité prohitlérienne et antifrançaise', *Liberté* (6 April 1945), p. 3; *Liberté* (26 April 1945), p. 3.
107 TNA: PRO FO 371/49275, British Consul-General, 29 April 1945.
108 Lévi-Valensi (ed.), *Camus at Combat*, pp. 216, 163–5; Zaretsky, *Camus*, pp. 72, 123; Martin Evans, *Algeria: France's Undeclared War* (Oxford: Oxford University, 2012), p. 82.
109 Camus, *Combat*, pp. 202–3.
110 « Libérez Messali, libérez les détenus. Indépendance », Interview with Mostefaï; Gallisot (ed.), *Algérie*, pp. 566–7.
111 TNA: PRO FO 371/49275, H. M. Consul-General to Foreign Office, 8 May 1945, and Z5591/900/69, Consul-General Carvel, 3 May 1945.
112 TNA: PRO FO 371/49275, H. M. Consul-General, 14 May 1945.
113 Ageron, *Histoire*, vol. 2, p. 572; Ruedy, *Modern Algeria*, p. 148; Sivan, *Communisme*, p. 139; Khalfa, Alleg and Benzine, *Aventure*, p. 39; Gallissot (ed.), *Algérie*, pp. 388–90.
114 Consul-General Carvel, 3 May 1945; « qui prend ses mots d'ordre à Berlin, chez Hitler », Rey-Goldzeiguer, *Origines*, p. 251, pp. 229, 241–2, 247–52.
115 Flanner, *Journal*, pp. 9, 46.

CHAPTER SIX

For an Algerian national front: unity and division in the liberation struggle

The Second World War's end led to a remapping of world politics. As the United States became the world's greatest power, Europe's territorial boundaries were redrawn and its colonial empires threatened. On 26 June 1945 representatives of fifty countries signed the United Nations Charter in San Francisco. The charter's first article called for international relations 'based on respect for the principle of equal rights and self-determination of peoples'. Yet the implementation of such rights was far from assured.[1]

With the Vichy regime's defeat in France, the French left – socialists and communists – became a majority in the post-war Constituent Assembly. A new constitution eventually agreed in October 1946 led to the formation of the Union française (French Union) 'based on equality of rights and obligations without distinction of race or religion'. But the colonial relationship remained intact. The new constitution allowed some representation of colonised peoples in the new National Assembly and French Union Assembly. Other reforms included the abolition of forced labour, the *indigénat*, and – except for Algeria – the dual college electoral system. The PCF, part of the government until May 1947, supported the French Union but opposed Algerian independence.[2]

With the prestige of its role in the Resistance, the PCF might have briefly felt close to state power. But in Algeria the PCA's relationship to the state was profoundly different. The anti-colonial movement was on the upswing as civil society became increasingly politicised and active. For the PCA, the war's end raised the prospect of again prioritising the anti-colonial struggle, whose marginalisation had alienated nationalists. The departure of the PCF delegation for France facilitated the PCA's autonomy, which increased as the PCF became increasingly concerned with Cold War politics. From 1946 the PCA pursued an aggressive policy of indigenisation that significantly increased Algerian membership while European membership declined.

As prospects for electoral reform proved barren, communists and nationalists faced the same dilemma: how to fight against colonialism and for democratic rights from within an increasingly authoritarian system that strove to nullify such efforts. Alongside the state's attacks on public political space, the nationalist movement's growing factionalism left little space for effective debate within its organisations. By contrast, the PCA allowed members space for discussion, which proved attractive for radicalised Algerian youth. The PCA pursued a multi-pronged campaign for democratic rights: firstly, through the launch of amnesty committees against repression; secondly, through the use of elections as forums to demand democratic rights; and thirdly, through the formation of organisationally pluralist united fronts for democratic rights and liberties. Throughout this period the PCA elaborated its vision of democratic rights through its press, its meetings and its campaigns. This vision reflected a dual notion of freedom – from repression and to develop. Yet it only arrived at this position after serious misjudgements of Algerian nationalism.[3]

The Constantinois massacre

As Europe's war ended, violence erupted in Algeria. While Algeria's Europeans celebrated VE day, Messali's PPA and Abbas' AML led demonstrations demanding their own liberation. There were no demonstrations in Algiers and Oran, where the 1 May violence had been followed by mass arrests, but in many other cities and towns the demonstrations were peaceful. Not so in Constantinois, however, where Algerians greatly outnumbered Europeans.[4]

In the politicised town of Sétif, some 8,000–10,000 demonstrators gathered on 8 May, inspired by the United Nations' formation.[5] While Ferhat Abbas and Chérif Saâdane waited in Algiers to congratulate Governor-General Chataigneau on the Allied victory, police in Sétif opened fire and killed some of the demonstrators for refusing to lower an Algerian banner. The British had a base at Sétif. 'When the procession which was quite orderly and under police control arrived opposite the office of "A" Company, 44th Infantry Battalion, of the South African Air Force', reported the British consul-general, 'a policeman attempted to seize the banner bearing the inscription "Libérez Messali Hadj". A scuffle then took place and a policeman drew his revolver and shot a native. More shots were fired both by the police and by French civilians who were watching the procession from balconies overlooking the street. Pandemonium then ensued.'[6] It was market day – peasants going to market, hearing the news, began attacking Europeans. By late morning, several dozen people had died; 28 Europeans were killed by stabbing or blows to the head from whatever was at hand to inflict them. Local nationalists quickly blamed the police.[7]

Amar Ouzegane and Harry Salem – by then called Henri Alleg – were driving back to Algiers that day. When they reached Sétif between noon and one p.m., its streets were strangely quiet. Only later did they learn that Albert Denier, the local communist leader they had planned to see, had been mutilated and that the socialist mayor Edouard Deluca, a friend of Abbas, had been shot and killed. Essentially a battle between Algerians and Europeans, intra-European politics also played a role: conservative Europeans in the region had vowed revenge for left-wing anti-corruption policies.[8]

Bus and car passengers carried the news. Leaving Sétif, Ouzegane and Alleg were stopped by a group of Algerians but allowed to continue; driving on, they passed military trucks proceeding towards the embattled region. A taxi carried the news to Périgotville. A crowd of peasants gathered; cries of *jihad* were heard. Europeans were killed, their bodies mutilated. Elsewhere, villagers attacked European settlements and symbols of colonial authority. At around five p.m. violence broke out in Guelma, a small town between Constantine and Bône, a region subjected to particularly heavy land dispossession. Guelma was about 80 per cent Muslim, and its sub-prefect André Achiary had banned demonstrations on 4 May, but a crowd carrying an Algerian flag met him head on. Police fired; the flag carrier and three others fell. The next day peasants from surrounding villages converged on Guelma, attacking European farms *en route.*[9]

The region erupted: 'the whole of the area between the sea and line running from Sétif to Souk Ahras flared up in open revolt.' Telephone lines were sabotaged; houses of the hated forest rangers were set on fire. Before departing for France, de Gaulle had ordered the repression of any insurgent activity that might undermine the war effort. Governor-General Chataigneau called in the army; on 9 May Achiary formed an 800-person civil militia that became a model for European communities. Some 10,000 troops, including Senegalese and Foreign Legion detachments, were dispatched to the region. Planes bombed and strafed villages and mountain settlements. There was 'considerable air activity', reported the British consul-general, with some '300 sorties ... by B.26's amd [sic] P.38's during the period May 8th – 14th. While it is said that 250-lb. bombs were used, it is thought that action was mostly confined to machine-gunning and the use of anti-personnel bombs. Reports from aerial observers indicate however that whole villages (Douars) have been destroyed.' Some 41 tons of bombs were dropped. By 10 May, he explained, 'the situation was well in hand, rebel activity being confined to the uplands situated South and South-West of Djidjelli, the hills surrounding Guelma and the mountainous region of Sédrata'. On 13 May, Constantine's prefect Lestrade-Carbonnel visited Guelma and with Achiary encouraged European civilians to attack unarmed Algerians. By then, 'order had been generally restored although isolated armed bands were still holding out in the mountains'. Two days later, 'whole villages formally submitted en masse, delivering up their arms and surrendering their leaders'.[10]

By mid-May the authorities had seemingly regained control of northern Constantinois. Nonetheless, the French asked the Supreme Headquarters Allied Expeditionary Force to send six Light Infantry Battalions and the Fifth French Armoured Division Reconnaissance Regiment to Sétif. The Reconnaissance Regiment was earmarked for Germany, however, and the American War Department seemed 'unfavourable'. PPA leaders in Algérois called for an insurrection to show solidarity with their compatriots. Government property was attacked in Oran on 18 May, and in Kabylia on 23 May; a plot to attack military headquarters at Cherchell was foiled. Eventually, the might of colonial forces squashed the rebellion.[11]

Nonetheless, European civilians continued slaughtering Algerians across Constantinois, village after village subjected to mass summary executions. The vigilance committee directing the Guelma militia included a large majority of leftists, including communists and Fighting France members. Achiary apparently bore direct or indirect responsibility for 2,000 to 3,000 deaths; several communists were reportedly involved in the murders. The magnitude of Algerian deaths would 'never be accurately known', the British consul-general informed the Foreign Office on 23 May. 'The Governor-General told me that the number of killed was between 900 and 1,000 but the French medical authorities have estimated that at least 6,000 were killed and 14,000 wounded. Other estimates are very much higher.' On 31 May he reported: 'the authorities are now prepared to admit that 1500 natives were killed', but 'it is alleged that they possess confidential information indicating that the total of killed may eventually be numbered as high as 20,000–30,000'. In towns most victims were traders, artisans and minor officials; in rural areas they were tenant farmers on European farms. Despite fewer European fatalities than in Sétif, the violence was especially fierce around Guelma, where European militias systematically murdered young Algerian men thought to be nationalists – almost 80 per cent were between fifteen and forty-five years old, constituting around 25 per cent of the adult male population. Individuals disappeared; families vanished.[12]

The mass *ratonnade* continued until early June. All told, some 103

Europeans died and unknown thousands of Algerians. In late June the PPA and AML put the Algerian toll at 35,000. Villages were bombed and set alight, and the French cruiser *Duguay-Trouin* fired fifty-eight salvos on the town of Djidjelli, they claimed. On 3 July two PPA representatives told the British consul-general that 35,000 was 'a conservative estimate'.[13] At Guelma 500 hastily buried bodies were dug up, trucked away and burned in a quicklime oven owned by a local European – so that the visiting Minister of the Interior Adrien Tixier would not know the extent of the slaughter.[14]

The Constantine uprising marked 'the first time', commented John Ruedy, that 'the dispossessed and pauperised masses of the countryside ... linked up for meaningful action with a nationalist movement that urban Algerians had created and which had been spreading in the cities for fifteen years'. Urban political elites succeeded in bringing their message to rural towns and villages, even if the uprising that erupted was brutally crushed. Open democratic protest was not possible for Algerians in Algeria – this was the massacre's extraordinarily cruel lesson.[15]

Had Algerians been able to, they would have declared war. They were convinced that France would never voluntarily accept Algerian independence. The immediate reaction was framed in terms of *jihad* – a war against the occupying Christians. Muslims wondered how it was that they constituted nine million, yet Christians, with only one million, could dominate. If each Muslim killed one Christian, the problem would be solved, the argument went. But such thoughts were only voiced within families, behind closed doors. A different sentiment emerged, especially amongst youth who, from schools, cinemas and newspapers, learned about European anti-fascist resistance and Italian, Polish, Irish and Indochinese struggles. Perhaps the Europeans leaving Constantinois for Algiers sensed these feelings.[16]

News of the massacre had spread like wildfire amongst Algerians. But the European press had been slow to report it – perhaps due to censorship. What was the communist response? The force of nationalism in that May 1945 undermined Thorez's thesis that Algeria was but a nation in formation; the murderous hatred shown by so many Europeans undermined the PCA's claims that ordinary Europeans were not the enemy. Nonetheless, like the PCF, the PCA initially saw the events through anti-fascist lenses. The PCA blamed the PPA for its 'Hitlerian' slogans; the PPA responded that the demonstrations had been peaceful and that Messali was neither anti-union nor pro-fascist but for national liberation.[17] Almost immediately after the initial Sétif events a delegation representing the PCA and PCF – Ouzegane, Caballero, Henriette Neveu and Victor Joannès – met with the governor-general and denounced 'the provocations of the PPA's and PPF's Hitlerian agents'. They castigated alleged imperialist agents in nationalist organisations, as well as 'the fascist lords of colonisation, the feudal Muslims and the high-level functionaries of the Vichy regime'.[18] On 10 May *Alger républican* published without comment a government communiqué stating that 'elements aimed at agitation using Hitlerian methods indulged in armed aggression on populations celebrating victory in the city of Sétif and surrounding areas'. Two days later, *L'Humanité* labelled Messali and the 'pseudo-nationalists' as 'criminal agents' who should be punished.[19]

By mid-May the PCA and PCF knew that Algerians were being slaughtered with machine guns, tanks and bombs. Yet they continued condemning even moderate nationalists. On 17 May *Liberté* published a report dated 13 May by Roger Esplaas, its special envoy to Sétif. 'The city is in mourning, the streets almost empty', he began. 'Everywhere, armed soldiers. Most of them are Algerian infantry. Machine guns and light machine guns at the most important crossroads.' He blamed the Fifth Column, 'that handful of miserable agents of Hitlerism (false nationalists, lords of colonisation, feudal landholders, agents of trusts).' Five censored lines followed. Esplaas argued that the 'disturbances' preceded the upcoming municipal elections and condemned them as orchestrated provocation, but noted that certain Muslims had saved Europeans from attacks by other Muslims.[20] Ouzegane similarly castigated 'false nationalists: informers, criminals and servants of fascism' and branded former-PCA member Ben Ali Boukort as a 'traitor'. Neveu called for unity to break the Fifth Column provocation and for the immediate suspension of Vichy-appointed administrators.[21]

Still in detention, Boukort wrote to Thorez to defend himself, stating that he still rejected overtures from other political parties. While he could understand denouncing Vichy supporters as fascists, to label the Muslim masses and their democratic political leaders in that manner was unacceptable. Political repression had touched virtually every Algerian family, and had 'become … one of the principal demands'. The Constantinois masses had not randomly attacked Europeans but instead had aimed at symbols of imperial authority. In that sense, he argued, the May events were anti-imperialist.[22]

Camus, in turn, stressed economic and political justice: 'the gravity of the Algerian affair does not stem solely from that fact that the Arabs are hungry. It also stems from the fact that their hunger is unjust … it is not enough to give Algeria the grain it needs; that grain must also be distributed equitably.' Grain, 'almost as scarce as gold', could be had on the black market for 7,000 to 16,000 francs per quintal – a far cry from the official 540 francs rate. Camus condemned the corrupt caïds: they 'act in a sense as stewards representing the French administration, [who] have all too often been entrusted with the tasks of overseeing the distribution of grain, and [whose] methods ... are often highly idiosyncratic'.[23] On 31 May, *L'Humanité* applauded the arrests of moderates Abbas and Saâdane, on whom it placed responsibility for the 'tragic events'. Astonishingly, the PCA tried to recruit the dissolved AML's membership, which only earned it more scorn from the nationalists.[24]

As the massacre's scale was revealed, however, the PCA could hardly help but reassess its position and condemn the repression.[25] Chastened by Boualem Khalfa, who had witnessed police attacks on unarmed Algerians at the 1 May Algiers demonstration, *Alger républicain*'s editor-in-chief Michel Rouzé clashed with the paper's printer – central committee member Joseph Parrès – over the publication of a tract titled *Messali l'hitlérien* (Messali the Hitlerite). Several weeks after the 8 May demonstration, Rouzé travelled to Constantinois. There he heard that tens of thousands had been slaughtered, that European militias had directed and engaged in the slaughter and that ovens had been built to burn the bodies. He informed communists in Algiers of the slaughter's mass scale. Gilberte Chemouilli learned of this through typing the central committee's reports. But getting the story out proved difficult. Rouzé's report was censored.[26] The communists and socialists called for the unity of Europeans and Algerians with the 'nouvelle [new] France'. The matter reached the Free French Consultative Assembly in July. However, like the communists, most found it convenient to attribute the initial events to fascists. Fajon stressed the pressing need for social and political reforms.[27]

Even in August the PCA's central committee maintained that the 'bloody events' had been the work of fascist provocation, insisting that Europeans and Algerians were 'becoming conscious of their solidarity based on the identity of their immediate interests and the will to forge a common fraternal future' – an amazing claim in light of the May events. Pointing to the development of a 'feeling of an original nationality linked to ideas of freedom', and taking up the issue raised by Boukort, Khalfa and other Algerians, it began campaigning against the heavy repression, organising amnesty committees around the country.[28]

Young Algerian men were vilified as criminals. The police detained any activist they could find. Some 5,560 Algerians were arrested; prison facilitated the development of political networks across the region. Some prisoners were eventually released; others were sentenced to varying terms – several hundred to life and estimates of some 100 or 120, to death. On 24 October 1945 the PCA's political bureau called for the organisation of amnesty committees to help free political prisoners, although Ouzegane evidently asked that PPA and AML leaders be exempted from amnesty on the grounds that they were *'antifrançais'*. *Liberté* – some of whose articles were censored – denounced the racist sentences. But only in late 1945 to early 1946 did the PCA cease its attacks on nationalist leaders.[29]

If Ouzegane castigated nationalist leaders as anti-French, there were good reasons for seeing the PCA as a French party, and for most Algerians it bore that stigma. By late 1945 the PCA's membership had swelled to eight or nine thousand, while *Liberté* had 25,000 subscribers and a print run of 115,000. But its members were still disproportionately European, and its new leaders had been trained by the 1943–44 PCF delegates. The party might accurately be described as the 'avant-garde' of anti-fascist resistance – but not of anti-colonial resistance, which the overwhelming majority of Algerians saw as their greatest need.[30]

The PCA had taken heart in the gains it made in the July 1945 municipal elections – gains possible because the PPA and AML, both illegal with their leaders imprisoned, refused to participate. About 40 per cent of potential Algerian voters abstained, but European voters came out solidly for the Fighting France candidates, who endorsed assimilation and the ordinance of 7 March 1944. The ethnic polarisation evidenced by the May 1945 massacre propelled the French government to consider political reforms. Three constituent assemblies were to deliberate on a successor to the Third Republic and future institutions. Algerians were legally entitled to vote for the same number of delegates as Europeans. Messali and Abbas urged their followers to boycott the October 1945 constituent assembly elections; 52 per cent of the potential electorate did not vote. The PCA contested the elections, winning 135,000 votes or close to 20 per cent of the total and first place in the first (European) electoral college with more than 80,000 votes. While most of the thirteen Algerians elected to the second college were assimilationists or government candidates, two communists, Ouzegane and Mohamed Chouadria, were elected. For the PCA, the results vindicated its policies.[31]

Several months later Ouzegane still described the May 1945 events as a fascist conspiracy, but squarely blamed those who organised the reprisals – Achiary, Lestrade-Carbonnel, Berque and General Duval, the former commander of the Constantine division – none of whom had been arrested. The PCA was thriving, Ouzegane noted. Its membership had tripled since before the war. Indeed, around Algiers and Médéa the Party was attracting young nationalists who had earlier been sceptical towards it, if not hostile. However, Ouzegane conceded, its recruitment of Muslim workers in ports, railways and on large farms was lagging. The pressing need was to work for democracy. As Stalin put it – Stalin had enormous prestige within the PCA, especially after the Red Army's victory over the Nazis – as democracy was strengthened, national oppression would become weaker. Thus, the PCA's stress was on amnesty campaigns for political prisoners. While the PCA supported the right to self-determination, Ouzegane argued, it was not in Algeria's interest to demand divorce from a democratic France that was fighting against the large economic trusts that were damaging Algeria. The PCA stressed four main points: reaffirmation of the Algerian personality by recognising the equal official status of Arabic; equal rights for all; abolition of repressive colonial regimes, especially in militarised zones; and increased agricultural production and rapid industrial development.[32] Still based mainly in European civil society, the PCA was committed to democratic rights for individuals and classes, but not to independence.

Algerianising the party

Despite the PCA's professed optimism, the Constantinois massacre compelled it to reassess its views on nationalism. The anti-colonial feelings that had developed following the Anglo-American landing and the Constantinois massacre were felt in the PCA as well as nationalist organisations. Young politicised Algerians found that nationalist organisations did not address poverty and economic inequality. The twenty years from 1930 to 1950 showed both a greater concentration of the largest European landholdings (Table 5) and a fragmentation of the smallest Algerian landholdings, a process accelerated by the war.

The tiny Algerian landed elite maintained its grip on the land (Table 6). But the middle peasants 'who could make ends meet' had declined, with only 2.62 per cent of Algerian properties in that category, down from almost six per cent twenty years earlier. The proportion of smaller landholdings had increased, especially amongst Algerians; some 96 per cent of Algerian landholdings were less than 49 hectares. Rural poverty was widespread.[33]

Some of the young Algerians concerned with these problems turned to communism. The PCA's demographic shift was reflected in its press. When the PCF deputies left for France at the war's end, the PCA took over *Liberté*, which enabled it to maintain continuity of technical staff and trade union coverage. Although a French-language paper, from 1946 *Liberté* gave greater coverage to Algerian politics and culture, in accordance with the aim of developing an Algerian identity reflecting the Arabo-Berber majority; it became known by its Arabic name, *El Hourriya*. An article by Bachir Hadj Ali argued that *medersa* students

Table 5 European landholdings in hectares, 1950

	No. of properties	Per cent of all properties	Area of land	Per cent of all land
Less than 10 ha	7,432	33.72	22,600	0.82
10 – 49 ha	5,585	25.39	135,300	4.96
50 – 99 ha	2,635	11.95	186,900	6.85
100 + ha	6,385	28.97	2,381,900	87.35
Total	22,037	100.03	2,726,700	99.98

Source: Adapted from Ageron, Histoire de l'Algérie contemporaine, vol 2 (1979), p. 495.

Table 6 Algerian landholdings in hectares, 1950

	No. of properties	Per cent of all properties	Area of land	Per cent of all land
Less than 10 ha	438,483	69.52	1,378,400	18.75
10 – 49 ha	167,170	26.50	3,185,800	43.34
50 – 99 ha	16,580	2.62	1,096,100	14.91
100 + ha	8,499	1.34	1,688,800	22.97
Total	630,732	99.98	7,349,100	99.97

Source: Adapted from Ageron, Histoire de l'Algérie contemporaine, vol 2 (1979), p. 495.

could form the elements of a cultural avant-garde and that, with educational and pedagogic reforms, *medersas* could transform themselves into universities.[34] Many issues carried Arab and Kabyle stories and articles on the need to make Arabic an official language, a matter of particular importance to Ouzegane; despite his antagonism towards nationalists, he wholeheartedly promoted Arabo-Berber culture as central to nation-building. *Liberté* presented the PCA's human face, publicising the photos and biographies of its leading figures. This face was multi-ethnic and increasingly representative of Algeria; by 1949, most of its leaders were Algerian men. *Alger républicain* similarly employed more Algerians and gave greater coverage to Algerian themes.[35]

The PCA's third congress took place on 21–24 March 1946. The party pointed to a significant success: on 1 March, following the impassioned interventions of communist deputy Mohamed Chouadria, the Constituent National Assembly approved an amnesty law – although many had already been executed and the law's application would be arbitrary.[36] The party had made progress Algerianising: its four-person secretariat comprised Ouzegane as political secretary; Caballero, assistant political secretary; Bouhali, secretary for mass work; and CGT activist Rachid Dalibey, organisational secretary. Most central committee members were European, but seven members of the thirteen-person political bureau were Algerian. The party's new slogan was 'Union for democracy'. It demanded bread for all, the formation of a broad movement for a democratic Algeria with more justice, happiness and freedom, and defence of peace – the latter demand reflecting the Soviet-inspired international peace movement.[37]

In April the Constituent Assembly debated the question of the second electoral college. Ouzegane presented the PCA's view. Although the 'Algerian personality' was growing stronger every day, he argued, the double electoral college was still best suited to the country. Communists could ask from an epoch no more than it could give – classic Marxist discourse used to justify caution. The PCA's hesitancy about electoral reform reflected its concern to appease European anxiety. It was imperative to avoid a repetition of the 'psychosis of fear' amongst Europeans that had produced the Constantinois massacre, Ouzegane contended. The 550,000 European voters would feel swamped by the 1,200,000 Muslim voters if there were a single electoral college. Colonialist newspapers such as the *Echo d'Alger* – dubbed *Echo de Vichy* – and the *Dépêche algérienne* – *Dépêche Hitlérienne* – could whip up hysteria with cries of 'Arab peril', 'Islamic fanaticism' and 'French thrown into the sea'.[38]

The party's electoral euphoria did not last. Abbas, released in March 1946, formed the Union démocratique du manifeste algérien (Democratic Union of the Algerian Manifesto, UDMA). In May a referendum narrowly rejected a proposed constitution for the French Republic. As a result, elections were held for a new Constituent Assembly in June 1946. The UDMA decided to contest these elections, even though the PPA continued the boycott. Amnestied in 1946, Boukort began working with the UDMA – 'a heterogeneous movement' – finding Messali too sectarian.[39] The PCA urged Algerians to vote. Styling itself the 'party of the future', it asked Algerians to spread the call for a democratic Algeria united with the French people to the most distant villages and oases. The proportion of non-voters declined slightly to 48 per cent. This time the nationalists beat the conservatives and the communists in the second (Algerian) electoral college: the UDMA won eleven out of the thirteen seats. The PCA won 53,000 votes, but this was just 8.4 per cent of the total, and it lost both its seats. It suffered a substantial drop in its stronghold of Algiers, down from 82,000 votes to 23,000. Nonetheless, now that French and European women had obtained the right to vote on 21 April 1944, the communist Alice Sportisse used her position to demand the franchise for Algerian women.[40]

The shock compelled the party to rethink its stance towards nationalism. It continued promoting the 'nation in formation' thesis, seeing its acceptance of Europeans as positive. However, recognising that the thesis' equal stress on all ethnic groups gave Europeans disproportionate weight, the PCA began interpreting it more flexibly. In July *Liberté* published the view of a Muslim reader who argued that the PCA was the French party closest to the sympathies of most Muslim Algerians. Ouzegane replied that the PCA was not a French party, but rather the only truly Algerian party and thus the only party able to represent all Algerians. The other parties were either French or Arab or Christian or Muslim, he wrote, but 'not yet Algerian'. A sophisticated response, but Ouzegane's imagined community did not make sense for those who saw the deep-rooted Arabo-Berber tradition as the core of the Algerian nation.[41]

On 21–22 July 1946 the PCA's enlarged central committee criticised the Party's earlier underestimation of the national question. The Party now aimed to be a 'truly Algerian party ... neither European, nor Muslim, nor Arab, nor French, nor Eastern, nor Western, but Algerian.' It sought to eliminate racism amongst Europeans and xenophobia amongst Muslims.[42] It insisted that Algerians of all origins were forming a stable community linked by common interests and the struggle against common class enemies – namely, the large trusts dominating the economy. Despite having shunned the nationalists throughout the war, the PCA now hoped to unite the PPA, the UDMA, the *'ulama*, the Socialists and the trade union movement in one big national democratic front to forge a free and democratic Algeria responsible for Algerian affairs, but willing to collaborate with France on external matters. Demanding Messali's return and the PPA's legalisation, it called for liberty, land and bread, to be financed by seizing the goods of Vichy collaborators and profiteers.[43]

The Party's greater concern with the national question was also seen in the publication – at long last – of an Arabic-language monthly, *El Djezaïr el Djedida* (*New Algeria*). Launched in April 1946, *El Djezaïr el Djedida*'s circulation reached 5,000–6,000 – average for an Arabic-language publication – and the PCA's fraternal organisations also launched Arabic-language publications. Nonetheless, French remained the language of most PCA publications. Colonial educational policy led to a much higher level of literacy amongst French-speakers, whether European or Algerian, and since many Algerians were illiterate, the demand for French-language publications exceeded that for Arabic publications. *Liberté*'s new orientation meant a sizeable drop in readership, but at a 15,000 print run it had almost three times as many readers as *El Djezaïr el Djedida*, a phenomenon also seen with nationalist publications. *Alger républicain* sold 27,000 copies daily.[44]

Alongside the Arabic-language monthly was a marked increase in Arabic oral propaganda. The party adapted the PPA's technique of 'flying meetings', preaching to assemblies of people gathered at markets or mosques, and held informal discussions in cafés, opening up new areas of political space. The communist-led UFA also adapted PPA methods, using cinema, theatre and female orchestras and interpreters to appeal to largely non-literate female audiences, and holding meetings at traditional women's activities – Turkish baths, weddings, baptisms and other ceremonies – enabling Muslim women to leave their homes. The UFA's Algerian membership rose rapidly in the late 1940s, and groups were formed in Algiers, Oran, Relizane, Sidi bel Abbès, Constantine, Bône and Sétif.[45]

The PCA began using Arabic at congresses, meetings and party schools, as well as at meetings of dock workers and peasants. It implemented bilingualism in mixed-language groups, although actual practice depended on the cell. In urban areas French remained dominant since most Europeans did not speak Arabic, while many Muslims and indigenous Jews spoke Arabic and French. In Oran, French and sometimes Spanish were used, and in Constantine, Arabic. In rural areas or where most members were Arab or Berber, Arabic was used more frequently; rural Europeans were more likely than their urban counterparts to speak Arabic, although only a few non-Muslims, such as the Larribères or the Sportisse brothers, addressed meetings in Arabic. Despite this flexibility, language remained a barrier. Although Gilberte Chemouilli's father and paternal grandmother spoke Arabic, the household was French-speaking, and Gilberte herself had studied English. Her Bab el Oued cell spoke French, and while Algerians might attend cell meetings for several weeks, they often drifted away, unable to follow rapid French discussions. Crucially, though, French was no longer privileged in oral communication, which certain Europeans found problematic.[46]

The growing tolerance towards nationalism was followed by changes in the fortunes of individual leaders – Ouzegane's overt anti-nationalism was seen as problematic. Yet the party's increasing concern for the national struggle made many European members uneasy, in particular those concerned mainly with socioeconomic issues and who had joined when the war-time conditions liberalised. Some left the party, a trend evident in 1946–47. Algerian communists, especially the younger ones, were concerned with fighting national oppression and increasingly intolerant of the lack of support from their European comrades. Chouadria had left the party in September 1946, claiming it was harming the national struggle and that one could not be Muslim and communist at the same time. Nonetheless, Algerians kept joining.[47]

Not only did they join, they occupied key positions that enabled them to gain experience and climb the party hierarchy (Table 7).

Table 7 Ethnic profile of PCA leadership: Algerians and Europeans

	Secretariat	Political Bureau	Central Committee
3rd Congress, March 1946			
Algerians	3	7	European
Europeans	1	6	majority
4th Congress, April 1947			
Algerians	3	9	23
Europeans	1	8	25
5th Congress, May 1949			
Algerians	3	7	30
Europeans	2	3	24
6th Congress, February 1952			
Algerians	3	8	30
Europeans	2	4	17

Source: Adapted from Sivan, *Communisme* (1976), p. 163.

Table 8 Generational profile of PCA leadership: old (pre-1942) and new (post-1942) members

	Political Bureau	Central Committee
3rd Congress, March 1946		
Old (pre-1942)	13	35
New (post-1942)	0	5
4th Congress, April 1947		
Old (pre-1942)	16	37
New (post-1942)	1	11
5th Congress, May 1949		
Old (pre-1942)	7	37
New (post-1942)	3	21
6th Congress, February 1952		
Old (pre-1942)	8	?
New (post-1942)	4	?
October 1954		
Old (pre-1942)	7	?
New (post-1942)	5	?

Source: Adapted from Sivan, *Communisme* (1976), p. 164.

Algerians became section secretaries in small and medium towns and cities, village group secretaries in rural areas, and regional and central committee members. Although Europeans were still the majority on the regional secretariats in the coastal cities of Algiers, Oran and Bône, Algerians were elected to regional secretariats in the hinterland cities of Tlemcen, Blida and Constantine. They saw no contradiction between their religion and their politics, and some paused for prayers during central committee meetings.

Although the PCA recruited comparatively few peasants, Tahar Ghomri, Mejdoub Berrahou and Mohammed Guerrouf were notable examples of rural activists. Born in 1909, Ghomri was a poor peasant from Ouchba village, northeast of Tlemcen. He joined the PCA in 1946, having earlier supported the 'ulama, and organised small peasants and agricultural workers. Berrahou was likewise from a peasant family in Ouchba. Orphaned at age eight, he was influenced by Ghomri and the Badsis. He began organising small cultivators in the mid-1930s, joined the PCA in 1940, was elected to its central committee in 1949 and was later sentenced to fifteen months in prison for his role in the 1951 agricultural strikes. His brother Abdelkader Berrahou joined the Party in 1945. Guerrouf was born around 1917–18 into a very poor peasant community at the foot of the Aurès. He studied to become a Koranic schoolmaster, then served in the Second World War and joined the PCA shortly after the war. By June 1949 he was a central committee member, organising peasants and working with Maurice Laban. Not surprisingly, Guerrouf referred equally to Islam and Marxism in his speeches.[48]

This ethnic transformation was accompanied by a generational change (Table 8). Most Algerians joining the party in the 1940s were young, reflecting both the age profile of the Muslim population and the recruitment success of the JC and UJDA, which became stepping stones for PCA membership.

Algerian workers generally joined the PCA via the CGT; communists organised dockers and miners, for example, which were primarily Algerian occupations. But by comparison with the plebeian background of older Algerian communists, the new members were generally more middle class. While older Algerian communists generally had a school certificate, the new entrants had often attended high school or teacher training colleges; some even had university degrees. As Sivan notes, the social and professional backgrounds of the new Algerian communist recruits was similar to that of young Algerians joining the PPA; indeed, many Algerian communists had family members in the nationalist movement. The growth in Algerian membership pushed the PCA to deal directly with the issue of national self-determination. In turn, the struggle for national self-determination in the context of increasing repression reinforced the struggle for individual democratic rights.[49]

For electoral reform and an Algerian Assembly

In the meantime, buoyed by the UDMA's electoral victory, Abbas proposed to the French government that Algeria become an autonomous republic within the French Union. This was rejected – a significant setback for the UDMA. A second referendum narrowly approved a new French constitution in October 1946; National Assembly elections were held in November. Burnt by its failure to secure Algeria's status an autonomous republic, the UDMA boycotted these elections. But Messali, released from internment, launched the Movement pour le triomphe des libertés démocratiques (Movement for the Triumph of Democratic Liberties, MTLD) and urged participation. Like the communists, nationalists used electoral participation tactically to advance their own partisan interests, rather than strategically to build a broad anti-colonial front.

Operating publicly alongside the underground PPA, the MTLD sought to build a plebeian base to rival the middle-class UDMA. Yet the MTLD did not have a clear class perspective. Rather, Mohammed Harbi suggests, it reflected an organic conception of society and a notion of unity as fusion that obscured class divisions: 'Allah is One, the Nation is One, the People are One, truth is One.' Nor did it have a doctrine, body of theory or schools for training cadre, as did the PCA. On colonialism, it was radical, on women's rights, conservative.[50] Notable amongst those attracted by the MTLD was Ahmed Ben Bella. Born in 1918 in Marnia (now Maghnia), near the Moroccan border, Ben Bella was the son of a small farmer and commercial trader. During the war he had served in the French army, had contact with the Italian resistance and received two medals for valour. But he was profoundly shocked and radicalised by the Constantinois massacre.[51] Boukort, finding the UDMA's atmosphere 'unbreathable', was approached by the MTLD to write for its newspaper.[52]

Despite the PCA's calls for a national democratic front, nationalists remained sceptical. In December the PPA called for a national union based on the coordinated efforts of 'specifically indigenous groups, without excluding its eventual enlargement'. This presumably meant the PCA's exclusion.[53] Generally, nationalists still harboured a profound distrust of the PCA as a result of its initial response to the Constantine massacre. When secondary school student Mohammed Harbi approached Abdallah Toumi in Philippeville (now Skikda) for advice on how to respond to the only Communist in his school, he was told that the PCA was not an Algerian party but a PCF offshoot that sacrificed Algerian interests to those of the USSR and that sought unity with the MTLD solely for its own benefit. Gradually, through a Trotskyist teacher from France, Harbi became interested in Marxism, if not the PCA.[54]

The stigma of being a French party was hard to dispel. In March 1947 the PCA's central committee called for the suppression of the colonial administrative apparatus and for universal franchise and an Algerian assembly. It argued that Algeria should be recognised as an associated territory within the French Union, allowing for collaboration on external affairs with a representative of the French republic.[55] Nonetheless, Ouzegane underlined once again that the PCA was 'a truly Algerian party'. It was not, he insisted, 'a *French* party in which "numerous Muslims [we]re already active"... Nor [wa]s it a *Muslim* party that accept[ed] Europeans. It [wa]s quite simply *Algerian*'. Perhaps it was the only truly Algerian party, he concluded, and its originality reflected that of the Algerian nation.[56]

Algerians continued climbing the PCA's ranks. The party's fourth congress, held at the Algiers suburb of Maison Carrée on 17–19 April 1947, called for 'a free, united and democratic Algeria'. The political bureau included nine Algerians and eight Europeans; the central committee consisted of twenty-three Algerians and twenty-five Europeans (see Table 7 above). The fortunes of individual leaders changed: Bouhali was elected as first secretary, Caballero as second and Ouzegane demoted to third. At the Party's 27–28 December central committee most interventions by both Europeans and Algerians were in French, but Tahar Ghomri and one Boudida spoke in Arabic. Ouzegane had gradually distanced himself and was expelled on 28 December.[57]

On 20 September 1947 the National Assembly had passed a much-debated Algerian Statute that allowed some reforms while conceding to settler interests – Communists had initially supported the bill but abstained in the final vote· The statute established an Algerian Assembly of 120 members with the power to vote on budgetary matters and modify laws applicable to Algeria. But its scope was very restricted, and it was still based on separate ethnically based electoral colleges; its double electoral college gave equal representation to the European minority and Algerian majority. Nonetheless, at the Algerian Assembly elections that October, the MTLD had gained a striking victory. In response, the French state cracked down on nationalists.

By the April 1948 Algerian Assembly elections, more than one-third of all MTLD candidates were in prison. Armed forces intimidated potential voters, and ballot boxes went missing. Election reform was exposed as a fraud.[58] Nonetheless, although demanding that the results be annulled, the PCA still advocated electoral participation. *Liberté* published an article on South Africa suggesting that the absence of black political representatives and the prison-like mining compounds meant that black South Africans were far worse off than Algerians. At least Algerians had some political representation, whereas in South Africa only whites were in Parliament, it argued.[59]

But the 1945 massacre and its aftermath told a different story. Conditions in late 1940s Constantine were heart-breaking. Peasants had lost their harvests and had no grain. 'One saw people coming from the countryside who were miserable, tired, very badly dressed. They had torn clothes,' recalled Noureddine Abdelmoumène. 'Within families we asked why, why were we living in this situation?' His family lived in an Arab neighbourhood called Sidi Bou Annaba. Although Algerians were forbidden to go to well-to-do European areas, they still saw the separate worlds of the rich and the poor. Constantine had a beautiful well-maintained garden for the rich with flowers, chairs and security guards, and a meagre garden for the poor. His uncle was a tramway worker and CGT delegate, and the young Abdelmoumène accompanied him when the workers were on strike. On one occasion all the workers were dismissed. Bringing their families, they occupied the trams to prevent people from boarding, crying: 'we want work and bread for our children.'[60]

The gruelling poverty intensified the fury over electoral fraud. Disillusionment with elections led to a rethink within the MTLD's ranks. Ben Bella joined the clandestine Organisation spéciale (OS). Launched in 1947 by Hocine Aït Ahmed, who came from a well-to-do Kabyle family, most of its members were from Kabylia, and it was strongest in the east. Like the underground PPA, the OS sought independence. Unlike the PPA, it was prepared to use violence. By 1949 Aït Ahmed and Ben Bella were its leading figures.[61]

The MTLD became rapidly factionalised. One faction reflected an urban Communist-influenced popular front strategy, a second Arabophone faction sympathised with Islamic reformism and a third Francophone faction, with republican ideals. But while ethnic tension within the PCA concerned the Algerian–European division, within the nationalist movement the Arab–Berber division was a lightning rod for intra-Algerian conflict. Ideological and ethnic tensions arose over an Islamic as opposed to a secular approach and an Arab as opposed to an Algerian movement encompassing Berbers, with Messali and Aït Ahmed representing the two sides of the dispute. Many Berbers objected to what they felt was Arab dominance; this became known as the Berber crisis. Sadek Hadjerès was shaped by this episode. By then a medical student at the University of Algiers and a leading figure in the

Association des étudiants musulmans d'Afrique du Nord (Association of North African Muslim Students, AEMAN), he was also a PPA–MTLD member. In December 1947 he had read – by candlelight as electricity workers were on strike – Marx's *Communist Manifesto* and Georges Politzer's *Principes élémentaires de philosophie*. He saw no contradiction between his nationalism and his social justice concerns, and he wanted space to discuss the Berber question and social justice issues. But increasingly concerned with the lack of internal democracy that made political discussion difficult, in late 1949 he left the PPA–MTLD. The MTLD's politics were further complicated by disputes between those advocating legal methods of struggle, who pointed in warning to the Sétif massacre, and those pointing to the failure of meaningful electoral reform who advocated greater militancy. On top of these tensions was the personality cult around Messali.[62]

The MTLD's factional wrangling facilitated the PCA's expansion. By late 1948 the Party claimed 12,000–15,000 members, mostly Algerians. According to one report, the PCA had five times the number of members that it had in 1939, and three times the number of late 1946.[63] Its growth was also helped by the PCF's Cold War priorities. The Communist Information Bureau (Cominform), launched by Stalin in September 1947, maintained that world politics was polarised into two antagonistic camps and adopted a critical stance towards nationalist movements that did not accept communist leadership. A Cominform member, and no longer in government, the PCF's priority was to ward off American aggression, especially in Europe and the Eastern bloc. Its diminishing involvement in Algeria was signalled with the departure of Henriette and Raymond Neveu, Jean Papeau and Théodore Mallet in early 1949. This left the PCA freer to develop its own positions, and its discourse became more militant. At the PCA's fifth congress held on 26–29 May 1949 in Oran, Hadj Ali called for national liberation, while Bouhali explained: 'in our country ... without distinction of race or religion, we want to build a democratic Algerian republic with its Constitution, its Parliament, its Government.' The French Union was put on the back burner.[64]

The PCA continued to benefit from the MTLD's disarray and the UDMA's declining membership. The Party offered a measuring rod against which young radicalised Algerians could evaluate the MTLD. Hadjerès joined in January 1951. He had recently published a series on the Cité Mahieddine shantytown near Belcourt, land that had formerly belonged to the feudal-like *bey* Mahieddine and that was now 'a thermometer of rural misery' and 'a hell in which many thousands of human beings lived'. Urban shantytowns were a colonial phenomenon, he argued, accommodating people from diverse *douars* and tribes who had fled hunger and injustice in the countryside only to find urban squalor. The new arrivals stayed in decrepit buildings surrounded by barbed wire that 'looked like concentration camps'. But such 'cities of hunger' were also cities of struggle, he concluded. The PCA organised in them, and the communist Rachid Dalibey had been elected to the Algiers general council by dockers from Cité Mahieddine and the *casbah*.[65]

Hadjerès's university cell was about 90 per cent European and included committed anti-fascists who had joined the party during the war, such as Daniel Timsit, who was starting his medical studies. Hadjerès wanted to organise a public talk in Arabic. The cell discussed it. Mohamed Dib – who came from a ruined but cultivated bourgeois family in Tlemcen and had been mentored as a child by the communist music teacher Roger Bellissant – questioned the need for Arabic, since students understood French. But the majority agreed with Hadjerès on the need for Arabic to attract Muslim students. When Hadjerès gave his talk in Arabic, the Muslim students were surprised – even nationalist student meetings at the time were generally conducted in French. As a result, the cell recruited more Muslims and formed a new predominantly Muslim cell. For Hadjerès, the experience signalled that the PCA was open to discussion and change – a marked difference from his PPA–MTLD experience.[66]

The PCA was extremely active in trade unions and anti-repression campaigns. Through trade unionists such as Dalibey, the party had influence in the ports, and in late 1949 and early 1950 dockers' strikes became 'endemic'. Indeed, early 1950 saw escalating strikes in many sectors in which communist trade unionists played important roles.[67] The CGT's May Day events were, in the British consul-general's words, 'mainly attended by ignorant native elements', while Europeans took the day as a holiday. 'The greater part of the communist following in this country is to be found among the native element of the population,' he reported in May. In late July the PCA's central committee resolved that the national liberation struggle must be the first and constant preoccupation of every communist, and that it was the duty of each communist to rally all Algerian patriots, irrespective of origin or religion, to that struggle.[68]

Strongest in urban areas, the PCA appointed a secretary to oversee rural membership. Recruitment drives took place around Tlemcen, in the Aurès and, later, in the area south of Orléansville, in Kabylia, and the eastern part of the southern territories. Village groups were formed – a cross between a communist cell and a section of the party's peripheral organisations – with local people in charge of propaganda and recruitment. The party's rural strongholds were around Tlemcen and

Orléansville; rural groups counted perhaps one thousand members.

Around Tlemcen communists had been involved in rural subsistence struggles since the mid-1940s. Central committee members Tahar Ghomri and Mejdoub Berrahou built up a communist network in and around Ouchba – Berrahou was a very effective propagandist. When Jacqueline Minne arrived from France in 1948 with her husband Pierre Minne, she was astonished to discover well-organised peasant groups in contact with urban labourers and railway workers. She was appointed as a teacher at Négrier (Chetouane), where she discovered Algerian and European agricultural workers in feudal-like conditions and sedentary nomads living harsh, impoverished lives. After clashing with the local colon, she was dismissed and began teaching at Aïn Fezza, a mixed European–Algerian school that was nonetheless marked by rigid discrimination. She and her husband divorced, and in 1950 she married Abdelkader Guerroudj, a teacher from Tlemcen. Born into a very poor peasant family – formerly a *'grande famille'* – Guerroudj had been raised in a nationalist atmosphere – his maternal grandfather was Messali's cousin. An apt student with an interest in language – he studied French, Latin and Greek – Guerroudj had attended the college of Tlemcen and started teaching in 1949. Abdelkader and Jacqueline Guerroudj joined the PCA in 1950 and travelled to different villages to hold meetings. Abdelkader Guerroudj also organised with Ahmed Inal, another communist teacher. Peasant communities may well have been interested in the party's positions on land and rural development, but conservative Muslims looked askance at the party's call for the vote for Muslim women. Nonetheless, Jacqueline Guerroudj felt accepted and was asked to advise rural women on nutrition and hygiene.[69]

The OS counted some 1,000–1,500 fighters. But in March 1950 it was decimated by a police crackdown: 363 members were arrested, and 197 imprisoned. 'The plot was apparently launched in the Department of Constantine, where some 150 arrests were made and small quantities of arms and ammunition were found early in April', reported the British consul-general. Further arrests were made in Algérois, 'where it [wa]s claimed that extensive, if not large, arms caches were unearthed'. The next month the OS raided Oran's main post office, taking over three million francs. Those not arrested fled to Egypt, France or the Aurès to form an underground *maquis* (rural resistance movement); Ben Bella escaped from prison and went to Cairo. With Messali's support, the MTLD's central committee declared the OS dissolved; for them, its destruction signalled the futility of armed methods. But the PCA and UFA campaigned actively on behalf of the OS arrestees. Raymonde Peschard, born in 1929 into a communist family in Algiers and later raised by her communist uncle in Constantine, threw herself into politics in the late 1940s. A social worker, she organised a women's campaign in Constantine to help OS prisoners; anti-repression campaigning overrode organisational divisions.[70]

United fronts...

Communism still functioned as an international community, and as part of this community PCA members travelled to other communist countries and participated in world peace movement forums. The October 1949 Chinese Revolution had a big impact on local communists, who were impressed by Mao Zedong's writings; heretofore, by some accounts, the PCF had filtered their selection of communist publications.[71] Baya Allaouchiche was elected UFA secretary-general and joined the PCA's central committee in that year. In December she went to China as part of an Algerian delegation and attended the Beijing Asian Women's Congress as an observer. Alice Sportisse, the National Assembly Deputy for Oran, visited the Soviet Union in early 1950. The UJDA's secretary, Hamou Kraba, attended the National Federation of Democratic Youth meeting in China in October 1950; in July he had been tried before a military court in Constantine for 'corrupting Army morale' as a result of UJDA-organised meetings demanding an end to the Vietnam war and repatriation of Algerian troops. An Algerian delegation attended the Second World Congress of the International Union of Students in Prague. These first-hand visits reinforced their belief in an international communist community.[72]

The PCA followed developments in Vietnam, Morocco and Tunisia closely; *Liberté*'s readers were familiar with those struggles and with debates about armed struggle. Japan had occupied Vietnam during the Second World War, and France saw its return as central to its plans for the French Union. But the Vietnamese fiercely contested French reoccupation. The PCA appealed to the MTLD and UDMA in October 1949 and March 1950 for a joint stand against war in Vietnam. The MTLD refused, the UDMA never replied, and some nationalists criticised the party for looking away from Algeria. The PCA had more success in organising Oran dockers to refuse to handle ships destined for Vietnam. The UFA had strong presence there, and Algerian women – as the wives and family members of dockers – were involved in the action, some even stoning the police.[73]

The PCA's headquarters were raided on 30 September 1950, and in November its central committee approached the MTLD and UDMA with a proposal for a *Charte d'unité et d'action* (Charter of union and action) to form a national democratic front to fight for independence – an Algerian democratic republic with its own constitution, parliament and government. Many nationalists saw little sense in unity when they themselves had much popular support. However, the grinding repression made some type of united action necessary, if not inevitable. 'A few words of solidarity' in support of popular struggles in Vietnam, Morocco and Tunisia, or 'the word "independence" used in a speech or an article' were enough to cause their author to be charged, tried and condemned for undermining state security. More and more activists were thrown in prison. Some withdrew from politics. Thus, attendance at UFA meetings had peaked in the late 1940s, but declined steadily in the early 1950s, presumably due to repression. Others threw themselves into a frenzy of activity, told by their leaders, both communists and nationalists, to focus on anti-repression campaigns. Political trials became the order of the day, and the accused used them as political space to present their views. The trial of Abane Ramdane and co-accused began on 25 January 1951, and the trial of those charged with the Oran post office raid, in February.[74]

Over time the PCA's appeals for united action finally bore fruit. Joint collaboration on amnesty committees and shared prison experiences helped to dispel nationalist suspicions. In March 1951 activists at Tébessa launched a committee against repression and appealed to the three main political organisations for united action. On 11 June another political trial, this time of 128, began in Bône. Legislative elections were scheduled for 17 June, during the trial of the 128. Once again, they were marred by massive fraud. The political trials brought the issue of torture to the public eye. Combined with electoral fraud, this drew the attention of French intellectuals to the Algerian situation.[75]

The next month representatives of the PCA, MTLD, UDMA and the *'ulama* met in Algiers to launch the Front Algérien pour la défense et le respect des libertés (Algerian Front for the Defence and Respect of Liberties). They pointed to the consistent mockery of Algerian rights since 1948, especially the right to vote and express opinions. The Algerian Front called for annulment of the 17 June elections, denounced the falsification of electoral results and police use of torture and demanded an end to repression. Its programme called for freedom to vote in the second college; freedom of belief, opinion, press and meetings; the release of all political prisoners; the lifting of the repressive measures imposed on Messali and the end of administrative interference in Muslim religious affairs. It was, reported *Liberté*, the 'first decisive step on the path to unity for national independence'.[76]

The Algerian Front's first general assembly took place on 5 August 1951. It appealed to all Algerians irrespective of opinion, religion or race to support its aims in publicising the lack of political rights for Algerians. Its mandate was narrow to avoid restricting the activities of the participating groups outside the front. The plan was to form committees around the country. These were to hold meetings, send resolutions and launch a press campaign in Algeria and France to publicise Algerian political conditions.[77]

To practice unity proved far more difficult than to call for it. The Algerian Front's first difficulty occurred when the PCA refused to support the nationalist boycott of the October 1951 departmental elections. At the urging of Bachir Hadj Ali and Ahmed Akkache, the PCA's central committee voted for boycott. But concerned that such an anti-colonialist action would jeopardise its own united front activities, the PCF sent Léon Feix to Algeria to convince the PCA to participate. Another central committee meeting was called, and sufficient numbers switched their position; clearly, the PCF still exerted moral authority over certain PCA members. By one account, Akkache was furious when the meeting ended and Bachir Hadj Ali had tears in his eyes. The PCF's influence on this occasion merely confirmed nationalist perceptions that the PCA was not really Algerian.[78]

The Algerian Front never recovered, yet when Akkache presented the front's first balance sheet in January 1952, he pointed to some successes. Due to the front's pressure, the sentences meted out to Descartes strikers had been reduced, the colonialist provocations in the Aurès had failed and hunger strikers in Oran and Orléansville had been helped. In the meantime, the PCA continued its amnesty campaign: November 1951 had seen the start of the OS trial of 56 in Blida, and the PCA demanded the prisoners' release.[79]

The PCA's sixth – and last – congress took place at Hussein Dey on 21–24 February 1952, with Marty in attendance. Preparatory regional conferences had already taken place at Blida, Bône and Algiers. The Party demanded bread, peace, land and national independence. The Algerian people's first concern was to live freely and independently, Bouhali began. In the Chinese Revolution's wake, the Vietnamese, Moroccan and Tunisian struggles indicated that colonised peoples were no longer willing to accept their slave conditions. Algeria's liberation would be the work of all Algerians, he stressed.[80] The struggle for a sovereign national assembly was paramount. This would be elected on the basis of direct, universal suffrage by all Algerians, irrespective of origin, through secret ballot. However, as a transitional step, the two principal ethnic groups would have proportionate representation – a significant if unacknowledged revision of the 'nation in formation' thesis. The national assembly would draw up a constitution for a democratic Algerian republic. It was in the interests of the Algerian and French peoples that a future Algerian republic should establish economic and cultural relations with France that were free and based on equal rights. The party would express its view on this matter, but it would not stipulate the relationship with France in advance.[81]

Algerianisation was reinforced. The ethnic composition of the political bureau and central committee had shifted considerably to reflect the increasing Algerian membership. The secretariat consisted of Bouhali, Hadj Ali, Caballero, Akkache and André Moine. Laïd Lamrani and Sadek Hadjerès were elected to the central committee – the former re-elected at the insistence of peasant delegates. The congress resolved to reorganise the party so that sections composed primarily of Algerians – whether in predominantly Algerian neighbourhoods or occupations, such as dockers, miners, tram workers or sanitation workers – received special support. *Liberté* published articles on racism in the party, and the congress resolved to expel European members engaged in discriminatory practices.[82] While some European members no doubt felt uncomfortable with these changes, Jewish communists were concerned about rising anti-Semitism in the USSR and Eastern Europe, which reached a peak with the arrest of Jewish doctors in Moscow – Stalin's 1951–53 'Jewish doctors' plot' – and the execution of Jewish communists in Prague in December 1952. Jewish PCA members who met together were reportedly advised not to do so. In 1953 some Jewish communists in Constantine refused to renew their party membership. Despite these internal tensions, the party was growing.[83]

Unity efforts continued. Algerian communists pressured the PCA to reformulate the 'nation in formation' thesis, even though they defended it in public. The MTLD and UDMA both envisioned an inclusive Algerian nation comprising all those who wished to belong to it, irrespective of race or religion. Algerians of European descent who became Algerian citizens would have equal rights, stressed the MTLD. Likewise 'liberatory nationalism' could never be based on 'a principle of action that was essentially religious in nature'. The national movement aspired to liberate Islam from colonialism, but not to convert people of different beliefs.[84] The MTLD and UDMA sought a regional alliance of nationalist parties in Algeria, Tunisia and Morocco – without communists. February 1952 saw the launch of the Committee of North African Union and Action, but regional coordination proved as elusive as unity within the country.

Organisational rivalries were not the only impediment to unity. The country's size and limited infrastructure were obstacles, although railway and road construction slowly provided an infrastructural basis for unity. By the 1950s a commercial bus service connected the Tell coastal areas and the northern Saharan oases, facilitating trade, travel and the diffusion of ideas. However, communist and nationalist ideas were slow to penetrate the Mzab. Tensions between the conservative religious establishment and reformist *'ulama* had deepened since the 1930s; by the early 1950s, the reformists were a majority. The reformist–conservative division was linked to differences about electoral participation. Reformists supported participation, but Sliman Boudjenah, still insisting that France honour its 1853 convention, sided with the conservatives. In February 1951 Boudjenah formed the Parti de l'union populaire de l'oued-M'zab (Popular Union Party of the Mzab Oasis, PUPOM). Advocating education and economic development, the PUPOM nonetheless felt that closer association with the Tell would lead to the Mzab's 'ruin and depopulation'. It envisioned a united, autonomous Mzab rather than a united Algerian nation.[85]

Unity efforts faced another setback with the Algerian Front's second breakdown, this time over Messali's May 1952 arrest and deportation to Niort, France. The MTLD called a strike for 23 May to protest both Messali's deportation and police brutality towards Muslim demonstrators in Orléansville. The PCA and CGT supported the strike, but not so the UDMA and the *'ulama*, worried about retaliation. Popular support was uneven. European workers, even those organised by the communists, generally failed to come out in support of Algerian rights.[86] The MTLD argued that the Algerian Front had not lived up to popular hopes and had devalued unity as a method of struggle. There was clearly a need for unity: its organ *Algérie libre* had been seized and the PCA's premises and those of *Liberté*, searched. Nonetheless, the Algerian Front lapsed into inactivity.[87]

Notwithstanding the Algerian Front's collapse, in late 1953 the PCA and MTLD signalled their desire to try again. In key respects their views on the demise of the Algerian Front and the pressing need for unity converged. On 1 November the PCA's central committee appealed for a national democratic Algerian front. Only a united people could end colonialism, it argued. Individual political parties could not succeed. The PCA proposed a new front based on a minimum programme that included:

- Amnesty for all victims of colonial repression, the release of progressive prisoners, the termination of Messali's exile and the end of discriminatory measures;
- Respect for democratic liberties recognised by the French constitution and application of the Algerian Statute's progressive measures, including suppression of mixed communes and southern territories;
- Support for popular socioeconomic demands, including those of urban and rural workers, peasants, artisans, small traders, former combatants and the unemployed;

- Education for all children, and official status and teaching of the Arabic language;
- Repatriation of Algerian troops from Vietnam and no further use of Algerians in imperialist wars;
- Defence of peace.[88]

The MTLD responded on 10 December, calling for an Algerian national congress to draw up a charter of the Algerian people. Its programme of action, similar to that of the PCA's, reflected four principles: first, Algeria was a nation; second, Algeria should have the right to self-determination recognised by the UN Charter, which France had signed; third, a sovereign national assembly should be elected by all Algerians based on direct universal suffrage; and fourth, a democratic and social republican state should be formed. Yet when the PCA pursued this, the MTLD stalled, arguing that it was precipitous to launch the national congress before the idea was popularised. The Algerian Front had failed, it claimed, precisely because it was a top-down *entente* of political parties rather than a mass organisation; any union not based on a popular foundation would likewise fail.[89]

The PCA continued its international initiatives, sending William Sportisse to Budapest that year to produce an Arabic-language radio programme called *sawt el istiqlal ou al selm* (the voice of independence and peace), which used Radio-Budapest's airwaves to broadcast across the Maghreb, creating new and expansive political space. Reflecting the joint collaboration of the three North African communist parties, Sportisse's colleagues included a Moroccan man and a Tunisian man who broadcast in 'Arabe moderne' and a Moroccan woman who broadcast in 'Arabe parlé' (spoken Arabic). The broadcasts were heard in Tunisia, Morocco and the south and plateau areas of Algeria from May 1954, enabling people across the region to learn about each other's struggles.[90]

...and fragmentation

People were angry, workers militant. The mood at a May Day demonstration in Constantine was grim. Unemployed workers were reportedly forbidden to look for work at the trade union centre; when assembled outside the police shot at them. They ran behind the building to claim the garden of the rich, chanting: 'we pay taxes so we want the garden', linking the economic and the political. Noureddine Abdelmoumène had been exposed to socialist ideas from a young age. He had learned about workers' struggles from his uncle, and his father was in the Force ouvrière, a socialist organisation that the son felt was too soft with the bosses. The head of Abdelmoumène's school was a communist with novel ideas, and Abdelmoumène had access to communist literature; he read about the campaign to save Ethel and Julius Rosenberg, executed by the United States in June 1953. He also attended meetings at the Ben Badis Circle, where they discussed North African developments.[91] People sought a way forward through ideas.

Yet political space within the MTLD had contracted to such an extent that discussion was impossible. Over the past year factions had crystallised around the central committee, or 'centralists', on the one side, and Messali and his followers, the Messalistes, on the other. In March 1954 a tiny group of OS members and sympathisers formed the Comité révolutionnaire pour l'unité et l'action (Revolutionary Committee for Unity and Action, CRUA) to reconcile the divided MTLD. In June Messali's supporters declared him MTLD president for life and dissolved the central committee; two months later the central committee expelled Messali and his followers. Each side's press underlined the unbridgeable divide. By mid-1954, the CRUA had 22 members, mostly young men from small towns or villages with elementary or secondary school education, but with political roots in the cities. Unable to end the MTLD's endless internal strife, it planned to launch guerrilla struggle and build a national liberation front. But infiltrated by a police mole, the group dissolved itself.[92]

On 5 July the PCA called for an assembly of all anti-colonialists to form a national front that would learn from the Algerian Front experience. It attributed the MTLD's split to Messali's refusal to convene a national congress proposed by the centralists. The PCA's concern was how to build unity in the face of the split. Amnesty remained the centre of its activity, and its list of democratic rights included the vote for Muslim women. Alongside Alice Sportisse's continued call for Muslim women's enfranchisement, the UFA organised demonstrations; in Sidi bel Abbès one thousand veiled women marched on the town hall with a petition demanding the vote.[93]

In September the PCA outlined its three fundamental political principles: firstly, that communists opposed all forms of national oppression; secondly, that communists supported the right of peoples to self-determination, including the right to separation; and thirdly, that separation was not positive in all cases. It argued that the form of national independence should be decided by a democratic election based on universal franchise for a sovereign national assembly, in which ethnic groups should have proportionate representation. The assembly would draw up a constitution, and the Algerian people could then freely determine their relationship with France. Algerians of European origin could become citizens in an independent Algeria or live in Algeria as French citizens, just as Algerian citizens lived in France.

Alongside national self-determination, it demanded the implementation of all rights available under the French constitution and, rather than an actual Algerian assembly, the election of a representative assembly to meet with French representatives to discuss Algerian institutions and French–Algerian relations. It also called for bread, peace and land and a united struggle in which groups could also fight for their own interests. These goals were to be won through multiple methods – petitions, demonstrations, strikes and electoral campaigns. The struggle's intensity would reflect the political maturity of the proletariat and the national movement. Compromise with the adversary would be acceptable if it advanced the struggle, but should otherwise be rejected.[94]

The PCA was not considering armed struggle – and indeed hoped to avoid bloodshed – yet *Liberté* provided regular coverage of Vietnam's guerrilla war led by the communist Ho Chi Minh. In late 1953, while preparing for peace talks with the Vietminh, French troops had attacked Dien Bien Phu in northwest Vietnam and built a garrison holding close to 16,000 troops, including North African soldiers. On 13 March 1954 the Vietminh attacked the garrison, sealing it off from the outside world. It finally fell on 7 May, signalling the end of French colonialism in Vietnam. *Liberté* drew the lessons. 'Here is the "secret" of the victories of the popular Vietnamese army', it reported, quoting the proclamations of Vietminh leaders: 'the people are our forest ... the people love the army'. Likewise, Bouhali – underground since December 1953 – stressed that the Vietnamese victory was due to its united struggle on national soil.[95] In short, the PCA was disseminating positive views on guerrilla war. Over the nine years since the Constantinois massacre, it had travelled a tremendous distance, both in its membership and its programme.

Despite the mounting repression, certain observers remained cautiously optimistic about the prospects for colonial reform. The British consul-general had toured the country in April–June 1954. In western Algérois, he observed, 'the astonishing contrast between the French farms in this rich wheat belt and those of comparable acreage owned by Moslems is incredible.' Tension was hardly surprising. Even in the remote town of Chellala, Messali's presence before his deportation to France 'had caused several disturbances'. Yet in Oranie, where, in the consul-general's view, the UDMA was the only significant Algerian party, 'complete economic parity between Europeans and Moslems [wa]s gradually producing a shift of wealth into Moslem hands'; indeed, in some parts there was 'more capital in Moslem than in European hands'. In the south, Ghardaïa's Mozabites – 'the puritans of Islam, rigid and austere, but with keen business acumen ... the grocers and tradesmen of North Africa' – still sought autonomy. The visit of the Minister of the Interior François Mitterand in October had 'brought a positive and stabilising factor to the Algerian political situation', he reported. Moreover, Algiers' Mayor Jacques Chevallier had 'unquestionably led to a real improvement in Franco-Moslem relations'.

The capital's population had exploded. Since 1930 more than one and one-half million rural Algerians had moved to Algiers; since 1942 the number of shantytowns had multiplied by ten. The vastly overcrowded urban areas were zones of nationalist discontent, the authorities feared. A proponent of assimilation, Chevallier's plan was to build ethnically mixed housing estates. Presently, noted the consul-general: 'a young Moslem couple who wish to become European are more or less stoned in the Arab quarter and ostracised in the European.' Thus, in his view, the importance of Chevallier's plans for mixed housing estates. Indeed, one local official had forecast that if the current regime could be maintained for thirty years, 'it would by then be irrevocably established and there could be no possibility of a reversal to any other policy than that of Franco-Moslem integration'.[96] But the idea of armed struggle was already in the air.

Notes

1 Transcript of United Nations Charter (1945), http://goo.gl/VGG1W3 (accessed 3 August 2010).
2 Evans, *Algeria*, pp. 99–101; Basil Davidson, *Modern Africa: A Social and Political History*, 2nd edn (Longman: London and New York: 1989), p. 127; Joly, *French Communist*, pp. 37–8.
3 Ian Carter, 'Positive and Negative Liberty', in Edward N. Zalta (ed.), *The Stanford Encyclopedia of Philosophy (Fall 2008 Edition)*, http://goo.gl/cDsTMX (accessed 14 August 2011).
4 This discussion draws on Planche, *Sétif*; Rey-Goldzeiguer, O*rigines*; Sivan, *Communisme*, pp. 139–54; Jean-Pierre Peyroulou, 'Sétif and Guelma (May 1945)', *Online Encyclopedia of Mass Violence*, 26 March 2008, pp. 1–13, http://goo.gl/5yWszl (accessed 11 August 2011); Alain Ruscio, 'Les Communistes et les massacres du Constantinois (mai–juin 1945)', *Vingtième Siècle. Revue d'histoire*, 94 (2/2007), pp. 217–29; Yves Benôt, *Massacres coloniaux, 1944–1950: La IVe République et la mise au pas des colonies françaises* (Paris: La Découverte, 1994), pp. 9–35, 54–64.
5 TNA: PRO FO 371/49275, *Aux autorités anglaises et alliés*, 8 May 1945.
6 TNA: PRO FO 371/49275, British Consul-General, 23 May 1945, notes that the account was substantiated by the officer commanding A Company, 44th Battalion, SAAF, and by French eye-witnesses. Other sources say it was a flag.
7 *Aux autorités anglaises*; Martin Thomas, 'Colonial Violence in Algeria and the Distorted Logic of State Retribution: The Sétif uprising of 1945', *Journal of Military History*, 75:1 (2011), 125–58, 139; Martin Thomas, 'Colonial Minds and Colonial Violence: The Sétif Uprising and the Savage Economics of Colonialism', in Martin Thomas (ed.), *The French Colonial Mind: Violence, Military Encounters and Colonialism*, vol. 2 (Lincoln, NE, and London, 2011), pp. 140–73.
8 Planche, *Sétif*, pp. 116–18; Alleg, *Mémoire*, p. 125; Ouzegane, *Meilleur Combat*, pp. 92–3; Benôt, *Massacres*, pp. 16–17; Ageron, *Histoire*, vol. 2, p. 573, puts the death toll

at 29 on that day.
9 Sivan, *Communisme*, pp. 140, 143, Gallissot (ed.), *Algérie*, pp. 44–5; Thomas, 'Colonial Violence', pp. 139–41.
10 TNA: PRO FO 371/49275, British Consul-General, 23 May 1945; Peyroulou, 'Sétif', pp. 4–5, 7; Thomas, 'Colonial Violence', p. 142; Gallissot (ed.), *Algérie*, pp. 44–5; Prochaska, *Making*, pp. 237–8.
11 TNA: PRO FO 371/49275, Telegram, War Cabinet Distribution, 17 May 1945; 'L'ordre est maintenant rétabli', and 'Pour maintenir en Algérie l'ordre français', *Echo d'Alger* (13–14, 16 May 1945), p. 1; Ruedy, *Modern Algeria*, p. 149.
12 TNA: PRO FO 371/49276, British Consul-General, 31 May 1945; Peyroulou, 'Sétif', p. 7; Gallissot (ed.), *Algérie*, pp. 44–5; Thomas, 'Colonial Violence', p. 144; interview with Abdelmoumène.
13 TNA: PRO FO 371/49276, British Consul-General, 28 June, 9 July 1945; *Frères algériens!*
14 The number of Algerian deaths remains hotly contested. Estimates range from 1,500 to 45,000; Planche, *Sétif*, pp. 218, 310–12 suggests 20,000–30,000. Sivan, *Communisme*, pp. 143–5; Gallissot (ed.), *Algérie*, p. 218; Peyroulou, 'Sétif', p. 8; Ageron, *Histoire*, vol. 2, pp. 573–4; Benôt, *Massacres*, pp. 13–14; Martha Crenshaw, 'The Effectiveness of Terrorism in the Algerian War', in Martha Crenshaw (ed.), *Terrorism in Context* (University Park, PA: Pennsylvania State University, 1995), 473–513, p, 479.
15 Ruedy, *Modern Algeria*, pp. 149–50; Ageron, *Histoire*, vol. 2, p. 57; sources vary on numbers arrested and sentenced.
16 Interview with Hadjerès.
17 TNA: PRO FO 371/49275, *A bas les provocateurs Hitleriens*; *Peuple algérien*.
18 « des provocations des agents hitlériens du PPA et du PPF ... des seigneurs fascistes de la colonisation, des féodaux musulmans et des hauts fonctionnaires vichyssois », Sivan, *Communisme*, p. 141.
19 « des éléments troubles d'inspiration et de méthodes hitlériennes se sont livrés à des agressions à main armée sur les populations qui fêtaient la victoire dans la ville de Sétif and dans les environs », Khalfa, Alleg and Benzine, *Aventure*, p. 37; TNA: PRO FO 371/49276, British Consul-General, 31 May 1945; Stora, *Messali*, pp. 191–6.
20 « La ville est un deuil, les rues sont presque vides. Partout, des soldats en armes. Ce sont, en majorité, des tirailleurs algériens. Aux carrefours les plus importants, des mitrailleurs et des fusils-mitrailleurs ... cette poignée de misérables agents de l'hitlérisme (faux nationalistes, seigneurs de la colonisation, féodaux terriens, agents des trusts) », Roger Esplaas, 'De Sétif', *Liberté* (17 May 1945), p. 1.
21 « faux nationalistes: mouchards, criminels et valets du fascisme », *Liberté* (17 May 1945), pp. 1, 3.
22 PCF 261J 7/, box 1, folder 3, « est devenue dans le pays une des principales revendications », Boukort to Thorez, 25 May 1945, p. 7.
23 Camus, *Combat*, p. 204; Todd, *Camus: Une vie*, pp. 518–23.
24 Alleg, *Mémoire*, pp. 123–4; Sivan, *Communisme*, pp. 140–2, 146; Khalfa, Alleg and Benzine, *Aventure*, p. 41; Jacqueline Lévi-Valensi (ed.), *Camus at Combat: Writing 1944–1947* (Princeton, NJ, and Oxford: Princeton University, 2006), pp. 212–14.
25 *Liberté* (24, 31 May 1945).
26 Khalfa, Alleg and Benzine, *Aventure*, pp. 39–41; Gallissot (ed.), *Algérie*, pp. 536–8; interview with Gilberte Sportisse.
27 TNA: PRO FO 371/49276, British Consul-General, 30 July 1945; *Assemblée consultative provisoire*, 10–11 July, 1350–1, 1373–5; PCF 261J 7/, box 3, 'Contre les trusts et le fascisme, union des populations d'Algérie européenne et musulmanes: Déclaration commune des Partis socialiste et communiste', *Liberté* (14 June 1945); *l'Humanité* (3, 11 July 1945).
28 « sanglants événements ... masses européennes et musulmanes de la ville et de la campagne prennent conscience de leur solidarité basée sur l'identité de leurs intérêts immédiats et sur la volonté de se forger un avenir commun fraternel ... sentiment d'une originalité nationale liée aux idées de liberté », Manifeste du Parti communiste algérien (12 août 1945), in Collot and Henry (eds), *Mouvement national*, pp. 208–12; Sivan, *Communisme*, p. 152; Rey-Goldzeiguer, *Origines*,

p. 359. In 1962 the PCA had still not accepted the depth of European racism, claiming in 'For a Free Algerian Republic', p. 35, that the massacre was 'carried out under de Gaulle's orders in May–June of 1945.'

29 *Liberté* (24 May 1945); Larbi Bouhali, 'Après les incidents de Sétif, la répression se trompe d'adresse', *Liberté* (31 May 1945), p. 1; Bennoune, 'Algerian Peasants', p. 7; Sivan, *Communisme*, p. 149; Ruscio, 'Communistes', p. 226; Ruedy, *Modern Algeria*, pp. 149–50; Hafid Khatib, *Le 1er juillet 1956: L'Accord FLN–PCA et l'intégration des « combattants de la libération » dans l'armée de libération nationale en Algérie* (Algiers: Office des Publications Universitaires, 1991), p. 10; Thomas, 'Colonial Violence', p. 150; interviews with William Sportisse. The sources vary on numbers sentenced.

30 Amar Ouzegane, 'Notes sur la situation politique en Algérie', *Cahiers du communisme*, 2 (January 1946), in Jurquet, *Révolution nationale*, vol. 4, 387–93, p. 388; Sivan, *Communisme*, p. 124.

31 Sivan, *Communisme*, p. 152; Ruedy, *Modern Algeria*, pp. 150–1; Lévi-Valensi, *Camus at Combat*, p. 234.

32 Ouzegane, 'Notes sur la situation', pp. 392–3; Alleg, *Mémoire*, p. 318; on Stalin, ANOM FR CAOM 9Fi300, 'Gloire immortelle à J. Staline', Flyer for public meeting, PCA, Oran, 1953, http://goo.gl/sKZ7lo (accessed 10 September 2013).

33 Ageron, *Histoire*, vol. 2, p. 495; Ruedy, *Modern Algeria*, pp. 122–3; Wolf, *Peasant Wars*, p. 235.

34 B. Hadj Ali, 'Les médersas peuvent-elles se transformer en universités?', *Liberté* (4 July 1946), p. 1.

35 *Liberté* (3, 10 January, 7 February, 9, 16 May 1946); Interview with Alleg, 23 June 2010; Sivan, *Communisme*, pp. 174–5.

36 PCF 261J 7/, Box 3, *Amnistie aux détenus politiques musulmans*: Discours des élus Communistes Mohamed Chouadria, député de Constantine, Camille Larribère, député d'Oran, Pierre Fayet, député d'Alger à l'Assemblée Nationale Constituante (1946); 'Le projet sur l'amnistie en Algérie est adopté à l'unanimité', *Oran Républicain* (2 March 1946), p. 1; Paul Caballero, 'Congres digne d'un Grand Parti', *Liberté* (28 March 1946), p. 1; Planche, *Sétif*, pp. 303–6; Sivan, *Communisme*, p. 163.

37 *Liberté* (28 March 1946) listed nine political bureau members: Ahmed Mahmoudi, Pierre Fayet, Nicolas Zannettacci, Alice Sportisse, Henriette Neveu, Roger Rouzeau, Cherif Djemad, Bouali Taleb, Abdelhamid Boudiaf.

38 Amar Ouzegane, 'Discours prononcé à l'Assemblée nationale constituante le 5 avril 1946 sur: « Double Collège, condition de l'Union des populations algériennes »', in Jurquet, *Révolution nationale*, vol. 4, 394–401, pp. 395–7, 400.

39 Boukort, *Souffle*, p. 122; Ruedy, *Modern Algeria*, p. 151; PCF 261J 7/, box 1, file 3, Boukort to président du Comité d'initiative pour l'amnistie en faveur des détenus politiques musulmans, 7 April 1946.

40 « parti de l'avenir », Appel du 3ᵉ Congrès du Parti communiste algérien (21 mars 1946), in Collet and Henry (eds), *Mouvement national*, 215–19, p. 218; Sivan, *Communisme*, pp. 153–4; Gallissot (ed.), *Algérie*, p. 561; MacMaster, *Burning*, pp. 33, 72.

41 Amar Ouzegane, 'Le parti communiste Algérien, parti de la nation Algérienne en formation', *Liberté* (18 July 1946), p. 1; interview with Hadjerès.

42 Marty, 'La Question algérienne', in Jurquet, *Révolution nationale*, vol. 4, p. 430.

43 *Liberté* (25 July, 1 August 1946); Khatib, Alleg and Benize, *Aventure*, p. 41; Khatib, *1er juillet*, pp. 10–11.

44 ANOM FM 81F/759, 'Collusions entre communistes et rebelles': *L'action du parti communiste dans la rébellion en Algérie* (supplément à la semaine en Algérie du 13 janvier 1957 au 20 janvier 1957), p. 3; Sivan, *Communisme*, pp. 173–4.

45 MacMaster, *Burning*, pp. 34–5, 37, 61, n. 44.

46 Interview with Alleg, 23 June 2010; interview with Gilberte Sportisse.

47 Sivan, *Communisme*, p. 169; Gallissot (ed.) *Algérie*, p. 218.

48 Gallissot (ed.), *Algérie*, pp. 78–9, 136, 307, 318; interview with Hadjerès.

49 Sivan, *Communisme*, pp. 162–6, 169; Pierre Haudiquet, 'L'Incendie', in Alleg (ed.), *Guerre*, vol. 2, 13–297, p. 113; interview with Alleg, 23 June 2010.

50 Harbi, *Vie*, pp. 73, 75, 134–5.

51 Horne, Savage War, pp. 74–5; Alf Andrew Heggoy, Insurgency and Counterinsurgency in Algeria (Bloomington., IN, and London: Indiana University Press, 1972), pp. 38–9, 53–4.
52 Ruedy, Modern Algeria, pp. 150–1; Boukort, Souffle, pp. 122, 124–5.
53 Appel du Comité central du Parti communiste algérien (21 juillet 1946) and Appel du Bureau politique du PPA pour l'union nationale (décembre 1946), both in Collot and Henry (eds), Mouvement national, pp. 228–32. Khatib, Alleg and Benzine, Aventure, p. 43.
54 Harbi, Vie, pp. 78–9, 85–6.
55 Paul Caballero, 'Le comité central du parti communiste adopte un projet de statut de l'Algérie', Liberté (13 March 1947), p. 1; Harbi, Vie, p. 77.
56 « un Parti français au sein duquel "militant déjà des nombreux musulmane" ... Il n'est pas non plus un Parti musulman au sein duquel on accepte des Européens. Il est tout simplement Algérien », Liberté (10 April 1947), emphasis in original.
57 'Un niveau de discussion élevé, une ardente volonté de lutte', Liberté (1 January 1948), p. 3; Khatib, 1er juillet, pp. 12–13; Sivan, Communisme, p. 173, n.43; Haudiquet, 'L'Incendie', p. 113; interviews with Alleg, 11, 23 June 2010, and Hadjerès; Gallissot (ed.), Algérie, pp. 501–2; interview with Fattouma Ouzegane, Algiers, 24 September 2011.
58 Ruedy, Modern Algeria, pp. 150–2; Horne, Savage War, pp. 39, 69–70; William H. Lewis, 'The Decline of Algeria's FLN', Middle East Journal, 20:2 (Spring 1966), 161–72, p. 163; Rey-Goldzeiguer, Origines, p. 360; Heggoy, Insurgency, pp. 30–2, 36; Khatib, 1er juillet, p. 20; Sivan, Communisme, p. 178; Liberté (22, 29 May, 5 June 1947).
59 'Choses vues en Afrique du Sud', Liberté (6 March 1947), p. 5; Liberté (22 April 1948), p. 1.
60 « On voyait des gens venant de la campagne qui étaient misérables, fatigués, très mal habillés, ils avaient les vêtements déchirés ... dans des familles on demandait pourquoi, pourquoi on vivait dans cette situation ... nous voulons du travail et du pain pour nos enfants », Interview with Abdelmoumène.
61 Ruedy, Modern Algeria, pp. 153–4; Mahfoud Bennoune, 'The Introduction of Nationalism into Rural Algeria: 1919–1954', Maghreb Review, 2:3 (1977), 1–12, p. 7; Horne, Savage War, p. 75; Heggoy, Insurgency, pp. 32–9, 54; Carlier, Nation, p. 106; Evans, Memory, pp. 26–7.
62 Interview with Hadjerès; Harbi, Vie, pp. 113–16; Ruedy, Modern Algeria, pp. 153–4.
63 Sivan, Communisme, p. 168, n. 24.
64 « dans notre pays ... sans distinction de race ni de religion, nous voulons ... édifier une République démocratique algérienne, ayant sa Constitution, son Parlement, son Gouvernement », Khatib, 1er juillet, p. 14; Liberté (2 June 1949); Sivan, Communisme, p. 178; Ageron, Histoire, vol. 2, p. 600; Joly, French Communist, pp. 43–4; Gaston Revel, Un instituteur communiste en Algérie: L'Engagement et le combat (1936–1965), ed. Alexis Sempé (Cahors: La Louve, 2013), pp. 203–14.
65 « un thermomètre de la misère des campagnes algériennes ... un enfer dans lequel vivent plusieurs milliers d'êtres humains ... l'air de camps de concentration », Rabat Serradj [Sadek Hadjerès], series on Cité Mahieddine, Liberté (July 1950). Hadjerès to author, 17 March 2013.
66 Gallissot (ed.), Algérie, pp. 102–3, 243–5; interview with Hadjerès.
67 TNA: PRO FO 371/80610, Bi-monthly political summary, January–February, March–April 1950, p. 2, Monthly political summary, May 1950.
68 TNA: PRO FO 371/80610, Bi-monthly political summary, 5 May 1950, pp. 1–2; Khatib, 1er juillet, p. 15.
69 Sivan, Communisme, pp. 169, 171–2; TNA: PRO FO 371/97079, Quarterly Political Review, period ending 31 December 1951, pp. 1–2; interview with Abdelkader Guerroudj, Algiers, 26 September 2011; Danièle Djamila Amrane-Minne, Des Femmes dans la guerre d'Algérie (n.p.: Edik, n.d.), p. 100; Dore-Audibert, Françaises, pp. 144–7; Gallissot (ed.), Algérie, p. 136.
70 TNA: PRO FO 371/80610, Bi-monthly political summary, March–April 1950, p. 2, and Monthly Political summary, May 1950, p. 2; Harbi, Vie, pp. 113–16; Ruedy,

Modern Algeria, pp. 153–4; Rebah, *Chemins*, pp. 160–1; Gallissot (ed.), *Algérie*, p. 507.
71 Interview with Hadjerès; Ouzegane, *Meilleur Combat*, pp. 42–3.
72 TNA: PRO FO 371/80610, 80620, Bi-monthly political summary, January–February 1950, p. 2, Monthly Political Summary, July 1950, p. 2, British Consulate-General to Foreign Office, 4 October 1950, pp. 1–2.
73 Martin Shipway, *Decolonization and its Impact: A Comparative Approach to the End of the Colonial Empires* (Oxford: Blackwell, 2008), pp. 87–113, esp. 88–90; Khatib, *1er juillet*, pp. 26–7, 80; MacMaster, *Burning*, p. 36; interview with Hadjerès.
74 'Quelques paroles de solidarités ... le mot « indépendance » utilisé dans un discours ou un article,' Alleg, 'Torrent', p. 275; Khatib, *1er juillet*, pp. 18–19; Harbi, *Vie*, p. 87; MacMaster, *Burning*, pp. 56–7, 318.
75 Henri J. Douzon, 'Les Occasions perdues', in Alleg (ed.), *Guerre*, vol. 1, pp. 284–595, 326–7, 357–9; TNA: PRO FO 371/80620, British Consul-General to Foreign Office, 4 October 1950, pp. 1–2.
76 « premier pas décisif dans la voie de l'union pour l'indépendance nationale », in Khatib, *1er juillet*, p. 29; 'Communiqué du comité d'initiative pour la formation d'un front algérien pour la défense et le respect de la Liberté (25 juillet 1951)', in Collot and Henry (eds), *Mouvement national*, pp. 289–90; Sivan, *Communisme*, p. 185; Alleg, 'Torrent', pp. 277–8; Gilbert Meynier, 'Le PPA–MTLD et le FLN–ALN, étude comparée', in Mohammed Harbi and Benjamin Stora (eds) *La Guerre d'Algérie* (Paris: Pluriel, 2010), 602–53, pp. 615–16.
77 'Programme d'action proposé par le Comité d'initiative et adopté par l'assemblée générale du 5 août 1951', pp. 290–1, and 'Résolution adoptée par l'assemblée générale de constitution du Front algérien le 5 août 1951', p. 291, both in Collot and Henry (eds), *Mouvement national*.
78 Interview with Hadjerès.
79 Sivan, *Communisme*, pp. 192–3; Ahmed Akkache, 'Premier bilan du Front Algérien', *Liberté* (3 January 1952), p. 1; 'Libérer les « 56 »', *Liberté* (10 January 1952), p. 1; Douzon, 'Occasions perdues', pp. 357–61.
80 *Liberté* (28 February 1952); TNA: PRO FO 371/97079, Political review of events in Algeria, quarter ended 31 March 1952.
81 'Appel du 6e Congrès national du Parti communiste algérien (23 février 1952)', in Collot and Henry (eds), *Mouvement national*, 297–300, pp. 298–9; Sivan, *Communisme*, pp. 181–2; Joly, *French Communist*, pp. 78–9.
82 Railway workers and functionaries, by contrast, were mainly European. Sivan, *Communisme*, pp. 163, 215, 218, 220–4; Khatib, *1er juillet*, pp. 15–16; Heggoy, *Insurgency*, p. 248; Einaudi, *Algérien*, pp. 120, 125; interview with Hadjerès.
83 ANOM FM 81F/759, 'PCA 1953', and on Jews, 'Février 1953'.
84 Harbi, *Vie*, p. 160; 'Principes directeurs de la lutte du mouvement national algérien' (M.T.L.D., décembre 1951), in Collot and Henry (eds), *Mouvement national*, pp. 300–4.
85 « ruine et dépeuplement », *Les Statuts du « Parti de l'Union Populaire de l'Oued-M'Zab »* (Algiers, 1951), p. 3; Benjamin E. Thomas, 'Motoring in the Sahara: The French Raids of 1951–1953', *Economic Geography*, 29, 4 (October 1953), 327–39, pp. 327–9; interviews with Mella, Bellalou and Mohamed Boudjenah.
86 Sivan, *Communisme*, pp. 184–6, 192–5, 210, 213–16; Khatib, *1er juillet*, pp. 28–30; Stora, *Messali*, pp. 212–19; cf. Harbi, *Vie*, pp. 90–1.
87 'Déclaration du M.T.L.D. à propos de l'union des forces nationales algériennes', in Collot and Henry (eds), *Mouvement national*, pp. 292–3; TNA: PRO FO 371/97079, Political reviews of events in Algeria for the quarters ended 31 March, 30 September 1952.
88 'Appel solennel du Comité central du Parti communiste algérien pour un Front national démocratique algérien (1er novembre 1953)', in Collet and Henry (eds), *Mouvement national*, 319–24, pp. 322–3; Khatib, *1er juillet*, p. 110.
89 'Appel du Comité central du M.T.L.D. pour un Congrès national algérien (10 décembre 1953)', pp. 324–30, esp. 329, and 'Réponse du M.T.L.D. à une lettre du P.C.A. à propos du Congres national algérien', p. 331, both in Collot and Henry (eds), *Mouvement*

national.
90 'Création du Front d'unité et d'action des Partis nationaux maghrébins' (2 février 1952), p. 292, and 'Pacte nord-africain (2-2-1952), pp. 292–3, both in Collot and Henry (eds), *Mouvement national;* TNA: PRO FO 371/97079, Political review of events in Algeria for the quarter ended 31 March 1952; Laszlo Nagy, 'Les «événements» du premier novembre et les premières réactions', 2 May 2012, p. 2, http://goo.gl/8Jw9yp (accessed 17 May 2013); interviews with William Sportisse, 24 June 2012; Harbi, *Vie,* p. 181.
91 Interview with Abdelmoumène.
92 Ruedy, *Modern Algeria,* pp. 153–4; Harbi, *Vie,* pp. 93–137; Stora, *Messali,* pp. 220–5; *Algérie libre* (3 September 1954), *La Nation algérienne* (3 September 1954), both in Collot and Henry (eds), *Mouvement national,* pp. 332–40.
93 'Les travaux de la session du comité central', *Liberté* (8 July 1954), p. 2; Boualem Khalfa, 'Que devient le problème de l'union après la scission au M.T.L.D.?', *Liberté* (9 September 1954); MacMaster, *Burning,* pp. 36, 52.
94 'La politique nationale du Parti communiste algérien', *Liberté* (9 September 1954), p. 2.
95 'Voici le "secret" des victoires de l'armée populaire Vietnamienne' and 'Interview de Vo N'guyen Giap sur la bataille de Dien-Bien-Phu', *Liberté* (13 May 1954); Larbi Bouhali, 'Raisons profondes des succès du peuple vietnamien', and Bachir Hadj Ali, 'Après la victoire de Dien-Bien-Phu', *Liberté* (27 May 1954), pp. 1, 3. On Bouhali, see Alleg, *Mémoire,* p. 309, and Christian Buono, *L'Olivier de Makouda* (n.p.: Art'Kange, 2007), p. 22.
96 TNA: PRO FO 371/108603, British Consul-General to Anthony Eden, 23 April, 18 May, 9 June 1954, and Political Survey of Algeria, November 1954; House, 'Displacements', pp. 4, 8.

CHAPTER SEVEN

Sparking an insurrection: pressure from the countryside

The mountainous *bled es siba* or dissident lands unleashed armed struggle against French colonialism at 1.15 a.m. on 1 November 1954, as the country's European Catholics celebrated All Saints' Day. The first African armed struggle launched since the outbreak of Kenya's 1952 Mau Mau uprising, Algeria's war of independence was inaugurated by a wave of some sixty synchronised sabotage attacks on police stations and garrisons around the country.[1] Its focal point was the Aurès mountains in eastern Algeria – 'a treeless wilderness where it looks as if nothing but stone will grow'. Stone villages in stone mountains provided camouflage for guerrillas and bandits, while travellers on the roads below felt 'observed by a thousand eyes in the invisible villages above'. Probably the country's poorest region, the overwhelmingly Berber population had suffered a tremendous decline in living standards over the previous fifteen years. Led by Mostefa Ben Boulaïd, the Aurès became the first military district, or *wilaya*, established by the men who called themselves the FLN and launched the Armée de libération nationale (ALN).[2]

So begin many accounts of Algeria's war of independence. But in the hearts and minds of those launching armed struggle, the war had begun on 8 May 1945, the day unleashing the Constantinois massacre. The All Saints' Day actions were the FLN's response. The 1945 events might have been the culmination of an urban-led movement spilling into the countryside, but in their wake activists fled to the mountains to plan armed struggle. While the 1945 events smashed Algerian hopes for peaceful reform, for the French and Europeans they signalled the potential for widespread rebellion. The state's militarisation as it sought to keep Algeria French was echoed by the FLN's militarisation.[3]

If the PCA's initial reaction to the 1945 massacre had been ambiguous at best, it played no role at all in the All Saints' Day events. Nor did communists have a forewarning of the date, even though some had a premonition. Most were far removed from the rural hinterland and the young men who launched the armed struggle. About one-third of the PCA's members were European, predominantly urban-based. Two-thirds were Algerian, many of whom lived in cities while retaining rural ties.[4] Caught off guard, the PCA's Algiers leadership saw the All Saints' attacks as individual sabotage and feared a Sétif-like reprisal. The party was flooded with enquiries, however, as Algerians contacted it to see if it was responsible for, or had news about, the events – after all, communists had supported armed struggles ranging from the French Resistance to Vietnam's guerrilla war.[5]

The PCA's political bureau published a statement on 2 November, apparently the only political organisation to do so. The colonialists obstinately pursued policies based on force that denied the Algerian people's legitimate aspirations, the statement read. The best means to avoid further bloodshed was to recognise their just and democratic aspirations. It condemned the governor-general's war-like methods, as well as 'these measures of terror that tend, by creating a climate of general insecurity, to open the way for general repression hitting all patriots and lovers of liberty and democracy'. Whether the statement meant state terrorism or individual acts of terror was unclear.[6] By 3 November authorities claimed that Algérois and Oranie were calm, although Constantinois was still bubbling.[7] *Alger républicain* demanded united efforts to achieve a democratic solution respecting the rights of all Algerians irrespective of race and religion – taking France's interests into account – and an end to colonial oppression, arbitrary arrests and police and army reinforcements.[8] More typical was the response of Louisette Ighilahriz's father, an MTLD supporter and retired police officer who ran a bakery. On 1 November he assembled his children and told them: 'it's the end of humiliation.' And eighteen-year-old Louisette knew that the events represented 'the end of humiliation, of scorn, of ratonnades'.[9]

But communists were far from united. André and Blanche Moine, both active in the world peace movement, claimed that armed struggle was counter-productive. In 1953, by one account, Maurice Laban, Chebba Mekki and Laïd Lamrani had been accused of factionalism. Some European communists now snubbed Laban because of his staunch support for armed struggle. Generally, those with military experience in the Spanish Civil War, the Second World War or the French army in Vietnam supported the armed initiatives. Generation was a factor: younger communists like Myriam Ben, 25 when the war began, were impatient with the leadership's wait-and-see attitude.[10]

Crucially, rural communists who worked with peasants and agricultural workers welcomed armed struggle from the start. This was so in the Aurès, where repression had been so fierce and the political climate so tense that guns were being sold in September. Laïd Lamrani, lawyer and president of the Bar in Batna, and Mohammed Guerrouf – central committee members and secretaries respectively of the Batna and Biskra sections – contacted FLN leaders Mostefa Ben Boulaïd, Si Slimane and Berrahil. On 7–8 November Guerrouf and Ben Boulaïd discussed Communist participation. On the 12th Guerrouf and Si Slimane met Caballero in Algiers, who agreed that the PCA would provide the Auressien guerrillas with funds and material support through Secours populaire algérien, led by Raffini. This was confirmed by Bachir Hadj Ali on the 15th, and Communist lawyers were instructed to take on FLN/ALN legal cases. The PCA would not commit to supplying personnel – Ben Boulaïd had requested Laban – but Guerrouf, Lamrani and Raffini helped the Aurès *maquis*. Laban supplied weapons on his own initiative. Thus, in the weeks following the All Saints' events, the PCA organised clandestine assistance without jeopardising its legal status with open support. It presumed, nevertheless, that the Aurès was a special case and did not issue a general call to arms.[11]

Likewise, around Tlemcen the response to armed struggle was immediate. Abdelkader Guerroudj worked in peasant communities; he knew that peasants 'lived colonialism'. So inhumane was their situation that they were imprisoned for collecting wood to make carbon to sell to buy food. After joining the PCA in 1951, Guerroudj attended a Party school in Algiers, as part of the national recruitment drive known as *la promotion Staline*; Guerroudj admired Stalin for fighting fascism and promoting Soviet industrial development. Guerroudj had organised Tlemcen carpet workers, but generally he worked with peasants in Ouchba, where he and other communists had built up a solid nucleus that included women. Halima Ghomri and Yamina Berrahou, the young daughters of Tahar Ghomri and Mejdoub Berrahou, organised about fifteen or twenty women, travelling from Ouchba to Oum Oulalou, Beni Ghazli and Terny. Rural elders opposed equal rights for women. But by ensuring that men and women met separately and that organising and fund raising were conducted amongst those of the same sex, these communists spread their message while respecting custom.[12]

As soon as they heard about the armed attacks, they knew 'the moment had come.' Within two days they made plans to get material for a sabotage campaign. Two peasants went to Sidi bel Abbès to meet René Justrabo, former mayor, PCA central committee member and communist delegate in the Algerian Assembly. But Justrabo told them that the Party had not yet decided to support the armed struggle, and they returned empty-handed to Ouchba. The fighting spirit was there, but, while disagreeing with Justrabo, they accepted party discipline, and the leadership chose to wait and see. Nonetheless, over the next year rural communists pressured their leaders to join the guerrillas. As the war's second year unfolded – a period characterised by a rural guerrilla campaign – most PCA members came to support the armed struggle.[13]

The PCF was far more removed from Algerian events. Immersed in the Cold War, its main concerns were containing American power and opposing German rearmament. It opposed American investment in North Africa and US military bases in Morocco and Vietnam, but Algeria was of secondary interest. Its thirteenth congress from 3 to 6 June 1954 at Ivry-sur-Seine, had maintained that France and its colonies had common interests against American imperialism and proposed a French Union of France and Algeria without colonial ties. Maintaining the 'nation in formation' thesis, it stressed that the right to divorce did not necessitate divorce.[14]

On 8 November the PCF's political bureau called for the immediate end to repression, the repatriation of French troops and police, the recognition of the just nature of Algerian demands and negotiations with Algerian representatives. The protection of French interests, it stressed, rested on an amicable relationship between the two peoples. There was no mention of independence. The next day *L'Humanité* stressed its support for Algerian rights while condemning terrorism. Although the FLN had not mentioned terrorism, the All Saints' events evoked a fear of terrorism, and the PCF would consistently oppose terrorism throughout the war.[15] Algerian communists such as Bachir Hadj Ali thought the PCF's slogans were imprecise, but it remained adamant.[16]

Despite the communists' tentative stance, state authorities saw the events through Cold War lenses that stressed the menace of international communism and the diffusion of Soviet influence into North Africa. They were particularly concerned about the PCA's potential as a cohesive organisation with a skilled membership and its prospects for collaboration with the FLN, and the PCA's public profile made it very vulnerable to repression. The Algerian Assembly debated a motion to suppress communism and prevent foreign interference. Repressive measures – 'draconic and ... judged by many as being excessive', reported the British consul-general – were rapidly implemented. Railway night services were cut, flights over Constantinois, prohibited and political parties, banned. There were house to house searches and widespread arrests. Several thousand reservists were brought in to reinforce the police.[17]

By mid-November the PCA's central committee acknowledged that the armed actions indicated multiple levels of struggle and demonstrated the FLN's popular support in the Aurès, although guerrillas elsewhere seemed isolated. The Aurès was at war, wrote *Liberté* in December. When Estorges visited the area where he had taught as a young man, the *montagnards* described themselves as a people who had always fought for their freedom, even before Roman times, and told him that it was absurd to claim that they were French. Parts of the Aurès were bombarded and the inhabitants forcibly moved. Guerrouf and comrades assisted village delegations appealing against forced removals and determined to resist collective punishments. At the French Assembly in Paris, Alice Sportisse demanded an end to colonialism and an Algerian republic.[18]

The FLN's origins

Hostile to and hardly influenced by communism, most of the men launching the war of independence had been in the short-lived CRUA, whose first full meeting had taken place on the day that Dien Bien Phu's fall was announced. The event had a decisive impact on their thinking. Some of their kin had fought with the French in Vietnam. When the Vietminh captured Algerians, they asked them why they were fighting for, rather than against, the colonisers. France's defeat at Nazi hands in 1940 had shocked many Algerians; the French defeat at Dien Bien Phu demonstrated to the CRUA that a colonised people could defeat an imperial power.[19]

The new FLN adopted CRUA's principle of collective leadership to avoid personality cults and to mediate Arab/Berber tensions. But the FLN lacked a mass base. Building on the OS's underground structure, it divided Algeria into five military districts: *wilaya* I, the Aurès and Nementcha mountains; *wilaya* II, north Constantinois; *wilaya* III, Kabylia; *wilaya* IV, Algérois; and *wilaya* V, Oranie. The area south of Algérois, including the Sahara, later became *wilaya* VI. The FLN's executive was led by Mohamed Boudia and included the five *wilaya* leaders. These six and three former OS members in exile, Ben Bella, Aït Ahmed and Mohamed Khider, became known as the war's nine historic leaders.

They envisioned the FLN as a revolutionary movement seeking to purify nationalism by eliminating corruption and reformism. The FLN's discourse reflected its MTLD lineage. But whereas the MTLD aspired to independence through parliamentary and political means, the FLN demanded independence through armed struggle. The Arabic word *thawra*, signifying revolt and insurrection, indicated their desire for revolution, rather than *harb* (war).[20] The FLN maintained that an Algerian state predated French colonisation. Its imagined Algerian nation was seen in its first aim: 'restoration of the sovereign, democratic, and social Algerian state within the framework of Islamic principles'. But its second aim reflected French republican values: 'Respect for all fundamental liberties without distinction of race or religion'. Europeans were promised the choice between Algerian nationality or 'their nationality of origin'. Relations with France were to be based on equality and mutual respect.[21]

The ALN's strength was modest – estimates the first year ranged from 900 to 3,000 guerrillas, about half of whom had guns. But its aims were ambitious and imbued with moral fervour. Its soldiers – *mujahidin* – were the 'mold in which the great moral forces of the past and the exalted hopes for the future blend'. They worked with the *musabilin* (those who fight God's battle), auxiliaries who did not wear uniforms and who could thus circulate openly, providing intelligence and logistical support and engaging in sabotage. Alongside these were the *fida'iyyin*, urban guerrillas who were seen as totally devoted to the cause; the term suggests religious sacrifice. The imagery was religious, but the war was against French colonial domination, its denigration of Islam and oppression of Muslims.[22]

Having gained their political experience in the cities – but with the Constantinois massacre in their hearts and minds, Fighting France in their memories and Vietnam before their eyes – the historic leaders launched their armed struggle in the rural hinterland. The FLN aspired to be the Algerian people's sole legitimate representative. Yet precisely because it had no popular base, it sought to build support through the armed struggle. Unity was needed to wage a successful war, and war became the means of imposing unity; this was the FLN's interpretation of the wartime slogan, 'a people united, an army united'. Yet peasants and *montagnards* had every reason to question the unknown FLN's claims to lead this war. The MTLD and UDMA had built their organisations through persuasion. While ALN guerrillas impressed many rural folk with their determination and bravery, not all of them wanted to help. They soon learned. Failure to give the FLN full support brought its full wrath.

The battle for the countryside

The newly formed FLN/ALN faced some 56,000 French soldiers stationed in Algeria. Against these odds, over the next two years the ALN established numerous rural guerrilla bases. Just as the Islamic reformists had made inroads amongst middle peasants, so did poor peasants furnish much of the ALN's rural base. After all, rural communities had been fighting the French ever since the conquest. They had less direct contact with French culture than did urbanites, and they felt the brunt of occupation more sharply. They had stocks of old weapons, some left behind by Allied Forces during the last world war, and they now put them to use.[23]

Some rural communities had been organised well before armed struggle was launched. The *djemâa* and underground *djemâas-occultes* provided the basis for local organisation. The *douar* of El Akbia, some 72 kilometres northwest of Constantine, had a history of organisation due particularly to two remarkable local activists: Si Lakhdar, a supporter of the AML and reformist *'ulama* who had organised against *caïds* and other collaborators since the 1940s, and Sfari Hocine, a migrant worker returned from France. Imprisoned at El Milia in 1945, Hocine met regional PPA leaders detained after the Constantinois massacre and agreed to start a PPA cell at El Akbia. Working together, Lakhdar and Hocine established a political network of peasants, miners – who were CGT members – and returned migrant workers who had gained trade union experience in France. The network grew rapidly, encompassing El Akbia, El Milia, Sidi Marouf and Yahmiden; its members participated in the All Saints' actions.[24]

As sabotage attacks spread west across the country, the FLN/ALN rallied support, first peasants and youths from small towns, and later, privileged urbanites. These recruits were overwhelmingly men. One estimate suggests about 326,000 men to 10,949 women – just over three per cent women – although this presumably underestimates female participation. Almost 78 per cent of female FLN members were from rural areas and generally illiterate in both Arabic and French. These *musabilat* typically provided refuge and support. Female urban guerrillas or *fida'iyyat*, mainly middle-class and French-educated, represented a tiny minority of female activists. The *mujahidat*, women who joined the ALN *maquis*, numbered about 1,755, or 16 per cent of women members. Often nurses and occasionally doctors who cared for the wounded and handled first aid, they also prepared food, acted as social assistants for nearby villages and sometimes engaged in propaganda and communication. Very few *mujahidat* engaged in combat, and they faced cruel, sexist practices, such as 'virginity testing' and forced marriage.[25] Nonetheless, far more than the *musabilat*, their very presence challenged the prevailing gender norms. The greater male participation did not mean that women felt the war less than men – far from it. Women with children could not flee when French troops arrived in rural villages, and they were subjected to the theft of their chickens, forced prostitution in exchange for food and systematic rape. They were also vulnerable to threats, intimidation and fines by ALN guerrillas.[26]

Violence was integral to the movement's development. At the war's outset, the FLN forbid violence against European civilians. Bulletins urged members not to kill women, children or elderly people, nor to rape or profane churches. Yet the FLN showed no such compunction when it came to Algerian civilians. Alongside belated French efforts to integrate Algeria into France, a Section administrative spécialisée (SAS), staffed by French soldiers, distributed aid and trained peasants in new agricultural techniques. Each adult family member was allocated eleven kilos of barley per month – insufficient for a family with children – leading to a 'pathological state of undernourishment of young children' and inadequate adult calorie intake. But SAS soldiers were often caught between Europeans and Algerians, while rural communities who welcomed their assistance found themselves targeted by the FLN for cooperating with the French.[27]

Violence became the means by which new ALN recruits proved themselves. Action, urged the FLN, will make you a new man. The ALN insisted that each new recruit kill an informer or spy as part of his initiation. The new member was followed to ensure that they fulfilled the task. 'An assassination marks the end of the apprenticeship of each candidate for the A.L.N.', baldly stated Belkacem Krim. The victims were mutilated and left in degrading and mocking poses. Some rural folk gladly helped the ALN, but violence was the punishment for those who vacillated and a warning for others.[28]

Conquered by the Nazis, defeated by the Vietminh, France refused to consider another defeat. On 22 December it launched operation *'Orange amère'* (bitter orange), sweeping up nationalist leaders irrespective of their politics and torturing them on suspicion of instigating the attacks. In Constantine, Noureddine Abdelmoumène's uncle was detained for trade union activities. The detainees were forced to walk home each night after curfew so that they could be shot at like rabbits. But along with the stick, the French dangled the carrot. When Jacques Soustelle became governer-general in January 1955, he promoted integration on the basis of equal rights. The idea was to develop a 'third force' of moderate, culturally French Algerians willing to keep Algeria French.[29]

To impede guerrillas from blending into communities, the authorities launched *regroupement*, the forced resettlement of small villages into larger units under military supervision. The countryside was divided into grids of so-called safe zones of resettled villages and forbidden areas where people were prohibited from settling or travelling under threat of being shot on sight. Sometimes communities were forcibly marched to new locations, only to find no infrastructure or accommodation. When there was infrastructure, it consisted of crowded, shoddily built houses with rudimentary facilities, surrounded by barbed wire and guarded by a military tower – a bleak and traumatising existence described by Simone de Beauvoir as 'death camps, serving on the side as brothels for elite troops'.[30]

Contact between guerrillas and communities became more difficult, but the miserable conditions meant that resettlement areas became fertile zones for nationalist ideas. The distance from their village to the resettlement camp might be only a few kilometres, but the new location was further down the mountainside, forcing the peasants to leave their fields and crops. Agriculture was abandoned; livestock died. Forced relocation undermined the extended family. Without the extended family's protection, women living near strangers often remained indoors, and many who had not previously worn the veil began to do so. Alongside this mass resettlement, people fleeing rural unrest flooded into urban shantytowns.[31]

The French quickly adapted their techniques. While their first troops lacked experience in guerrilla warfare, this changed with the arrival of the *parachutistes* (paratroopers) or *paras*, as they were known, who introduced tactics learned from Vietnam. Repeated states of emergency enabled the transfer of power from civil authority to the military. The balance sheet at the end of the winter of 1954–55 showed the armed struggle's heavy human costs for the FLN; its leaders were either killed or in prison, and its soldiers forced ever higher into the mountains. Its soldiers were tough; small units would ambush French forces and disappear into the mountains, sometimes trekking seventy kilometres in one day. But they paid dearly, both physically and mentally.[32]

Frantz Fanon, the Martinique-born, French-trained psychiatrist, had arrived in Algeria in November 1953 to work at the Blida-Joinville Hospital. Already known for his influential book *Black Skin, White Masks* and his article on 'The "North African Syndrome"', he began treating ALN soldiers for mental problems in early 1955.[33] Fanon discovered that Algeria's religious and national compartmentalisation had penetrated the medical profession and hoped to undo the destructive impact of racism and colonialism by transforming the alienating nature of the psychiatric hospital. His unequivocal and loudly voiced anti-colonialism became quickly known to the FLN, which sorely needed sympathetic doctors.[34]

Neutralising opponents

FLN campaigns against Algerians who failed to support it or who worked within the French system escalated during spring 1955. The FLN showed extreme intolerance towards political parties refusing its authority – patriotic unity necessitated the dissolution of existing parties and the adherence of their members to the FLN. Although the FLN's intimidation alienated many peasant communities, the ALN's endurance earned it recruits. The French response was frequently indiscriminate and disproportionate: mass arrests, military sweeps, collective punishment and forced relocation. French soldiers engaged wholeheartedly in *ratissages*, in which communities suspected of hiding guerrillas were encircled and thoroughly searched. Over time French brutality drove Algerians to the FLN. On 1 April 1955 the FLN appealed to the Algerian people to join the struggle. Two days later the government imposed a state of emergency. This allowed a shift from civilian to military courts, gave the governer-general powers of confinement over individuals deemed dangerous to public order and increased control over the media. That month, however, the FLN made an international breakthrough, obtaining an invitation to the Bandung conference of non-aligned states, which unanimously upheld Algeria's right to self-determination.[35]

The people indeed joined the struggle. But the FLN's relations with Messali Hadj and his followers showed the limits of compulsion. The war intensified old antagonisms. Messali had been furious when he learned about the All Saints' sabotage – but he nonetheless sought credit for it. In the first confusing days after the armed struggle's launch, organisational boundaries were in flux, and Messali loyalists made donations to the armed struggle. But on 5 November 1954 the MTLD was banned, its leaders detained. Many MTLD centralists switched to the FLN.[36]

Messali and his loyalists restyled themselves as the Mouvement national algérien (MNA). Launched in France that December and supported by French Trotskyists and anarchists, it surfaced in Algiers some weeks later. The MNA supported the armed struggle – if not the FLN – in its underground organ, *La Voix du peuple* (*The People's Voice*). It garnered support amongst Algerians in France and in Kabylia, where it began forming a *maquis*. But it would not endorse the use of terror against civilians that the FLN's charismatic intellectual, Abane Ramdane, was promoting. The MNA asked the FLN to join its ranks, but the FLN was growing and had no such need. By May 1955 the two organisations were maligning each other; that summer the FLN fought MNA supporters in Kabylia. If the FLN's rural base enabled it to operate away from French eyes, in Algiers the MNA was subjected to intense political repression as police informants penetrated the organisation.[37]

The FLN was also wary of the PCA, which on 13 January 1955 had warned that individual action risked playing into colonialist hands. Yet the party discreetly aided the insurrection. Its Arabic-language radio broadcasts from Budapest were so successful that Aït Ahmed sent the FLN's congratulations via the Egyptian ambassador. In February 1955 a PCA delegation including Rachid Dalibey, Guerrouf, Justrabo, Lamrani, Azzedine Mazri and Alice Sportisse had travelled through the Aurès. They found an occupied region full of tanks and machine guns, parts of which had been reduced to a 'concentration camp' where the laws of war were ignored. Villages had been burned and local communities subjected to harsh collective displacements. Batna was still under civil authority, and the delegation circulated relatively freely, despite being stopped and grilled about their plans. From Batna they went to Bou-el-Freiss, fifty kilometres away, where displaced Auressiens had been relocated, and where they met with a group of peasants, one of whom had worked in France and another of whom was in the UDMA. The so-called pacification, *Liberté* reported, was actually a military operation. Guerrouf was arrested soon after. An FLN agent had been picked up with a letter from Hocine Berhail to Guerrouf, asking him to come immediately to discuss joint lines of action and supplies for the guerrillas. What the state security apparatus called '*l'affaire Guerrouf*' and their discovery that Secours populaire algérien was funding the Auressien rebels strengthened their belief in FLN–PCA collaboration, although at this point localised in the Aurès.[38]

The FLN's initiative in launching armed struggle put tremendous pressure on the PCA. Although individual communists had joined the Aurès *maquis*, the longer the PCA sat on the sidelines, the greater the risk of marginalisation. Certainly, the PCA hoped to continue its public activities for as long as possible and contested local elections, which offered political space in which to expose the conditions underpinning the armed struggle. Yet communists disagreed on the value of electoral campaigns. Laïd Lamrani and Abdelkader Guerroudj still believed that they offered useful propaganda forums; but Abdelhamid Boudiaf, a rural organiser from a peasant family near M'sila, thought them a waste of time once armed struggle began. The PCA's public and clandestine activities were used by state authorities to demonstrate communist activity in the Aurès, which deepened FLN resentment of the PCA.[39]

As the guerrilla struggle gained momentum, pressure within the PCA to openly support armed struggle mounted. The leadership thus began formalising what was already happening in practice, a process that occurred in several stages. In February 1955, having been unable to contact the FLN, the PCA secretariat – Hadj Ali, Bouhali, Caballero, Ahmed Akkache and André Moine – had decided that the party should form its own detachments.[40]

In Tlemcen, notwithstanding Justrabo's initial admonition, communists had hidden provisions and military supplies in the mountains as soon as the authorities began rounding up political activists and trade unionists, recounted Mejdoub Berrahou. Like Lamrani in Batna and Biskra, Abdelkader Guerroudj campaigned as a communist candidate for the second college elections scheduled for 17 April 1955. His campaign slogan – 'Forward for combat' – left no doubt about his stance. The party leadership carefully reproached him. He met with Akkache, who maintained the party's position of behind-the-scenes support for armed struggle. Abdelkader Guerroudj, Jacqueline Guerroudj and Tahar Ghomri were arrested shortly after the election. The Guerroudjes were deported to France; they returned to Algeria after a legal battle, but were banned from Oranie.[41]

Repression was intense. *Liberté* and *El Djezaïr el Djedida* were seized as soon as they appeared; *Alger républicain* was prohibited in Constantinois and Oranie in May 1955. In late April or May the political bureau ratified the secretariat's decision to form armed detachments – the Combattants de la libération (Liberation soldiers, CDL) – and adopted the slogan, 'All for the armed struggle'. On 20 June the central committee met at Bab el Oued. It unanimously agreed that the party would form armed units, participate directly in the guerrilla struggle wherever it had sufficient numbers and increase its support for the guerrillas.[42]

The 'Yvanez affair' deepened the state's concern about communist involvement in the armed struggle. On 17 June – a few days before the central committee's decision – communist Roland Yvanez met with PCA, UDMA and MTLD–PPA activists in Oran. He informed them that he had been authorised to reveal that the PCA was represented in armed groups in the Aurès. Soon after, PCA secretary Caballero was arrested carrying an internal PCA document attributing the party's delay in joining the armed struggle to its European members. The party planned to reallocate tasks and give Algerians greater responsibilities so that it could lead the liberation struggle. Henri Alleg was arrested in July 1955 and spent six weeks in Serkadji Prison, where he met Caballero, serving two years for distributing an FLN tract. The 'Caballero affair' confirmed the state's belief of a communist plan to capture the struggle. The Americans were concerned about communist–nationalist collusion and requested further information. The governor-general's office informed the French Minister of the Interior of the Guerrouf, Yvanez and Caballero affairs as evidence of this collusion.[43]

Spiralling violence

Over time, the FLN's violence towards Algerians who did not support it eroded the distinction between civilians and combatants. Many ALN leaders had initially been sceptical about violence against civilians. But they found it increasingly unacceptable that Europeans went about their lives normally, an issue raised repeatedly by Abane Ramdane. Between 11.30 a.m. and 12.30 p.m. on 20 August 1955 – a date chosen to express solidarity with the Moroccan struggle – some two thousand guerrillas in north Constantinois launched synchronised attacks in 25 towns and villages, including Constantine city centre, hoping to spark a mass insurrection.[44] The targets were symbols of colonial authority – police stations, army camps, aerodromes, public buildings and mining infrastructure – but in some cases European and moderate Algerian civilians were not spared. Never before had the *'hors-la-loi'* (outlaws) been so bold; never before had the country seen 'so many rebel hordes remarkably organised and going to combat in the strict sense of the term', reported one journalist. Some eighty guerrillas attacked the pyrite mining village of El Alia, near Philippeville, killing men, women, children, babies, indiscriminately, before fleeing into the mountains. ALN losses were heavy indeed: 521 deaths, 79 wounded and 1,022 prisoners. By comparison, French military casualties numbered 26 deaths and 115 wounded; European civilian casualties comprised 69 deaths and 51 wounded; and for 'French-Muslims', the numbers were 15 deaths and 40 wounded.[45]

The French response was draconian, the polarisation of Europeans and Algerians inevitable, and the possibility for negotiation over. Soustelle called for military reinforcements. 'Nine mechtas, home of the rebellion ... totally destroyed by our troops after evacuation of women and children', reported the press.[46] Europeans formed civilian militias – an echo of the 1945 massacre. Algerians were summarily executed. The official death toll was 1,273; the FLN claimed 12,000 deaths. Algerian survivors fled; the ALN offered them food and safety. Algerians could hardly forget the 1945 massacre, and the FLN/ALN gained recruits and supporters. Europeans vacated certain areas and abandoned forest stations; for the ALN, this was a success. In marked contrast to the MNA, the PCA's underground press saluted the FLN and announced its desire for cooperation. Indeed, state authorities were convinced that the communists had been involved through the CGT, which organised mine workers at El Alia. But the FLN remained aloof and sceptical towards the communists.[47]

Political allegiances shifted rapidly. On 26 September 1955 Algerian deputies issued a 'Declaration of the Sixty-One' claiming that Algerians overwhelmingly believed in an Algerian nation. On their behalf, the long-time socialist and journalist Aziz Kessous launched the *Communauté algérienne*, an eclectic review aspiring to create common ground between Algerians and Europeans. Camus had already informed the Comité Messali Hadj that he disagreed 'totally with terrorism that hit civilian populations' and felt the same about counter-terrorism. He now despaired to Kessous of 'the storm of death that has struck our country'. His letter appeared in *Communauté algérienne*'s first issue: 'We know nothing of the human heart if we imagine that the Algerian French can now forget the massacres at Philippeville and elsewhere. And it is another form of madness to imagine that repression can make the Arab masses feel confidence and esteem for France.' He urged both sides to 'preach pacification'. The teacher and novelist Mouloud Feraoun admired Camus and sympathised with his non-violent stance, but nonetheless criticised his refusal to recognise that 'this country [wa]s indeed called Algeria and its inhabitants [we]re called Algerians'.[48]

Already reeling from the FLN's propaganda war, the MNA's Algiers leaders were captured by police on 2 November, a devastating blow. Newspapers reported daily on skirmishes with guerrilla groups. An atmosphere of fear pressed down on the country, recorded Feraoun from Kabylia, where he taught school at Fort-National. 'Military vehicles plowed through the streets, swooped down into the valleys, crawled up to the villages, stopped in fields, rounded up "suspects," and, at times, came under gunfire.' The city was 'still and secluded, cunning, hostile, and frightened'. At the Béni Douala market, 'held behind tangles of twisted barbed wire, soldiers ... bus[ied] themselves around jeeps, trucks, and tanks'. Feraoun noted cynically: 'the cannons and machine guns pointed at the sky are there to convince you that you are with fine people who know how to live and proclaim the benefits of a motorized and armoured civilization.' Meanwhile, terrified Kabyles 'slip by quickly like ghosts.' The FLN was felt as a source both of strength and intimidation, prohibiting tobacco, alcohol and cinema, along with dominoes, cards and gambling. Tobacco and alcohol boycotts would hurt the colonial economy, its leaflets explained, while their consumption indicated a dissipated lifestyle. Austerity, discipline and obedience were the orders of the day.[49]

The progressive Association des amis du théâtre Arabe (Association of Friends of Arabic Theatre) invited Camus to Algiers to speak. His old comrade Amar Ouzegane was a member; the FLN had approached Ouzegane, and he was using his organising skills on its behalf. The PCF, in the meantime, isolated as the Cold War swept across France, unsuccessfully sought an alliance with the Socialist Party. It hoped to form a bridge between the French government and the FLN and to unite French workers and oppressed Algerians. Instead, the Republican

Front, a centre-left coalition led by the Socialist Party, won the general elections of 2 January 1956. On 16 January the PCF's Léon Feix declared that Algeria's nation in formation was now a nation in fact – *le fait national algérien* – and called for negotiations with the FLN. The socialist Guy Mollet became Prime Minister; his government called for reform and a negotiated end to the war.[50]

On 22 January Camus addressed the Circle of Progress in Algiers hoping to convince Algerians and Europeans to agree to a truce. The hall was packed – Camus was a draw. Outside, a line of security forces separated swarming settler diehards from FLN supporters. Inside, Camus proposed: 'without making any change in the present situation ... we refrain from what makes it unforgiveable – the murder of the innocent.' If Europeans and Algerians united in this aim they could succeed.[51] Many in the audience were moved, but the young European psychiatrist Charles Geromini was shocked at Camus' seeming refusal to take a stand. Active in defence of civil liberties, Geromini was drawn towards the FLN, which insisted on the prior recognition of Algerian independence before the cessation of violence. He and his comrades had admired Camus and expected him to speak unequivocally against colonialism. Instead, they heard 'a sweet-sister speech'. Camus stressed the need to protect civilians, yet 'he was categorically against fund raising in favor of the innocent families of political prisoners. We in the hall were dumbfounded.'[52]

Few heeded Camus' appeal. Schools were burning down; Egyptian and Tunisian papers had just been banned in Algeria; the public political space in which such idealistic hopes could be voiced was shrinking rapidly. The Friends of Arabic Theatre was one of the very few groups in Algiers within which Algerians and Europeans mixed. A few moderates stood behind Camus as he spoke – a Catholic priest, a Protestant minister and the Muslim Abdelaziz Khalid – and Ferhat Abbas greeted him on stage. But fearing that the mob outside would break into the hall, Camus rushed through his speech and out of the country.

Despite the PCA's antipathy towards Camus, it, too, hoped to avoid further bloodshed. Optimistic about the centre-left victory in France, it nonetheless categorically rejected Mollet's proposals for a negotiated peace. Any cease-fire negotiations, it argued, must recognise Algerian national aspirations, and negotiations must include all political representatives without exception. Peace would have to be followed by free elections under the aegis of a representative assembly based on universal suffrage and proportional representation through the two electoral colleges. It called for a national democratic front of fighting forces.[53]

On 5–6 February 1956 Prime Minister Mollet visited Algeria, to be met by European demonstrators hurling tomatoes, categorically rejecting his reform efforts.[54] Algeria 'will run with blood', Fanon warned. He was presumably thinking of the European–Algerian conflict, not conflict amongst Algerians, but the FLN's castigation of Messali as 'Algeria's number one enemy' and its claim that 'every conscious Messaliste must be shot without trial' – underlined his warning.[55]

Organisational rivalry extended to the trade union movement. Two years earlier, in June 1954, the Algerian CGT had restyled itself as the Union générale des syndicats algériens (General Union of Algerian Trade Unions, UGSA), led by the communist trade unionist Lakhdar Kaïdi. While retaining CGT affiliation, it affiliated directly to the World Federation of Trade Unions (WFTU). It concentrated on the overwhelmingly Algerian occupational sectors, such as miners, dockers and agricultural workers. But some of its European leaders had been hesitant about armed struggle, and its European members began leaving, while its Algerian members moved towards the FLN. In February 1956, the MNA launched the Union syndicale des travailleurs algériens (Syndicalist Union of Algerian Workers, USTA). This affiliated to the International Confederation of Free Trade Unions (ICFTU), which had split from the WFTU once the Cold War developed. A few days later the FLN launched the Union générale des travailleurs algériens (General Union of Algerian Workers, UGTA). UGTA structures were often built on top of UGSA structures, especially in Constantine and Oran. The UGTA demanded that the UGSA disband, which it refused to do – although its Communist leaders later regretted this decision.[56]

By then, Algeria was a major issue in French politics. The UN General Assembly had already placed Algeria on its agenda on 29 September 1955; the French National Assembly had been compelled to debate the matter in October, with communist delegates calling for negotiation with all representative Algerian groups.[57] In February 1956 the French government introduced a bill giving it special powers in Algeria to do everything necessary to maintain law and order at the expense of civil liberties – Camus' hoped-for middle ground vanished. 'Algeria is not a province like the others but neither is it a Muslim State', argued Mollet.[58] Although the French left had generally opposed Parliamentary 'decree-laws' that gave governments special powers, this changed after 1948, rationalised by efficiency; however undemocratic, special powers allowed rapid action. On 12 March 1956 the French National Assembly passed the special powers bill by a huge majority that included the PCF. Jacques Duclos summed up the PCF's position, which was premised on a supposed threat of fascism. The PCF opposed the use of special powers to increase military repression, he noted. However, the ultra-colonialists or ultras, as they were called – were behind the recent and, in the PCF's view, fascist anti-Mollet demonstrations. They wanted to prolong the war, undermine independence prospects in Morocco and Tunisia and replace the French socialist government. The preservation and consolidation of socialist and communist unity against this threat was vital, Duclos contended. The French government must pursue a negotiated cease-fire and an end to repression. Special powers, he argued, would facilitate this.[59]

The PCF believed that support for special powers would enable it to influence government policy and encourage the socialists to pursue détente with the USSR. However, its support for the bill angered many young French leftists, who – in the aftermath of Soviet leader Nikita Khrushchev's February revelations about Stalin's terror – linked their disenchantment with the PCF's stance on Algeria to a broader critique of the Soviet system.[60] The PCA press did not discuss the decision, but Algerian communists were angry and sorely disappointed. By then, however, they were preparing their own armed detachments. They would be very hard hit by the new act.[61]

The act gave the government sweeping powers to use all means needed to re-establish order – including the suspension of elected officials who allegedly impeded the state. The military was given control over specified zones. France sped up negotiations with Tunisian and Moroccan nationalists – to the benefit of the FLN, which set up bases after the two countries became independent in March 1956. Yet that breakthrough exacerbated tensions between the FLN's internal and external wings. The guerrillas needed arms. Their leaders criticised the external representatives for inadequate military procurement, for negotiating with France without internal consultation and for acting as if external work was more important than the armed struggle. By then the FLN had about 8,500 fighters and 21,000 auxiliaries and controlled close to one-third of the country. Guerrillas were entrenched in the mountainous regions. Ambushes, attacks and bombs became daily occurrences. 'The soldiers are ruthless; their actions have become acceptable, normal', observed Feraoun that March. 'The fellagha are ruthless; their actions have become acceptable, normal. For either of them, the readily designated enemy, the suspect to be threatened or manhandled, the accomplice to be shot, to be hit with a fine, or to be led to jail can be found in a Kabyle village … The people in the villages are terrified.'[62]

The Algerian Assembly was an early special powers casualty. In March 1956, Abbas' UDMA had called for the assembly's dissolution on the grounds that negotiations had reached an impasse; it was dissolved on 12 April. From then on, a resident minister (replacing the governor-general) ruled the country by decree. Sweeping administrative reforms followed. Alongside the SAS, the policy of *quadrillage*, linked to forced resettlement, entailed the division of the country into small units controlled by French garrisons. *Douars* were abolished, along with the office of the *caïd*, producing a political vacuum in many localities. Abbas dissolved the UDMA and announced his adhesion to the FLN.[63] Sliman Boudjenah's Mozabite political party had faded, but French troops often surrounded his Ghardaïa home, and since the torture centre was close by, his family heard people shrieking. After a report that his house was to be searched, his wife Fafa Boudjenah removed his pistol, hiding it under her veil. Not surprisingly, when FLN recruiters contacted Boudjenah, he pledged his support. 'The Algerian rising is gaining unity', wrote Nevill Barbour. To the authorities in Algeria – and even the British consul-general – foreign journalists were too sympathetic to the nationalist cause.[64]

Student support for the FLN grew rapidly. Algerian university and school students boycotted classes. Constantine high school students went on strike against the murders of fellow-students. On 19 May the FLN-aligned Union générale des étudiants musulmans algériens (General Union of Muslim Algerian Students, UGEMA) called on students to strike and join the ALN. Noureddine Abdelmoumène joined the FLN, but went to study in France because conditions in Constantine were impossible. Others wondered what use their diplomas were and joined the *maquis*.[65] They included young urban women; their presence created further stresses for the predominantly rural male guerrillas. Zoulikha Bekaddour joined the war at this time. Born 1939 in Casablanca and raised in Tlemcen, Bekaddour enrolled at the University of Algiers in October 1955 and became a student leader, despite being a newcomer and one of the very few Algerian women students. By January 1956 university students were disappearing; it was impossible to study. A few days after the student strike, Bekaddour travelled to Oran where, hoping to join the *maquis*, she trained for several weeks as an auxiliary nurse with Dr Mohamed Seghir Nekkache, a former MTLD member who spearheaded the launch of the ALN's health services. But Dr Nekkache was forced to flee, and Bekaddour's training was interrupted. She worked with the FLN in Oran, meeting radical Catholic activists.[66]

Louisette Ighilahriz left school to work underground. Since women could move about with slightly more ease than men, her father had asked her to be a liaison, and she carried documents, medicines or arms from one part of Algiers to another. Ighilahriz tried wearing a veil. But unaccustomed, she could not master the technique, and her mother feared she would stand out. So she dressed as usual *à l'Européenne* and went around with her material hidden in bread from the family bakery. Later she adopted a masculine demeanour: flat shoes, slacks, her hair combed with her fingers – 'A curtain had fallen over my femininity.' Amar Ouzegane's niece Fattouma Ouzegane had grown up in the Algiers *casbah* discussing politics with her uncle; she became part of an underground UGTA network. Group meetings risked arrest and torture; contacts were one to one. By the spring of 1956, the FLN had the youth.[67]

As the FLN went on the offensive, so did the French. By April, massive troop increases, with up to 210,000 *harkis*, had contained the rural revolt. *Harkis* were originally locally based Algerian auxiliaries to the French army. As the war developed, they served alongside French troops, providing knowledge of local terrain and sometimes torturing other Algerians. Some aided the French voluntarily; others were forced. The FLN's response was unequivocal. 'Brother Algerian', began a flyer circulated by the ALN's war staff on 6 June 1956. 'We are passing through a grave and decisive hour. All relations with the enemy must be discontinued. In consequence you must stop working in the next 48 hours at your job of traitor. All disobedience will be avenged by capital punishment.' The *harkis'* fate was sealed.[68]

The Combattants de la liberation (CDL)

Next on the FLN's agenda were the communists. At the PCA's 20 June 1955 central committee meeting ratifying armed units, a minority had argued that the party should dissolve and its members join the FLN, but the majority agreed on the need for an independent communist party. The PCA prided itself in being the only non-racial and non-ethnic political party able to attract European workers. The PCA's role was to provide a proletarian perspective, whereas the armed struggle, in the central committee's view, was primarily a peasant-based struggle. But most *combattants* felt that the leadership had dallied too long over armed struggle, and they thus saw themselves as a distinctive group within the party. As Jacqueline Guerroudj recalled, the *combattants*, 'having chosen an extreme engagement, naturally also had extreme positions'.[69]

Back from France, Abdelkader Guerroudj convinced Hadj Ali to authorise a *maquis* near Tlemcen and on 14 July headed clandestinely to the mountains near Tlemcen. By the time he arrived, news of the central committee's decision had reached Tahar Ghomri and Hilali Moussa. With Berrahou, they organised the *maquis*, obtaining medicine and equipment from the PCA in Oran. Their numbers varied from six or seven to ten or twenty. They cut electrical lines, burned the *colons'* agricultural material and killed people deemed to be French agents. Ghomri's daughter Halima was fifteen when the *maquis* was formed. Literate in Arabic, she was responsible for reading messages from the *maquisards*; she and two other women prepared food for them.[70]

Communists were thus engaging in sabotage while the party was still legal. They hoped to continue open political and trade union work for as long as possible – for example, supporting the FLN's tobacco and alcohol boycott, which targeted European farm owners, and organising a dockers' strike against unloading weapons. But the central committee prepared for the party's eventual banning by organising an underground printing press. André Moine headed the operation; Rachid Dalibey proposed the Minerva printing machine that the party had used just after the Allied landing when it was still semi-underground. The machine was noisy, but they found an isolated villa, and began producing underground tracts in September. Moine worked with Mahmoud Merdaci, and Ahmed Akkache set up a clandestine distribution system. It was tricky work; they had to separate the sites of production and distribution to protect the machine from possible seizure. They produced flyers and, from September or October, the roneoed monthly *La Voix du soldat*, aimed at French army conscripts and secretly distributed by French communist soldiers.[71]

Notwithstanding the Party's efforts to attract Europeans, they left in droves. Nonetheless, a few idealists still joined, such as Elyette Loup, the daughter of *colons* in rural Mitidja. Strongly influenced by her mother Jeanne Loup, a humanitarian and communist sympathiser who had visited the USSR in 1936 and assisted French and Spanish communists during the Second World War, Elyette Loup was shocked by the ruthless exploitation of farm workers. At secondary school in Algiers, she sought kindred souls and began frequenting the PCA's bookshop. She joined the party around 1953, became an underground liaison in 1955 and worked on the printing press. Safe accommodation was difficult; Loup, Moine and Merdaci ended up living in an apartment at El Biar. The printing machine was moved there, and they put blankets on the walls and doors to cover the noise. It was claustrophobic, and tempers frayed due to the stress of clandestinity. Nonetheless, each day they read and discussed Politzer's *Principes élémentaires de philosophie*.[72]

Similarly, although Annie Fiorio-Steiner had not been politically engaged before the war, she was increasingly unhappy with the injustices she witnessed and spontaneously applauded when she learned of the All Saints' explosions. She worked at the library of the *Centres Sociaux*, a French socio-educational network spearheaded in 1955 by the ethnologist Germaine Tillion that worked in slums and squatter camps. Fiorio-Steiner wanted to help the FLN, but lacking contacts, she spoke to the man who ran the PCA bookshop and was introduced to Hadj Ali. Although not a communist, she became a liaison for the PCA, with Hadjerès her contact.[73]

In the meantime, preparations for the CDL began apace. The CDL's national leadership included army veteran Hadj Ali; army veteran and aeronautics expert Jacques Salort; Hadjerès and Lucette Larribère Manaranche. Decorated army veteran Dr Camille Larribère was the military advisor. There were three regional leaders: Boualem Khalfa, in charge of Oranie, assisted by Antoine Salmeron; Mohammedia Hamouda, in charge of Constantinois, assisted by Antoine Martinez; and Abdelhamid Benzine, in charge of Algérois, assisted by Bab el Oued-born Georges Acampora, a fire fighter who had joined the PCA in 1950, and French-born André Castel.[74]

On 12 September 1955 – reflecting its belief that communists had been involved in the 20 August uprising – the government dissolved the PCA and seized its property. The next day the party produced its first underground tract, which stated: 'The Algerian Communist Party cannot be dissolved. Nothing nor any person will prevent it from pursuing its patriotic task of liberation.' Eight of the party's twelve political bureau members were arrested, and *Liberté*, *El Djezaïr el Djedijda* and *Alger républicain*, banned. The UFA and other allied organisations were dissolved on 17 September.[75]

The Tlemcen *maquis* had been launched in July 1955, and in Blida, where the PCA had a well-established base amongst urban workers, agricultural labourers and peasants, Abdelkader Babou was preparing the *maquis*. A railway worker and local CGT leader, Babou had served in the navy during the Second World War. He joined the PCA central committee in 1948 and visited the USSR and China in 1950–51 as part of a PCA delegation. At Blida he developed a network of some seventy activists, including Odet Voirin, a turner and UJDA and PCA member who became the Party's regional secretary in 1953. Babou organised an agricultural strike in July–August 1955 to prepare the CDL's launch. In August he was seconded by the CGT for a period of six months – of which the Blida police were aware – presumably to develop the *maquis*.[76]

Abdelhamid Benzine organised the Algiers CDL from September to December 1955. Benzine was born in 1926 at Beni Ourtilane, Kabylia, into a family with social standing. His grandfather had been a *cadi*, his father, secretary to a *cadi*, and he attended French and Islamic schools before college in Sétif. Joining the PPA in 1940, he became an energetic organiser, travelling to Tunis and Paris, where he was influenced by MTLD members associated with Pierre Lambert's Fourth International. The CGT sent him to Moscow, where he was so impressed by the USSR's state-led industrialisation that in 1952 he joined the PCA and began working at *Alger républicain*. The young UJDA activist Nour Eddine Rebah, who had attended international youth congresses in Prague and Berlin, joined the Algiers CDL in October 1955.[77]

In Constantine Ali Boulahrouz, Raymonde Peschard, Laban, Lamrani and other communists met clandestinely in October. Lamrani arrived from the Aurès where, he reported, many communists had already torn up their PCA membership cards and joined the ALN – there was no doubt as to the rank-and-file pressure on the PCA leadership. He proposed that they begin sabotage in north Constantinois to ease the burden on the Aurès *maquis*. A CDL unit was formed, but by December 1955 its members had been arrested or had fled to the *maquis*.[78]

Guerroudj left the Tlemcen *maquis* on 20 December 1955, proceeding to Algiers, where once again he met Hadj Ali and argued that the PCA should publicly support the armed struggle. Benzine left for the Aurès, and Guerroudj took charge of the Algiers CDL. Guerroudj was responsible for about ten members, who sabotaged electric transformers and telephone lines, set fires or killed collaborators, colonial representatives or military leaders – including an abortive assassination of General Massu. In addition to Acampora and Castel, the group included Jean Farrugia, a plumber, trade union activist and Dachau prisoner from May 1944 to April 1945; the idealistic Fernand Iveton, a UGSA delegate for the EGA plant at Hamma, Algiers; Jean Yahia Briki, a journalist at *Alger républicain*, son of a Kabyle Protestant pastor and brother of trade unionist David Yusuf Briki; and Jacques Salort. Daniel Timsit and other activists with scientific or technical backgrounds prepared explosives in an underground laboratory. Jacqueline Guerroudj was a liaison, transmitting written and oral information, documents, false papers, arms and, on occasion, bombs.[79]

Other CDL units were launched between January and March 1956. A *maquis* with several units was set up in the Chelif river valley, around the coastal town of Ténès and the inland city of Orléansville (now Chlef), where the ALN had not established a presence. With some thirty communist *maquisards*, the area became known as the '*maquis rouge*' and 'little Moscow'. The PCA's Ténès cell had dwindled over the years. Its Kabyle secretary Rabah Benhamou, introduced to politics in Tizi Ouzou by the leather-worker and artisan Caracéna, felt isolated from the local Arabic traditions. But he revived the cell following Gaston Donnat's arrival. Donnat had led a peripatetic life. After teaching at La Bouzaréah, in 1935 he was transferred to a school in Tizi Ouzou, where he too met Caracéna. During the war he was mobilised into the navy and in 1944 transferred to Cameroon. There he became head of a school in Douala, launched a Marxist study circle in Yaoundé and organised two trade unions. From 1947 to 1951 he was a communist councillor for the French Union, before returning to Algeria. Ever the activist, once in Vieux Ténès he built up the school and linked up with local communists. Benhamou had reputedly been ready to fight since November 1954 and was waiting for the party's word.

After his work at Blida, Abdelkader Babou was tasked with forming armed groups around the Chelif. The CGT extended his secondment for another six months 'to fulfill trade union functions'; the Blida police reported that he was no longer in Blida, but had been seen at Menerville in early April 1956.[80] Babou contacted two local communists, the French-born Arabic-speaking Dr Jean Masseboeuf of Ténès and Dr Martini, the chief surgeon at Orléansville Hospital. They set up a *maquis* at Beni Boudouane, near Lamartine, and were joined by Maurice Laban and Abdelhamid Gherab, a reserve army officer from Blida. The region was mountainous and pocketed with valleys and ravines, allowing reasonably secure movement. Small numbers of communists had been active between Ténès and Cherchell on the coast and from Orléansville to the village of Duperré (now Ain Defla) inland. The area behind the nearby iron mining village of Francis Garnier, where the miners had a well-organised union and lived in dispersed settlements, was well situated for a guerrilla base. That guerrilla group could link up relatively easily with the region around Cherchell, Zaccar and Miliana, another mining area where the PCA had contacts. Benhamou and a local FLN activist were imprisoned, but Benhamou escaped, and in early February 1956 he became head of a CDL group near Francis Garnier.[81]

Laban formed another group near Orléansville and Duperré, where the PCA had a presence. Mohammed Marouf had organised peasants and agricultural workers in the region. The distribution of aid following the 9 September 1954 earthquake that had left some 1,400 dead allowed communists, trade unionists and UFA members scope for organising without arousing police suspicion; the UFA's Baya Allaouchiche had led an active aid campaign there. *Alger républicain* journalists reported on the dire conditions of the badly hit villages with the aim of mobilising its readers against the indifference and inefficiency of municipal and, more broadly, colonial authorities. The CGT's *La Vie ouvrière* (*Working Life*) stressed French and European worker solidarity with Algerian workers and peasants. Moreover, the PCA's Budapest radio broadcasts spotlighted the plight of Tunisian prisoners of war held at Orléansville and demanded their release. These propaganda approaches were complementary and allowed activists to develop diffused and intersecting networks. The population was radicalised; even before

[202]

the November 1954 events supplies had been hidden in mountainous areas. Following numerous arrests on 25 May 1955 – including that of communist municipal councillor Ahmed Keddar, who had organised local peasants and supported the struggles of miners at Zaccar – a group of peasants and miners ransacked a police station and seized weapons. Orléansville, in sum, was a logical base to set up an armed unit.[82]

Laban was joined by Mustapha Saadoun. Born into a well-to-do and politically active peasant family in Cherchell, Saadoun had joined the PCA in 1946. He organised farm workers and peasants on the Mitidja and the Chenoua and Dahra massifs and was arrested for this in 1950. He was elected to the PCA central committee in 1952. Saadoun thought communists should have joined the ALN at the outset; on All Saints' Day in 1954 he had gone to the market at Damous, where mountain-dwellers from Dahra gathered every Saturday to shop and exchange news, to discuss forming a *maquis* in the mining area of Bréira.[83]

The *maquis rouge* was supplied by Henri Maillot, a close friend of Iveton's; they had both grown up in the largely Muslim neighbourhood of Clos Salembier, Algiers. A JC leader during the Vichy years, Maillot later worked at *Alger républicain* with Alleg. Called to serve in the French army during the Algerian war, Maillot became a cadet officer. After returning from Hungary, William Sportisse stayed with Maillot's mother in Clos Salembier; he had met Maillot in 1948–50, when he organised the UJDA in Algiers. Maillot contacted Sportisse in Clos Salembier and told him that he did not want to fight for the French and that he had the possibility of stealing arms. Sportisse relayed the information to Bachir Hadj Ali. Maillot deserted on 4 April 1956 with a truck of weapons – machine guns, revolvers, fusils, grenades and ammunitions. Jacqueline Guerroudj, amongst others, helped transport these weapons, sometimes on her own, sometimes with Jean Farrugia. The PCA's endorsement of Maillot's desertion was a significant departure from the PCF's policy of propaganda within the army.[84]

If the media publicised Maillot's action, so did the CDL, issuing a communiqué from '*quelque part*' (somewhere) in Algeria explaining that the action commemorated the 4 April 1871 Kabylia insurrection and detailing the inventory. Maillot issued his own statement: 'I am not Muslim, but I am Algerian of European origin. I consider Algeria as my country.' He was tried *in absentia* by a military tribunal on 22 May and sentenced to death. For nine-year-old Jean-Pierre Lledo – whose father, PCA activist Noël Lledo, was of Spanish descent and whose mother was a Berber Jew – Maillot proved that Europeans could be completely committed to the Algerian struggle, and he pointed this out to his Arab friends.[85] Nonetheless, the CDL's launch and the publicity they generated hardly eased the FLN's resentment. Soon thereafter, the Ténès

CDL learned that the ALN's regional commander was demanding the group's dissolution – or it would be attacked.[86]

But at the FLN's national level, pragmatics prevailed; the PCA clearly had access to military supplies that its guerrillas desperately needed. That May the FLN and the PCA began talks. The PCA's central committee initially proposed the formation of a *Conseil national algérien de la Résistance* (Algerian National Resistance Council), allowing both organisations autonomy, but the FLN insisted that the party disband. Since the PCA's central committee was unable to meet because of security risks, groups of two or three met to discuss matters. Although a minority favoured the PCA's dissolution, most felt, as they had the year before, that the PCA should not dissolve. An independent communist party was the only guarantee that after independence, workers and peasants would be able to progress towards real social, economic and cultural liberation, they argued. It was needed to build solidarity with the French working class and anti-imperialist forces; dissolution would only serve the interests of the FLN's bourgeois and petty bourgeois sections. Moreover, many communists had engaged in clandestine work during the Second World War, and dissolution would have meant renouncing their underground past and risking condemnation from communists and sympathisers around the world. Political repression made it impossible to call a congress to discuss the matter, but had this been feasible, the central committee would have advised against dissolution. The question, however, remained open for discussion.[87]

The French security forces, in the meantime, were well aware that Maillot would distribute the weapons. Immediately after his desertion, the prefect of Algiers wrote to local authorities across the country asking them to report on communist activity in their regions. On 9 April Orléansville authorities reported that local communists had gone on an eight-day training programme near Mont Chenoua and been instructed to explain their absence as a family visit. On the same day, Miliana police reported the arrival of the well-known Orléansville communist Marcel Montagné and an unknown Algerian. On 10 April Blida police reported that communists Mustapha Saadoun, Georges Counillon and Abdelhamid Gherab had vanished. On 11 April the police in Algiers provided details of Maillot's possible political contacts; on the 12th they reported that rank-and-file communists had been informed that the party was preparing a *maquis*. On 21 April authorities in Algiers learned that the PCA had installed a training camp at the *douars* of Beni Bou Melluk and Tachta, that Orléansville activists had been invited and that Orléansville communist Ahmed Chaoui was the liaison; the brothers supplying the *maquis'* food informed the police. On 23 April the Miliana sub-prefect informed the prefect of Algiers that Miliana and Duperré had long been zones of communist activity: the CGT had organised the miners at Zaccar, and Maillot had cultivated local military circles and knew the region well, he explained. On 5 May Miliana authorities reported the arrival of two communist sympathisers. Tracking every communist move, the state put its men in place.[88]

On 5 June 1956 the French army decimated Laban's *maquisards* after the pro-France Bachaga Boualem provided precise information on their whereabouts. Laban, Maillot, Belkacem Hamoun and Djillali Moussaoui died immediately. Abdelkader Zalmaï was captured the next day and executed. Mohamed Boualem, the leader of the Oran dockers, Saadoun, Gherab and others escaped.[89] The PCA had expected that the *maquis rouge* would provide leverage in its negotiations with the FLN. Its loss was a heavy blow. That month the PCA's central committee agreed to military unity and increased cooperation with the ALN. Hadj Ali and Hadjerès presented the party's position to the FLN's Abane Ramdane and Benyoussef Ben Khedda, bringing with them a truck of weapons – part of Maillot's stolen stock. They agreed that with effect from 1 July 1956 groups of *combattants* would integrate into the ALN with their weapons and accept the FLN's authority. Some communists had already joined the ALN; they and the *combattants* were to cut all organic links with the PCA for the war's duration, but without renouncing their political convictions. The PCA and FLN would cooperate on such matters as the political education of French soldiers through the diffusion of *La Voix du soldat*. The PCA would provide technical assistance, such as the use of its printing press to make false identity papers. But it refused to dissolve, arguing that this would be against the interests of the working class and the Algerian people, and it continued its independent propaganda.[90]

Two hundred communists, mostly Algerians, were integrated into the ALN that July. Europeans who joined the ALN fell into two broad groups. First were those who had been part of the 1940–41 underground structure and who sympathised with the national movement. Second were intellectuals and professionals – students, teachers, doctors, engineers and journalists, especially those at *Alger républicain*.[91] Generally the CDL cells were incorporated into the ALN with their structure intact. There were two reasons for this, speculated Jacqueline Guerroudj. The first was efficiency – it was not prudent to disrupt operational CDL cells. The second was the FLN's concern that individual communists integrated into nationalist cells might influence other members. Keeping the original CDL cells intact but separate would minimise ideological influence. Once in the ALN, the cells were under the authority of an FLN leader. However, initiatives for operations could come either from the FLN leader or from the unit itself, with the leader's permission.[92]

Abdelkader Babou was visibly relieved at the integration of Ténès *combattants* into the ALN, while Guerroudj believed that many rank-and-file communists would have been willing to disband and join the FLN. Similarly, around Constantine, relations between communists and nationalists had always been fluid, according to William Sportisse, who had returned to reconstitute the PCA's underground. Many *combattants* had been killed by the French army; others had been forced to flee. Sportisse believed that those remaining would have joined the ALN even without the accord. The FLN wished to keep its relationship with the PCA secret, arguing that public knowledge would diminish support from anti-communist regimes and slow down the provision of arms. While not accepting this reasoning, the PCA agreed in order to ensure the FLN of its commitment.[93]

Meanwhile, the intensification of French efforts compelled the internal FLN to re-evaluate its position – a need reinforced by the 16 June announcement of Saharan oil discoveries. Algiers suffocated in a 'stifling atmosphere', wrote Feraoun. 'People have the same worried and scared look. There, however, one is lost in the crowd. One does not really get the feeling of being targeted'. How different in villages, where people feared a night-time knock on the door. At a police crackdown one market day that July, there was an 'endless line of people with hands in the air ... The old men moved like crabs and looked pitiful. The young looked ashamed and submissive. The whole group resembled a pathetic herd that the policemen shoved, hit, and insulted.' Terror and humiliation drove the struggle forward. Those in the countryside still felt this first.[94]

The Soummam congress

In August–September 1956 – one year after the north Constantinois actions – sixteen FLN leaders met at a forester's lodge overlooking the Soummam valley in Kabylia. The twenty-day Soummam congress was the inspiration of Abane Ramdane, who had rapidly climbed the internal FLN ranks after his release from prison in 1955. Ramdane and Larbi Ben M'Hidi were committed to urban terrorism to catalyse mass support. Regional representation at the congress was uneven. Constantinois and Kabylia had the most delegates. The Aurès was not represented; conditions there were anarchic. Although the FLN's leaders in Cairo wanted to attend, their attempts went awry, to their anger.[95]

From the FLN's perspective, the FLN–PCA accord was purely expedient – its guerrillas needed military supplies. The external FLN would certainly have preferred to refuse communist aid, especially in light of US concerns about communist–nationalist links. The Soummam congress scathingly described the PCA as absent from the struggle – a claim clearly belied by Laban's *maquis rouge* and the other CDL units. The PCA's leadership slavishly followed the PCF, it claimed. Although the congress acknowledged that individual communists could join the FLN and ALN, it was convinced that the PCA would use those individuals to mask its own isolation. Crucially, it contended, the PCA refused to acknowledge the peasantry's revolutionary potential, instead seeking to defend the Algerian working class from the domination of the '"bourgeoisie arabe", as if Algeria's national independence had to follow the path of failed revolutions'. However, aware that their hunger for land could only be satisfied through independence, peasants, sharecroppers and agricultural workers comprised the dominant proportion of *mujahidin* and *musabilin*. The revolution necessitated the politicisation of the *maquis* and the relentless pursuit of armed struggle to achieve a general insurrection.[96]

The congress produced a forty-page document that outlined the struggle's objectives and reorganised political and military structures; the former communist Ouzegane had evidently played a major role in developing the ideas. Its aim was *'the renaissance of an Algerian State under the form of a democratic and social republic and not the restoration of a monarchy or a past theocracy'*. It refused to accept a cease-fire until France accepted the principle of independence.[97] A Comité de coordination et d'exécution (CCE) was to coordinate the activities of the *wilayas*. A Conseil national de la révolution Algérienne (CNRA) was to be Algeria's first sovereign parliament. The CNRA comprised seventeen former CRUA members, six former MTLD centralists, two former UDMA members and two reformist *'ulama*. The ALN was restructured under a high command headquartered in Algeria, with Algiers an autonomous zone. To avoid personality cults around generals the highest rank was colonel. The congress underlined the authority of political over military leadership and the primacy of the internal over the external struggle. It endorsed collegiality, opposed regionalism, rejected pluralism and refused to tolerate organisations that did not accept the FLN's hegemony.[98]

Despite the FLN's disdain for the PCA, it had nonetheless accepted its support.[99] The PCA had moved closer to the FLN – and distanced itself from the PCF – fully supporting the armed struggle and conceding the appeal of violence or 'punishments adequate with the gravity of acts committed' against collaborators: 'the good popular opinion of guerrillas and partisans has been stirred by a varied and original scale of punishments', including 'the hair cut off the collaborator women during the liberation of France, and ... the nose divided for the unrepentant collaborators in the Algerian campaign'. But a fundamental strategic difference remained: while the FLN propounded the peasantry's revolutionary potential, the PCA stressed proletarian leadership. Peasants were prone to 'an ideology that expresses itself occasionally in acts of a distorted character, to the discredit of the just character of the national struggle ... creating the impression of a chauvinist, racist, fanatical struggle'. This spontaneous violence must be contained by working-class political leadership.[100] A fair and lasting peace was possible if France ceased its policy of violence, recognised Algeria's right to self-determination and engaged in negotiations over the cease-fire terms with the ALN and Algerian representatives from all organisations to discuss Algeria's future institutions.[101]

On 22 October, in flagrant violation of international law, the French army forced a Moroccan plane carrying four external FLN leaders – Ben Bella, Aït Ahmed, Mohammed Khider and Mohamed Boudiaf – and prominent intellectual Mostefa Lacheraf to land in Algeria. The five were imprisoned in France. Although the FLN's internal leadership condemned the action, some of them, not least Abane Ramdane, were reputedly relieved: the arrests resolved the internal–external rivalry and left the Soummam Charter, with its stress on the primacy of internal struggle, seemingly unchallenged.[102]

Whatever the intentions of the Soummam congress, the FLN's intolerance and violence had earned it Algerian critics. Feraoun confided to his journal: '[the FLN's] prestige is eroding ... Did someone not tell me back home that they are now behaving like masters?' Nonetheless, fear produced unity. By late November, Feraoun observed: 'a major part of Kabylia has been declared a forbidden zone. Only the civil servants, employees, and business owners are allowed in. The dominating presence in the streets is that of soldiers wearing green fatigues.'[103]

With state and society increasingly militarised, the impact of the Soummam congress was to uphold the lesson of 20 August 1955 – guerrilla insurgency and terror paid. By then much of Algerian society was organised into underground networks. Uneven in coverage and effectiveness, these networks nonetheless encompassed a military structure and elements of an alternative civil administration: judicial structures, civil and tax authorities, and pension and family assistance organised by the FLN. But the French army was making inroads in the countryside. Accordingly, the FLN shifted its focus to urban terrorism against Europeans, planning to capture the capital – the symbol of French colonialism – and divert the French army from the countryside.

This, believed the FLN, would spark the hoped-for insurrection.[104]

CDL units had already engaged in urban guerrilla actions. Once integrated into the ALN, communist experience varied greatly. In parts of Algérois and Oranie, communists and nationalists worked together with mutual respect. In Algiers the integration went relatively well, even though the FLN's Saâdi Yacef, who headed operations in the *casbah*, was anti-communist. Around Tlemcen, where communists had a long presence, they integrated into the ALN with relative ease. In Blida and Oran, communists engaged in anti-military propaganda amongst French soldiers, sabotaged war provisions in factories and organised supplies, medical aid and shelter for urban guerrillas.[105]

The PCA was caught between the French state's fear of Soviet expansion and the FLN's intolerance of communism and political pluralism. Thus, communists often remained suspect in the eyes of ALN leaders, a suspicion that deepened after the Soummam congress. The FLN–PCA accord stipulated that communists joining the ALN renounce contact with the PCA until independence. But in practice the FLN also insisted that communists denounce the PCA. In Kabylia and the Aurès, Lamrani, Raffini and others were executed for refusing to renounce their views. Around the Chelif river valley and the Ouarsenis mountain range, communists were disarmed and stripped of responsibilities. In other cases, communists were isolated from the local population and given the most dangerous assignments. As a result, communist deaths were particularly high. Seven central committee members and regional secretaries died – Lamrani, Raffini, Laban, Ghomri, Mustapha Fodil and Bouali Taleb – as did many rank-and-file members. Integration did not mean tolerance.[106]

Notes

1. « A la même heure (1 h. 15), dans la nuit de dimanche à lundi, des terroristes ont opéré en divers points du territoire algérien », *Dépêche quotidienne d'Algérien* (2 November 1954), p. 1.
2. Horne, *Savage War*, pp. 48, 88, 109–10. See also, *inter alia*, Yves Courrière, *La Guerre d'Algérie*, 4 vols. (Paris: Fayard, 1968–71); Heggoy, *Insurgency*; Ruedy, *Modern Algeria*, pp. 156–94; Wolf, *Peasant Wars*, pp. 211–47; Benjamin Stora, *Histoire de la guerre d'Algérie (1954–1962)* (Paris: La Découverte, 1993); Evans, *Memory*; Evans, *Algeria*.
3. Ruedy, *Modern Algeria*, pp. 149–50; Crenshaw, 'Effectiveness', p. 479; Lazreg, *Torture*, p. 35; Macey, *Fanon*, p. 205.
4. Horne, *Savage War*, p. 136; Haudiquet, 'L'Incendie', p. 111; Ruth First Papers, Institute of Commonwealth Studies, London (hereafter RF) 1/5/15, Ruth First, interview with Henri Alleg, 11 March 1967; Alleg, *Mémoire*, p. 180; André Moine, *Ma guerre d'Algérie* (Paris: Editions Sociales, 1979), pp. 24–6; Bashir [sic] Hadj Ali, 'Lessons of the Algerian Struggle,' in William J. Pomery (ed.), *Guerrilla Warfare and Marxism* (London: Lawrence and Wishart, 1969), 254–60, p. 259.
5. ANOM FM 81F/759. *L'action du Parti communiste dans la rébellion en Algérie*

(supplément à la semaine en Algérie du 13 janvier 1957 au 20 janvier 1957, p. 4; Jean-Louis Planche, 'De la solidarité militante à l'affrontement armé. M.N.A. et F.L.N. à Alger, 1954–1955', in J.-Ch. Jeauffret and M. Vaïsse (eds), *Militaires et guérilla dans la guerre d'Algérie* (Editions Complexe, 2001), 219–36, p. 29; Pierre-Jean Le Foll-Luciani, 'Un microcosme de l'Algérie nouvelle? Le Parti communiste algérien en clandestin à Constantine pendant la guerre d'indépendance (1954–1962)', *Atala*, 16 (2013), 245–58, pp. 245–7; Harbi, *Vie*, p. 150.

6 « ces mesures de terreur qui tendent, en créant un climat d'insécurité générale à ouvrir la voie à une répression généralisée frappant tous les patriotes, tous les hommes épris de liberté et de démocratie », 'Voici les véritables responsables des événements actuels', *Liberté* (4 November 1954), p. 1; 'Déclaration du Bureau politique du P. C. algérien', 1 November 1954, in Alleg (ed.), *Guerre*, vol. 3, pp. 513–4; cf. Benjamin Stora, *La Gangrène et l'oubli: La Mémoire de la guerre d'Algérie* (Paris: La Découverte, 1991, 1998), p. 146.

7 « Le calme semble revenu dans l'Algérois et en Oranie, mais l'effervescence persiste dans le Constantinois », *Dépêche quotidienne d'Algérie* (2 November 1954), p. 1.

8 Douzon, 'Occasions', p. 478; Sivan, *Communisme*, p. 229; Alleg, *Mémoire*, p. 159; Khatib, *1er juillet*, p. 48; 'Les blindés sont entrés en action contre les hors-la-loi de l'Aurès', *Dépêche quotidienne d'Algérie* (5 November 1954), p. 1.

9 « c'est la fin de l'humiliation ... du mépris, des "ratonnades" », Louisette Ighilahriz, *Algérienne* (Algiers: Casbah, 2006), pp. 46, 48; interview with Louisette Ighilahriz, Algiers, 20 September 2011.

10 Yves Courrière, *La Guerre d'Algérie: Le Temps des léopards*, vol. 2 (Paris: Fayard, 1969), p. 294; Dore-Audibert, *Françaises*, p. 171; Nagy, 'Les « événements »', p. 5; Gallissot (ed.), *Algérie*, pp. 465, 486; Einaudi, *Algérien*, pp. 125, 130–3, 138–9.

11 ANOM, FM 81F/759, G. Pontal, Directeur, Sûreté nationale en Algérie, *Le Parti communiste algérien dans la clandestinité* [6 December 1955]; Interview with Hadjerès; First, interview with Alleg, p. 3; Lucette Larribère Hadj Ali, *Itinéraire d'une Militante algérienne* (Blida: Editions du Tell, 2011), p. 85; Sivan, *Communisme*, pp. 231–2; Douzon, 'Occasions', p. 478; Donnat, *Afin que*, p. 307; Harbi, *Vie*, pp. 93–4; Einaudi, *Algérien*, pp. 132–3, 138–9.

12 « ils ont vécu colonialisme », interviews with Abdelkader Guerroudj, Algiers, 26, 28 September 2011; Jacqueline Guerroudj, in Amrane-Minne, *Femmes*, pp. 181–7, 183; Dore-Audibert, *Françaises*, p. 147; Courrière, *Léopards*, p. 294; Sivan, *Communisme*, pp. 231–2.

13 « le moment est arrivé », interviews with Guerroudj; Gallissot (ed.), *Algérie*, pp. 369–70.

14 Joly, *French Communist*, pp. 43–4; Irwin M. Wall, 'The French Communists and the Algerian War', *Journal of Contemporary History*, 12 (1977), 521–43, pp. 522–3; Harbi, *Vie*, pp. 152–3.

15 Déclaration du Parti communiste français sur la situation en Algérie, 8 November 1954, in Alleg (ed.), *Guerre*, vol. 3, pp. 511–12; Alleg, *Mémoire*, p. 182; Moine, *Ma guerre*, pp. 195–9; Horne, *Savage War*, p. 98; Wall, 'French Communists', pp. 524–5; Evans, *Memory*, p. 91; Macey, *Fanon*, pp. 243–4; Heggoy, *Insurgency*, pp. 251–2; Todd Shepard, *The Invention of Decolonization: The Algerian War and the Remaking of France* (Ithaca, NY, and London: Cornell, 2006), p. 44.

16 Interview with Hadjerès.

17 *Liberté* (25 November 1954); TNA: PRO FO 371/10863, British Consul-General to Anthony Eden, 24 November 1954; ANOM FM 81F/759, *L'action du Parti communiste dans la rébellion*, pp. 11, 14; Connelly, *Diplomatic Revolution*, p. 84; Le Foll-Luciani, 'Un microcosme de l'Algérie nouvelle?', pp. 247–8.

18 *Liberté* (14 November, 9, 16, 30 December 1954).

19 Meynier, 'PPA-MTLD', p. 611; Wolf, *Peasant Wars*, p. 187; Macey, *Fanon*, pp. 246–7; Horne, *Savage War*, pp. 78–9; Hadj Ali, 'Lessons', p. 255; Benjamin Stora, 'Commentaire', in Pierre Journoud and Hugues Tertrais (eds), *1954–2004: La Bataille de Dien Bien Phu, entre histoire et mémoire* (Paris: Société française d'histoire d'outre-mer, 2004), pp. 251–3. Alleg, interview, 11 June 2010, met Algerians who had served in Vietnam, claiming to have been recruited with promises of special benefits.

20 Meynier, 'PPA-MTLD', p. 622; Daho Djerbal, 'Les effets des manifestations de décembre 1960 sur les maquis algériens', in *11 décembre 1960: Le Diên Biên Phú Politique de la Guerre d'Algérie* (Algiers: NAQD, 2010), 63–92, p. 65.
21 « La restauration de l'Etat algérien souverain, démocratique et social dans le cadre des principes islamiques ... Le respect de toutes libertés fondamentales sans distinction de race ni de confession ... leur nationalité d'origine », 'Proclamation du F.L.N.', 1 November 1954 in Alleg (ed.), *Guerre*, vol. 3, 507–10, p. 509; Ruedy, *Modern Algeria*, pp. 157–60; Heggoy, *Insurgency*, pp. 63–6; Shepard, *Invention*, pp. 43, 46.
22 Heggoy, *Insurgency*, pp. 113–15, quotes pp. 293–4, n. 16; Wolf, *Peasant Wars*, p. 238; Macey, *Fanon*, pp. 251–3; Lazreg, *Torture*, pp. 210, 222; Djerbal, 'Effets', p. 68.
23 Launay, *Paysans*, pp. 175–6; Heggoy, *Insurgency*, p. 79; Wolf, *Peasant Wars*, p. 230; First, interview with Alleg; Ruedy, *Modern Algeria*, p. 163; Bennoune, 'Introduction of Nationalism', p. 5; Hadj Ali, 'Lessons', p. 255; Lazreg, *Torture*, p. 222; Djerbal, 'Effets', p. 68.
24 Bennoune, 'Introduction', pp. 2, 4–10. PCF 261J 7/, box 4, République algérienne, Ministère de l'Information, *A travers les wilayas d'Algérie* (November 1960), p. 36 notes that the local population was very strongly politicised before 1954.
25 Estimates are based on registration with the Ministry of War Veterans for pensions, jobs or promotions, which was harder for women than men. See Lazreg, *Eloquence*, pp. 119–20, 124–5; Ryme Seferdjeli, 'Rethinking the History of the *Mujahidat* during the Algerian War: Competing Voices, Reconstructed Memories and Contrasting Historiographies', *Interventions*, 14:2 (2012), 238–55; 240–41, 247–9; MacMaster, *Burning*, pp. 319–21; Natalya Vince, 'Transgressing Boundaries: Gender, Race, Religion, and "Françaises musulmanes" during the Algerian War of Independence', *French Historical Studies*, 33, 3 (Summer 2010), 445–74; interview with Zoulikha Bekaddour, Algiers, 26 September 2011.
26 Lazreg, *Torture*, pp. 155–6; Heggoy, *Insurgency*, p. 97; Mouloud Feraoun, *Journal, 1955-1962: Reflections on the French-Algerian War* [1962] (Lincoln, NE, and London: University of Nebraska, 2000), pp. 131, 140–1.
27 Lazreg, *Torture*, pp. 59, 76–86; Patrick Rotman, *L'Ennemi intime* (Paris: Editions du Seuil, 2007), pp. 41–9; Heggoy, *Insurgency*, pp. 90, 95–6, 188–211; Ruedy, *Modern Algeria*, p. 162.
28 Horne, *Savage War*, pp. 134–5; Stora, *Gangrène*, pp. 166–7.
29 Lazreg, *Torture*, pp. 36–60; Ryme Seferdjeli, 'French "Reforms" and Muslim Women's Emancipation during the Algerian War', *Journal of North African Studies*, 9:4 (Winter 2004), 19–61, pp. 43–4; interview with Abdelmoumène.
30 Francis and Gontier, *de Beauvoir*, p. 299.
31 'Une notice officielle fixe les règles de l' « action psychologique » dans les camps d'hébergement', *Le Monde*, 23 January 1958, p. 4; PCF 261 J7/ box 1, file 6, République Algérienne, Ministère de l'Information, *Génocide en Algérie ... Les camps de regroupement* (October 1960); RF 1/5/15, K. Sutton and R. I. Lawless, 'Population Regroupment in Algeria – Traumatic Change and the Rural Settlement Pattern', paper presented at the symposium on 'Settlement and conflict in the Mediterranean world', I.B.G., Newcastle (6 January 1977), esp. pp. 1–14.
32 Heggoy, *Insurgency*, pp. 213–16; Lazreg, *Torture*, pp. 36–7, 48–50, 58–60; PCF 261 J7/, box 1, folder 2, 'Appel de 120 enseignants et avocats d'Oran', 15 June 1955.
33 Ruedy, *Modern Algeria*, p. 161; Horne, *Savage War*, pp. 100–4; Crenshaw, 'Effectiveness', p. 479.
34 Macey, *Fanon*, pp. 264–6; Alice Cherki, *Frantz Fanon: Portrait* (Paris: Seuil, 2000), pp. 38–42, 59, 70–1, 83, 115–16.
35 Ruedy, *Modern Algeria*, p. 161; Horne, *Savage War*, pp. 111–12; Heggoy, *Insurgency*, pp. 91–2; Lazreg, *Torture*, p. 36; *Directives du F.L.N. au sujet de la conférence de Bandoeng*, 1 Juin 1955, and *Front de libération nationale. Appel de l'armée de libération nationale*, 1 Avril 1955, both Alleg (ed.), *Guerre*, vol. 3, pp. 515–17.
36 Planche, 'Solidarité', pp. 219–21; Heggoy, *Insurgency*, p. 108; Meyner, 'PPA–MTLD and FLN–ALN', p. 610.
37 Planche, 'Solidarité', pp. 221–5; Stora, *Gangrène*, pp. 48, 138–44; Ruedy, *Modern*

  Algeria, p. 162; Horne, *Savage War*, p. 97.
38 ANOM FM 81F/759, Pontal, *Parti communiste*, p. 2; *Liberté* (24 February, 3, 10, 17, 24 March 1955); Gallissot (ed.), *Algérie*, p. 318; Nagy, 'Les « événements »', p. 5.
39 *Liberté* (3 March 1955); Khatib, *1er juillet*, p. 50; Rebah, *Chemins*, p. 37; Gallissot (ed.), *Algérie*, pp. 150–1.
40 Interview with Hadjerès.
41 « En avant pour le combat », interview with Guerroudj, 26 September 2011.
42 « Tout pour la lutte armée », Jacqueline Guerroudj, *Des Douars et des prisons* (n.p.: Bouchene, n.d.) p. 34; Haudiquet, 'L'Incendie', pp. 113–14; Alleg, *Mémoire*, pp. 197–8; interview with Hadjerès.
43 ANOM FM 81F/759, Pontal, *Parti communiste*, p. 3, GGA to Ministère de l'Intérieur, 24 June 1955, Cabinet GGA, 4 July 1955; Connelly, *Diplomatic Revolution*, pp. 84, 312, n. 85, suggests the Americans thought the French overstated the PCA strength and its relationship with the FLN.
44 See République algérienne, *A travers les wilayas*, pp. 36–7, esp. re preparation; Horne, *Savage War*, pp. 119–22; Ruedy, *Modern Algeria*, p. 162; Benjamin Stora, *Algeria, 1830–2000: A short history* (Ithaca, NY, and London: Cornell, 2001), pp. 43–4; Revel, *Instituteur*, p. 400; *Bilan des actions de l'A.L.N. du 20 août 1955 dans le Nord-Constantinois*, in Alleg (ed.), *Guerre*, vol. 3, pp. 518–20; Crenshaw, 'Effectiveness', p. 479; Macey, *Fanon*, pp. 267–8. Jean-Pierre Lledo's film, *Algérie: Histoires à ne pas dire* (2008) discusses the 1955 massacre; see Mohamed Harbi, 'Je pense qu'il faut défendre ce film', http://goo.gl/IARhah (accessed 23 November 2008).
45 « autant de hordes de rebelles remarquablement organisées et allant au combat au sens propre de ce terme », *Dépêche quotidienne d'Algérie* (21–2 August), p. 1 (23 August 1955), p. 4; 'Sanglant échec d'une tentative d'insurrection dans le Constantinois', *Dépêche Constantine* (21–2 August 1955), p. 1; 'Le terrorisme dans le Constantinois', *Dépêche Constantine* (21–2, 23 August 1955), p. 1.
46 « Neuf mechtas, foyer de rébellion … totalement détruites par nos troupes après évacuation des femmes et des enfants », *Dépêche quotidienne d'Algérie* (23 August), p. 1 (1 September 1955); *Dépêche Constantine* (23, 24, 25, 26 August 1955), p. 1. The *mechtas* were in the *communes mixtes* of Oued Zenati and Jemmapes; République Algérienne, *A travers les wilayas*, p. 36, mentions Jemmapes.
47 Bennoune, 'Introduction', p. 11, and République algérienne, *A travers les wilayas*, p. 37, state that the ALN gained control of the area. ANOM FM 81F/759, *L'action du Parti communiste dans la rébellion*, p. 6; Nasser Djabi, *Kaïdi Lakhdar: Une histoire du syndicalisme Algérien* (n.p.: Chihab, 2005), pp. 199–203; Ruedy, *Modern Algeria*, p. 163; Horne, *Savage War*, p. 137; Djerbal, 'Effets', p. 71. Secondary sources suggest wilaya II had few guerrillas before this episode, but newspaper accounts express surprise that there were two thousand. *A travers les wilayas*, p. 36, states that the wilaya had gone through a difficult period in April–June 1955.
48 « je désapprouve totalement le terrorisme qui touche aux populations civiles », Albert Camus, Lettre au 'Comité Messali Hadj', 25 March 1955, in Albert Camus, *Œuvres Complètes, III, 1949–1956* (Paris: Gallimard, 2008), p. 1110; 'Letter to an Algerian Militant' [1 October 1955], in Albert Camus, *Resistance, Rebellion, and Death* (New York: Modern Library, 1960), 93–7, pp. 94–5; Guy Pervillé, 'Mohammed el Aziz Kessous (1985)', 5 May 2007, http://goo.gl/UpPOu6 (accessed 19 April 2010); Feraoun, *Journal*, p. 71.
49 Feraoun, *Journal*, pp. 32–3, 16, 45, 47–8, 51; on guerrilla activity, *Echo d'Alger* (January 1956); 'Boycott du tabac, des débits de boissons alcoolisées et des salles de spectacle', [c. April 1956], in Mohammed Harbi and Gilbert Meynier (eds), *Le FLN: Documents et histoire, 1954–1962* (n.p.: Fayard, 2004), pp. 112–13.
50 Wall, 'French Communists', p. 526; Zaretsky, *Camus*, pp. 132–4; Stora, *Gangrène*, pp. 74–5; interview with Ouzegane.
51 'Appeal for a Civilian Truce', in Camus, *Resistance*, 97–106, pp. 97, 102–3; Zaretsky, *Camus*, pp. 120–1, 129–30; Todd, *Camus: A Life*, pp. 336–7; Todd, *Camus: Une vie*, pp. 857–67.
52 Frantz Fanon, *A Dying Colonialism* (New York: Grove, 1967), pp. 163–76, 172;

Charles F. Peterson, *Dubois, Fanon, Cabral: The Margins of Elite Anti-Colonial Leadership* (Lanham, MD, and Plymouth: Lexington, 2007), p. 98.
53 « Reconnaître le droit de l'Algérie à la libre disposition », 23 January 1956, in Harbi and Meynier (eds), *FLN*, pp. 227–8.
54 « L'arrivée de M. Guy MOLLET à Alger a été marquée par de violents incidents », *L'Echo d'Alger* (7 February 1956), p. 1.
55 Macey, *Fanon*, p. 272; « Il est devenu l'ennemi n° 1 de l'Algérie », Lettre à la délégation extérieure du FLN du Caire de Abbane, 20 September 1955; « tout messaliste conscient devra être fusillé sans jugement », Lettre d'Abane à la délégation extérieure FLN du Caire, 29 February 1956, both in Harbi and Meynier (eds), *FLN*, pp. 207–8; TNA: PRO FO 371/119422 re banning of foreign papers; Zaretsky, *Camus*, pp. 129, 134–7; Feraoun, *Journal*, pp. 59, 72.
56 Meynier, 'PPA–MTLD', p. 617; Stora, *Messali*, pp. 245–8; Haudiquet, 'L'Incendie', pp. 198–203; Douzon, 'Occasions', p. 550; Djabi, *Kaïdi Lakhdar*, pp. 203–14; Gallissot (ed.), *Algérie*, pp. 373–9.
57 PCF 261J 7/, box 4, Jacques Duclos, 'La France et l'Algérie: Discours prononcé à l'Assemblée Nationale le 11 octobre 1955', in Maurice Thorez, Jacques Duclos and François Billoux, *La France et l'Afrique du Nord* (Paris: Editions de France Nouvelle, n.d. [1955]), pp. 3–32.
58 « Le gouvernement pourra pratiquement instituer l'état de siège en Algérie », *L'Echo d'Alger* (2 March 1956), p. 1; « M. Guy MOLLET posera la question de confiance sur les pouvoirs spéciaux », *L'Echo d'Alger* (3 March 1956), p. 1; « Algérie n'est pas une province comme les autres mais elle n'est pas non plus un Etat musulman », *L'Echo d'Alger* (10 March 1956), p. 4; Heggoy, *Insurgency*, pp. 254–5; Connelly, *Diplomatic Revolution*, p. 81; Shepard, *Invention*, p. 44, n. 72.
59 Assemblée nationale, Séance du 12 Mars 1956, *Journal officiel de la République française, Débats parlementaires* (13 March 1956), pp. 854–5; *L'Echo d'Alger* (13 March 1956), p. 1; Williams, *Crisis*, pp. 270–5; Stora, *Gangrène*, pp. 52–3, 75–6.
60 Joly, *French Communist*, pp. 106–12; Heggoy, *Insurgency*, pp. 188–9; Evans, *Memory*, pp. 27–8, 88–9, 99, 138–9; Shepard, *Invention*, p. 112; Wall, 'French Communists', pp. 526–7; Larribère Hadj Ali, *Itinéraire*, p. 94.
61 Interview with Hadjerès; Donnat, *Afin que*, p. 334; Stora, *Gangrène*, pp. 75–8. A child during the war, Riad Benchikh-el-Fougoun (interview, Constantine, 23 September 2011) recollected that local Communists denounced special powers. Guerroudj (interview, 26 September 2011) fiercely opposed special powers and thought the PCA leadership too accommodating with the PCF.
62 Feraoun, *Journal*, p. 82; Ruedy, *Modern Algeria*, pp. 165–6; Horne, *Savage War*, pp. 123–4; Heggoy, *Insurgency*, pp. 76, 98–100; Stora, *Gangrène*, p. 75; *New York Times* (1 October 1955).
63 Heggoy, *Insurgency*, pp. 188–95, 199; Lazreg, *Torture*, p. 37; Ruedy, *Modern Algeria*, pp. 163–5; Horne, *Savage War*, pp. 123–4; Crenshaw, 'Effectiveness', p. 484, n. 16; Laurent Schwartz, 'L'engagement de Pierre Vidal-Naquet dans la guerre d'Algérie', in François Hartog, Pauline Schmitt-Pantel and Alain Schnapp (eds), *Pierre Vidal-Naquet: Un historien dans la cité* (Paris: La Découverte, 2007), pp. 24–41, 32; Francis and Gontier, *de Beauvoir*, pp. 297–8; RF 1/5/15, [Ruth First], 'Armed struggle in Algeria', p. 5.
64 TNA: PRO FO 371/119422, *Observer* (29 April 1956), p. 6; interviews with Fafa Boudjenah, Hadj Aissa Bellalou.
65 Interview with Abdelmoumène; TNA: PRO FO 371/119422, *Arab News Letter*, 8 (1 June 1956).
66 MacMaster, *Burning*, pp. 320–1; interview with Bekaddour; discussion with Bekaddour and Elyette Loup, Algiers, 29 September 2011.
67 « Un rideau était tombé sur ma féminité », Ighilahriz, *Algérienne*, p. 72; interviews with Ighilahriz, Abdelmoumène, Ouzegane; Ali Mebtouche, 'L'Histoire d'une grève: Ralliement des étudiants à la Révolution algérienne', *Liberté* (19 May 2009) http://goo.gl/Gfya7L (accessed 19 November 2012); Hafida Ameyar, *La Moudjahida Annie Fiorio-Steiner: Une vie pour l'Algérie* (Algiers: Association les amis de Abdelhamid Benzine, 2011), pp. 83, 99; Rebah, *Chemins*, p. 83.

68 ALN War Staff, flyer (6 June 1956), in *True Aspects of the Algerian Rebellion* (Algiers: Cabinet du gouverneur général, 1957), exhibit at 'Francis Bacon: A Centenary Retrospective', Metropolitan Museum of Art, New York, 5 August 2009; Stora, *Gangrène*, pp. 163–6.
69 « ayant choisi un engagement extrême, avaient naturellement aussi des positions extrêmes », Guerroudj, *Douars*, p. 38; Moine, *Ma guerre*, p. 85; Alleg, *Mémoire*, pp. 197–8.
70 Interview with Guerroudj, 28 September 2011; Haudiquet, 'L'Incendie', pp. 113–14; Amrane-Minne, *Femmes*, pp. 100–3.
71 Moine, *Ma guerre*, pp. 83–4, 91–2; Haudiquet, 'L'Incendie', pp. 113–14; Parti communiste algérien à la direction du Front de libération nationale, 12 July 1956, in Alleg (ed.), *Guerre*, vol. 3, pp. 532–4; Heggoy, *Insurgency*, p. 249; cf. Larribère Hadj Ali, *Itinéraire*, pp. 85–6; Roger Bourderon, 'Un journal clandestin pour les appelés: « La Voix du soldat »: Entretien avec Alfred Gerson, Lucien Hanoun, André Moine', *Cahiers d'histoire de l'Institut de recherches marxistes*, 8 (1982), 89–111. Hadjerès to author, 23 March 2012.
72 Planche, 'Solidarité', p. 228; Amrane-Minne, *Femmes*, pp. 188–91; Larribère Hadj Ali, *Itinéraire*, pp. 105–6; Gallissot (ed.), *Algérie*, pp. 433–4; Moine, *Ma guerre*, pp. 98–103, 107–15; interview with Elyette Loup, Algiers, 29 September 2011.
73 Ameyar, *Moudjahida*, pp. 26–9, 34–5, n. 10, 38–9; MacMaster, *Burning*, p. 100.
74 Haudiquet, 'L'Incendie', pp. 189–90; Khatib, *1er juillet*, pp. 72–8; Larribère Hadj Ali, *Itinéraire*, p. 86; Gallissot (ed.), *Algérie*, pp. 44, 193–4.
75 *Journal officiel de l'Algérie: Lois et décrets* (23 September 1955), p. 1883 (27 September 1955), p. 1926; « On ne dissout pas le Parti Communiste Algérien. Rien ni personne ne pourra l'empêcher de poursuivre sa tâche patriote de libération », Moine, *Ma guerre*, pp. 199–200; ANOM FM 81F/785; ANOM 1K 580/1, 'Dissolution'; TNA: PRO FO 371/113796 , 'Collusion entre nationalistes et communistes algériens', 6 September 1955; *Déclaration du bureau politique du Parti communiste français après la dissolution du Parti communiste algérien* (Paris: 13 September 1955); 'Against the ban on the Algerian Communist Party', *African Communist*, 2:3 (April–June 1963), 27–39, p. 28; Sivan, *Communisme*, pp. 231, 233; Alleg, *Mémoire*, pp. 184–5, 188–90, 195–6; Dore-Audibert, *Françaises*, p. 34; MacMaster, *Burning*, p. 72; Courrière, *Léopards*, p. 293; Heggoy, *Insurgency*, p. 250.
76 ANOM 1K 580/1, J. Dupeyron, L'Officier de police, Blida, to Commissaire divisionnaire, Algiers, 12 April 1956; cf. Einaudi, *Algérien*, p. 16. PCF 261J 7/, box 1, « Organisateur du maquis rouge de Béni-Boudouane, Abdelkader Babou membre du bureau politique du P.C.A. a été capturé dans les rangs rebelles », *L'Echo d'Alger* (18 February 1958); Gallissot (ed.), *Algérie*, p. 77.
77 Dore-Audibert, *Françaises*, p. 172; Rebah, *Chemins*, pp. 117–33, 163–6; Donnat, *Afin que*, pp. 329, 335; Gallissot (ed.), *Algérie*, pp. 131–5; Nagy, 'Les « événements »', p. 6.
78 Revel, *Instituteur*, pp. 405–6; Sportisse, *Camp*, p. 199; interviews with William Sportisse; Douzon, 'Occasions', p. 479; Le Foll-Luciani, 'Un microcosme de l'Algérie nouvelle?', pp. 248–50, dates the launch of this first group to summer 1955.
79 EGA was the Electricité et gaz d'Algérie. Interviews with Guerroudj; Guerroudj, *Douars*, pp. 35–6; Khatib, *1er juillet*, pp. 76–7; Dore-Audibert, *Françaises*, pp. 148–9; Gallissot (ed.), *Algérie*, pp. 568–70. Einaudi, *Pour l'exemple*, pp. 63–7, 158.
80 « d'exercer des fonction syndicales », ANOM FM 81F/759, Dupeyron, to Commissaire divisionnaire, 12, 18 April 1956.
81 Donnat, *Afin que*, pp. 303, 306, 329–30; Gallissot (ed.), *Algérie*, pp. 113–14, 251–5, 304–5; « Organisateur du maquis rouge », *L'Echo d'Alger* (18 February 1958).
82 *Liberté* (3 January 1952, 16 September 1954); Yaël Simpson Fletcher, 'The Politics of Solidarity: Radical French and Algerian Journalists and the 1954 Orléansville Earthquake', in Patricia M. E. Lorcin (ed.), *Algeria and France, 1800–2000: Identity, Memory, Nostalgia* (Syrcuse: Syracuse University, 2006), pp. 84–98; Gallissot (ed.), *Algérie*, pp. 158, 384, 460; Haudiquet, 'L'Incendie', pp. 112–13; Larribère Hadj Ali, *Itinéraire*, pp. 88–9; interviews with William Sportisse.
83 Gallissot (ed.), *Algérie*, pp. 541–3; Rebah, *Chemins*, p. 44; Einaudi, *Pour l'exemple*,

pp. 71–2. « Mustapha Saadoun n'est plus », *El Watan.com* (28 January 2009), http://goo.gl/6bIMft (accessed 22 December 2012).

84 « Un aspirant de réserve (chef de cellule communiste) a libéré un camion d'armes aux rebelles », *Aurore* (6 April 1956); Sivan, *Communisme*, pp. 234, 236–8, 244; Guerroudj, *Douars*, p. 36; interviews with William Sportisse; Sivan, *Communisme*, p. 244; Haudiquet, 'L'Incendie', pp. 126–7.

85 ANOM 1K 580/1, Combattants de la libération, *Communiqué* [n.d.], « Je ne suis pas musulman, mais je suis Algérien, d'origine européen. Je considère l'Algérie comme ma patrie », « Henri MAILLOT explique son geste » (April 1956); PCF 261 J7 /, box 1, file 5, « La presse publie une lettre de l'aspirant Henri Maillot » [May 1956]; Courrière, *Léopards*, pp. 294–5; Heggoy, *Insurgency*, p. 250; Alleg, *Mémoire*, pp. 196–7; interviews with Lledo; interview, Alleg, 11 June 2010.

86 Donnat, *Afin que*, p. 335.

87 Parti communiste algérien à la direction du Front de libération nationale, 12 July 1956; Alleg, *Mémoire*, pp. 197–9; Khatib, *1er juillet*, p. 79; interview with Alleg, 11 June 2010; interviews with Guerroudj; discussion with Ouadi.

88 ANOM 1K 580/1, L. Bernadie, l'Officier de police, Miliana, 9 April, 5 May 1956; *Notes de renseignements*, Orléansville, 9, 21 April 1956; J. Dupeyron, l'Officier de Police, Blida à Commissaire divisionnaire, police, Algiers, 10 April 1956; J. M. Gonzalez, Commissaire divisionnaire, chef de la police, Algiers, 11, 12 April 1956; Gallissot (ed.), *Algérie*, pp. 488–9.

89 Khatib, *1er juillet*, pp. 80–6; « Maillot, l'aspirant félon aurait été abattu à 40 km. D'Orléansville », *France-Soir* (7 June 1956); « Henri Maillot et Maurice Laban, héros "oubliés" », El Watan.com (18 June 2007), http://goo.gl/pChru1 (accessed 17 February 2012); 'Au fronton de l'histoire: le camion d'armes d'Henri Maillot', El Watan.com (1 April 2011), http://goo.gl/NDHgbE (accessed 18 February 2012).

90 Combattants de la libération, *Communiqué*, 1 July 1956, in Harbi and Meynier (eds), *FLN*, p. 230; Parti communiste algérien à la direction du Front de libération nationale, 12 July 1956; Haudiquet, 'L'Incendie', pp. 126–9; Khatib, *1er juillet*, p. 103; Larribère Hadj Ali, *Itinéraire*, pp. 87–8; Heggoy, *Insurgency*, pp. 250–1; Alleg, *Mémoire*, pp. 199–200; Djabi, *Kaïdi Lakhdar*, pp. 223–7; interviews with Hadjerès and William Sportisse; cf. Courrière, *Léopards*, pp. 294–9.

91 Sivan, *Communisme*, pp. 238–40, estimates 200. This may be an underestimation. His estimates are largely based on arrests, which captured many activists, but not all. Moreover, he claims the Oranie network comprised forty communists, but events discussed in Chapter 8 indicate that it was much larger, as was likewise the case for the Blida network.

92 Guerroudj, *Douars*, pp. 38–41.

93 Le Foll-Luciani, 'Un microcosme de l'Algérie nouvelle?', p. 250; Parti communiste algérien à la Direction du Front de libération nationale, 16 August 1956, in Alleg (ed.), *Guerre*, vol. 3, pp. 534–5; Alleg, *Mémoire*, pp. 199–200. The PCA's 12 July and 16 August 1956 letters to the FLN were published in *Pour une nation algérienne libre, souveraine et heureuse* (March 1957). The claims of Courrière, *Léopards*, p. 299, and Ruedy, *Modern Algeria*, p. 165, that the PCA voted itself out of existence on 1 July 1956 are inaccurate.

94 Feraoun, *Journal*, pp. 123, 127.

95 Courrière, *Léopards*, pp. 371–9; Horne, *Savage War*, pp. 143–6; Ruedy, *Modern Algeria*, p. 156; Stora, *Gangrène*, p. 147; Einaudi, *Algérien*, pp. 158–9.

96 « comme si l'indépendance nationale de l'Algérie devait suivre forcément le chemin des révolutions manquées », *Plate-forme de la Soummam pour assurer le triomphe de la Révolution algérienne*, in *Les Textes fondamentaux de la Révolution* (Editions ANEP, n.d.), pp. 11–68, pp. 23–4, 26, 36–7, 40, 42–3; ANOM FM 81/F759, SDECE [Service de documentation extérieure et de contre-espionnage], *Le F.L.N. et l'affaire de l'aspirant Maillot*, 24 September 1956; Khatib, *1er juillet*, p. 105; Marie Elbe, 'Le rôle du P.C.A. dans la rébellion', *Echo d'Alger* (26 October 1957), assesses the FLN–PCA relationship; see her series in *Echo d'Alger* (31 October, 1, 5, 8 November 1957).

97 « la renaissance d'un Etat algérien sous la forme d'une république démocratique

et sociale et non la restauration d'une monarchie ou d'une théocratie révolues », *Plate-forme de la Soummam* p. 19 (emphasis in original); Ruedy, *Modern Algeria*, pp. 166–7; Heggoy, *Insurgency*, pp. 162–3, 168–9; Crenshaw, 'Effectiveness', pp. 486–7; Wall, 'French Communists', p. 527; Fanon, *Dying*, pp. 90–2; interview with Ouzegane.

98 'Procès-verbal du congrès de la Soummam' and 'Plate-forme de la Soummam', in Harbi and Meynier (eds), *FLN*, pp. 241–9, 243; Le Congrès de la Soumman: Procès verbale de la réunion du 20 août 1956', 'Conseil national de la Révolution algérienne du Congrès de la Soummam (20 août 1956)', Ramdane Abane, 'Un nouveau chapitre de la Révolution algérienne s'ouvre', *El Moudjahid*, 3 (September 1956), all in Alleg (ed.), *Guerre*, vol. 3, pp. 535–45; Alleg, *Mémoire*, p. 197; Horne, *Savage War*, pp. 133–5, 184–5; Heggoy, *Insurgency*, p. 164; Ruedy, *Modern Algeria*, pp. 164, 166; Stora, *Gangrène*, p. 148.

99 Sivan, *Communisme*, p. 241; Parti communiste algérien à la direction du Front de libération nationale, 16 August 1956.

100 *Réalités algériennes et Marxisme*, 1 (November–December 1956), extracted as 'Algeria: Features of the Armed Struggle', in William J. Pomeroy (ed.), *Guerrilla Warfare and Marxism* (London: Lawrence and Wishart, 1969), 249–54, pp. 252–3. See Sivan's discussion of six key points in which the PCA's stance differed from that of the PCF, *Communisme*, pp. 243–58; Courrière, *Léopards*, pp. 298–9; Wall, 'French Communists', p. 528; First, interview with Alleg; Alleg, *Mémoire*, pp. 197–200; Douzon, 'Occasions', pp. 478–9; Moine, *Ma guerre*, pp. 199–200.

101 PCA, Réponse à MM. Guy Mollet and Robert Lacoste, 31 October 1956, in Harbi and Meynier (eds), *FLN*, pp. 231–2.

102 Ruedy, *Modern Algeria*, pp. 157, 159; Horne, *Savage War*, pp. 146, 159–61; Feraoun, *Journal*, p. 143. On Lacheraf, Fanny Colonna, 'The Nation's "Unknowing Other": Three intellectuals and the culture(s) of being Algerian, or the impossibility of subaltern studies in Algeria', *Journal of North African Studies*, 8:1 (2003), 155–70.

103 Feraoun, *Journal*, pp. 85, 152.

104 Ruedy, *Modern Algeria*, pp. 157, 159, 163; Hadj Ali, 'Lessons', pp. 252, 257; Horne, *Savage War*, pp. 146, 159–61; Heggoy, *Insurgency*, pp. 168–71, 232–3; Crenshaw, 'Effectiveness', p. 488; Macey, *Fanon*, p. 292; [First], 'Armed struggle', pp. 5–6; Douzon, 'Occasions', p. 545.

105 Haudiquet, 'L'Incendie', pp. 128–9; Jacques de Bonis, 'A la recherche du dernier quart d'heure', in Henri Alleg (ed.) *La Guerre d'Algérie* vol. 1 (Paris: Editions Messidor, 1981), 299–591, p. 481.

106 Bachir Hadj Ali au Gouvernement provisoire de la République algérienne, 15 July 1959, in *Lettres adressées au G.P.R.A. au cours de la guerre pour l'indépendance au nom du comité central du Parti communiste algérien* (Algiers: Al Houriya, 1962), pp. 21–4, http://goo.gl/2EcyPX (accessed 24 June 2011); Alleg, *Memoire*, pp. 199–200; interview with Alleg, 11 June 2010; Guerroudj, *Douars*, p. 39; Khatib, *1er juillet*, pp. 103–4; Rebah, *Chemins*, pp. 57–8. Einaudi, *Algérien*, pp. 158–9, states that anti-communism in the maquis worsened after the deaths of Ben Boulaïd and his secretary Abdelhamid Lamrani – Laïd Lamrani's younger brother – in March 1956.

CHAPTER EIGHT

'Our people will overcome':
to the cities and the prisons

Armed struggle moved to the cities. Public political space closed down. While the Soummam congress promoted the primacy of the political struggle over the military, the war had its own logic. Posing the political and military in opposition accentuated the tension between the FLN's political and military wings. However, the FLN's ruthless drive for unity masked its internal power struggle, and waves of young people joined. The FLN's ascendancy seemingly left little political space for the PCA, which was seriously weakened by mass arrests – although the arrests and trials kept its name in the press. Nonetheless, communists fought in the ALN, organised in prisons and continued their underground propaganda.

What some call the Battle of Algiers and others the Great Repression was heralded by a crescendo of tit-for-tat attacks by French and Algerian forces in the late summer and early autumn of 1956.[1] Abane Ramdane commanded the Algiers zone, where bombings in crowded civilian areas became a daily occurrence. He was assisted by Larbi Ben M'Hidi and Saâdi Yacef. The *casbah*, home of some 100,000 people, was their centre of operations. Yacef worked closely with Ali Ammar – Ali la Pointe – who had joined the FLN in 1955 in Serkadji prison. Yacef created a matrix of secret passages, hiding places and bomb factories in the *casbah*, organising some 1,400 operatives, including sixty-five women.

Despite their tiny numbers, the *fida'iyyat* were celebrated because of their spectacular actions. From known and trusted nationalist families, they were generally in their twenties and part of the first generation of Algerian women who attended French or French–Arabic schools. They seldom wore a veil and continually confronted their male comrades' belief that war was not women's affair. Women became symbols of the power struggle between the French state and the FLN. For the French, the veil symbolised female oppression; for the FLN, women's family role symbolised Algerian tradition and culture. As part of its integration policy, France promoted equality for Muslim women and made several high-level female appointments. The FLN responded that women's equality depended on national liberation. The French initiatives never rivalled the popular impact of the *fida'iyyat*.[2]

Women arriving at the Serkadji prison gate to visit sons, husbands or brothers were often the first to learn of executions, signalled by bloody water running under the gate. As veiled women gathered and exchanged news, the prison perimeters became public, gendered political space. Baya Allaouchiche had been organising women's demonstrations outside the prison gates since 1955; female solidarity gradually transformed into political demands for better prison conditions and visiting rights. Impressed by her work, the FLN approached her, but she was arrested and, as a French citizen, deported to Marseille. There the PCF criticized her support for armed struggle, so she contacted the FLN.[3]

The execution of two FLN activists at Serkadji prison on 19 June 1956 had precipitated a spiral of violence: the FLN retaliated by killing two French soldiers, while European terrorists bombed a presumed FLN safe house in the *casbah*, killing close to one hundred. On 30 September three well-educated young women from bourgeois families – Zohra Drif, Djamila Bouhired and Samia Lakhdari – planted bombs in European locales. The communist bomb-maker Daniel Timsit, who feared an Algerian–European bloodbath, was arrested on 8 October.[4] European outrage followed. When FLN sympathiser Dr Pierre Chaulet expressed his repugnance to Abane Ramdane, his friend did not mince words: 'I see hardly any difference between the girl who places a bomb in the Milk-Bar and the French aviator who bombards a *mechta* [village neighbourhood] nor who drops napalm on a *zone interdite*.'[5]

International tension peaked in that year: Soviet tanks entered Hungary on 24 October, an action supported by the PCF, but which intensified the French Socialist Party's anti-communism; Israel, backed by France and Britain, invaded Egypt on 29 October, precipitating the Suez Crisis. But Algerians faced more immediate concerns as indiscriminate terrorism multiplied exponentially, with some 120 attacks in December alone. Ali la Pointe was chosen to assassinate First World War veteran Amédée Froger, Boufarik's mayor and president of the Federation of Mayors of Algeria. Froger was killed on 28 December; European reprisals followed.[6]

'Algiers radio modestly reports that serious confrontations have taken place at Government Square: five terrorists killed, twenty cars burned out, and several stores vandalised', wrote Feraoun the next day. Listening, he looked out at 'the Arab district filled with Muslims who, being more or less clothed in rags, were more or less considered suspect, and who, being more or less dark-skinned, were viewed as more or less unpleasant'. Relations between Europeans and Algerians were ever-more hostile. Feraoun watched Muslims fleeing from 'well-behaved, correct, well-dressed young people who were nonetheless indignant at the ... odious crimes of a fanatic mob ... so indignant that instead of seeing brown they saw red. It was as if in their eyes each Arab had been transformed into a gigantic red fez, and it was necessary to tear up all these red hats in a rage.'[7]

France fought back ferociously. 'Few armies in the world possess a generation of officers who have fought so much,' observed Le Monde. General Raoul Salan arrived on 14 December. He was assisted by General Jacques Massu, who had led the 10th Para Division in Suez. Massu won the first major confrontation – the breaking of a widely supported general strike called by the FLN for the week of 28 January 1957, when the UN General Assembly was scheduled to debate the Algerian question. Ramdane had hoped the strike would compel the French to negotiate. Not so. Force was countered by more bombings. Pitched battles went on in parts of the city, mass rapes in other regions.[8]

Although Resident Minister Lacoste could implement reforms to win over moderate Algerians, the French army became Algiers' *de facto* government. The line between civilian and military rule was increasingly blurred. By one account, 'the army executes those its informers denounce, even when the magistrate has released them'. The *parachutistes* used horrific torture; Fanon had seen the effects of torture – psychosis and depersonalisation – on both victims and perpetrators in his practice at the Blida-Joinville hospital, known for its sympathy towards guerrillas. Fanon's involvement with the FLN had deepened. Chaulet arranged a meeting between Fanon, Ramdane and Ben Khedda, which took place on 29–30 December. By then Fanon had resigned from the hospital. Expelled from Algeria as of 1 February 1957, he hurriedly left the country. In late February Ramdane and other CCE members fled the capital and the country, leaving a furious Yacef in charge of Algiers. The CCE's flight into exile was a portent of things to come. Between February and October 1957 French forces destroyed the FLN's internal organisation, cutting the internal–external link.[9]

Nor did the French state spare the banned PCA, whose political and paramilitary networks in Oranie were discovered and destroyed in September 1956. Gabrielle Gimenez was in charge of the political network, and Boualem Khalfa, who after *Alger républicain* had become the editor of *Liberté*, developed the Oranie *maquis*. There were sixty arrests in Oranie, twenty of which were in Oran. These included Drs Martini and Massebouef, Maître Rezkallah, Mohammed Marouf and

Aline Larribère of the activist family. The operation led to the dismantling of the PCA's Algérois–Oranie network – again highlighting the PCA's activism. The FLN's Oran networks were dismantled next: Zoulikha Bekaddour was arrested on 11 November; Benalla Hadj, responsible for Oran, soon after.[10]

In Algiers, Abdelkader Guerroudj's ALN cell continued its sabotage and assassinations, but their room to manoeuvre was constantly shrinking. On the one side, the Main rouge (Red Hand), a shadowy terrorist organisation set up by the French security forces to cut the ALN's supply lines and assassinate its activists, was a continuous threat.[11] On the other, it became almost impossible to avoid arrest. Georges Acampora was arrested and sentenced to death with Mourad Akkache for an attack on a police station at La Redoute; an Arabic-speaker, Acampora served as translator in Serkadji. Fernand Iveton was arrested in late October after an abortive attempt to bomb the EGA plant and deprive Algiers of electricity – meticulously planned to avoid deaths. Fiori-Steiner was arrested in the same month, and Yahia Briki in December 1956.[12] In November Lacoste had ordered all administrative departments to cut ties with the Communist-aligned CGT and UGSA. Those not detained went underground. Month after month the communists were in the press, to the FLN's anger. France's labels for guerrillas had shifted, it claimed, from 'rebels' and 'outlaws' to communists. How could a country where one-quarter of the electorate voted communist and whose National Assembly had many communist delegates be worried about a communist threat in Algeria, it asked.[13]

The French were winning the battle for Algiers. The city became one huge armed camp. The army listed each and every resident in a card-index system. With an informer in almost every street, it was virtually impossible to move without the army's knowledge. 'Guarded, motorised, militarised Algiers', thought Feraoun when he visited in February 1957. At the end of March – the first month without a bomb – it appeared that the French had won.[14] Indeed, the FLN was consumed by murders and purges. On 29 May, ALN soldiers massacred pro-MNA peasants at Melouza in southern Kabylia. ALN leaflets in the region claimed responsibility; the FLN in Tunis denied responsibility. Melouza became Fanon's first test of organisational loyalty. Practising psychiatry in Tunis, he became the FLN's spokesperson, writing for its organ, *El Moudjahid*. Despite knowing the ALN's role at Melouza, he blamed the French army to protect the FLN's image, his account accepted by French and Algerian communists.[15]

By then, most schools in Kabylia had been burned down. 'From now on', despaired Feraoun, 'what name can those who promised accountability evoke in order to be able to speak? Who will be able to believe them?' By mid-1957 the FLN had seemingly neutralised the MNA as a political threat in Algeria, if not France.[16] Yacef struck again in June – 'three bombs exploded at rush hour in three of the main thoroughfares in Algiers: ten dead, a hundred wounded ... French and Arab.' That same week there was 'a skirmish in Kabylia near Michelet, near Fort-National: one hundred and twenty-five rebels dead. So this is war.' To escape the fighting, in July Feraoun transferred to a school in the Algiers suburb of Clos Salembier, 'a very populated Muslim neighbourhood where poverty exist[ed] alongside opulence; corrugated shacks next to beautiful bourgeois villas'.[17]

The PCA carried on despite its losses. Larbi Bouhali had secretly left the country in September 1956 to represent the PCA at the eighth congress of the Chinese Communist Party, before travelling to Albania and France. Bouhali planned to establish an external PCA office to promote the party's perspective and obtain external support for the internal struggle. Until then PCA activists in Europe had worked through the PCF, but they felt that the PCF wanted to sideline the PCA. The FLN had already launched the influential Fédération de France du FLN (FFFLN), and Bouhali negotiated with the PCF to launch the Fédération de France du PCA (FFPCA).[18] In December 1956 Bouhali settled in Prague to direct the PCA's international work. He was joined, amongst others, by Gilberte Chemouilli, who had been expelled from Algeria. In January 1957 the Party launched *Réalités algériennes et Marxisme*. A theoretical journal, the first issue was produced in Algeria, but the seizure of their press, arrests of numerous comrades and difficulties of underground work made production inside the country impossible. The Prague office took over the journal, which was published in East Germany and sent clandestinely to Algeria. The second issue, originally planned for March 1957, appeared in July 1958; production continued through the war. It was a miniature journal with minute print written on very fine paper to fit into a small envelope and thus escape the authorities' prying eyes. The PCA's external work was subsidised by the PCF and the communist parties of Czechoslovakia, East Germany and the Soviet Union.[19]

In the prisons

Massu's efforts to break the ALN led to further arrests. The prisoners were first taken to torture centres, such as El Biar in Algiers and Ameziane farm near Constantine. Beatings, rape, electrical shock, waterboarding and psychological torture were routine. After this, they were incarcerated to await their military tribunal. Serkadji prisoners were relatively privileged in that the proximity of foreign journalists and consulates ensured some degree of international scrutiny. Yet there, as elsewhere, they were surrounded by death, bathed in the guillotine's blood.[20]

Abdelkader Guerroudj was arrested on 4 January 1957, tortured and sent to Serkadji on 9 January; his wife Jacqueline was sent to Serkadji's women's quarter. Hélène Timsit and Emma Nahon, liaison agents who transported bombs, were arrested and sent to France. The French state saw Iveton as a symbol of European and communist support for armed struggle. Although Iveton had deliberately timed the bomb to avoid human casualties, and the bomb had not exploded, he was nonetheless horrifically tortured and, along with the FLN's Mohamed Lakhnèche and Mohamed Ouennouri, guillotined at Serkadji on 11 February 1957 – the only European and communist to be executed.[21] 'The life of one man, mine, counts little. What counts is Algeria, its future', he stated before his execution. To Camus, Iveton's execution reflected political expediency: the French government sought to assuage French fears of terrorism, while showing Arabs that the guillotine was equally for Europeans.[22]

Late March saw the 'doctors' trial' of the three Timsit brothers – all doctors – the engineer Georgio Arbib, Fiorio-Steiner and others. Then came the dismantling of the *Voix du soldat* and Blida networks. Elyette Loup was arrested on 2 April, tortured and sent to Serkadji, then André Moine and Ahmed Akkache. Later, when Moine found his wife Blanche she had been so badly tortured that she was 'aged, unrecognisable'. On 23 March Hadjerès was sentenced *in absentia* to twenty years of forced labour for his work in a bomb factory.[23]

Serkadji's numbers swelled. Built to hold 700, by 1957 it had 2,400, its walls covered with 'Vive le F.L.N.' Prisoners were split into divisions and kept in cells of up to three people, while those in solitary confinement went mad, their shrieks piercing the air. The colonial hierarchy was structured into prison life, with the worst jobs reserved for Muslims. Prisoners were politically segregated, activists and intellectuals isolated from other prisoners, communists, from non-communists. The communists formed a solid bloc and in March–April barricaded themselves in their hall to prevent prison authorities from removing PCA secretary Ahmed Akkache so that he could be tortured again. Eventually the guards won and removed Akkache, but news of the event leaked outside and Akkache was returned without being tortured. The prison authorities learned quickly: from then on communists were dispersed into small groups or isolated. Prisoners were frequently moved and their cells searched, making organisation extremely difficult, although the infirmary provided a space for exchanging news. Somehow they set up a clandestine news network called *Nidham*.[24]

But they could not suppress the ever-present thoughts of the guillotine.

'Blessed are the mornings without the guillotine, when the men's prayer wakes us', wrote one woman prisoner. In early 1957 Sekardji's women's quarter had very few political prisoners. Jacqueline Guerroudj, Baya Hocine and Djoher Akrour joined three nurses from the *maquis*. As their numbers grew, so their quarter became noisy and cramped. Yet they humanised their surroundings, even managing to study on two tables in their courtyard. Some taught Arabic literature, another gave French dictation. The Algerian women learned to read and write Arabic and French; the Europeans learned spoken Arabic. Try as they might, however, they could not block out the endless killing: 'The thought of death never leaves us', the woman confided to her journal. After each execution there followed a hunger strike. 'The days when blood does not run, it's like a victory of life over death.'[25]

Zoulikha Bekaddour had been transferred to the Maison Carrée prison, where the fifteen Algerian and European women political prisoners were isolated from other women prisoners. Bekaddour had been the only Algerian girl at her primary and secondary girls' schools, and although she spoke perfect French and looked European, none of the other girls had ever spoken to her. Her prison experience was the first time she had any positive contact with European women. Communist women nursed her and fed her with a spoon after she had been tortured.[26]

Alleg was arrested on 12 June 1957 at the home of comrade Maurice Audin, a University of Algiers mathematics lecturer arrested the previous day. They saw each other at the El Biar torture centre. Audin, badly tortured, could only say, *'C'est dur, Henri'* – 'It's hard' – before vanishing without a trace.[27] Alleg spent a month at El Biar, subjected to beatings, electric shocks, waterboarding, biochemical torture with 'truth serum', psychological torture – the sounds of others shrieking – revealing nothing. The experience cemented his identity as an Algerian and a communist.

From El Biar Alleg was sent to Lodi camp, one hundred kilometres southwest of Algiers, where Europeans and French who favoured Algerian independence were interned without charge, trial, sentence or any knowledge of when they would be released. A former holiday camp hastily converted with barbed wire, Lodi had three dormitories housing 50 prisoners each. The first prisoners had arrived in autumn 1955, to be greeted with excruciating daily monotony. Iveton's lawyer, Albert Smadja, had been arrested on 13 February 1957 – two days after his client's execution – and sent to Lodi. Needing to break the silence surrounding torture, at Lodi Alleg wrote a five-page letter detailing his experience at El Biar. Transferred to Serkadji in August, Alleg passed through Algiers, 'a tortured city, under tight surveillance, controlled and searched in every street, every train, every "suspect" neighbourhood strangled by barbed wire', its streets patrolled by armed guards ready to shoot.[28]

The PCF's lawyer Léo Matarasso urged Alleg to continue writing about his torture. His cell mates agreed. The world must know that torture was typical of the French military in Algeria – not exceptional. But how to avoid the guards' prying eyes and cell searches? For hours at a time Alleg kneeled in the only corner not visible to the guards, composing in phonetic French with Cyrillic characters in tiny writing, hiding the pages in his clothes. In the evenings the prisoners had their 'Radio Serkadji' when they could speak to each other after the guards had gone home. Christian Buono was one of Alleg's cell mates, condemned to five years. A teacher introduced to socialism by Audin, Buono had joined the PCA in November 1955. Alleg, Buono and their cell mates discussed the work as it proceeded. 'It's too dry', one of them said, to be told, 'It's not a work of art, but a cry of alarm.' The style should be simple to make a serious impact. Why not mention an event if it's true? It was too incredible for belief, came the response. Even jokes. Someone mentioned that it took Flaubert fifteen years to edit one page. Alleg's response: Flaubert was lucky. They agreed on the title – *La Question* – and the manuscript was smuggled out and sent to Alleg's wife Gilberte Serfaty Salem, who had been exiled and was in Paris.[29]

Conditions at Lambèse, Algeria's largest penitentiary, were unimaginably worse. Alleg's comrade Abdelhamid Benzine, captured in battle in September 1956 and sentenced to twenty years at an Oran military tribunal, arrived at Lambèse in September 1957, chained to his fellow prisoners, their wrists bloody from being wrenched, starving and sleepless after three days of travel. The Lambèse regime was premised on total dehumanisation. Upon arrival, prisoners were severely beaten, given torn clothing and numbers and forbidden to use their names. They were 'conditioned to be only numbers', Benzine recalled, and even those were expressed in the coloniser's language. During showers, they were beaten and forced to stand under scalding water. Some were severely burned; a well-connected French conscientious objector was evacuated to France. Sometimes they were kept in large halls – 250 men with four holes in the floor that served as toilets – so tightly packed that they had to creep over each other to use the toilet; tricky, since diarrhoea was common. One-person cells generally housed two or three. Prisoners slept on straw mattresses, and when three shared a cell, one of the mattresses invariably ended up on the hole used as a toilet. Many prisoners had fleas. In glacial winters they were made to stand in the snow, and in searing summers to stand in the sun and often forced to harvest esparto grass until they dropped and died. Hunger was their constant companion. The food was horrific: one man consumed a good portion of his soup to discover pieces of excrement in it. Physical maltreatment led to mental disorders. One prisoner told Benzine that he understood how the Nazis had compelled death-camp inmates to go to their death: they were simply too depleted to resist. In what was called the devil's infirmary the European doctor – a Batna landowner – refused to treat those with broken bones and pus-filled infections, many of whom later died from lack of care. No need for the guillotine here.[30]

More arrests were made in August 1957. A mass trial of communists took place in Oran, the 'ringleaders' given severe sentences. The British consul estimated PCA membership at about 1,000, mainly in Oran and mainly European. Before the armed struggle many of the PCA's rank-and-file members had been workers, the consul reported, but 'the split ... along racial lines which ha[d] been precipitated by the present events ha[d] reduced the majority of these European workers to silence'. He noted: 'Those who now remain in the party are for the most part intellectuals and members of the liberal professions, such as doctors and schoolteachers.' The consul saw only the PCA's public face. The party still had key members in the electricity and gas industries, as well as post offices, docks and railways, some of whom clandestinely disseminated propaganda, but most Algerian communists still at large were underground or in the *maquis*.[31] Nour Eddine Rebah, for one, had transferred into the ALN following the FLN–PCA accord. He and Hamid Allouache were sent to the mountainous area around Palestro–Fondouk–Larbaâ–Tablat. They found themselves ostracised for their Marxist views, however, and Rebah was sent from one area to another, before dying in battle in September 1957.[32]

The waves of arrests left Hadj Ali and Hadjerès as the two remaining political bureau members directing the PCA's activities inside the country – deep underground. The party published occasional flyers and newspapers. Feraoun had seen a leaflet in August – 'the first in more than a year. Bravo!' He found the communists 'absolutely sincere': they 'act clandestinely, like fish in water, whereas the average mortal would suffocate'. Hadj Ali and Hadjerès wrote for *Liberté* and *Réalités algériennes et Marxisme*, while Lucette Larribère was a liaison, handling correspondence with Bouhali and other exiles. *Liberté* was produced on stencils smuggled in baskets of vegetables to be mimeographed with a time-consuming roneo machine. In Constantine Sportisse's underground group had organised a rudimentary but effective underground press and published *Le Patriote* and *Etudes et documents*. The three North African communist parties met in November – Bouhali and Dalibey represented the PCA – to coordinate their actions for Algeria's liberation.

If the PCA relied on its French counterpart for financial help, the FLN was 'looking decisively toward Moscow', thought Feraoun.[33] But while the external FLN courted Moscow, its internal organisation was fighting for its life. The *parachutistes* finally captured Yacef on 24 September. The next month, on 8 October 1957, Ali la Pointe and comrades died in a massive explosion in the *casbah*, marking the end of the battle for Algiers. It was a major defeat for the FLN, signalling the failure of its political strategy and costing some 7,000 lives, through direct confrontation, summary executions without trial and death from torture. The Algiers underground was effectively smashed. Urban terrorism had not sparked a general uprising; the guerrilla army could not defeat the French army.[34]

More mass arrests followed. Louisette Ighilahriz was arrested and systematically raped and tortured for two and one-half months from 4 October to 15 December 1957. She learned that rape was *'une arme de guerre'* (a weapon of war). Rape of women, rape of men, gang rape, rape with bottles and other objects were routine. Transferred to Serkadji, she found her mother, grandmother and sister Malika. Such was the stigma of rape that Louisette felt that her mother would rather she had died in prison than be raped. She must never speak of it, her mother told her. Her father, she learned, was also in prison. Another sister was in a regroupment centre, and two uncles imprisoned at Affrènes. Her activist family had all been scooped up.[35]

Women were pulled into the war. The guerrillas relied on village women for food and shelter, and in the absence of men, 'they forced them to take on all tasks and responsibilities'. While the French state demanded equal rights for women, the French army infiltrated women's groups; growing numbers of women were arrested. 'The fellagha slit the throats of women who betray them; the army shoots, arrests, or tortures women who work for the organisation.' Both sides raped them – rape was an unspeakable trauma; silence, the only way to cope. With men underground, imprisoned or in the *maquis*, Algerian women in cities became more publicly defiant. 'Perhaps a new world is being constructed out of ruins', speculated Feraoun, 'a world where women will be wearing the pants, literally and figuratively, a world where what remains of the old traditions that adhere to the inviolability of women, both literally and figuratively, will be viewed as a nuisance and swept away.'[36]

Students and intellectuals, men and women, boys and girls, fled the city to become guerrillas. Some were 'turned' by the French who, to foment mistrust, made much of this to the *wilaya* leaders. Convinced that his troops had been infiltrated, the *wilaya* III leader Amirouche Aït Hamouda – known as Colonel Amirouche – murdered the intellectuals. Roughly two thousand Algerians – many the school and university students who had joined after the May 1956 student strike – were killed by their *wilaya* leaders.[37] Although the ALN used village women to cook and clean, in late 1957 and early 1958 *wilaya* leaders began removing female guerrillas from the *maquis* and sending them to Tunisia and Morocco, where they were kept in restrictive conditions. The reasons are unclear: some sources suggest tensions concerning the arrival of educated, urbanised young women into the *maquis*; others, that the war's mounting ferocity meant the loss of stable guerrilla bases to accommodate women.[38]

The communist Raymonde Peschard, banned from Constantine in 1955, had gone underground after Iveton's arrest, wrongly suspected of being his accomplice and of being responsible for the Milk Bar bombing. She joined the *maquis* as a nurse and social worker. Part of a unit ordered to Tunisia by Amirouche, she was captured and executed by the French on 26 November 1957, the only European woman to die in this manner. For months rumours of her whereabouts and false reports of her capture in March 1957 had dominated the press. Now it ran articles about contestations over her corpse. Close by, three communist women – Dr Néfissa Hamouda, who founded the Red Crescent in Algeria, nurse Louise Attouche and Danielle Minne, daughter of Jacqueline Guerroudj – were captured alive. For the French state their case demonstrated further nationalist–communist collusion and growing female participation in the *maquis*.[39]

Serkadji's guillotine kept chopping. 'A lone, sharp cry pierces the silence ... the call of a man who is going to die to his brothers ... enveloped in the warmth of a hundred other voices of those condemned to die ... The entire prison joins them. Suddenly, replying to our cries, the savage, terrible song of the women explodes ... a hommage to the martyr.' In such a manner the prisoners humanised their inhuman conditions.[40]

The military tribunal of Abdelkader Guerroudj's ALN cell – FLN chemistry student Abderramane Taleb, Jacqueline Guerroudj, Briki, Farrugia, Salort, Georges Marcelli and Jocelyne Chatain – took place on 4–7 December 1957. Denying the right of French tribunals to judge Algerian combatants, the prisoners used the military court as political space. Denouncing colonialism, Abdelkader Guerroudj spoke passionately about France's revolutionary tradition and stated that he joined the armed struggle because non-violence had proved futile. Jacqueline Guerroudj, a Jew, had been briefly interned in a concentration camp during the Nazi occupation of France. From that experience she learned that sometimes one had to take a stand.[41] Salort explained that coming from a poor family, he quickly realised the just aspirations of the Algerian people and made them his own. 'I am here with my brothers of struggle', he stated. Called as a witness, Yacef tried to help them. There had been so many bombs, he stated, that he could not recall which had gone to the communists. After the Milk Bar explosion, Taleb had been on the verge of suicide because of the loss of human life. But Yacef would not allow him to pull out – he was his best chemist. Taleb only agreed to help if there were no further victims. He did not deserve the death penalty, Yacef insisted.

Although the bombs had not been intended to hurt people and had not exploded, the Guerroudjes and Taleb were sentenced to death. 'For Algerians', replied Taleb, 'the guillotine will henceforth have the same significance as the cross in your churches.' Briki and Farrugia were sentenced to forced labour in perpetuity, Salort to twenty years and Marcelli to eight. Chatain was acquitted and deported.[42] Jacqueline Guerroudj joined Djamila Bouhired, Djamila Bouaza, Baya Hocine and Djoher Akrour on Serkadji's women's death row. Jacqueline Guerroudj had studied with Simone de Beauvoir, who organised an international clemency campaign. The Guerroudjes were spared, but Taleb was to be executed on 24 April 1958, one of five guillotined over two days.[43]

The external FLN and the propaganda wars

The FLN's defeat in Algiers shifted the terrain of struggle back to the rural areas. But the guerrillas were starved of food and resources. The Algiers defeat also strengthened the external FLN, which turned for help to newly independent Tunisia and Morocco, who allowed it to set up recruitment and training centres.[44] The separation of the internal and external ALN was graphically symbolised by France's Morice Line, completed in September 1957. This was a gruesome structure – a barbed wire fence, 2.5 metres high and 3 metres wide, with electrified wires in the middle that ran along the Moroccan and Tunisian frontiers from the sea to the Sahara desert. The fence was decorated with 'electrocuted animals – dogs, sheep, goats and even occasionally a pathetic little donkey'. Thousands of Algerians were killed trying to cross the border. Each side was bordered with 46 metres of anti-personnel mines and barbed wire. Armed patrols with searchlights kept watch. Algerians discovered that they could dig under it or divert the current with jumper cables and cut the electrified wire. Even so, electrical devises pinpointed their location, and they were targeted with automatic fire while mobile troops moved in. The French were obsessed with protecting the line, the FLN, with breaching it. About 10,000 ALN troops stood at the Tunisian frontier, armed with weapons from around the world while the *wilayas* were starved of people and weapons.[45]

With the CCE now in Tunis, contact with and coordination among the *wilayas* became virtually impossible. While *wilaya* leaders disparaged the CCE's failure to direct the struggle, Ramdane criticised what he called *'wilayism'* or the political autonomy of the *wilayas*. Ramdane was murdered on 26 December 1957; the FLN reported his death months later as the result of a French army encounter. That was a cover-up. When the CCE left Algiers, Ramdane went to Morocco, where he clashed with *wilaya* V's Abdelhafid Boussouf, whose right-hand man was Houari Boumediène. Boussouf organised Ramdane's murder, but by then Ramdane had alienated other FLN leaders.[46] The murder marked the ascendancy of military over political leaders, already indicated by the predominance of military leaders within the CNRA. It was also Fanon's second test of loyalty. Of all the FLN leaders, Fanon had felt closest to Ramdane who, like Fanon, envisioned an independent and multicultural Algeria. Most other FLN leaders, Fanon had discovered, thought only of independence, not about the nature of the revolution and future society. For Fanon, Ramdane's death symbolised the loss of revolutionary vision.[47]

The violence in Algeria drew the attention of journalists, human rights activists and political leaders around the world.[48] For its first two years the FLN's military and political wings had been relatively integrated. However, as the internal wing declined, the external wing responsible for diplomatic and propaganda activities became more important. The urban middle-class leaders who fled into exile captured this external apparatus, becoming more influential as the guerrilla forces weakened. With the influx of new and politically diverse members, the FLN became a loose organisation embracing multiple and conflicting interests. The separation of the internal and external wings heightened the tensions arising from these conflicting interests.[49]

As the balance of power within the FLN shifted to its external wing, the international propaganda war became ever more important. Some of this concerned organisational rivalry: the FLN tried to discredit PCA activists as *'tous français'* (all French), despite the obvious falseness of this claim. Moreover, in 1958 the PCA set up a base in East Germany, much to the resentment of the FLN members stationed there; the East Germans evidently used the PCA to pressure the FLN.[50]

More often, the propaganda war concerned torture and terror. French reservists coming home recounted tales of torture. The PCF still condemned the FLN's use of terror, but, hoping to retain some influence with the Mollet government, downplayed French use of torture. But from spring 1957 intellectuals organised anti-torture committees, challenging the PCF's dominance of the left. A staunchly pro-independence current developed around Jean-Paul Sartre and Simone de Beauvoir's *Les Temps modernes*, while a new left current campaigned against torture from a republican perspective, believing that Algerians could be assimilated into France. Resentment over conscription and the high costs of fighting made the war increasingly unpopular.[51]

Camus had been silent over the war since his unhappy experience at the Circle of Progress. In October 1957 he was awarded the Nobel Prize for literature. For the Swedish Academy, his work 'illuminated the problems of the human conscience in our times'. In December Camus went to Stockholm for the ceremony. An Algerian student asked him to explain his silence over Algeria, when he did not hesitate to speak about the Soviet invasion of Hungary. He had always supported a just and democratic Algeria, Camus replied, but his further intervention risked inflaming the situation. 'I have always condemned terror', he stated. 'I must also condemn terrorism that strikes blindly, for example in the streets of Algiers, and which might strike my mother and family. I believe in justice, but I'll defend my mother before justice.' His mother and family, 'poor and without hatred', lived in fear of being hurt or killed by random bombs. His response, a plea for embodied human rights over abstract principles, inflamed the French left, deepening the rift between Camus and Sartre and de Beauvoir that had developed since Camus' publication of *The Rebel* and his criticisms of the USSR.[52]

Camus' refusal to accept a conquered people's demand for independence notwithstanding, his rejection of the violence plaguing Algeria reflected a compassion for real people. Feraoun shared Camus' abhorrence of violence, despite having political differences with him. In eastern Algeria, Feraoun wrote of skirmishes, mass evacuations, villages razed, dozens of suspects shot each day. In Algiers, he observes: 'terrorism in the city is being reorganised: attacks are recurring in various places, and there has been a proliferation of neighborhood inspections and mass arrests. Every day the radio reports widespread fighting, violent encounters, bloody hand-to-hand fighting, "important rebel bands".' And yet, despite the French propaganda, French soldiers were beginning to recognise that Algeria was 'not France but, rather, the property of France.'[53]

Alleg's *La Question*, published in France on 12 February 1958, sold 65,000 copies in five weeks. But reprints and reviews were censored, and in late March French authorities seized the publisher's remaining copies. Sartre, Malraux, Roger Martin du Gard and François Mauriac published a protest in *L'Express*, *L'Humanité* and *Le Monde*. Through

Alleg's book the PCA had scored a significant propaganda victory. Nonetheless, when the news reached Serkadji, the prisoners were stripped and searched, their papers seized. Notebooks were banned by military authority. 'And if we wrote on the walls, would they get rid of those?', asked one prisoner. In France the revelation of systematic torture sparked an uproar. In a widely circulated underground essay Sartre drew on Alleg's book to argue that colonialism's degradation of the colonised laid the basis for systematic torture – putting further pressure on the French state to implement reforms.[54]

As part of this reform agenda, a new law – the *loi-cadre* of 5 February 1958 – ended the double electoral college and gave Algerian men and women equal rights as French citizens. This had little immediate impact. Algerians were squeezed between the French army and the ALN, whose numbers were growing. 'The maquis, now better armed and more numerous, are still enforcing the harsh punishment of hanging and cutting throats', reported Feraoun in March. 'The soldiers of pacification are hitting harder and harder, with less and less discrimination and pity ... planting a definitive hatred for the French in the hearts of the Kabyles.'[55] Algerians may have feared the ALN, but for most, their hatred of the French was stronger. The legal reforms meant nothing in Serkadji – nine executions in less than a month. 'The prison is bathed in an atmosphere of death and mourning.'[56]

With the obvious concern about torture and terror, the national question remained secondary. An article in *Réalités algériennes et Marxisme* posited the view of the nation as a continually evolving social formation. Algerian nationalism was rooted in love of land and liberty, values which could be traced back to the Berbers, the author began. The Arabs had introduced Islam, while allowing the Berbers to retain their customs and social organisation, laying the basis for an Algerian nation embracing multiple cultures.[57] The development of Algerian nationalism was comparable to 'a river's course, at first a stream, which grows as it passes through new lands, narrow in the gorges that embrace it, calm and wide in the plains, enriching the terrain and enriched by tributaries from the nearby mountains'.[58] Capitalism had facilitated the territory's economic unification. But colonialism – by closing mosques and independent schools, decreeing Arabic as a foreign language and imposing French – had been a step back for Algerian nationalism. Nonetheless, Algerian nationalism had leaped forward during the Second World War and been further fuelled by the 1945 massacre. The Algerian nation displayed Stalin's criteria of nationhood, the author contended – a stable community with a common national character and language, an integrated, coherent economy within a single territory.[59]

While the Arabo-Berber population fit Stalin's criteria of nationhood, the author sought to envision the conditions that would enable Jews and Europeans to become part of a larger multicultural nation, predominantly, but not exclusively, Arabo-Berber. The key concerned the subjective factor of identity. Although Jews had lived in North Africa for centuries, the Crémieux decree had split them off from the Algerian nation. But by identifying as Algerian, they could become part of the Algerian nation and state. While European settlers would not be at home in France, the *ultra* idea of an Algeria independent of France was premised on the suppression of the indigenous people. 'On that they base their dream of another South Africa where the "small whites", separated from the uncomprehending metropole, would reign as masters.' Nonetheless, Europeans could be integrated into the Algerian state as citizens and workers, and progressive Europeans, as part of the Algerian nation.[60]

The PCA had interpreted Thorez's 'nation in formation' thesis dogmatically to mean that the nation's formation depended on the prior fusion of its supposed twenty races, the author claimed. That interpretation reflected the PCA's underestimation of Algerian nationalism, a legacy of communism's arrival in Algeria, carried by European trade unions concerned with class rather than national issues. Communists had overestimated European workers' anti-colonialism, while underestimating the impact of their superior conditions on their political consciousness. But as Ben Badis had insisted, Algeria was incontestably Arab; this would inevitably increase after independence, enabling an Arabic cultural renaissance. Algerians would never accept de Gaulle's notion of integration; any positive relationship between the two countries necessitated that France recognise the Algerian nation. The equality of Algerians and Europeans was impossible under the colonial economic framework. That framework must be broken, a task that fell to Algerians, concluded the author. This was an important contribution, although its impact at the time is not known.[61]

The war precipitated the Fourth Republic's collapse in May 1958. On 13 May the army organised demonstrations in Algeria to honour French soldiers killed in combat. That evening European demonstrators rocked the capital. Lacoste was removed from office. A Committee of Public Safety was formed, led by General Massu with three colonels and seven civilians as liaisons between the military and the civilian population. 'The army is with you wholeheartedly,' Massu told the crowd. Serkadji prisoners heard the noise – horns, trucks with loudspeakers – and saw the traffic jams. Serkadji and Lodi were targets; flyers circulated that called on Europeans to 'avenge the blood of soldiers executed by the F.L.N.' Women prisoners at Serkadji feared that the ultras would get inside and go for those on death row. 'Grave hours in Algiers', reported *Le Parisien* the next day as some 50,000 Europeans and even some Algerians demonstrated in support of *Algérie française*. Thousands marched in solidarity in Paris. On the 18th, Algerian women joined the demonstrations and participated in an unveiling led by General Massu's wife, becoming symbols of the 'keep Algeria French' movement. But other Algerian women organised counter-demonstrations to protest against the French presence. 'Revolution is in the air', wrote Feraoun; 'people have barricaded their homes; protesters are moving along the large thoroughfares of the city; stores are closed.'[62]

Charles de Gaulle was voted into office as Prime Minister the next month on the back of the threatened coup and mass settler demonstrations and, in the PCF's view, supported by French financial capital investors eager to exploit Algerian oil reserves. Yet de Gaulle's declaration – 'I have understood you' – aroused settler hopes, and he convinced many Algerians of his support for change.[63] Keeping track of the events, Communists in Serkadji put together a little newsletter – *Barberousse républicain* – made from surreptitiously obtained newspaper cuttings and folded to fit into the bottom of a matchbox. But it was soon discovered, and prison authorities cracked down, still smarting from *La Question*.[64]

The news reached Lambèse, where prisoners were fighting their dehumanisation. When Benzine had arrived, the prisoners – mostly political – had no defence committees and were easily divided and atomised. At the war's outset, most prisoners had come from the Aurès and Constantinois, but from summer 1957, convoys arrived from Oran and Algiers. The FLN, MNA and PCA were all represented, and some criminals gradually became politicised. Stealthily, they organised an underground network, using the matchbox system. In late 1957 prisoners led a successful strike over esparto grass production. In early 1958 they convinced certain guards to help them obtain messages, news and newspapers, and later that year half the prisoners went on hunger strike demanding an end to violence, better food and health care and access to mail. Some were forced to eat under threat of being shot, but they won two important victories: firstly, that prisoners would be in charge of their own discipline; secondly, that prisoners would designate the most serious cases for the infirmary. Hunger strikes became their most potent weapon.[65]

Prison campaigns spread. The former Dachau prisoner Farrugia had been transferred from Lodi to Berrouaghia penitentiary in the south. The inmates were subjected to a brutal regime of forced labour on large landed estates that produced esparto grass, tobacco and wine. Their guards included Vichy and Red Hand supporters and even former criminals. Some prisoners went mad; others hanged themselves. Farrugia began a letter-writing campaign to expose the conditions. In France Algerian prisoners won improvements. When Serkadji prisoners asked the assistant director why those improvements could not be applied in Algeria, he replied: 'France is France, and Algeria is Algeria' – a tacit recognition that Algeria was indeed another country.[66]

De Gaulle launched an aggressive campaign to integrate Algeria into France. His constitutional referendum to inaugurate a new Fifth Republic, scheduled for 28 September, was to be based in Algeria on universal suffrage in a single electoral college. Voting for the first time, Algerian women were intimidated by both sides as the French and the FLN vied for their support. For the French, the enfranchisement of Algerian women symbolised integration; yet it was an achievement for which the UFA had campaigned since 1944. The PCF opposed the proposed constitution, while the FLN threatened to kill Algerians who voted. The FLN launched more terrorist attacks in Algiers and brought them to France. From 24 August to 28 September, when it called a halt, there were 242 attacks on people and 181 on property in France. Nonetheless, de Gaulle won. In France 84.9 per cent of the electorate turned out, and 66.41 per cent voted yes. Despite FLN's boycott call, almost 80 per cent of Algerians voted, 96.6 per cent of them for the new constitution – a significant FLN defeat. On 3 October de Gaulle went to Constantine to unveil a five-year development plan that included educational expansion, redistribution of 250,000 hectares of state-owned land and industrial investment designed to create 400,000 new jobs. The Constantine Plan accented social, economic and educational opportunities for women.[67]

To regain the initiative, on 19 September 1958 the FLN had formed the Gouvernement provisoire de la République algérienne (GPRA), a provisional government in exile replacing the CCE and presided over by the moderate Ferhat Abbas, who proposed a cease-fire. De Gaulle countered on 23 October offering reconciliation on the basis of un-conditional surrender – a *paix des braves*, or peace under honourable conditions – that was rejected by the FLN and criticised by both left and right. The 1st of November saw a general strike to honour the anniversary of the armed struggle's launch, which was celebrated in prisons and internment camps. Algerian patriotism was growing, and de Gaulle's influence declining. At the 30 November parliamentary elections, only 65 per cent of eligible Algerian voters turned out, and no significant Algerian political figure stood for office, although of the 67 deputies elected, 46 were Algerian and 21 European. More broadly, the election was a triumph for the Gaullists and a disaster for a divided and demoralised left. The PCF was devastated by a combination of anti-communist sentiment and a new electoral law. Only ten communists sat in the new National Assembly.[68]

However, in Algeria the election was a propaganda defeat for de Gaulle, who began to separate military and civil authority in Algeria. The French military had gained almost total control of Algeria, its leaders sympathised with the settlers and its loyalty to the French government was questionable. De Gaulle purged the army. The all-powerful General Salan, embittered, was recalled to Paris. He was replaced by a military duumvirate to ensure that civil and military powers would be divided and controlled from Paris. General Maurice Challe took charge.[69]

The PCA, decimated by waves of arrests, pledged its full support to the GPRA. Nonetheless, in November the PCA's central committee expressed concern with 'the almost total absence for more than a year of any other form of struggle apart from armed struggle'. While acknowledging armed struggle's centrality, it noted that not all Algerians could participate in that manner. The mass actions of 1956-57 – strikes, boycotts, demonstrations – showed that political activities could broaden and deepen the national liberation struggle. By 1958 the virtual impossibility of movement in Algiers and the French military presence across the country meant that space for open mass action was very heavily curtailed. Nonetheless, the PCA foresaw the implications of the FLN's militarisation at the expense of civil society organisation.[70]

The African continent moves

The FLN seized the tide of change sweeping across Africa in the late 1950s. As the Cold War intensified and pressures on imperial powers mounted, the African political terrain underwent profound upheavals. Ghana, the first sub-Saharan African country to win independence, became a focal point for this anti-colonial groundswell. In April 1958 its leader Kwame Nkrumah, assisted by the pan-Africanist and anti-Stalinist George Padmore, had organised a conference of independent African states that paired Algeria and South Africa as two pivotal European bastions in Africa. Nkrumah championed non-violent 'positive action'. Algeria's armed struggle challenged this non-violent paradigm.[71]

In December, Ghana hosted an All-Africa People's Conference for nationalist parties across Africa. The conference promoted an 'African Personality based on ... Pan-African Socialism as the ideology of the African Non-Violent Revolution'. Ahmed Boumendjel, Dr Chawki Mostefaï and Fanon – as Dr Fanon Omar – represented Algeria.[72] Fanon argued that Algeria's armed struggle should be a guide for other African struggles and that Africans had to form 'a national front, against inhumanity and poverty', using all available means, including 'force and violence'. He was cheered, but the discussion became so heated that the North Africans threatened to leave. To restore calm the Kenyan trade unionist and anti-colonialist Tom Mboya made a 'brief but captivating commentary on the Algerian Question', noting that Western arms were used to suppress Algerians fighting for their human rights. If the West were worried about communist influence, he argued, it must support democratic struggles.[73]

The conference resolution reflected Fanon's intervention. Condemning legislation that considered 'those who fight for their independence and freedom as ordinary criminals', it pledged 'full support ... to all those who resort to peaceful means of non-violence and civil disobedience as well as to those who are compelled to retaliate against violence to attain national independence and freedom of the people'. Fanon knew many African intellectuals from his student days; no longer FLN spokesperson since the GPRA's formation, he became the FLN's voice for Africa.[74]

The Ghana conference was another FLN propaganda coup. Yet 1959 saw ever more misery for Algerians. Paranoia became normal, observed Feraoun: 'every day traitors are discovered, then put to death; and those who kill them also end up dead ... It is absolutely certain that the [Kabyle] maquis were infiltrated, and this explains their lack of success and the drastic cuts that the army was able to inflict each time.'[75] Weapons shortages necessitated changes in ALN tactics. Thus, an ALN company 'would have had eight machine-guns' a year ago, reported the British consul-general in January, but 'they were now operating with only two and ... shot-guns were again making their appearance, since the Kabyles could make the ammunition for them themselves'. But the ALN did not reduce its military campaigns – which seemed to be increasing – amidst speculation that it was stockpiling unused machine-guns in caves for the future.[76]

In Serkadji, the announcement came in January 1959 of no more executions. 'We breathe as if the walls no longer existed', wrote Alleg. 'The prison is freed from the gigantic grip that was strangling it. The guillotine, the nightmares of bloody nights ... all of that in the past? We would no longer live in a tomb?' But no; the guillotine was replaced by firing squads.[77] At Lambèse, though, there were real victories. In the second half of 1959 more than two thousand prisoners went on strike after a guard attacked Shaykh Mohamed. They had organised the University of Lambèse, as the prisoners called the prison schools they started. Literacy was the main focus – most of the prisoners were poor peasants, illiterate in both Arabic and French – and the communist Etienne Neplaz taught hundreds to read and write. Those studying Arabic had three grammar books, and they used what they called the 'Chinese method': when one group finished the first book, they would start the second while teaching beginners the first book. An ALN attack just outside the prison confirmed their hopes that the revolution was still alive.[78]

In the same year, General Challe implemented his military vision – 'integral pacification' – 500,000 troops engaging in 'hunt commandos' to break the ALN. Challe's troops wiped out many *maquis*. Millions of peasants were displaced; some accepted the French out of exhaustion. In July Feraoun's mother wrote that his village had sided with the French. 'The village is surrounded by a wire fence, and we are at peace. We have been set free. The general came and threw a party for us. He gave us guns in exchange for our men. They are going to create a school for girls and boys here. We are at peace.'[79]

Fanon's propaganda war

Back in Tunis, Fanon promoted the FLN despite his doubts about its politics. Its leadership was dominated by Belkacem Krim, Abdelhafid Boussouf and Lakhdar Bentobbal. 'They want power ... but to what ends', Fanon wondered, upset over Amirouche's murders of intellectuals – Amirouche himself had been killed on 28 March 1959. Like the communists, Fanon worried about the FLN's seemingly unstoppable militarisation. That spring he worked intensely on an analysis of the Algerian Revolution. He finished the preface in July; the book was published that autumn as *L'An V de la révolution algérienne* (Year V of the Algerian Revolution).[80]

The book was Fanon's reply to FLN critics who 'like to claim that the men who lead the Algerian Revolution are impelled by a thirst for blood'. Fanon acknowledged the movement's 'excesses', recognising that 'things that should have been avoided have transpired on the national soil'. The revolutionary movement must take moral responsibility for such actions: 'the colonised people must win, but they must do so cleanly, without "barbarity".' Hence, the GPRA's intention to punish, even by 'capital measures', those who violated the leadership's directives and engaged in such excesses.

Yet out of such violence the Algerian nation was being born, Fanon contended. Colonialism's penetration into every aspect of Algerian society had reinforced tradition as the colonised tried to 'flee from the occupier', both mentally and physically. The war overturned those defensive responses, producing the revolutionary process that stimulated the development of Algerian national consciousness: 'The thesis that men change at the same time that they change the world has never been so manifest as it is now in Algeria.' Unlike colonial situations where nationalist parties achieve formal political independence and then begin forging a national consciousness out of different ethnic communities, 'in Algeria it is the national consciousness, the collective sufferings and terrors that make it inevitable that the people must take its destiny into its own hands'.[81]

While Feraoun noted the war's traumatic impact on women, Fanon stressed its positive consequences. French attempts to use the veil to divide men and women had backfired, he argued. This was due to 'one of the laws of the psychology of colonisation' – where initially, 'the action, the plans of the occupier ... determine the centers of resistance around which a people's will to survive becomes organised'. Urban women guerrillas used the veil instrumentally. Dress became camouflage; women relearned the use of their bodies in public space. The French realisation that Algerian women carried explosives marked a turning point: this was no longer a war between armies, but a revolutionary war embracing all members of society. From that point on, everyone – men, women, Algerian, European – became suspect in French eyes and was treated accordingly. Women's involvement as terrorists, nurses or rape victims transformed families. The war ripped apart the traditional family, enabling new family relationships to develop – a view echoed by Algerian communists. Yet Fanon was silent on the FLN's treatment of the *mujahidat*.[82]

New attitudes towards the radio reflected the growth of national consciousness, Fanon contended. Earlier generations had 'avidly read' the anti-colonialist Francophone press but shunned the radio as 'a symbol of French presence'. When the anti-colonialist press was censored, Algerians turned to the radio for news about struggles in Tunisia and Morocco. Thus, when the FLN launched the 'Voice of Free Algeria' in late 1956, demand for radios and receivers skyrocketed. Through the radio Algerians imagined themselves as a nation and as part of a revolution. The FLN's decision to broadcast in multiple languages – Arabic, Berber and French – was 'the expression of a non-racial conception' linking Arabs and Berbers and destigmatising French as the oppressor's language. Significantly, Fanon did not mention the communist broadcasts from Budapest, which had ceased in October 1955 after France pressured Hungary to stop them.[83]

Algerians also displayed a rapid change in consciousness about health care, Fanon noted. The dehumanisation of Algerian patients, already routine before the war, was accentuated by the war. European doctors 'prepared' torture victims for each new round of torture. Health professionals were required to report wounded Algerians. Pharmacists were forbidden to provide drugs to Algerians; many died agonising deaths in consequence. However, when conventional health visits ceased, the FLN set up public health facilities across the country, and Algerians scrupulously learned hygiene, sanitation and basic health care – brought to them through the revolution, which compelled them to rethink their attitudes.[84]

There were certainly affinities between Fanon's analysis and communist views, notably on gender, non-racialism and changing consciousness.[85] Yet despite losing his illusions about the FLN, Fanon nonetheless emphasised only the war's positive aspects, assuming the spontaneous development of popular consciousness and underestimating the need for political education. The failure to discuss the war's negative consequences – the FLN's stress on military over political means, the masking of criminal violence as political and the internal FLN/ALN power struggles – necessarily meant inadequate attention to rectifying such problems. Fanon's communist friend Dr Georges Counillon had distributed medicine in the Aurès during struggles between rival warlords; he was assassinated in 1955 or 1956 for his communist views. What was Fanon's reaction, wondered Sadek Hadjerès. The FLN constructed political difference as anti-revolutionary; this prevented Fanon from expressing his concerns in public. The PCA could criticise such excesses precisely because it maintained its organisational autonomy, argued Hadjerès.[86]

Winning self-determination

The PCF finally accepted the idea of Algerian autonomy: on 31 May 1959 Thorez suggested that France would benefit from an autonomous Algeria controlling its own oil resources. The PCA likewise acknowledged its long-term underestimation of Algerian nationalism. The police reported that during 1958, repression had reduced contacts amongst those PCA members still at large to almost nothing, but by February 1959 contacts were reviving. That spring communists tried unsuccessfully to revive trade union activity at Bab el Oued and Hussein Dey, but found that mass action was still virtually impossible. In June, however, Larbi Bouhali made a fruitful fund-raising trip to the Eastern bloc countries, obtaining a commitment to provide training for Algerian youth and funds for the FLN, on condition that the GPRA made an official appeal to the relevant Eastern bloc governments.[87]

Flushed with that success, on 15 July the PCA wrote to the GPRA to improve relations. The Soummam congress had cast a cloud of suspicion on communists. Many communist guerrillas had been marginalised and stripped of their weapons. Yet the PCA and FLN shared the goal of independence, the PCA stressed. Events in Indochina, Cuba and elsewhere had demonstrated that organisational autonomy and ideological tolerance were not obstacles to liberation. It urged the GPRA and FLN to cast aside anti-communist attitudes and to unite the country's diverse political currents.[88] But anti-communist attitudes were still felt, and survival in prison or the *maquis* sometimes compelled communists to distance themselves from the PCA. However, Abdelkader Guerroudj thought that communists sometimes used anti-communism as a pretext to justify their decision to remain outside the FLN. Transferred to Marseille, in late 1959 he announced his resignation from the PCA. In spite of the FLN-PCA accords, he wrote, the PCA used the names of *combattants* who had joined the ALN to promote itself. Instead, it should have dissolved itself alongside the CDL.[89]

De Gaulle finally conceded the possibility of self-determination on 16 September 1959. He foresaw three choices to be put directly to the electorate in Algeria: secession, which he thought unrealistic; integration with France; or association based on the federal organisation of Algeria into ethnic communities – French, Arab, Kabyle and Mozabite.[90] De Gaulle did not anticipate negotiations with the FLN, which he saw as one organisation among many. Indeed, many Algerians were terrified of the FLN's ruthlessness. As the British consul-general remarked, it was 'the old depressing story of the F.L.N. controlling the country at night and the French Army during the day'. Yet the ALN never lacked for volunteers. Its success at obtaining French army uniforms caused real problems for the French, and it evidently now had access to military equipment inside the country. Its guerrillas possessed the latest military supplies – weapons, ammunition, jeeps, walkie-talkies, wireless sets, even uniforms – and they seemingly obtained them at the same time as the French army.[91]

De Gaulle's proposal satisfied no one. Alleg wondered whether anything had really changed: with two new executions in eight days, it was 'as if each step forward towards the solution had to be punctuated with bloodstains'. Serkadji prisoners launched a four-day hunger strike – only MNA prisoners refused to join.[92] The trial of the Blida comrades took place in late November. Abdelkader Babou, who had organised the CDL's integration into the *wilaya* IV ALN after the destruction of the Orléansville *maquis rouge*, had been captured in February 1958 with great media fanfare. Babou thought the trial went well: he was able to say what he wanted, and the sentences were as expected – twenty, fifteen, ten years. 'Pas de surprise' (No surprise). The PCA pledged its support to the GPRA, and the PCF decided to increase its financial support to the FFPCA.[93]

The year 1960 began in turmoil. On 19 January de Gaulle sacked Massu for criticising his policy. On the 24th, 'Barricades Week' was launched – an abortive insurrection against de Gaulle by army leaders in Algiers. Two days later the mutineers were 'still swaggering around behind their barricades', reported Feraoun. 'The center of the city is in a state of war, the European residents are visiting their heroes and feeding them supplies without much trouble' – with the aim of 'keeping Algeria French forever'. By the 29th, though, the revolt had collapsed, its leaders to be put on trial in Paris.[94] Nonetheless, 'Barricades Week' overshadowed the second All African People's conference taking place in Tunis. When Tunisia's President Habib Bourguiba opened the conference on 25 January, his call to support the Algerian struggle met with cheers. Despite the rigid settler resistance at either end of the continent, 1960 became the year of African freedom as roughly half of the continent won independence.

Yet by late April 1960 the ALN's guerrillas were seemingly defeated. Exhausted, from a high of some 30,000, their numbers had dropped to 12,000; the number of military actions declined accordingly. In Morocco and Tunisia, by contrast, the ALN's numbers swelled with a continuing influx of guerrillas and refugees, and its supplies were augmented by Eastern bloc weapons. It was now controlled by Colonel Houari Boumediène, who was reorganising it under control of a general staff.[95] Algerians still had hope. Freedom would 'result from fatigue and be confused with victory', predicted Feraoun.[96]

A military tribunal of PCA leaders took place on 13 June 1960 – three years after Alleg's arrest. Along with Alleg, the accused were Ahmed Akkache, Fernand Boillat, Buono, Caballero, Georges Catogni, André Moine and Constant Tiffou. Akkache vehemently rejected the French tribunal's right to judge him; he categorically refused the French citizenship being imposed on him against his will. Alleg castigated the military and judicial police. The two men were removed. Bouillat and Tiffou were released, the others sentenced to prison. A hearing on Maurice Audin's disappearance opened in Rennes on 28 June; Alleg was transferred to the Rennes prison to testify.[97]

In France anti-war protest mounted as Fanon's new book heightened criticism of French colonialism. Pierre Vidal-Naquet launched a committee on Audin's disappearance; de Beauvoir organised a campaign for Djamila Boupacha; captured, tortured, raped and sentenced to death, Boupacha was represented by the radical lawyer, Jacques Vergès.[98] Leading intellectuals signed the *Manifesto of the 121* in support of military deserters, which appeared in *Les Temps modernes* that August.

While for most French, opposition to torture did not lead to support for the FLN, for a tiny number it did. The Jeanson network, known as *les porteurs de valise* (suitcase carriers) organised safe houses and obtained forged identity documents for FLN activists in Europe. Francis Jeanson's underground network had been broken in February 1960, its members charged with treason. Jeanson himself escaped capture but was later condemned *in absentia*. The left was split. While the PCF argued that imperialism was the primary enemy and continued urging legal protest – communist propaganda within the army rather than desertion – the new left and anti-war movement supported the FLN and endorsed desertion. The manifesto's signatories were banned from radio and television, and the October issue of *Les Temps modernes* was seized.[99]

De Gaulle tried playing off disgruntled FLN factions against each other, but an attempt to negotiate with disillusioned *wilaya* IV leaders backfired. The war dragged on. De Gaulle finally agreed to negotiate with the GPRA, which ordered a halt to terrorism in France, despite dissension in its French wing. The talks took place in June 1960 at Melun in France, and although the PCF endorsed them, the new left and the anti-war movement had little hope in the process. By August the talks had collapsed, and the PCF found itself isolated on the French left.[100]

Just as the PCF's strategy of alliance with the socialists had foundered, so had the PCA's hopes of an alliance with the FLN been dashed. The PCA publicly criticised the FLN for stressing the military over the political, for failing to look towards progressive forces in France and for marginalising communists. Yet some Algerian communists detected a softening in the FLN's attitude towards them – compared with the sometimes virulent anti-communism of the war's earlier years – presumably reflecting a pragmatic need for support. In early 1960 the PCA had sent a report to the Soviet Consulate in Paris highlighting the dismal conditions of internees at Lodi and asking for help to improve the situation. Soon after, communist lawyers were expelled from Algeria. However, Lodi was closed in October 1960, its internees released, and the police soon picked up signs of their activity in Bab el Oued.[101] Along with periodic publications, in July someone painted the PCA's emblem of hammer, sickle and crescent in red along walls between Saoula and Douéra, south of Algiers. It was hoping to influence Algerian youth, and rumours flew amongst young Algerian intellectuals that the GPRA would be expanded to include representatives of the PCA, UGTA and UGEMA; some even put forward the names of Bachir Hadj Ali and Larbi Bouhali.[102]

'Our people will overcome'

On 18 November the PCA published a 48-page pamphlet called *Notre peuple vaincra* [Our people will overcome][103]. Sadek Hadjerès had read a Vietnamese brochure entitled *Le peuple vaincra* that argued that successful anti-colonial struggle must be based on political success. The PCA had cautioned the GPRA that armed struggle had to be combined with political work. Since the Barricades Week, young Algerians had been calling for demonstrations, a demand the PCA supported. Trade union actions, student protests and popular demonstrations would build political consciousness and send a message to the French government. With the Vietnamese brochure in mind, Hadjerès drafted a pamphlet. He and Hadj Ali met secretly to discuss the work. A central theme was the refutation of the hard-line FLN position that it was now time to sit and wait for the opposition to collapse. The GPRA moderates, by contrast, still hoped to pursue negotiations, despite the breakdown of talks at Melun.[104]

The Algerian nation demanded its right to existence, the pamphlet began. The ALN was waging a just war reflecting the aspirations of the Algerian people, who had already achieved major political successes – the GPRA's constitution in September 1958, de Gaulle's recognition of Algeria's right to self-determination in September 1959 and his recent admission on 4 November 1960 that an Algerian Algeria would one day exist. Each event represented an important step towards liberation.

The continuing civil society protest in Algeria and France posed mounting problems for colonialism, the pamphlet argued. Yet Algeria was a decisive French bastion and its European minority could be swayed by *ultra* propaganda, on the one hand, and used to influence metropolitan opinion, on the other. Neither the French army nor the ALN had defeated each other militarily. But the ALN wanted to keep the French army in check to obtain a political victory. The PCA pledged to support all GPRA efforts to reach a political victory, but cautioned that future negotiations must not repeat the errors at Melun. It criticised the FLN's narrow conception of unity and its underestimation of political work and denounced the MNA as counter-revolutionary.

To achieve victory, the PCA argued, the liberation movement must pursue both underground and mass work for total independence. The flow of supplies from the borders to the interior and the number of armed actions must be increased. The political training of guerrillas must be intensified, alongside political agitation within the enemy army. This must be accompanied by political mobilisation of the masses. A united leadership does not negate the independent existence of organisations that form the national liberation movement; this had been a principle in Vietnam and China, where communists led the national liberation struggles. As the party of peasants and workers, the PCA could not be dissolved. But its priority was independence, not socialism.[105]

On 9 December 1960 de Gaulle visited Algeria, provoking 'an explosion in each of the two races, the European settlers and the Arab natives'.[106] Avoiding the dangerously heated atmosphere of Algiers and Oran, he proceeded to Tlemcen, where European demonstrators booed him and Algerian demonstrators demanded an 'Algerian Algeria'. The event caught the popular imagination. Across the country, from west to east, many thousands of Algerians, many of them boys and girls aged ten, twelve, fourteen years – much of their childhood spent in wartime – swept into the streets and took them back – a seemingly spontaneous mass uprising, but one embodying years of frustration. As the inhabitants of one town descended into the streets, so did those of the next – from Tlemcen and Aïn Témouchent on 9 December to Oran, Cherchell, Belcourt and Orléansville on the 10th; Algiers, Constantine, Blida, Bougie, on the 11th; Saïda, Philippeville and Biskra on the 12th; Bône and Sidi bel Abbès on the 13th; Sétif on the 15th, Batna on the 16th; Béchar on the 21st; and still others. The centre of power had shifted to the cities.[107]

In Algiers the ultras demonstrated against de Gaulle on 9–10 December. On the 11th, Algerians 'swarmed out of their casbash – the clamor of their voices by the thousands screaming "Independence! Ferhat Abbas to power! Free Algeria!"', while flourishing 'their green-white-and-red Algerian rebel flags'. Algerian women were more publicly militant in 1959–60; men were a minority. These were the mass demonstrations described by Flanner as 'the awful, bloody events in Algeria ... [when] three myths died' – the first, that Algeria was French; the second, that only a small minority of Algerians wanted independence; the last, that de Gaulle could make peace. In just three days, 'the Europeans' rebellion against de Gaulle gave more aid to Ferhat Abbas than he had received in three years from the subversive rebel war', opined the conservative Catholic daily, *Le Figaro*. Europeans shot and ran over Algerians. Recently appointed as inspector for the *Centres sociaux*, Feraoun witnessed the events: 'People are breaking windows, raising clubs, setting fires ... and starting to kill others.' Algerians were being shot 'by the very people who claim to defend them, to watch over them, and to fraternise with them'. He watched 'dozens and dozens of military trucks pass by on their way to re-establish order by shooting into a crowd dressed in rags'. France had lost the capital.[108]

The communists who had recently been released from internment camps and prisons participated. Hadj Ali thought the December events 'marked the turning point in the war of liberation', while for Hadjerès they vindicated the PCA's call for political work. This was the message the PCA sent to the PCF on 12 December. While it appreciated the PCF's continued support for negotiations with the GPRA based on guarantees for self-determination, only by mass action could justice for Algeria be achieved. The next day the PCA called for an extension of mass struggle. Irrespective of the repression that communists had endured, their idealism was still intact.[109]

Talks in earnest finally began. Indeed, the referendum that took place on 8 January 1961 – 'Do you approve the Bill submitted to the French people by the President of the Republic and the organisation of the public powers in Algeria prior to self-determination?' – gave de Gaulle the support that he needed for negotiations. In France some 75.5 per cent voted, with 76.25 per cent giving support to de Gaulle, vindicating his position *vis-à-vis* the generals. But in Algeria he received 55 per cent of a much lower turnout. Many Algerians had followed the FLN's call to abstain, having already made their stand in the city streets.[110]

Notes

1 'La Grande répression de 1957, dite la 'Bataille d'Alger', in Harbi and Meynier (eds), *FLN*, pp. 136–42. Ruedy, *Modern Algeria*, p. 168, dates it from 30 September 1956; Djerbal, 'Effets', p. 73, from February 1957.
2 MacMaster, *Burning*, pp. 315–17; Vince, 'Transgressing', p. 446; Evans, *Algeria*, p. 203; Lazreg, *Eloquence*, pp. 121–2; 124–5; Heggoy, *Insurgency*, pp. 230–8; Seferdjeli, 'Rethinking', pp. 240–3; Seferdjeli, 'French "Reforms"', pp. 47–54.
3 Danièle Djamila Amrane-Minne, 'Women at War: The Representation of Women in *The Battle of Algiers*', *Interventions*, 9:3 (2007), 340–9, p. 343; MacMaster, *Burning*, pp. 323, 353; Gallissot (ed.), *Algérie*, p. 158.
4 Horne, *Savage War*, pp. 184–6; Crenshaw, 'Effectiveness', p. 485; Macey, *Fanon*, pp. 284–5, 291–2; Simone de Beauvoir and Gisèle Halimi (eds), *Djamila Boupacha* (Paris: Gallimard, 1962); Gallissot (ed.), *Algérie*, p. 569; Wood, 'Remembering', p. 261.
5 Horne, *Savage War*, pp. 186–7.
6 Evans, *Algeria*, states 122 attacks, pp. 189–90, 195–6; Crenshaw, 'Effectiveness', p. 489; Macey, *Fanon*, pp. 259–60; Cherki, *Fanon*, p. 130.
7 Feraoun, *Journal*, p. 163; Boukort, *Souffle*, p. 132, also describes European attacks on Algerian bystanders.
8 PCF 261J 7/, box 1, 'Mémoire du F.L.N. à l'O.N.U.', and 'La question algérienne devant l'O.N.U.', *Résistance algérienne* (10, 20 January 1957), p. 1; Horne, *Savage War*, pp. 165, 178; Feraoun, *Journal*, p. 166; Vince, 'Transgressing', pp. 459–63; Evans, *Algeria*, pp. 201, 207.
9 Feraoun, *Journal*, p. 201; Evans, *Algeria*, p. 209; Horne, *Savage War*, pp. 188, 190–204; Seferdjeli, 'French "Reforms"', p. 44; Meynier, 'PPA–MTLD', p. 646; Crenshaw, 'Effectiveness', pp. 488–9; Macey, *Fanon*, pp. 299–300, 311–12; Cherki, *Fanon*, pp. 131–2; First, 'Armed struggle', p. 6.
10 PCF 261J 7/, box 1, file 5, 'Khalfat Boualem "l'Homme aux deux pseudonyms" arrêté par la D.S.T. d'Oran', *L'Echo d'Alger* [n.d.]; « Soixante arrestations ont été opérées dans le département d'Oran », *Le Monde*, 20 September 1956; Gallissot (ed.), *Algérie*, pp. 308, 389; interview with Bekaddour.
11 Thomas Riegler, 'The State as a Terrorist: France and the Red Hand', *Perspectives on Terrorism*, 6:6 (2012), http://goo.gl/tNBASq (accessed 4 October 2013).

12 « La femme d'un architecte algérois Mme Steiner et un instituteur, Etienne Nepas "travaillaient" avec Hadjeres Sadok [sic] et l'ingénieur Arbib Giorgio », *Dépêche quotidienne d'Algérie* (19 October 1956); Ameyar, *Moudjahida*, p. 28; Einaudi, *Pour l'exemple*, pp. 121–5. « Le communiste Fernand Yveton est surpris cachant une bombe à retardement à l'usine à gaz du Hamma », *L'Echo d'Alger* (15 November 1956); *Echo d'Alger* (29, 30 October 1957); *Dépêche quotidienne d'Algérie* (22, 23 October 1957).

13 'Le disque usé ou le danger communiste en Algérie', *Résistance algérienne* (20 January 1957), p. 3; interviews with Guerroudj; Guerroudj, *Douars*, pp. 40–1; Moine, *Ma guerre*, pp. 136–9; Henri Alleg, *Prisonniers de guerre* (Paris: Minuit, 1961), pp. 40–1.

14 Feraoun, *Journal*, p. 183; Evans, *Algeria*, p. 205; discussion, Boussad Ouadi.

15 PCF 261J 7/, box 5, 'Melouza', *Résistance algérienne* (10 June 1957), pp. 1–2, 4–5, 8; 'Tracts du FLN sur la tuerie dite de Melouza', in Harbi and Meynier (eds), *FLN*, pp. 199–202; Stora, *Messali*, pp. 263–4; Cherki, *Fanon*, pp. 148–50, 155; Evans, *Algeria*, p. 217; Harbi, *Vie*, pp. 199–200.

16 Feraoun, *Journal*, pp. 208, 211–12; Ruedy, *Modern Algeria*, p. 164; Horne, *Savage War*, pp. 207, 260; Crenshaw, 'Effectiveness', pp. 483–4; Macey, *Fanon*, pp. 353–5; Evans, *Memory*, pp. 173–4.

17 Feraoun, *Journal*, pp. 212, 216, xiii.

18 PCF 261J 7/, box 3, *Bulletin édité par la Fédération de France du Parti communiste algérien*, 4 (1959).

19 Buono, *L'Olivier*, p. 26; Alleg, *Mémoire*, pp. 309–11, 313–15; *Réalités algériennes et Marxisme*, 1 (January 1957); ANOM ALG 91 3F/75.

20 Jean-Luc Einaudi, *La Ferme améziane: Enquête sur un centre de torture pendant la guerre d'Algérie* (Constantine: Media-Plus, 1993 and Paris: Harmattan, 1991), pp. 9–11; Alleg, *Prisonniers*, p. 7.

21 PCF 261J 7/, box 1, folder 5, Joë Nordmann to Emile Kahn, Ligue des droits de l'homme, 21 December 1956; « Fernand Yveton: Peine de mort », news clipping [n.p., n.d.]; Etienne Fajon, 'La triple exécution d'Alger' and 'Trois Algériens guillotinés', *L'Humanité* (12 February 1957); de Bonis, 'A la recherche', pp. 364–9.

22 PCF 261J 7/, box 1, folder 5, « La vie d'un homme, la mienne, compte peu. Ce qui compte, c'est l'Algérie, son avenir », « Je suis persuadé que bientôt l'amitié entre les Français et les Algériens se ressoudera », news clipping [n.p., n.d.]; Albert Camus, 'Reflections on the Guillotine', in Albert Camus, *The Plague, The Fall, Exile and the Kingdom, and Selected Essays* (New York, etc: Alfred A. Knopf, 2004), 607–56, p. 641; Einaudi, *Pour l'exemple*, pp. 126–207.

23 Marie Elbe, 'L'Idée-bombe et la « relance » des communistes en 1956 dans la « Bataille d'Alger »', *Echo Constantine* (5 November 1957); interviews with Guerroudj; Rebah, *Chemins*, p. 173; Alleg, *Mémoire*, p. 202; Ameyar, *Moudjahida*, pp. 43–5; de Bonis, 'A la recherche', pp. 485–6, 488–92; Moine, *Ma guerre*, p. 138; Extrait des Minutes du Greffe (23 March 1957), courtesy Sadek Hadjerès.

24 Nidham (system, organisation). Alleg, *Prisonniers*, pp. 20–21, 28–9, 31, 43, 47–8.

25 « Bénis soient les matins sans guillotine, quand la prière des hommes nous réveille ... La pensée de la mort ne nous quitte pas ... Les jours où le sang ne coule pas, c'est comme une victoire de la vie sur la mort », in *Serkadji, Quartier des Femmes* (Algiers: Al Houriyya, 1961), PDF, pp. 1–2, 4, http://goo.gl/ITtwV0 (accessed 23 December 2012).

26 Discussion with Bekaddour and Loup.

27 Henri Alleg, *La Question* (Paris: Minuit, 1958), p. 35.

28 « ville torturée, quadrillée, contrôlée et fouillée à chaque rue, dans chaque train, aux quartiers "suspects" étranglés de fils de fer barbelés », Alleg, *Prisonniers*, p. 17; Alleg, *Question*, pp. 8–9; Horne, *Savage War*, pp. 200–1; Heggoy, *Insurgency*, p. 237; Evans, *Memory*, p. 143; Donald Reid, 'Review Article: The Question of Henri Alleg', *International History Review*, 29:3 (September 2007), 573–86, pp. 577–8; Nathalie Funès, 'Lodi, le camp des oubliés', *Nouvel Observateur* (18 March 2010), http://goo.gl/nkJqzm (accessed 2 October 2013).

29 Christian Buono, 'J'ai assisté à la naissance de « La Question », de Henri Alleg', *Réalités algériennes et Marxisme*, 7 (16 September 1961), 42–5; Allison Drew, 'An Interview with Henri Alleg', *Socialist History*, 39 (2011), 42–59; Gallissot (ed.), *Algérie*, pp. 173–4.
30 Benzine, *Lambèse*, pp. 8–9, 49, 59, 64–5, 70, 85–8, 97, 144–5.
31 TNA: PRO FO 371/125922, British Consulate-General to Selwyn Lloyd, 6 August 1957, p. 1, and *Communism in Algeria* (Annual Report), p. 2; Le Foll-Luciani, 'Un microcosme de l'Algérie nouvelle?', pp. 253–4.
32 Rebah, *Chemins*, pp. 89, 109–43.
33 Feraoun, *Journal*, pp. 221–2; Larribère Hadj Ali, *Itinéraire*, pp. 103–4; Le Foll-Luciani, 'Un microcosme de l'Algérie nouvelle?', pp. 253–4; PCF 261J 7/ box 3, folder 1, *Déclaration des Partis communistes algérien, marocain et tunisien*, n.d., [November 1957].
34 Serge Bromberger, 'Saadi Yacef – chef du terrorisme à Alger – arrêté dans la casbah', *Figaro*, 25 September 1957; Horne, *Savage War*, pp. 211–18; Heggoy, *Insurgency*, p. 239; Evans, *Algeria*, p. 221, states 7 October.
35 Interview with Ighilahriz; *Serkadji*, p. 6; Vince, 'Transgressing', 462; MacMaster, *Burning*, p. 317.
36 Feraoun, *Journal*, pp. 261–2, 242; MacMaster, *Burning*, p. 352.
37 TNA: PRO FO 371/138585, British Consulate-General to African Department, 12 January 1959; Horne, *Savage War*, p. 219; Hadj Ali, 'Lessons', p. 257; First, 'Armed Struggle', p. 6.
38 MacMaster, *Burning*, pp. 331–2; Vince, 'Transgressing', pp. 463–4, 466–9; Seferdjeli, 'Rethinking', pp. 242–4.
39 Gallissot (ed.), *Algérie*, p. 507; Rebah, *Chemins*, pp. 160–2; Sportisse, *Camp*, p. 221, n. 34; « Arrestation de la terroriste communiste Raymonde Peschard », *Figaro* (26 March 1957); *Echo d'Alger*, 26 March 1957; « Raymonde Peschard tuée en combattant au sein d'un maquis rebelle », *Aurore* (29 November 1957); « Le corps de la militante communiste algérienne Raymonde Peschard découvert parmi des cadavres de rebelle », *Figaro* (29 November 1957); « Raymond Peschard tuée dans un combat avec un maquis F.L.N. », *Le Populaire* (29 November 1957); Marcel Thiébault, « Plusieurs militantes communistes aux côtés de Raymonde Peschard dans le maquis ou elle a été tuée », *Le Monde* (30 November 1957); René Janon, « Le F.L.N. a lancé des assauts répétés pour tenter de reprendre le corps de Raymonde Peschard », *Figaro* (30 November–1 December 1957).
40 « Solitaire, aigu, un cri déchire le silence ... l'appel d'un homme qui va mourir, à ses frères ... enveloppé dans la chaleur de cent autres voix, celles des condamnés à mort ... La prison entière se joint à eux ... Soudain, répondant à nos cris, éclate, sauvage et terrible, le chant des femmes ... un hommage au martyr », Alleg, *Prisonniers*, pp. 78–9.
41 de Bonis, 'A la recherche', pp. 486–8; Marcel Thiébault, 'Au procès des « combattants de la libération »', *Le Monde* (6 December 1957); René Janon, 'Le procès des « combattants de la libération »', *Figaro* (6 December 1957).
42 « Je suis ici avec mes frères de lutte », « Pour les Algériens, la guillotine a désormais la même signification que la croix dans vos églises », « Trois condamnés à mort devant le tribunal militaire », *L'Humanité* (11 December 1957); Dore-Audibert, *Françaises*, pp. 151–6; *Serkadji*, p. 3; Alleg, *Prisonniers*, p. 163.
43 On the clemency campaign, see *Les Guerroudj et Taleb ne doivent pas mourir* (Paris: February 1958); *L'Ecole et la nation* (January 1958); *l'Humanité* (24 December 1957, 20, 25, 26, 27 March, 3 May 1958); *Le Monde* (23 March 1958).
44 Djerbal, 'Effets', pp. 82, 86–7; Horne, *Savage War*, pp. 190–2; Crenshaw, 'Effectiveness', pp. 492–3; Wolf, *Peasant Wars*, pp. 236, 238–9.
45 Horne, *Savage War*, pp. 264, 266; Museum of the Armed Forces, Algiers, Morice Line Exhibit, 23 September 2011.
46 Horne, *Savage War*, pp. 228–30; Evans, *Algeria*, pp. 226–8.
47 Evans, *Algeria*, pp. 228–9; Macey, *Fanon*, pp. 313–14, 355–7; Cherki, *Fanon*, pp. 150–3.

48 TNA: PRO FO 371/125949, British Embassy, Paris to Foreign Office, 30 July 1957; British Consulate, Algiers to Foreign Office, 21 August 1957; Birmingham Peace Council to Selwyn Lloyd, 6 September 1957; Fédération démocratique internationale des femmes to UN Secretary-General, 2 September 1957; '"Pick-and-shovel peacemakers" arrested in Algeria', n.d.; « Délégués de la commission contre le régime concentrationnaire publient leur rapport sur l'Algérie », *Le Monde* (27 July 1957).

49 Heggoy, *Insurgency*, pp. 240–4; William H. Lewis, 'The Decline of Algeria's FLN', *Middle East Journal*, 20:2 (Spring 1966), 161–72, p. 164; Ruth First, *The Barrel of a Gun: Political Power in Africa and the Coup d'Etat* (Harmondsworth, Middlesex: Penguin, 1970), pp. 90–2.

50 'Un devoir national: Faire échec au chantage anti-communiste des impérialistes', *Liberté* (September–October 1957), courtesy Sadek Hadjerès; Rapport de la Mission Aït Chaalal en DDR (June 1960), in Harbi and Meynier (eds), *FLN*, 807–10, p. 808.

51 PCF 261J 7/, box 4, Secours populaires français, *Vérités sur les Tortures* (Paris: n.d.); Wall, 'French Communists', p. 528; Francis and Gontier, *de Beauvoir*, pp. 272, 274; Cherki, *Fanon*, pp. 137–40; Shepard, *Invention*, pp. 63–8; Evans, *Algeria*, pp. 223–5; Stora, *Gangrène*, pp. 62–3, 76–7.

52 « J'ai toujours condamné la terreur. Je dois condamner aussi un terrorisme qui s'exerce aveuglément, dans les rues d'Alger par exemple, et qui un jour peut frapper ma mère ou ma famille. Je crois à la justice, mais je défendrai ma mère avant la justice », Zaretsky, *Albert Camus*, pp. 144–5; Albert Camus, Letter to Amrouche, 19 November [1954?], Albert Camus, *Notebooks, 1951–1959* (Chicago, IL: Ivan R. Dee, 2008), pp. 217–18; Todd, *Camus: A Life*, pp. 362, 365, 378–9; Camus, *First Man*, pp. 58–9; Francis and Gontier, *de Beauvoir*, pp. 257–9.

53 Feraoun, *Journal*, pp. 235–6, 244.

54 « Et si nous écrivions sur les murs, est-ce qu'ils nous les supprimeraient ? », Alleg, *Prisonniers*, p. 140; Crenshaw, 'Effectiveness', p. 480; Evans, *Memory*, pp. 82, 142–3; Flanner, *Paris Journal*, p. 362; Lacouture, *Malraux*, pp. 391–2; Lazreg, *Torture*, pp. 213–18; Stora, *Gangrène*, pp. 67–71; Stora, *Algeria*, p. 68.

55 'Organisateur du maquis rouge', *L'Echo d'Alger* (18 February 1958); Feraoun, *Journal*, p. 240; Seferdjeli, 'French "Reforms"', p. 25.

56 « La prison baigne dans une atmosphère de mort et de deuil », Alleg, *Prisonniers*, p. 140.

57 'Essai sur la nation algérienne', *Réalités Algériennes et Marxisme*, 2 (July 1958), 3–35, reproduced in *Cahiers du Communisme* (supplement), 8 (August 1958); cf. Sivan, *Communisme*, pp. 250–3.

58 « cours d'un fleuve, d'abord ruisseau qui grandit au fur et à mesure qu'il traverse des contrées nouvelles, étroit dans les gorges qui l'enserrent, calme et large dans les plaines, enrichissant les terres et enrichi d'affluents venus des montagnes voisines », 'Essai sur la nation', 4, 9. Compare Neville Alexander, *An Ordinary Country: Issues in the Transition from Apartheid to Democracy in South Africa* (Pietermaritzburg: University of Natal, 2002), pp. 106–7: 'South African society ... has come about through the flowing together – mostly violently, sometimes in a relatively peaceful manner – of three main "tributaries" carrying different cultural traditions, practices, customs beliefs ... [The Garieb] traverses the whole of South Africa and its tributaries have their catchment areas in all parts of the country. It is a dynamic metaphor which gets us away from the sense of unchanging, eternal and god-given identities ... [and] represents the decisive notion ... that the mainstream is constituted by the confluence of all the tributaries, that is, that no single current dominates, that all the tributaries in their ever-changing forms continue to exist as such, even as they continue to constitute and reconstitute the mainstream.'

59 'Essai sur la nation', p. 17.

60 « C'est sur lui qu'ils fondent leur rêve d'une nouvelle Afrique du Sud, où les "petits blancs", séparés d'une métropole peu compréhensive, régneraient en maîtres », 'Essai sur la nation', p. 21.

61 'Essai sur la nation', pp. 23–9; Alleg, 'Torrent', p. 245, n. 59.

62 « L'armée est de cœur avec vous ... venger le sang des soldats exécutés par le F.L.N », Alleg, *Prisonniers*, pp. 170, 167–8; *Serkadji*, p. 13; 'Heures graves à Alger', *Le Parisien* (14 May 1958), pp. 1, 9; Feraoun, *Journal*, pp. 246–7; Funès, 'Lodi'; Seferdjeli, 'French "Reforms"', pp. 44–5; MacMaster, *Burning*, p. 352.
63 « *Je vous ai compris!* », Evans, *Algeria*, pp. 235–8; Wall, 'French Communists', p. 530; Lacouture, *Malraux*, pp. 395–402; Francis and Gontier, *de Beauvoir*, pp. 276–7; Alleg, *Prisonniers*, pp. 175–6, 181–2.
64 Alleg, *Prisonniers*, 183.
65 Benzine, *Lambèse*, pp. 56, 160–1, 164, 166–70.
66 PCA 261 J7/, box 1, file 6, Jean Farrugia, 'Cinq mois de terreur à la Centrale de Berrouaghia', *La Défense*, [n.d.] pp. 4–5; 'A la centrale de Lambèse comme à Berrouaghia', *La Defense*, [n.d.], p. 5; Gallissot (ed.), *Algérie*, p. 282; « La France, c'est la France, et l'Algérie c'est l'Algérie », Alleg, *Prisonniers*, p. 210.
67 Evans, *Algeria*, pp. 235–8, 243; MacMaster, *Burning*, pp. 273–80; Horne, *Savage War*, pp. 200, 301; Ruedy, *Modern Algeria*, p. 173; Feraoun, *Journal*, pp. 248–9; Wall, 'French Communists', p. 530; Lacouture, *Malraux*, pp. 393–5; Francis and Gontier, *de Beauvoir*, pp. 279–80; Wolf, *Peasant Wars*, p. 242; Shepard, *Invention*, pp. 74–6; Seferdjeli, 'French "Reforms"', pp. 25–7, 56.
68 Evans, *Algeria*, pp. 242–4; Horne, *Savage War*, pp. 315, 318; Stora, *Histoire de la guerre*, p. 62; Feraoun, *Journal*, pp. 249–50; Flanner, *Paris Journal*, p. 386; Francis and Gontier, *de Beauvoir*, p. 280; *Serkadji*, p. 6; Charles de Gaulle, 'Que vienne la paix des braves', Vidéo Ina, http://goo.gl/c48sVv (accessed 17 February 2010).
69 Ruedy, *Modern Algeria*, pp. 174–5; Horne, *Savage War*, pp. 308–10; Crenshaw, 'Effectiveness', p. 480; Flanner, *Journal*, p. 391; Feraoun, *Journal*, p. 256; Stora, *Algeria*, p. 75.
70 ANOM ALG 91 3F/43, PCA, *Plus que jamais tous unis derrière le G.P.R.A.* (1 October 1959); Bachir Hadj Ali to GPRA, 15 November 1958, in *Lettres adressées au G.P.R.A. au cours de la guerre pour l'indépendance au nom du comité central du Parti communiste algérien* (Algiers: Editions Al Houriya, 1962), pp. 4–20, 11, http://goo.gl/OS4bFH (accessed 24 June 2011). The letter was evidently transmitted to the FLN in May 1959.
71 University of York, Borthwick Institute for Archives, Southern African Archives, Duncan Papers (hereafter CSAS DU) 8.14.4, *Conference of Independent African States – Declarations and Resolutions*, resolutions 3–4, 22 April 1958.
72 CSAS DU 8.14.2, *Provisional Agenda of the All African People's Conference*; CSAS DU 8.14.3, *All African People's Conference Souvenir Programme*, Accra, 5–12 December 1958; Imanuel Geiss, *The Pan-African Movement: A History of Pan-Africanism in America, Europe, and Africa* (New York: Africana, 1974), pp. 419–20; C. J. Driver, *Patrick Duncan: South African and Pan-African* [1980] (Cape Town: David Philip, and Oxford: James Currey, 2000), pp. 156–7.
73 CSAS DU 8.14.23, Heads of Today's Proceedings (9 December 1958), p. 2; CSAS DU 8.14.30, *Daily Graphic* (10 December 1958), pp. 1, 3; *Ghana Times* (10 December 1958), pp. 9, 12; Macey, *Fanon*, pp. 348–50, 368–70; Cherki, *Fanon*, pp. 144–5, 176–7, 202–5.
74 CSAS DU 8.14.6, All-African People's Conference, *Conference Resolution on Imperialism and Colonialism* (5–13 December 1958), p. 2; Cherki, *Fanon*, p. 180.
75 Feraoun, *Journal*, p. 261.
76 TNA: PRO FO 371/138585, British Consulate-General to African Department, 12 January 1959, to Foreign Office, 30 June 1959, Calendar of Events, Algeria - 1959.
77 « On respire comme si les murs n'existaient plus. La prison est libérée de l'étreinte gigantesque qui l'étranglait. La guillotine, les cauchemars des nuits sanglantes ... tout cela, du passé? On ne vivrait plus dans un tombeau? », Alleg, *Prisonniers*, pp. 201–2, 206.
78 Benzine, *Lambèse*, pp. 10, 73, 164, 171–2, 178.
79 Feraoun, *Journal*, p. 267; Stora, *Algeria*, pp. 74–5.
80 Cherki, *Fanon*, pp. 162, 178; Macey, *Fanon*, pp. 397–411; Stora, *Algeria*, p. 75; TNA: PRO FO 371/138585, British Consul-General to Brigadier J. A. H. Mitchell, Paris, 6 April 1959.

81 Fanon, *Dying*, pp. 23–5, 49, 30, 28.
82 Fanon, *Dying*, pp. 47, 57–61, 107; 'Gloires aux femmes', *Liberté*, 18 February 1961; cf. MacMaster, *Burning*, pp. 332–4, 340–41; Vince, 'Transgressing', pp. 454, 457.
83 Fanon, *Dying*, pp. 73, 76–7; 82–84, 89, 93–4.
84 Fanon, *Dying*, pp. 124, n. 1, 132–145.
85 Fanon, *Dying*, pp. 150–78.
86 Sadek Hadjerès, 'La Pensée de Fanon: Quelques uns de ses impacts dans la sphère socio-politique algérienne', intervention au colloque de l'ACB du 9 Mai 2009, http://goo.gl/7C2I0U (accessed 24 June 2011); Gallissot (ed.), *Algérie*, p. 222.
87 ANOM ALG 91 3F/43, Notes de renseignement, 11 February, 2, 10 June 1959.
88 Hadj Ali, 'Au gouvernement provisoire de la République algérienne', 15 July 1959, p. 23; Rebah, *Chemins*, pp. 57–8, 60–2; Fanon, *Dying*, pp. 151–2.
89 'Lettre d'un ex-responsable Cxommuniste [sic]', 7 December 1959, in Harbi and Meynier (eds), *FLN*, pp. 236–8; interview with Guerroudj, 26 September 2011; cf. Guerroudj, *Douars*, p. 39.
90 Wall, 'French Communists', p. 534; Shepard, *Invention*, pp. 114–15; Lacouture, *Malraux*, pp. 403–9; Stora, *Gangrène*, pp. 79–82.
91 TNA: PRO FO 371/138585, British Consul-General to African Department, Foreign Office, 22 September 1959, to Brigadier J. A. H. Mitchell, Paris, 8 September 1959, Calendar of Events, Algeria – 1959; Feraoun, *Journal*, p. 268.
92 « comme si chaque pas en avant vers la solution devait se ponctuer de taches de sang », Alleg, *Prisonniers*, pp. 223–5, 232.
93 ANOM ALG 91 3F/43, PCA, *Plus que jamais tous unis derrière le G.P.R.A.*, 1 October 1959; Préfecture d'Alger, Note de renseignement, 16 October 1959; Préfecture d'Alger, 30 October 1959; « Organisateur du maquis rouge de Béni-Boudouane, Abdelkader Babou membre du bureau politique du P.C.A. a été capturé dans les rangs rebelles », *L'Echo d'Alger* (18 February 1958); Gallissot (ed.), *Algérie*, p. 77.
94 Feraoun, *Journal*, p. 273; Horne, *Savage War*, pp. 344–6; Crenshaw, 'Effectiveness', p. 498; Stora, *Histoire de la guerre*, p. 62; Flanner, *Paris Journal*, pp. 459–60.
95 Ruedy, *Modern Algeria*, pp. 177, 175. First, interview with Alleg.
96 Feraoun, *Journal*, p. 275.
97 ANOM ALG 91 3F/43, Commissaire divisionnaire, Alger, to Directeur, Sûreté nationale, Algérie, 13 June 1960; Alleg, *Mémoire*, pp. 259–73.
98 Pierre Vidal-Naquet, *L'Affaire Audin* (Paris: Editions de Minuit, 1958); Schwartz, 'L'Engagement'; Francis and Gontier, *de Beauvoir*, pp. 295, 298–9; Lazreg, *Torture*, p. 54.
99 Wall, 'French Communists', pp. 532–5; Francis and Gontier, *de Beauvoir*, pp. 293, 295–6; Rosa Moussaoui, 'An Insubordinate Named Francis Jeanson', *L'Humanité in English*, http://goo.gl/CwV6Km (accessed 14 March 2010), Alleg, *Mémoires*, pp. 272–3.
100 Horne, *Savage War*, pp. 304–8, 337, 340, 387–97; Evans, *Memory*, pp. 141–71; First, interview with Alleg.
101 ANOM ALG 91 3F/43, *Note de renseignement*, 15 January, 12 February 1960; *Dépêche quotidienne d'Algérie* (27 March 1960); 'Plusieurs responsables communistes libérés en Algérie', *Paris-Presse* (29 Septembre 1960); interview with Hadjerès; Le Foll-Luciani, 'Un microcosme de l'Algérie nouvelle?', p. 254.
102 Sadek Hadjerès, 'Réflexions d'un témoin-acteur communiste', paper presented at Forum on 'Quelques conceptions et pratiques de pouvoir en Algérie', Delphes, 27–30 October 1995, 18, http://goo.gl/JisYUA (accessed 4 July 2011); interview with Hadjerès; 'Le P.C.A. clandestin se manifeste dans le Sahel', *Dépêche quotidienne d'Algérie*, 29 July 1960; ANOM ALG 91 3F/75, Etat d'esprit de la population musulmane [date stamped 24 November 1960]; Wall, 'French Communists', pp. 535–6, 538.
103 PCA, *Notre peuple vaincra* (18 November 1960), http://goo.gl/pUqDVc (accessed 30 April 2011).
104 PCA, *Notre peuple*; interview with Hadjerès; Ruedy, *Modern Algeria*, pp. 177–8.
105 PCA, *Notre peuple*, esp. pp. 1–4, 6–8, 13–19, 22–3, 29, 31–5, 46.

106 Flanner, *Paris Journal*, pp. 461–3.
107 Evans, *Algeria*, pp. 286–9; Hocine Hamouma, *Les Enfants de décembre*, vol. 2 (Reghaia: ENAG, 2007), p. 39; Djerbal, 'Effets', p. 87. According to *Echo d'Alger* (10 December 1960), p. 1, de Gaulle was welcomed to Aïn-Timouchent and Tlemcen with cries of « Algérie française » and many Muslims carried banners saying: « Ici la France. Nous voulons rester Français »
108 Flanner, *Journal*, pp. 461–3, 441–2; Feraoun, *Journal*, pp. 279–82, 287, xiii; Ruedy, *Modern Algeria*, pp. 178–9; MacMaster, *Burning*, p. 353.
109 ANOM ALG 91 3F/44, PCA, *A l'exemple d'Alger, d'Oran et du Constantine étendre les luttes de masse pour en finir avec le colonialisme assassin* (13 December 1960), and Albert Rauzy, Sûreté nationale, to Préfet de police, Algiers, 12 June 1961; *Message du Parti communiste algérien au Parti communiste français* (12 December 1960); Hadj Ali, 'Lessons', p. 258.
110 'De Gaulle well satisfied with Algeria votes', *Guardian* (9 January 1961); Ruedy, *Modern Algeria*, p. 179; Evans, *Algeria*, pp. 290–1. The sources vary on election figures.

CHAPTER NINE

'We need a country that talks': imagining the future Algeria

'Today's children don't go to class. They are writing the history of a free Algeria,' wrote Zhor Zerari of the December 1960 demonstrations that propelled negotiations forward.[1] A week after the January 1961 referendum the GPRA signalled its readiness to negotiate. Algerian cities saw more demonstrations, but negotiations shifted the political momentum back to the French state and the external FLN, which was concerned about the popular dynamic unleashed in the streets.[2] The year saw the rise of the Organisation armée secrète (OAS), which announced itself with a plastic bomb campaign in February. Led by the disgraced generals Salan, Susini and Lagaillarde, its aim was to keep Algeria French, using terror to undermine the negotiations scheduled to begin 7 April at the French spa town of Evian-les-Bains.

If the internal FLN and its guerrilla army were fragmented and seemingly defeated, so was the PCA. At a glance it seemed virtually smashed – certainly, the state's security forces thought so. Many communists had been killed, imprisoned, interned or exiled. Those still at large were so far underground that they had only occasional face-to-face contact with one or two comrades at any one time. Contact outside a tiny circle was virtually impossible. PCA groups in Paris and Prague faced the same difficulties of communicating with comrades in Algeria as did the external and internal FLN. But communists had been energised by the December 1960 demonstrations, and the PCA stepped up its propaganda work, turning its efforts to young Algerians. In Moscow, Larbi Bouhali thought the moment ripe for communist influence of the mass struggle, reported security agents.[3]

Yet the FLN claimed to be the sole legitimate representative of the Algerian people. The week before negotiations were due to begin, the GPRA adamantly refused to allow the participation of any other Algerian organisation – specifically the MNA. Algerians had varied interests and loyalties, but the FLN undoubtedly had mass support.

The French conceded to the demand. But on 31 March Evian's mayor was assassinated by pro-French Algeria forces – bringing negotiations to a halt.[4]

Despite this setback, Algerians were discussing their country's future. In Paris Noureddine Abdelmoumène recruited students to the Fédération de France du FLN. But when he tried to discuss Algeria's post-independence future, the FFFLN leaders asked him whether he was moving towards the Americans. When he questioned why the FLN criticised the communists, despite receiving Eastern bloc support, he was asked whether he was a communist. When he denied being a communist, he was told that all communists would be liquidated when they were back in Algeria. He could not understand why they would kill people who had participated in the liberation war simply because they did not have the same ideas. Concerned for his own safety, when he was later instructed to go to Tunisia, he did not, fearing that he would be liquidated. Similarly, after her release from prison and under threats to her life from the Red Hand, Fattouma Ouzegane went to Paris and worked on behalf of the FFFLN. But she discovered that the FFFLN was threatening Algerians in Paris. Since she had not fled the Red Hand in Algeria to be threatened in Paris, she went to Tunis.[5]

Concerned about the FLN's failure to discuss post-independence Algeria, Fanon worked feverishly on the manuscript that became *Les Damnés de la terre* (*The Wretched of the Earth*), a searing indictment of colonialism, which he described as a Manichean system maintained through direct force that precluded any conciliation between colonised and coloniser. If colonialism was based on violence, then so must be its antidote, decolonisation, which meant in essence that 'the last shall be first and the first last'. More than half of the book consisted of material published before 1961; Fanon dictated the remainder to his wife Josie Fanon during that spring and summer.[6]

Although informed by Marxism, Fanon differed strongly with the PCA. While communists urged the political organisation of urban civil society alongside armed struggle, Fanon deprecated activity conducted 'in a highly peaceful fashion, through stoppages of work in the few industries which ha[d] been set up in the towns, mass demonstrations to cheer the leaders, and the boycotting of buses or of imported commodities'. Acknowledging that such activity could be positive, he nonetheless described it as 'therapy by hibernation' and a 'sleep-cure'.

The PCA saw urban working-class struggle as central; Fanon saw it as secondary. The working class in colonised societies help to run the 'colonial machine', he argued. By virtue of its relatively privileged position *vis-à-vis* the impoverished peasantry, it has 'everything to lose'. While nationalist parties count on skilled workers as their 'most faithful followers', they neglect peasants, who 'alone are revolutionary, for they have nothing to lose and everything to gain. The starving peasant, outside the class system, is the first among the exploited to discover that only violence pays.' The peasantry's revolutionary potential stems from its desire to regain the land. For colonised people, 'the most essential value, because the most concrete, is first and foremost the land: the land which will bring them bread and, above all, dignity'.[7]

Yet Fanon did not ask what would happen once peasants attained their land, although he understood that an overly militarised struggle could unleash a cycle of violence and that nationalist parties could manipulate peasants to support violence. Peasants felt 'that violence alone w[ould] free them' because political organisations 'invoke violence in their slogans and call the masses to embark on armed struggle'. But he also saw violence as productive. While colonialism was 'separatist and regionalist', revolutionary violence was 'all-inclusive and national ... [and] closely involved in the liquidation of regionalism and of tribalism'.[8]

Yet whether revolutionary or counter-revolutionary, violence was destructive. Panicking at the prospect of independence, in early April the OAS launched a full-fledged terror campaign of bombings and assassinations. General Salan seemingly sought a South African style solution – 'a kind of Apartheid for Algeria'. On 12 April de Gaulle announced that if Algeria broke completely with France, it would cut all aid. On 22 April the OAS staged a putsch in Algiers; General Challe claimed the military was in charge. The next day, de Gaulle called for all means necessary to thwart the putsch. On the 25th, Challe surrendered; the putsch was over. However, the OAS initiated a wave of bombings in Paris, destroying the offices of *France observateur* and threatening those who had signed the *Manifesto of the 121*.[9]

The PCA tried to raise its profile. Larbi Bouhali and Abdelhamid Boudiaf met with the PCF and the three North African communist parties that month; a message from Bachir Hadj Ali was read at the PCF's 16th congress held from 11 to 14 May at Saint-Denis. *Liberté/El-Hourriya* which had been irregular, now appeared monthly, and the PCF launched *Secteur postal Algérie*, an informative newspaper that carried no identifying information. The PCA began producing several roneotyped flyers per month, generally sending a few hundred copies each to Algerian neighbourhoods, while the FFPCA sent flyers from Paris. Despite the increased propaganda activity, however, the PCA seemed to have no organisational life within the country, although there were reports of small nuclei of activists in Algiers, in Mouzaïaville, near Blida, and in Constantine.[10]

The Evian negotiations, derailed by terror, were rescheduled for

20 May to 28 July. The PCA welcomed the talks, again pledging full support to the GPRA and demanding peace on the basis of the full equality and sovereignty of both nations. But France threatened partition. 'De Gaulle wants to confront our people and our government with an unacceptable choice: neo-colonial bonds and truncated independence or true independence and truncated territory', the PCA warned. Negotiations resumed, but collapsed over the rights of Europeans. They restarted, but collapsed again over the Sahara. In early July the FLN launched a massively successful general strike supported by the PCA for the unity of Algeria and the Sahara.[11]

OAS explosives terrorised Paris and produced virtual anarchy in Algeria's cities. The wounded *en route* to hospitals were stopped and killed; funeral processions *en route* to cemeteries were machine-gunned. In Algiers, the university library, the national library and the municipal library were burned; schools were pulverised; Algerian-run establishments in European neighbourhoods were destroyed – restaurants, cafés, Turkish baths, hairdressers, sports halls and Koranic schools. Jews, who had been leaving Algeria in noticeable numbers since 1960, stepped up their departure in 1961. The OAS represented encroaching fascism, warned the PCF.[12]

The negotiations and their breakdowns were parallelled by the FLN's continuing strife. On the one side stood the GPRA, on the other, Boumediène and the ALN. The GPRA castigated Boumediène's military inactivity as a betrayal of the guerrilla struggle. Boumediène resented the GPRA's claim to authority over the ALN and complained of corruption, bourgeois domination and its soft approach at the Evian negotiations. It was impossible to conduct negotiations without involving Ben Bella and his four fellow political prisoners, who had gradually been allowed greater communication with the outside world, and Boumediène eventually gained Ben Bella's support. When the fourth CNRA met at Tripoli, Libya, on 5 August, the GPRA–ALN rivalry and the collapse of negotiations dominated the discussion. The GPRA's leadership was reorganised. The moderate Abbas was replaced by Benyoussef Ben Khedda, who hoped to ensure civilian control over the military. But Ben Bella obtained concessions to appease Boumediène and his staff. The 'hard-liners', thought Feraoun, had gained control.[13]

Needing to end the never-ending war, in September de Gaulle finally conceded Algeria's right to the Sahara. Yet Paris remained beset with violence. French police became renowned for their brutality against peaceful anti-war demonstrations and sit-ins. Vidal-Naquet and other Comité Audin members suffered sanctions for their work. On 17 October 1961 a peaceful Algerian demonstration turned into a nightmare as police engaged in a frenzied attack – for days afterwards bodies were fished out of the Seine.[14] Police attacks on Algerians in France were followed by OAS attacks in Algiers. During the night of 31 October, 60 bombs exploded in Algiers. The next day saw massive demonstrations of Algerians, with more than 80 deaths; Ben Bella and fellow detainees began a hunger strike. On 9 December France stepped up legal proceedings and police activity against the OAS. In a momentary interlude, on 12 December ALN representatives met with GPRA vice-president Belkacem Krim to bury Frantz Fanon, who had died from leukaemia on 6 December 1961; his last wish was to be buried in Algeria. He had lived to see the publication of *Wretched of the Earth*, which predicted the political bankruptcy of the national bourgeoisie that would come to power.[15]

Prison struggles continued. Over several years Lambèse prisoners had won gains: they played sports, listened to radio and even produced a monthly newsletter, *La Voix du prisonnier* [*The Prisoner's Voice*]. But for some, conditions deteriorated. In late January 1961 seventy Lambèse prisoners had been transferred to Camp Morand at Boghari. They had no status – neither prisoners of war, nor political nor criminal prisoners – and thus no legal protection. They slept on straw in hastily made dugouts, with no blankets, no lights and no spoons. Guarded by legionnaires and former-Nazis, they endured psychological and physical torture that Abdelhamid Benzine had not imagined, forced to engage in continuous vigorous movement – to crawl, run up and down, do endless press-ups, do more running, beat each other and endure constant insults. The point of torture during interrogations was to gain information. But this torture regime, Benzine speculated, was predicated on creating a 'third force', namely, the recruitment of Algerian prisoners as *harkis* by psychologically breaking them. Yet with negotiations under way, the third force strategy was no longer relevant. Now, it was purely a question of sadism. After several months Benzine got word to his comrades. A lawyer arrived in April. Slowly, their conditions improved.[16]

With the PCF's help, in 1961 two high-profile communists escaped from French prisons: Boualem Khalfa and two FLN prisoners from Caen, and Alleg from Rennes. Khalfa took charge of the FFPCA in Paris, while Alleg headed to Prague. There Alleg discovered Larbi Bouhali; Mustapha Saadoun and Mohamed Boualem, both from the Orléansville *maquis rouge*; Abdelhamid Boudiaf, from the ALN *maquis* in Oranie; Abdelhamid Guerab from *Alger républicain* days; Paul and Simone Boiziz, Oran attorneys who helped political prisoners; and Gilberte Taleb, widow of Bouali Taleb, who had died in battle. All had crossed into Morocco; all were publicising the PCA's views within the socialist bloc and internationally, presumably closely watched by

Czech security services. Well known because of *La Question*, Alleg travelled widely in Eastern bloc countries, finding that those he met did not wish to discuss Stalin's personality cult.[17]

Saadoun's experience illustrated the continuing marginalisation of communists within the ALN, which he had joined following the slaughter of the Orléansville *maquis rouge*. But once the Soummam congress delegates returned, he felt ostracised. In March 1957 he learned that Abane Ramdane had enquired whether he was engaging in 'fractional work'. Accused by nameless individuals, he was sent to Kabylia, which was heavily penetrated by the French army. The local people had been relocated to tightly controlled regroupment centres; it was impossible to make contacts in such conditions. Isolated, Saadoun was sent on similar missions, and in late 1960 he was ordered to Morocco. The entire country was at war, but he went on foot, without weapons. He met fellow communist Abdelhamid Boudiaf, and together they crossed the Moroccan border. From there they were sent to Prague. This saved Saadoun's life, but he had wanted to stay and fight.[18]

In October 1961 the PCA celebrated its twenty-fifth anniversary. A commemorative article presented an impressive account of the party's role in urban and rural struggles that alluded to the difficulties of 'managing to keep alive in the tempest of this war', while avoiding mention of the 'nation in formation' thesis and the party's initial response to the Sétif massacre. Reiterating its demands for literacy and the recognition of Arabic as an official language, it endorsed the idea of an Arab cultural renaissance, arguing that 'cultural revival is not a matter of simple contemplation of the values of the past, but an enrichment and rebirth of these values for a genuinely national, progressive, popular and scientific culture'. Political victory depended on intensifying armed struggle alongside negotiations, it stressed, urging Algerians to make 1962 the year of independence.[19]

De Gaulle agreed, announcing on 29 December that 1962 would see the end of French Algeria – to the shock of Europeans in Algeria. On 5 January 1962 the OAS attacked the PCF's headquarters. The PCF and other organisations of the left began mobilising against further attacks. In Algeria, assassinations became normal: 'Every morning, you learn about the death of a friend, someone you knew, a good man, an innocent', commented Feraoun. The next month, on 8 February, police violence against an anti-OAS demonstration in Paris culminated in the death of eight communists. On the 13th more than half a million demonstrators marched through Paris to commemorate the victims.[20]

Negotiations resumed in February. Violence against Algerians escalated. 'Attacks on Moslems in Algiers result in over 60 deaths', reported the British consulate-general for 24–25 February. 'For two days I have been holed up at home to avoid the ratonnades', recounted Feraoun on the 28th. 'There was a large attack on Muslims at Bab el Oued, with scores of casualties and wounded ... The day before yesterday ... I watched the gunfire ... crowds, flying bullets, and the reckless flight of bystanders ... state police in a jeep ... turn their backs on the murderers.' More anti-Algerian attacks in Algiers and Oran. The situation was unbearable. Yet people bore it.[21]

The second set of Evian talks took place between 7 and 18 March 1962. With negotiations proceeding, Algeria drew the attention of Africans across the continent. Nelson Mandela and Robert Resha of South Africa's African National Congress (ANC) were on a mission to raise funds for their own recently launched armed struggle. Arriving in Casablanca on 6 March, on the 9th they met Dr Chawki Mostefaï, who headed the GPRA's mission in Morocco. Inspired by Vietnam's victory at Dien Bien Phu, Mostefaï explained, the FLN had initially planned to overthrow French rule by military force. Over time it realised that a military victory was impossible; it hoped that the guerrilla struggle would force the French to negotiate.[22]

The FLN's internal divisions notwithstanding, Mostefaï stressed unity. 'A revolution cannot move with two heads ... one bad head is better than two good ones', Mandela jotted in his notebook. The political organisation had to 'be in complete control of the people and their activity', and soldiers 'must live amongst the people like fish in water'. The entire movement must unite behind a single leadership and vision based on a 'general plan'.[23] The movement's strategy included military, political and psychological objectives, which in turn might produce new conditions necessitating the general plan's revision. The strategy incorporated multiple tactics, including military operations, the development of political consciousness amongst the masses and the mobilisation of international allies. The aim was 'to destroy the legality of the Government and to institute that of the people. There must be parallel authority in the administration of justice, in administration and in supplies.'[24]

In Algeria people were subjected to daily terrorist attacks: on one single morning the OAS showered Algiers with 117 plastic bombs. 'Terror reigns', Feraoun wrote on 14 March. 'Yet people still go out ... They leave without being too sure whether they will come back or fall in the street ... every time that anyone goes out, he comes back to describe a murder or report a victim.' The next day Feraoun and five other Centres sociaux colleagues were lined up and assassinated by an OAS commando squad. Schools stopped holding classes in mourning. The Evian Accords were signed on 18 March; a cease-fire was declared on the 19th. News films that day showed Boumediène's ALN, 'tough, scruffily dressed men', standing in silence to commemorate the one million Algerians who had lost their lives in the war.[25]

Back in Morocco Mandela and Resha took the train to Oujda, fifteen kilometres west of the Algerian border and near the ALN's base at Ben M'Hidi. They visited the Zegangan training base, where they saw the army museum and the soldiers' theatre, listening to music and political sketches that, in Mandela's view, contained 'terrific propaganda against French rule in Alg.'. Despite the PCA's concerns about the ALN's limited political education, the South Africans were impressed by 'the high level of political consciousness amongst the members of the Aln' and 'were pestered with questions on [their] political organs, the country and its peoples. On non violence, etc.'[26]

Returning to Oujda they went to the ALN printing works and transmission headquarters, then to the northern division battalion headquarters at Bouliker, 'situated suitably in the most strategic area and heavily guarded'. They visited a battalion on the border, where refugees teemed around the camp. At Oujda they met a Captain Harbi, who stressed that leaders must recognise the masses as society's 'most important investment', that all operations and activities must include intellectuals, workers and peasants, and that the FLN 'did not start their own revolution before they had achieved unity of intent'. The Algerians followed events in Cuba, whose first military supplies to the ALN had just arrived in January 1962. The Cuban Revolution had suffered because of its 'failure to achieve unity of all forces before the start was made', Harbi contended. The Algerians 'succeeded in doing what the Cubans failed to do. Formation of an integrated party to head the revolution.'[27] But the Cuban Revolution had followed its own dynamics. In December 1956, Fidel Castro's 26 July Movement had launched guerrilla war against Fulgencio Batista's dictatorship – without the backing of the Popular Socialist Party, the descendant of the original Communist Party of Cuba. Two years later, in January 1959, Batista fled, and Castro took power. In April 1961 Castro declared that the Cuban Revolution was socialist; in July 1961 his 26 July Movement merged with the Popular Socialist Party.[28]

But the PCA's steadfast refusal to disband was testimony of the FLN's failure to subsume all political currents. Following the Evian Accords, Alleg held a press conference in Prague to announce his plans to restart *Alger républicain*. The FLN despatched a representative from Tunis to counsel him against this. He was informed that political assassinations would no doubt continue to be used to settle problems in Africa – echoing the threat made to Noureddine Abdelmoumène. Alleg had underestimated how profoundly the common aim of preventing non-FLN views overrode the FLN's internal divisions.[29] Irrespective of the PCA's severely weakened state, the FLN still considered it a potential rival.

At Oujda a military parade in honour of Ben Bella, just out of prison, was planned for 25 March. Mandela was overwhelmed by the 'enthusiasm' of the 'fantastic crowds' and awed by the ALN troops. This was not Ethiopia's 'crisp, well-drilled, handsomely uniformed force ... but a kind of walking history of the guerrilla movement in Algeria', he thought. The parade was led by 'proud, battle-hardened veterans in turbans, long tunics and sandals, who had started the struggle many years before. They carried the weapons they had used: sabres, old flintlock rifles, battle-axes and assegais.' He realised that South Africa's liberation army 'would be more like these troops here in Oujda'. But Mandela did not know that many of the troops he saw that day had been stationed outside Algeria and had never seen battle. Most likely these were the 'younger soldiers, all carrying modern arms ... Some held heavy anti-tank and anti-aircraft guns'.[30]

Despite the cease-fire, violence still tore Algeria apart. On 8 April a referendum in metropolitan France signalled agreement for an independent Algeria. Europeans prepared to leave. The French government announced the court martial of any settler involved in terrorism. But the impact was swiftly undercut, in Flanner's view, by the amnesty agreement that included those Europeans who continued to engage in their 'blood-drunk *raton[n]ades*, or rat hunts, on the Algerian city sidewalks, in which rich bourgeois *colons*' sons shot down passing *ratons* ... The realistic, historical wisdom behind this implicit amnesty – or so some French feel – is that there is no difference between soldiers and civilians in a bitter civil war; both kill.' Salan was arrested on 20 April. His trial in Paris, thought Flanner, would 'be the most important and disturbing trial in modern France since that of Marshal Pétain, because once more it w[ould] involve the Army'.[31]

The PCA published its independence programme in that April. The future Algeria would belong not to a single class or party but to all Algerians working together for the national good, it stressed. Algeria would be an independent sovereign democratic republic with a formal constitution, an independent judiciary, regular parliamentary elections every four years and representative local assemblies. The constitution would enshrine human rights for all, the neutrality and non-interference of the state in religion, the mutual respect and tolerance of religious beliefs, the prohibition of racial discrimination and the full equality of women in all domains, including the abolition of polygamy, unilateral repudiation and unequal inheritance. Learning and culture should be promoted across the land. The people must make their voices heard: 'We need *a country that talks*, mouths that open freely at the village assembly just as in the National Assembly, in neighbourhood committees as in trade unions and political parties, in offices as at depots. In newspapers, on the radio, on the television, we need to popularise and highlight initiatives, encourage the exchange of experiences from one end of the country to another.' The PCA envisioned an engaged, vocal civil society filling public political space.[32]

The PCA stated that it would support a single-party system that was based on working-class and peasant interests. In this respect, it conceded to the Soviet one-party-state model. However, it added, Algeria's social system was not sufficiently developed to make that possible. Accordingly, it opposed a one-party system in Algeria. Even if such a party had a popular base, it contended, it would inevitably become the instrument of bourgeois domination over workers and peasants – as was the case in Egypt. Thus, the PCA promoted a pluralist political system that would include bourgeois and petty-bourgeois parties alongside an autonomous communist party.[33]

Although Algeria did not yet have the conditions for socialism, the economy could be directed along a non-capitalist path, the PCA argued. The comparative experiences of India and China indicated that a socialist path promoted rapid industrial development far more effectively than a capitalist path, it claimed, pointing to their production indices for steel and electricity.[34] Similarly, the experiences of North and South Vietnam indicated that socialist planning benefited small countries as well (see Tables 9 and 10).

While nationalisation and socialisation of the principal means of production and collectivisation of agriculture were not sufficient

Table 9 Comparative industrialisation, India and China

	Steel (kg per inhabitant)		Electricity (kWh per inhabitant)
	1950	1960	1950
India	4.1	7.5	14.0
China	1.1	27.0	8.3

Source: Adapted from *Programme du Parti communiste algérien* (April 1962), p. 20.

Table 10 Comparative electrification, North and South Vietnam

	Production of electricity per inhabitant (kWh)	
	1955	1960
North Vietnam (socialist path)	3.5	17.0
South Vietnam (capitalist path)	17.0	22.0

Source: Adapted from *Programme du Parti communiste algérien* (April 1962), p. 21.

conditions for socialism, the PCA maintained, they would provide its basis. Thus, it advocated the expropriation of large landholdings without compensation. This included those of the 7,000 largest European settlers and of the traditional Algerian landed elite, with particular emphasis on those deemed to have betrayed the revolution.[35]

The FLN's independence programme was adopted at the CNRA's conference in Tripoli from 28 May to 7 June 1962. The conference planned to draw up a political agenda and design the future political institutions. But the struggle for power within the FLN was feverish, and the CNRA's deliberations, heated. On one side stood Ben Bella, Boumediène, Abbas; on the other, the GPRA, the FFFLN, Aït Ahmed and others. Ben Bella and his allies dominated the proceedings. The Tripoli programme was infused with socialist ideas, in part responding to the PCA and reflecting socialism's popularity in Africa. The authors were familiar with Fanon's arguments about revolutionary consciousness and the PCA's criticisms of the FLN's inadequate political education. Their criticisms of the leadership's behaviour during the war – a pointed attack on the GPRA – indicated significant internal dissatisfaction, glossed over by the programme's glorification of unity.[36]

The Tripoli programme stressed that the Evian Accords signified 'an irreversible political victory ending the colonial regime and foreign secular domination'. Through their combined action, the Algerian people had consolidated their national unity and developed 'perspectives of a radical social transformation'. Yet the FLN leadership had overlooked the people's creative efforts and their revolutionary potential, noted the programme with concern.[37] Moreover, despite the political victory, the accords represented a neo-colonialist solution. What the French called 'coopération' was, in fact, economic dependency. French corporations gained privileged access to the country's oil and gas reserves, while the French armed forces, some of which were to remain in Algeria, could play divide-and-rule by manipulating the European minority and playing off FLN factions against each other.[38]

The challenges of post-war reconstruction were enormous, the programme noted. First was the country's feudal legacy. This took economic form through the pre-colonial pattern of land distribution, dominated by the large landowners who had collaborated with the French, and political form through the caïds, marabouts and clientelist relations made possible due to the widespread lack of education. The country was exhausted, the urban population crushed by poverty, and large parts of the once vibrant countryside desolate. Two million Algerians, mainly women and children, were leaving regroupment centres, and hundreds of thousands of refugees in Morocco and Tunisia awaited repatriation. These challenges could only be addressed by a popular democratic revolution based on the leadership of the rural masses supported by the urban poor and middle class and reflecting socialist and collectivist values. Like the delegates at the Soummam congress, like Fanon, the Tripoli programme's authors saw the peasantry as the leading political force.[39]

This popular democratic revolution was first and foremost an agrarian revolution with three principal tasks: agrarian reform, agricultural modernisation, and restoration and conservation of natural resources. Industrialisation would be based on the nationalisation of key sectors, including credit and foreign trade.[40] The new government would promote education and culture that were national, revolutionary and scientific; Islam, freed of superstitions, could contribute to the development of culture and national identity. The participation of women in the war had created the conditions for their full liberation, and their organisations should be supported. The socialist-bloc ties developed during the war would be strengthened to fight imperialism.

Glaringly absent was any mention of political institutions or political pluralism. Although the terms unity, party and vanguard resonated throughout, the FLN's overemphasis on the military struggle had allowed the very idea and content of the party to atrophy, as the PCA had warned. Without an ideology developed through contact with the masses and their lived experiences, a revolutionary party could not exist, the programme's authors acknowledged. Indeed, it was widely recognised that the FLN and its structures had degenerated during the war.[41]

With Algeria on the brink of independence, two broadly socialist programmes had been put forward; the PCA's espoused political pluralism, and the FLN's, a one-party state. Yet despite the FLN's public stance on unity – the necessary illusion to hold the fractious FLN together and justify its quest for complete control – it was on the verge of erupting. The CNRA overwhelmingly adopted the Tripoli Programme but refused to pass Ben Bella's proposal for a political bureau to replace the GPRA. This proposed political bureau was to include one *wilaya* leader, one member of the existing GPRA and the five former political prisoners – hardly representative of all those who had struggled for so many years. The matter was never put to the vote, and the meeting adjourned without having set up the expected institutions. Thus, the FLN's political structures remained fragmented and divided, with at least ten centres of power: the six interior *wilayas*, the ALN forces in Tunisia and Morocco, the GPRA, seen by many as the country's legal representative, the FFFLN, which had raised more funds than any other FLN section, and the five former political prisoners, seen as bearers of moral authority. Of all these, the external ALN was the most cohesive.

Alongside these were the FLN-aligned UGTA and UGEMA.[42]

The FLN's internal power struggles mirrored the country's seemingly endless violence. May had brought further OAS attacks in Algeria. On 2 May some fifty Algerian dockers were killed and more than one hundred wounded in an explosion at the Port of Algiers. More attacks on Muslims occurred the next week. A bloodbath followed: OAS versus FLN. In June the OAS ordered all Europeans to leave the country and began a scorched earth policy. In Algiers, the main hospital, the town hall and the civil aviation office were destroyed. On 17 June the OAS and FLN agreed to a cease-fire – the Mostefaï–Susini Agreement. But in Bône and Oran the OAS rejected the cease-fire and blew up the respective town halls. The mass European exodus had already begun. Despite the Evian guarantees, one-third of the European population had left by April. Some 350,000 left in June. On the 30th the GPRA dismissed Boumediène and dissolved his general staff. None of this seemed to matter in the euphoria of the moment. On 1 July 1962 Algerians voted resoundingly for independence. Two days later de Gaulle conceded the result. On 5 July the GPRA declared Algeria independent.[43]

Notes

1. « Des enfants aujourd'hui ne vont pas en classe. Ils écrivent l'histoire de l'Algérie libre », Zhor Zerari, 'L'école de la liberté', in Hamouma, *Enfants*, p. 216.
2. MacMaster, *Burning*, pp. 354–5, 366, n. 28.
3. ANOM ALG 91 3F/44, *Activités politiques d'inspiration séparatiste – activités communistes*, 28 December 1960, Rauzy to Préfet of police, and PCA, *En avant pour l'indépendance*, Appel du parti communiste algérien à la jeunesse algérienne (Algiers, 28 September 1961).
4. TNA: PRO FO 371/165607, British Consulate-General, 'Summary of Events – 1961'; Evans, *Algeria*, pp. 291–2; Stora, *Messali*, pp. 277–8.
5. Interviews with Abdelmoumène and Ouzegane.
6. Fanon, *Wretched*, pp. 37, 38–9, 41.
7. Fanon, *Wretched*, pp. 66, 109, 61, 45.
8. Fanon, *Wretched*, pp. 23, 94, 109.
9. Horne, *Savage War*, p. 485; Feraoun, *Journal*, p. 274; TNA: PRO FO 371/165607.
10. ANOM ALG 91 3F/43, Note de renseignements, 16, 29 May, 26 August 1961; Note d'information, 8 August 1961; PCF 261J 7/ box 3, file 1, FFPCA, *Un impératif décisif: Gagner davantage encore le soutien des masses françaises* (28 June 1961); Le Foll-Luciani, 'Un microcosme de l'Algérie nouvelle?', pp. 254–7; Bourderon, 'Journal clandestin', p. 110; Ciné-archives, Images du 16ème congrès du Parti communiste français, Saint-Denis (11–14 May 1961), http://goo.gl/2YNjKT (accessed 22 September 2013).
11. 'The talks on Algeria', Statement by the Algerian Communist Party (21 May 1961), *African Communist*, 6 (July 1961), 18; ANOM ALG 91 3F/44, PCA, *5 juillet: Journée nationale de lutte contre le partage* (1 July 1961).
12. TNA: PRO FO 371/165607; Evans, *Algeria*, pp. 300–2; Feraoun, *Journal*, pp. 289–90, 297; Boukort, *Souffle*, p. 167; Horne, *Savage War*, pp. 440–1; Wall, 'French Communists', p. 537; Francis and Gontier, *de Beauvoir*, pp. 298–9; Wolf, *Peasant Wars*, p. 242; Shepard, *Invention*, p. 174.
13. Feraoun, *Journal*, p. 298; Evans, *Algeria*, pp. 302–3; Ruedy, *Modern Algeria*, pp. 181, 184–5.

14 Perhaps two hundred died; the number is disputed. The 17 October demonstrators were mostly men; women and children demonstrated on 20 October (Jim House to author, 18 June 2013); Evans, *Algeria*, pp. 303–4, 308–10; Schwartz, 'L'engagement', pp. 36–7; Shepard, *Invention*, p. 84, n. 6.
15 TNA: PRO FO 371/165607; Fanon, *Wretched*, pp. 37, 148–205; Macey, *Fanon*, pp. 3–7, 447–92.
16 Abdelhamid Benzine, *Le Camp* (Paris: Editions Sociales, 1962), pp. 17, 21, 25, 30–3, 38–9, 41–3, 80, 86 ; 'Bibliographie', *Le Monde* (15 March 1962).
17 'For a Free Algerian Republic', p. 38; ANOM ALG 91 3F/43, *Appel de Henri Alleg aux Européens et aux Israelites* (30 November 1961), *Extraits d'une conférence de presse d'Henri Alleg, organisée le 4 décembre à Prague par l'Union des journalistes tchécoslovaques* [1961]; Gallissot (ed.), *Algérie*, pp. 388–90; Alleg, *Mémoire*, pp. 310–18 ; Benzine, *Lambèse*, pp. 171, 227.
18 Rebah, *Chemins*, pp. 59–64.
19 'For a Free Algerian Republic', p. 39; PCF 261J 7/, box 3, PCA, *Pour éclairer et déblayer le chemin de la paix et de l'indépendance* (Algiers: 7 November 1961).
20 PCF 261J 7/, box 4, *8 février, 13 février 1962* (Paris: Union des Syndicats de la région Parisienne, 1962); Wall, 'French Communists', p. 538; Francis and Gontier, *de Beauvoir*, pp. 299–300; Shepard, *Invention*, pp. 85–6; Feraoun, *Journal*, p. 311.
21 TNA: PRO FO 371/17312, '1962 Annual Review'; Feraoun, *Journal*, p. 313.
22 Nelson Mandela Centre of Memory, Johannesburg (hereafter NMCM), 385/33/17/32, Nelson Mandela, Africa Diary (8–9 March 1962), 385/33/17/34, 14 March 1962. My thanks to Razia Saleh; Nelson Mandela, *Long Walk to Freedom: The Autobiography of Nelson Mandela* (London: Little, Brown, 1994), pp. 286–7; Mostefaï, interview; www.mostefai.net/biographie.html (accessed 9 November 2007).
23 NMCM 385/33/16, Mandela, Notebook, pp. 56–7, 54.
24 NMCM 385/33/16, Mandela, Notebook, p. 56.
25 Feraoun, *Journal*, pp. 313–14, xxv, xli–xlii; Horne, *Savage War*, pp. 23–5; TNA: PRO FO 371/173125. For the Evian Accords text see Yves Courrière, *La Guerre d'Algérie: Les Feux du désespoir*, vol. 4 (Paris: Fayard, 1971), pp. 649–72.
26 NMCM 385/33/16, Mandela, Notebook, pp. 2, 4–5; NMCM 385/33/17/35, Mandela, Africa Diary, 18–19 March 1962.
27 NMCM 385/33/16, Mandela, Notebook, pp. 6–7, 8–11; NMCM 385/33/17/35–36, Mandela, Africa Diary (19–21 March 1962). Piero Gleijeses, 'Cuba's First Venture in Africa: Algeria, 1961–1965', *Journal of Latin American Studies*, 28 (1996), 159–95, p. 160; Fidel Castro with Ignacio Ramonet, *My Life*, trans. by Andrew Hurley (London: Allen Lane, 2007), pp. 298, 309–10, 312, 690, n. 4.
28 Castro with Ramonet, *My Life*, pp. 635–9; William J. Pomeroy, 'Introduction', 9–49, pp. 37–9, and Ernesto Che Guevara, 'Lessons of the Cuban Revolution', pp. 287–8, both Pomeroy (ed.), *Guerrilla Warfare*.
29 Alleg, *Mémoire*, pp. 322–6.
30 NMCM, 385/33/17/37–38, Mandela, Africa Diary (23–25 March 1962); Mandela, *Long Walk*, p. 287.
31 Flanner, *Journal*, pp. 517, 514, 525; Francis and Gontier, *de Beauvoir*, p. 301; TNA: PRO FO 371/173125.
32 « Il faut *un pays qui parle*, des bouches qui s'ouvrent librement à la djemâa comme à l'Assemblée Nationale, dans les comités de quartier comme dans les syndicats et les partis politiques, dans les bureaux comme sur les chantiers. Dans les journaux, à la radio, à la télévision, il faut populariser et mettre en valeur les initiatives, encourager l'échange d'expériences d'un bout à l'autre du pays » (emphasis in original). *Programme du Parti communiste algérien pour l'indépendance totale* (Algiers: El Houriyya, 18 April 1962), p. 17.
33 *Programme du Parti communiste*, pp. 17, 3–6, 13. Post-1945 East European communist parties initially collaborated with other political parties but later absorbed them. In some cases they had the backing of, or arguably were the instrument of, the Soviet army. However, Anna M. Grzymala-Busse, *Redeeming the Communist Past: The Regeneration of Communist Parties in East Central Europe* (Cambridge: Cam-

bridge University, 2002), points to the primacy of distinctive conditions at the time of political transition that shaped the parties' subsequent actions, arguing, p. 27, that 'as the critical formative moments, the initial takeovers had the greatest influence on the choice of these organizational practices and hence on subsequent elite political resources'.

34 Although these figures did not indicate democratic practice or quality of life, research suggests that China has consistently outperformed India on a range of socio-economic indicators. Amartya Sen, 'Quality of Life: India vs. China, *New York Review of Books* (12 May 2011), http://goo.gl/Cl6SiD (accessed 13 February 2013).
35 *Programme du Parti communiste*, pp. 8–9, 16–17, 19.
36 *Projet de programme pour la réalisation de la révolution démocratique populaire (adopté à l'unanimité par le CNRA à Tripoli en juin 1962*, in *Les Textes fondamentaux de la révolution* (Editions ANEP, n.d.), pp. 69–134; PCF 261J 7/, box 5, 'L'expérience révolutionnaire algérienne', *El Moudjahid*, 89 (16 January 1962), pp. 8–9, drew on Fanon's arguments; Extracts from *Damnés de la terre* were published in that and the previous issue (nos. 88–9); Ruth First, *The Barrel of a Gun: Political Power in Africa and the Coup d'Etat* (Harmondsworth: Penguin, 1970), pp. 446–7; David and Marina Ottaway, *Algeria: The Politics of a Socialist Revolution* (Berkeley and Los Angeles, CA: University of California, 1970), p. 17, n. 19; William B. Quandt, *Revolution and Political Leadership: Algeria, 1954–1968* (Cambridge, MA, and London: MIT, 1969), p. 166; Evans, *Algeria*, p. 333; Harbi, *Vie*, pp. 297–8.
37 « une victoire politique irréversible qui met fin au régime colonial et à la domination séculaire de l'étranger ... perspectives d'une transformation radicale de la société », *Projet de programme*, pp. 69–71, 84; Quandt, *Revolution*, p. 166.
38 *Projet de programme*, pp. 74–5, 79, 87–9; Jeffrey James Byrne, 'Our Own Special Brand of Socialism: Algeria and the Contest of Modernity in the 1960s', *Diplomatic History*, 33:3 (June 2009), 427–47, p. 431.
39 *Projet de programme*, pp. 81–2.
40 *Projet de programme*, pp. 112–13.
41 *Projet de programme*, pp. 90, 120–3, 127–34; Quandt, *Revolution*, p. 166.
42 Quandt, *Revolution*, pp. 166–8; Ruedy, *Modern Algeria*, pp. 181, 190–2; Lewis, 'Decline', p. 166; Wolf, *Peasant Wars*, p. 241.
43 « Un cessez-le-feu effectif concrétise l'accord FLN–OAS', *Oran républicain* (19 June 1962), p. 1 ; « Le Colonel Boumedienne et le Commandant Mendjli dégradés par le GPRA sont en fuite », *Dépêche quotidienne d'Algérie* (1–2 July 1962); Evans, *Algeria*, pp. 318–20; Horne, *Savage War*, pp. 530–4; Stora, *Messali*, pp. 279–80; Shepard, *Invention*, pp. 207–47; TNA: PRO FO 371/173125.

CONCLUSION

Algerian communists and the new Algeria

The new Algeria joined the international state system shortly before the Cuban missile crisis. World politics seemed frozen into a bipolar, ideologically driven rivalry between the United States and the Soviet Union, although Sino-Soviet tensions were undermining the Eastern bloc's seeming unity. When the armed struggle was launched, Africa was almost entirely under colonial rule. By July 1962, much of Africa was independent, and the colonial era effectively over – with the notable exceptions of Lusophone Africa and Southern Africa's white settler states. The end of colonial empires fuelled Cold War competition, as the superpowers vied for the sympathies of newly independent African states. Although socialism appealed to many African leaders, a significant number adopted a non-aligned African socialist path between East and West. This was indeed a new world order in the making.

But the latest member of the state system had been devastated by war. OAS explosives had damaged or destroyed many buildings. The war-time capital flight accelerated after independence. During the three years between 1960 and 1963, the gross domestic product shrank by more than one-third. The manufacturing, construction and public works sectors declined, and by 1963 about 70 per cent of the adult male workforce was either unemployed or underemployed. Tax collection proved very difficult, and the new state was dependent on foreign aid, first and foremost from France. The magnitude of the problem necessitated state-led reconstruction and development.

Class stratification was proceeding apace. If the political strength of urban relative to rural classes is an indicator of democratic potential, Algeria was not in a propitious condition; 70 per cent of Algerians still lived in rural areas. The Muslim landed elite was intact; many had moved to the cities or to France until stability was restored, and some sought to marry their daughters to ALN officers to solidify their position in the new order. About 25,000 families owned estates of more than 100 hectares – comprising half of Algeria's arable land. Money and education were generally more important than lineage in the development of this landed class. In Oranie Launay found several types of well-to-do Muslim landowners: the traditional landed elites; the middle-class professionals of cities and villages, including bureaucrats, doctors, pharmacists and intellectuals, who had acquired land; and prosperous peasants or traders, who had profited from the war and acquired land. The peasantry, by contrast, had been profoundly proletarianised. Some 170,000 peasant families – a supposed middle stratum – had landholdings of ten to fifty hectares; 450,000 owned less than ten hectares, and about 120,000 of those had less than one hectare. About 130,000 people were full-time farm workers, and 450,000, seasonal workers.

Impoverished rural people swarmed into overcrowded urban slums, which housed some two million unemployed and underemployed people. Of the remaining urban population, 110,000 were full-time workers; 180,000 were small shopkeepers, artisans, civil servants and service personnel; and 50,000 were entrepreneurs, landlords, managers and professionals. The mass European exodus meant the loss of skilled technicians and professionals. Civil service vacancies were filled by Algerians – linking their interests to the state, although 15,000 coopérants – left-wing French aid workers also known as *pieds-rouges* (red feet) – filled some posts. The *pieds-rouges* brought leftist ideas and reinforced the French language, to the dismay of religious leaders. Civil servants and those with cash snapped up vacant houses, flats, shops and farms, strengthening the middle class and landed elite. Algerians moved *en masse* into buildings hastily vacated by Europeans.[1]

The country teetered on the brink of civil war – reflecting not class struggle but political and economic ambition. People celebrated for days on end in July 1962, but popular euphoria notwithstanding, the FLN's internal power struggles erupted into the open. Three aspiring governments vied for power: the provisional executive set up at Evian; the GPRA, led by President Ben Khedda and seven ministers; and Ben Bella's political bureau. Although the Tripoli conference had not ratified the political bureau, Ben Bella refused to back down, and he gained the support of Boumediène and the external army, clearly post-war Algeria's most cohesive organisation. On 3 July violence erupted in Algiers at parades welcoming Ben Khedda and the GPRA. On the 11th Ben Bella entered Algeria and set up base at Tlemcen, supported by members of the political bureau, general staff and external army leaders. A rival Tizi Ouzou group was set up in Kabylia. The groups began negotiating but were stymied by resistance from the leaders of *wilayas* II, III and IV, who, along with FFFLN leaders, opposed Boumediène and the political bureau. The Tripoli programme called for ALN guerrillas to either disarm or merge into a new Armée nationale populaire, a proposal which they staunchly opposed. While on the one hand, Ruedy notes, *wilaya* leaders may have wished to preserve their own power, on the other, 'the subordination of the forces who had borne the brunt of the fighting to leaders, many of whom had seen none, was in many eyes almost counterrevolutionary'. Undeterred, Boumediène moved his troops from Morocco and Tunisia into Algeria. Ben Bella and his political bureau took charge. The GPRA conceded to the political bureau in early August. A list of electoral candidates for the National Constituent Assembly was unveiled on 20 August.[2]

The transition from de facto colony to politically independent state was a moment of political flux. Public political space opened up. People flocked to the victorious FLN, whose ranks swelled with those attracted by power. Nonetheless, the loss of many of the country's future intellectuals – the students slaughtered by Amirouche and others during the war – was palpable precisely because of their absence. Mohammed Harbi realised that the FLN's conception of a united struggle against a 'colonial totalitarianism' had discouraged individuals from developing and expressing their own views. Many had been 'consenting hostages'. After independence the FLN/ALN's upper echelons remained concerned by the younger generation's propensity to ask questions. In rural Oranie political and military elites viewed youth leaders suspiciously – they talked too much and were too intellectual.[3]

In the first heady days of independence, the PCA quickly re-entered public space. Despite Sivan's claim that the PCA's support for the anti-colonial struggle was both belated and abrupt, thereby contributing to its collapse, in fact, the Party's decline as the war unfolded reflected the ferocity of state repression against its activists. Its ranks had been severely depleted through arrest, internment, imprisonment and death, and some communists had joined the FLN. Indeed, the party's leaders acknowledged, 'during the war there was a time when the Party became "embryonic" as a result of its terrible losses'. Inevitably, the war had undermined the party's internal democratic procedures. Its last congress had been in February 1952. It functioned with essentially the same leadership as before the war, although new members had been periodically added to its central committee and political bureau to replace those who had died, been imprisoned or exiled. Unable to hold a congress, its central committee and political bureau members were reconfirmed.[4]

Did this indicate that the PCA's decision to maintain its organisational autonomy during the war had been politically short-sighted, even if politically principled? Not necessarily. The war had made the question of organisational autonomy or merger into the FLN ever more acute. At some points the PCA's very organisational existence was in doubt. However, the depth of anti-communism amongst many FLN leaders would presumably have made entryism as difficult an option as organisational autonomy – as some communists who joined the FLN discovered. Most communists saw themselves as part of a movement that, even if temporarily smashed, could nonetheless revive and rebuild under more auspicious circumstances. They hoped that independence would offer such a possibility. The PCA was scarcely a threat to the FLN in terms of numbers or organisational capacity. Its challenge lay in its ideas and its willingness to voice them and, in so doing, to push the boundaries of public political space.

Yet the PCA was again caught between international and national forces. During the Popular Front and Second World War years, international developments had facilitated the PCF's dominance over the PCA. But the extraordinary post-war repression compelled the PCA to fight for the rights of individuals and collectives – workers, peasants, women, Muslims and the Algerian nation. From the late 1940s Algerians had joined the party in growing numbers, pushing it to address the national question. Thus, the PCA's struggle against state repression led it to a deeper consideration of the national question. In the 1950s the guerrilla struggle's intensity pulled the PCA into the war. Increasingly autonomous *vis-à-vis* the PCF, the PCA committed itself fully to the national struggle, while Algerian communists in Eastern bloc countries strengthened the party's ties with the Soviet Union and its allies. The French state had viewed the PCA as a regimented, well-oiled machine representing a Soviet-backed international communist threat and had subjected it to ruthless repression – constant surveillance, arrest, internment and imprisonment. As a result, the party suffered extremely heavy losses relative to its size.

Algeria's independence shifted the balance of international and national pressures on the battered party. Western and Eastern powers competed for Algeria's attention, attracted as much by its oil and gas reserves as by its status in the emergent Third World. The FLN was relatively agnostic about the Sino-Soviet split – although slightly more sympathetic to China, but the PCA remained steadfastly pro-Soviet. Algerian communists were not blind to Soviet injustices. Rather, Abdelhamid Benzine explained, 'In the socialist world, in spite of sometimes dramatic errors ... one was building a new society, without capitalism, without exploitation of man by man.'[5]

The PCA's voice was heard through *El-Hourriya*, which now appeared weekly. *Alger républicain* reappeared, following the Soviet stance on foreign affairs and benefiting from the FLN's divisions and the absence of an official state newspaper. Alleg was the first of its staff to return; Khalfa was still in France, and Benzine was recovering from his internment. Veteran communists – Salort, Zannettacci, Sportisse,

CONCLUSION

Gilberte Chemouilli, the trade unionist Kaïdi Lakhdar and Djaafar Inal, back from his studies in the USSR, amongst others – joined Alleg. They worked at the office of the communist architect Abderrahmane Bouchama, and for a time were joined by the novelist Kateb Yacine. *Oran républicain* now styled itself as *'le quotidien de la démocratie'*, carrying daily reports on terrorist actions and provocatively asking why the ALN was bypassing the GPRA and appealing directly to public opinion. Despite the daily violence, Algeria became a Third World Mecca for revolutionaries congratulating and seeking aid from the new Algeria. Alleg was visited by radicals from around the world, including South African communists Yusuf Dadoo and Michael Harmel.[6]

Young people disenchanted with the FLN's lack of democracy and interested in socialism were attracted to the PCA. One of these was Noureddine Abdelmoumène, who was still in France in July when the FFFLN brought together its cadre for a seminar on independence. Some thirty people attended. For the first time Abdelmoumène learned the names of other FFFLN activists. It was an extraordinary experience. They heatedly discussed the GPRA and raised demands about nationalisation, agrarian reform and cooperatives. Yet Abdelmoumène sensed a power struggle amongst the leaders, who acted as if the ordinary members counted for nothing; his seminar participation was his last act for the FLN. At the September *Fête de L'Humanité*, he joined the PCA. The FFPCA asked him to organise new recruits, as he had done for the FFFLN. These recruits feared the FLN, the OAS and the *harkis*, and he himself had received threats, so he contacted the PCF for protection and help arranging safe meeting rooms. Soon thereafter, Boualem Khalfa asked him to return to Algeria to work on *Alger républicain*.[7]

Yet even as public political space expanded, it contracted. For the FLN's factionalised leadership, any potential opposition was a threat. This included the PCA, which had quickly begun pushing the boundaries of political space and was showing signs of reviving. Precisely because the moment was politically fluid, Ben Bella's political bureau sought to eliminate potential opposition. Abbas Khidder, the political bureau's general secretary, had initially supported the PCA's organisational autonomy. Ben Bella indicated there was no intention to ban the party, but suggested that communists join the FLN as individuals. Larbi Bouhali was subsequently informed, however, that the party should cease independent activity until after the FLN's congress. Ben Bella was impressed by Cuba, where the guerrillas and socialists had merged. Why not follow the Cuban model, communists were asked? Their response was that the Cuban exemplar would only be relevant if the Algerian Revolution followed the Cuban path. *El-Hourriya*'s third issue was seized from news agents, although publication continued. Ben Bella called in Abdelhamid Benzine, who had become *Alger républicain*'s editor-in-chief, to criticise the newspaper's alleged negativity towards the new regime. State officials criticised the newspaper for printing letters and exposés about the growing corruption. Benzine, Khalfa and Alleg proclaimed their loyalty to the government, arguing that any disagreement concerned the means by which the people's needs could best be served.[8]

Anarchy loomed. *Harkis* were arrested, tortured and killed, often with French troops standing by and preventing bystanders from intervening – yet de Gaulle refused the *harkis* entry into France. One estimate suggests that there were 55,000 to 75,000 deaths in the spring and summer of 1962. In Algiers MNA forces attacked FLN leaders. The OAS continued its scorched-earth policy. In Oran it had seemingly been contained by late June – but not before it had set alight the British Petroleum plant. The flares leapt more than 100 metres above the city, covering it with a black cloud. People marched for peace. But shots were fired at the independence celebrations. Despite calls to save the tenuous reconciliation, Algerians retaliated by attacking Europeans, precipitating yet another European flight that depopulated the city centre. In late August the verbal aggression between the political bureau, the GPRA and the *wilaya* leaders turned into armed attacks in Algiers. On the 29th, armed confrontations erupted between the political bureau and *wilaya* IV partisans. Ben Bella arrived triumphantly, proclaiming peace.[9]

Once again, the masses took to the streets, many of them energised by the UGTA, this time crying *'Sebaa s'nine! Barakat!'* (Seven years! Enough!).[10] People wanted peace. The war had deprived civil society of public space and freedom to build organisations and networks. It had few resources to continue contesting state power, whether colonial or post-colonial. Ben Bella arrived in Algiers on 4 September; on 5 September the dissident *wilaya* leaders accepted the political bureau's authority; on the 9th Boumediène and his tanks entered the capital, the events culminating in several thousand deaths. A new electoral list was unveiled, and national constituent assembly elections took place on the 20th. On 25 September the Democratic and Popular Republic of Algeria came into being. Ben Bella became prime minister. Order was restored.[11]

The PCA stressed its intention to continue as an autonomous organisation. To this end, on 30 September the PCA and PCF issued a joint communiqué emphasising the PCA's role in the armed struggle. A month later Abdelmoumène was back in Algiers to start work at *Alger républicain*. By then, the censor's hand was visible in the newspaper's white spaces, as was the case with *Oran républicain*. On 3 November Ben Bella attacked the PCA's insistence on autonomy as an attempt to destroy unity. Then came the banning of two public PCA meetings – a press conference and a meeting in Sétif – a portent of future developments.[12] On 29 November the PCA and *El-Hourriya* were banned – the Party claimed 8,000 to 10,000 members and sympathisers. There was 'no place for the Communist Party in Algeria now', announced Minister of Information Hadj Hamou, The government was not anti-communist, Hadj Hamou explained. Rather, the decision was in accordance with the Tripoli programme, which opposed political pluralism as divisive. Indeed, as the British Embassy pointed out, the government distinguished between the PCA and the Eastern bloc; Egypt had already set a precedent in suppressing local Communists while seeking Eastern bloc aid.[13]

The Soviet Communist Party saw the PCA's banning through Cold War lenses. *Alger républicain* reprinted a *Pravda* article claiming that the banning reflected the FLN's desire to appease the American and French governments. A few brave Algerian souls condemned the banning, notably Abdelkader Guerroudj, now in the FLN, and Hocine Aït Ahmed, who argued in the Algerian Assembly that socialist groups stimulated political debate. In February 1963 Hadjerès, Hadj Ali and Babou met with the Soviet Premier and CPSU Secretary Nikita Khrushchev in Moscow, reported the British Embassy.[14]

For the third time in its existence, the PCA faced illegality. The party had not held a congress or worked out procedures for the new situation. Nonetheless, it had no intention of ceasing its activities, and its activists were not completely underground. It was pointless to support a single party under duress, it argued: 'if the single party is realised only by agreement between leaders, it will not survive. It is necessary for democracy to penetrate the lives of all Algerians', who should certainly not 'toss aside liberties of which they were once cruelly deprived and the value of which they have come to know and appreciate'. Far from being a unifying force, a single party would be divisive. 'If revolutionary and anti-imperialist forces, representing social groups, should prefer to keep their separate autonomous organisations, or should refuse to participate in the building of a single party aiming at socialism ... [then] their rights must be respected', it cautioned. These diverse forces should organise a united front 'formed voluntarily, without constraint, and on a clear basis of policy: that the people, through people's committees of the front, would be better able to judge the policy and actions of every force and current within it'. Thus, a politically pluralist participatory democracy was fundamental to the PCA's conception of the Algerian nation.[15]

As a tiny party, the PCA would have benefited from a multiparty political system. Yet its stance could not be dismissed as self-serving. It had struggled against state repression and for political pluralism for years. Once in operation, political pluralism would create its own dynamics – most importantly, tolerance of diversity and expectations of continued pluralism. The critical question was whether the Soviet one-party model would override the distinctive conditions in which the PCA had developed and that had shaped its political perspectives. The party's record was ambiguous. Algeria's social, political and structural conditions, compounded by its geopolitical position had contributed to the weakness of its socialist and communist movements. The PCA had been particularly vulnerable to external forces. Nonetheless, in the critical post-1945 period, as more Algerians joined the PCA and as the national and anti-colonial struggle intensified, the party had developed an autonomous practice *vis-à-vis* the PCF and resisted the FLN's call to disband. This suggests that the Algerian communist movement had the potential to break from the Soviet model and to promote pluralist democracy.

Within this pluralist system, a Marxist–Leninist party was needed to build socialism, argued the PCA. The FLN's understanding of socialism was unclear. It favoured Nasser's Arab socialism, yet Nasser's notion of national unity acted to prevent class struggle. Just as nationalisation and agrarian reform were preconditions for socialism, the PCA contended, so was a Marxist–Leninist party. Although the peasantry had formed the revolution's backbone, Algerian peasant production was individually based. The peasantry, therefore, could not lead a collective socialist project. A Marxist–Leninist party must be led by the working class, supported by the peasantry. This alliance was necessary to fight against colonial land ownership, feudalist and neo-colonial elements and war profiteers and to raise the living standards of rural and urban poor.[16]

As the PCA pointed out, the suppression of communist parties was invariably followed by the suppression of trade unions. Indeed, the PCA was not the FLN's only target. The government moved to control the major civil society organisations, beginning with the trade union movement. During the war both the UGSA and UGTA had been decapitated by mass arrests; in 1957 the UGSA leadership had called on its members to join the UGTA, which set up headquarters in Tunis with the FLN. The UGTA called for full social and economic transformation, including nationalisation, restrictions on property and complete agrarian reform, claiming that the revolution was 'inseparable from independence'.[17] While supporting the Tripoli Charter, its leaders had expected some autonomy, and when the July power struggles broke out, the UGTA had supported Ben Khedda's faction. On 1 November the UGTA's organ L'Ouvrier algérien (Algerian Worker) published an editorial on the need for trade union autonomy; it was quickly seized. Nonetheless, in December 1962 the UGTA agreed to coordinate its policy with that of the FLN, which was to recognise the federation's 'organic and managerial autonomy'. The UGTA affiliated to the ICFTU, while pursuing friendly ties with the communist-aligned WFTU.[18]

The UGTA's first national congress on 17–20 January 1963 was a test of its freedom to manoeuvre under the FLN regime. Attended by some 385 delegates, the congress was clouded by claims of procedural irregularities in the elections of certain delegates. Ben Bella's opening address warned against 'ouvriérisme' (workerism) and a labour elite that pursued its own interests while the country's majority remained impoverished. When peasants constituted 80 per cent of the congress, he stated, 'the UGTA will have accomplished its mission ... I want to see 80% turbans here.'[19] But Ben Bella's support was far from unanimous. Over the next two days a sizeable opposition, with communist support, challenged the political bureau positions. Nonetheless, on the third day the political bureau called in its supporters to pack the congress and imposed a new executive committee. The brazen manoeuvring shocked foreign observers, and some sixty or seventy delegates withdrew in protest, estimated the British embassy's labour attaché. But the remainder carried on, indicating that the federation would follow government policy. For Kaïdi Lakhdar the central problem concerned the imposition of a leadership against the wishes of the workers.[20] The matter was summed up in the UGTA's statutes, which stated that the FLN was 'charged with the control of the said movement' and that UGTA membership was 'incompatible with the membership of any political organisation other than the F.L.N.' Nonetheless, reported the British embassy, 'the displaced elements were not completely silenced. They have now been given a clearer sense of grievance and placed more distinctly in opposition. They may thus still give trouble.'[21]

A day later the women's movement met a similar fate. During the war the UFA and other women's groups had been banned. In the absence of a publicly organised women's movement at independence, even the *mujahidat* refrained from politics. Patriarchal attitudes resurfaced, attacking the gains women had made during the war. In January 1963 *Alger républicain* published a debate about women's rights, with male writers denouncing feminism as European and anti-Islamic. Such attitudes were buttressed by Ben Bella's courting of conservative religious leaders. When the UFA held its first post-war congress on 20–21 January, its name was changed to the Union nationale des femmes algériennes (National Union of Algerian Women), and a new leadership slate of FLN heroines took office. The new organisation withered. The state – Ben Bella and his political bureau supported by the army – now controlled the main civil society organisations.[22]

The 1963 Constitution – drafted by Ben Bella – proclaimed the FLN as the sole legal party. Algeria was declared a socialist state with equal rights for men and women; Arabic was the official language; Islam, the official religion – Ben Badis' slogan reinterpreted in a new context. Indeed, the complexities of national identity in a war-torn society had already surfaced. At first, just a minor event when Alleg's son recounted that an Algerian chum told him: 'I spit at Europeans, I spit at Jews, I spit at Communists.' Alleg himself had never experienced such prejudice from Algerians. But that year Algerian nationality became legally defined in terms of national origin and religion. Europeans and Jews were not considered Algerian and had to apply individually for citizenship. Some did; others refused.[23]

In September 1963 Ben Bella was elected president, the sole candidate to run. He was now head of state, head of government and head of the FLN. Of the six historic chiefs who had survived the war, three were in exile, one banished to the Sahara and another, Aït Ahmed, organising opposition in Kabylia. Ben Bella's supporters depended on him for their political careers, but like Ben Bella himself they lacked substantial constituencies.[24] Ben Bella turned to the worker-led *autogestion* movement, a largely spontaneous reaction to the European exodus. Encouraged by the UGTA, farm workers on large estates abandoned by their European owners organised themselves collectively to harvest and market crops, while industrial workers ran abandoned factories – economic self-determination in practice. Ben Bella championed *autogestion* as a means to promote economic development through self-management, holding congresses of agricultural and industrial workers and, in autumn 1963, nationalising French-owned farms. It won him popularity in rural areas, but a black market in abandoned farms, shops and enterprises sprung up and operated alongside the state-supported *autogestion* movement.[25]

From 16 to 21 April 1964 the FLN held its first congress since independence – not until he was assured of his own power would Ben Bella convene a congress. Ben Bella's men dominated the preparations and controlled the rules and agenda; the event was boycotted by most of the historic chiefs, although certain *wilaya* leaders attended. The left-wing congress programme, known as the Algiers Charter, maintained that socialism was consistent with the society's Arabic and Islamic tradition. But this was an economic vision of socialism as large-scale economic development. Alongside the development of heavy industry and the nationalisation of the financial sector, it supported *autogestion*

CONCLUSION

as the basis for cooperative agricultural production.

Since independence the FLN's ranks had swelled to more than 150,000, representing a broad social and economic cross-section. The charter called for a purge of the 'non-revolutionary' elements to ensure that the social revolution would move forward. Whatever the attempts to contain dissent, the congress was marked by class, clan and regional divisions. The British Embassy speculated that Moscow had urged Algerian communists to be less confrontational in order to regain Ben Bella's favour. But if the PCA had tried this tactic, it clearly had not succeeded. *Alger républicain*'s Benzine was an official observer. The congress proclaimed the newspaper as the FLN's official organ. Algerian communists lost their last public voice.[26]

Yet Algeria was courted by rival communist powers even as its own communists were pushed further underground. Notwithstanding the FLN's political intolerance, Algiers' many international festivals and conferences made for a lively political and cultural scene, thought South African iconoclast Patrick Duncan.[27] He had arrived in March to represent the Pan Africanist Congress – a South African rival to the ANC. The army was busy with reconstruction, protecting the environment and fighting soil erosion through collective tree planting. This impressed Duncan, as did *autogestion* – despite his anti-socialism. So committed was he to the new regime that he refused Amnesty International's August 1964 request to investigate political arrests, 'arguing that strict control was an inevitable consequence of the revolution'.[28] Nonetheless, he was dismayed by police violence and by religious puritanism regarding women. On 8 March 1965 tens of thousands of women marched through Algiers celebrating international women's day. Some days later their leaders were summoned by the local police commissioner, who denounced their demonstration and demands as 'indecent'.[29]

With public political activity impossible, the PCA functioned solely in underground political space. Certain communists pointed to Cuba's experience, arguing that the Algiers Charter's socialist orientation allowed possibilities for influencing the FLN from within. The PCA's political bureau discussed the possibility of dissolving the party and asking its members to join the FLN as individuals. Alleg, for one, argued vigorously against this. In the Cuban case the victorious 26 July guerrillas, under the shadow of US imperialism and concerned to strengthen ties with the USSR, chose to merge with the socialists; in the Algerian case, the victorious FLN banned the communists. Alleg convinced the majority; the PCA did not dissolve. Many communists were, in fact, refused membership in the FLN and progressively ostracised from leadership posts in trade unions and other popular groups.

Indeed, although *Alger républicain* was now an FLN organ, its directors were denied FLN membership. The FLN decided that the far more successful *Alger républicain* was to merge with *Le Peuple* to form *El Moudjahid*, scheduled to appear on the third anniversary of independence. But on the night of 18–19 June 1965, Boumediène seized power and imprisoned Ben Bella. Most of his political bureau cast their lot with Boumediène. A new government was formed on 10 July.[30]

Civil society seemed apathetic, exhausted by war, alienated by the FLN's factional battles. Communists and FLN leftists were rounded up, imprisoned and tortured. They formed the Organisation de la résistance populaire (Organisation of Popular Resistance), which was smashed by September. The following January they launched the Parti d'avant-garde socialiste (Socialist Vanguard Party).[31] The FLN, born to unite the Algerian people through war, had now come full circle. The absolute unity promulgated during the war as necessary for victory became a model for the new Algeria. The army, formed to wage a merciless war premised on this unity, now controlled the party. Force became the arbiter of all matters political – as it had under the militarised French state. The post-colonial state controlled all public political space. If civil society could not contest this, neither could the tiny communist movement. Its history was marginalised and forgotten, but not erased. Self-consciously intellectual, the PCA left many traces – of its work in trade unions and other popular organisations, its promotion of a free press, its campaigns against repression and its prison writings. All of these indicate its extraordinary efforts to imagine a pluralist, democratic and socialist Algeria – one based on dense networks of civil society organisations – that would allow people to talk and ideas to flourish.

Notes

1 Ruedy, *Modern Algeria*, pp. 185, 195, 197, 214–15; Launay, *Paysans*, pp. 396–8, 402; MacMaster, *Burning*, pp. 369–70; Byrne, 'Our Own Special Brand', 434–5; Planche to author, 4 July 2013.
2 Ruedy, *Modern Algeria*, p. 193; Quandt, *Revolution*, pp. 168–71; First, *Barrel*, pp. 92, 216–17; Harbi, *Vie*, pp. 356–63.
3 « otages consentants ... totalitarisme colonial », Harbi, *Vie*, p. 370; Launay, *Paysans*, pp. 376–7.
4 'The Algerian Communists and the Single Party', *African Communist*, 2, 3 (April 1963), 29–39, p. 35; Alleg, *Mémoire*, pp. 364–5; Djabi, *Kaïdi Lakhdar*, p. 301; Sivan, *Communisme*, p. 242; Sivan, p. 239, estimates that the PCA had about one hundred members at independence, but, as Chapter 7 indicates, Sivan probably underestimated party membership.
5 « Dans le monde socialiste, en dépit d'erreurs parfois dramatiques ... on construit une société nouvelle, sans capitalisme, sans exploitation de l'homme par l'homme », Benzine, *Lambèse*, p. 35; TNA: PRO FO 371/173132, Report from British Embassy, Algiers, 12 March 1963; Byrne, Our Own Special Brand', pp. 427–8, 436, 441.

CONCLUSION

6 Khalfa, Alleg and Benzine, *Aventure*, pp. 203, 206–7, 213, 220–1; Alleg, *Mémoire*, p. 335; Djabi, *Lakhdar*, p. 299; Sportisse, *Camp*, p. 250; « Pourquoi l'ALN prend-elle contact avec l'opinion publique en dehors du GPRA? », *Oran Républicain* (28 April 1962), p. 1.
7 Khalfa, Alleg and Benzine, *Aventure*, pp. 206–7, 210, 213, 220–2; p. 196 shows *Alger républicain*'s censored front pages of 17–18 July, 23 August, 30 August 1962; interviews with Abdelmoumène and William Sportisse.
8 Khalfa, Alleg and Benzine, *Aventure*, p. 233; Gleijeses, 'Cuba's First Venture', p. 163.
9 Stora, *Gangrène*, pp. 193, 200–2, 206–8, 324; Lledo, *Algérie: Histoires à ne pas dire* (film); 'Des chefs FLN tombent dans une embuscade MNA', and 'Opération « terre brûlée » durant le week-end à Oran', *Oran républicain* (24–25 June 1962), pp. 1, 3; 'Incendie terrifiant dans le port d'Oran', *Oran républicain* (27 June 1962), p. 1; 'Des explosions nombreuses ont encore retenti hier à Oran', *Oran républicain* (28 June 1962), p. 4; *Oran Républicain* (29 June 1962); 'Mot d'ordre impérieux pour Oran: Sauver la réconciliation', *Oran Républicain* (6–9 July 1962), p. 1; 'Je ne désespère pas de la possibilité d'une solution pacifique', *Oran Républicain* (13 July 1962), p. 1; Ruedy, *Modern Algeria*, p. 193; Khalfa, Alleg and Benzine, *Aventure*, pp. 201, 229; Evans, *Algeria*, pp. 320, 325–8.
10 Khalfa, Alleg and Benzine, *Aventure*, p. 196 shows *Alger Républican*, 30 August 1962 with that call; Quandt, *Revolution*, p. 171.
11 Horne, *Savage War*, pp. 536–7; Ruedy, *Modern Algeria*, pp. 192–3; Quandt, *Revolution*, p. 171; Lewis, 'Decline', p. 167; Macey, *Fanon*, pp. 497–8; Shepard, *Invention*, p. 125.
12 'Algerian Communists and the Single Party', p. 29; Khalfa, Alleg and Benzine, *Aventure*, p. 235; interview with Abdelmoumène.
13 « Il n'y a pas de place actuellement, en Algérie, pour le parti communiste »; « Le Parti communiste interdit en Algérie », *La Dépêche d'Algérie*, pp. 1, 8; TNA: PRO FO 371/165650, Algiers to Foreign Office, 30 November, 1 December 1962, A. V. Hayday to J. W. R. Shakespeare, Foreign Office, 12 December 1962, 'Algeria Bans Communist Party', December 1962; 'Against the Ban on the Algerian Communist Party', *African Communist*, 2:3 (April–June 1963), 27–9, p. 28; Alleg, *Mémoire*, pp. 363, 367–9; Sportisse, *Camp*, p. 242.
14 Report from British Embassy, 12 March 1963, pp. 1–2; Sportisse, *Camp*, pp. 244–5.
15 'Algerian Communists and the Single Party', pp. 34–5, 30; Djabi, *Lakhdar*, p. 301; Sportisse, *Camp*, pp. 245–6, 248.
16 'Algerian Communists and the Single Party', pp. 31–3.
17 Djabi, *Lakhdar*, pp. 252–3; PCF 261J 7/ box 3, A. Ali-Yahia, *Déclaration de l'U.G.T.A.* (Tunis, 17 March 1962).
18 « autonomie organique et de gestion », TNA: PRO FO 371/173182, First National Congress of the Union générale des travailleurs algériens, 17–20 January 1963, Report of W. R. Thomson, Labour Attaché, British Embassy, Algiers; Ruedy, *Modern Algeria*, p. 198.
19 « Quand il y aura dans ce congrès 80% de fellahs, l'U.G.T.A. aura accompli sa mission ... Je veux voir ici 80% de turbans »; « M. Ben Bella fait appel », *Dépêche d'Algérie* (18 January 1963), p. 1. The 17 January issue reported close to 500 delegates.
20 A German journalist reportedly compared the events to the Nazi Party's 1933 takeover of German trade unions. TNA: PRO FO 371/173182, First National Congress; Algiers to Foreign Office, 24 January 1963; Djabi, *Lakhdar*, pp. 298–9; Sportisse, *Camp*, pp. 248–9.
21 TNA: PRO FO 371/173182, British Embassy Algiers, 25 January 1963; Letter to Foreign Office, 28 January 1963, p. 2, First National Congress; Ruedy, *Modern Algeria*, p. 198.
22 « L'Union nationale des femmes algériennes affirme sa volonté de participer à la consolidation de l'Algérie indépendante et à la construction d'un état socialiste », *Dépêche d'Algérie*, 22 January 1963, p. 8; TNA: PRO FO 371/173182, British Embassy Algiers, 25 January 1963; MacMaster, *Burning*, pp. 380–1, 386–7.
23 Alleg, *Mémoire*, p. 363; Sivan, *Communisme*, pp. 255–6; Sportisse, *Camp*, pp. 253–9; MacMaster, *Burning*, p. 373.

24 Ruedy, *Modern Algeria*, pp. 199–202.
25 Ruedy, *Modern Algeria*, pp. 198–9, 202–4; First, *Barrel*, pp. 447–8; Alleg, *Mémoire*, p. 366.
26 Ruedy, *Modern Algeria*, pp. 203–4; Byrne, 'Our Own Special Brand', pp. 433–5; Alleg, *Mémoire*, pp. 375–6, 378–9; Report from British Embassy, Algiers, 12 March 1963.
27 Driver, *Duncan*, pp. 243–4; *Révolution Université*, March 1965, in Duncan Papers, CSAS DU 9.6; Byrne, 'Our Own Special Brand', pp. 440–1.
28 Driver, *Duncan*, pp. 245–6.
29 Driver, *Duncan*, pp. 245–6, 262, 241; Alleg, *Mémoire*, pp. 372–3.
30 Alleg, *Mémoire*, pp. 376–7, 379–81; Djabi, *Lakhdar*, pp. 302–4; Ruedy, *Modern Algeria*, p. 207.
31 Interviews with Abdelmoumène and with Riad Benchikh-el-Fougoun, Constantine, 23 September 2011; Djabi, *Lakhdar*, pp. 314–15, 318; cf. Sportisse, *Camp*, pp. 263–6.

BIBLIOGRAPHY

Archives and libraries

Archives Nationales d'Outre-Mer, Aix-en-Provence
Bibliothèque François Mitterand, Paris
Bibliothèque Marxiste, Paris
British Library and British Newspaper Library, London
Centre des Archives Contemporaines, Fontainebleau
Ciné-archives, Fonds audiovisuel du PCF, Archives françaises du film, Forum des Images, Archives départementales de Seine-Saint-Denis, Bobigny
Comintern Archives, Russian State Archive of Socio-Political History, Moscow
Duncan Papers, Southern African Archives, Borthwick Institute for Archives, University of York
Foreign Office Papers, The National Archives, London
Institut d'Histoire Sociale, Nanterre
League against Imperialism Archives, International Institute of Social History, Amsterdam
Nelson Mandela Centre of Memory, Johannesburg
Parti Communiste Français Archives, Archives départementales de la Seine-Saint-Denis, Bobigny
Ruth First Papers, Institute of Commonwealth Studies, London

Interviews by author

Abdelmoumène, Noureddine (Algiers, 25 September 2011)
Alleg, Henri (Paliseau, 11 May 2001, 11, 23 June 2010)
Bakelli, A. (Ghardaïa, 7 September 2011)
Bekaddour, Zoulikha (Algiers, 26 September 2011)
Bellalou, Hadj Aissa (Ghardaïa, 5 September 2011)
Benchikh-el-Fougoun, Riad (Constantine, 23 September 2011)
Boudjenah, Fafa (Ghardaïa, 6 September 2011)
Boudjenah, Mohamed, with Slimane Tounsi (Ghardaïa, 3 September 2011)
Guerroudj, Abdelkader (Algiers, 26, 28 September 2011)
Hadjerès, Sadek (Paris, 24 March 2011)
Ighilahriz, Louisette (Algiers, 20 September 2011)
Lledo, Jean-Pierre (Cambridge, England, 29 November 2008; Paris, 21 June 2010)
Loup, Elyette (Algiers, 29 September 2011)
Mella, Mustafa (Ghardaïa 5, 6 September 2011)
Mostefaï, Dr Chawki (El Mouradja, Algiers, 19 September 2011)
Ouadi, Boussad (discussion, Algiers, 24 September 2011)
Ouzegane, Fattouma (Algiers, 24 September 2011)
Soufi, Fouad, and Boussad Ouadi (discussion, Algiers, 25 September 2011)

Sportisse, Gilberte Chemouilli (Paris, 24 June 2012)
Sportisse, William (Paris, 18 June 2001, 24 June 2012)
Todd, Olivier (discussion, Paris, 25 May 2001)

Interviews by others

First, Ruth (interview with Henri Alleg, 11 March 1967)
Naceur, Mohammed ben Saleh (questions posed to Sliman Boudjenah by the intermediary of Ahmed Fersouce, Ghardaïa, 24 September 1973)

Newspapers consulted

Alger républicain
Alger socialiste
Al-Lioua-Al-Ahmar (1926)
Al-Raïat-Al-hamra (1927)
Aurore
Bulletin (ed. Fédération de France du Parti communiste algérien) (1959)
La Caserne/El Kazirna (1923–24)
Combat social (1927)
Demain
Dépêche d'Algérie
Dépêche de Constantine
Dépêche quotidienne d'Algérie
Echo d'Alger
Figaro
L'Humanité
L'Humanité nouvelle
Liberté
Liberté (clandestine, 1955–62)
Lutte sociale
Le Monde
El Moudjahid
Oran républicain
Le Parisien
Le Populaire
Résistance algérienne
Le Tell
El Watan.com

Official papers

Gouvernement général de l'Algérie, Direction générale des finances, Service de statistique générale, *Annuaire statistique de l'Algérie*, new series, vol. 1, 1939–49 (Algiers, 1949).
Journal officiel de l'Algérie: Lois et décrets (23, 27 September 1955).

BIBLIOGRAPHY

Journal officiel de la République française, Débats parlementaires, Chambre de Députés: Réponses des ministres aux questions écrites (May 1934).
Journal officiel de la République française, Débats parlementaires, Assemblée nationale (13 March 1956).

PCA documents

Pour la formation d'un front de la liberté en Algérie contre la pénétration allemande en Afrique du nord, n.d.
Pour le salut du peuple d'Algérie: Manifeste adopté par le Congrès du Parti communiste d'Algérie, 1936 (Algiers: Bureau d'Editions, 1936).
Le Parti communiste au service des populations d'Algérie, Report by Amar Ouzegane to the PCA central conference, 23 September 1944 (Algiers: Liberté, 23 September 1944).
Amnistie aux détenus politiques musulmans, Speeches by communist deputies Mohamed Chouadria, Camille Larribère and Pierre Fayet to the Constituent National Assembly (1946).
La voie à suivre: Appel du comité central du Parti communiste algérien (Algiers, 4 July 1954).
Pour une nation algérienne libre, souveraine et heureuse (March 1957).
Lettre aux Européens d'Algérie (7 October 1957).
Déclaration des Partis communistes algérien, marocain et tunisien (n.d., [November 1957]).
'Essai sur la nation algérienne', *Réalités algériennes et Marxisme* 2 (July 1958) and *Cahiers du communisme* (supplement), 8 (August 1958).
Plus que jamais tous unis derrière le G.P.R.A. (1 October 1959).
Le Parti communiste algérien dans la guerre pour l'indépendance nationale (Algiers, Imprimerie spéciale du PCA, December 1959).
Notre Peuple vaincra, 18 November 1960, PDF available at http://goo.gl/pUqDVc (accessed 30 April 2011).
Message du Parti communiste algérien au Parti communiste français (12 December 1960).
Serkadji, quartier des femmes (Algiers: Al Houriyya, 1961) http://goo.gl/ITtwV0 (accessed 23 December 2012).
Un impératif décisif: Gagner davantage encore le soutien des masses françaises (FFPCA, 28 June 1961).
'The talks on Algeria', Statement by the Algerian Communist Party (21 May 1961), *African Communist*, 6 (July 1961).
5 juillet: Journée nationale de lutte contre le partage (1 July 1961).
En avant pour l'indépendance, Appeal to Algerian youth (Algiers, 28 September 1961).
Pour éclairer et déblayer le chemin de la paix et de l'indépendance (Algiers: 7 November 1961).
Lettres adressées au G.P.R.A. au cours de la guerre pour l'indépendance au nom du comité central du Parti communiste algérien (Algiers: Al Houriya, 1962) http://goo.gl/2EcyPX (accessed 24 June 2011).
Programme du Parti communiste algérien pour l'indépendance totale (Algiers:

El Houriyya, 18 April 1962).
'For a Free Algerian Republic: The 25th Anniversary of the Algerian Communist Party' [1961], *African Communist* (April 1962), 26–40.
'The Algerian Communists and the Single Party', *African Communist*, 2:3 (April–June 1963), 29–39.
'Algeria: Features of the Armed Struggle', in William J. Pomeroy (ed.), *Guerrilla Warfare and Marxism* (London: Lawrence and Wishart, 1969), pp. 249–54.

PCF documents

Le Congrès de Tours: 18ᵉ Congrès national du Parti socialiste [1920], ed. Jean Charles, Jacques Girault, Jean-Louis Robert, Danielle Tartakowsky and Claude Willard (Paris: Editions Sociales, 1980).
Algérie! La France te parle! Speech by Marcel Gitton to PCA congress, October 1936 (Algiers: Franco-Italienne, [1936]).
Le Peuple algérien uni autour de la France: Speech by Maurice Thorez, 11 February 1939, Algiers, *La Brochure populaire*, no. 7 (Paris: April 1939).
Déclaration du bureau politique du Parti communiste français après la dissolution du Parti communiste algérien (Paris: 13 September 1955).
Jacques Duclos, 'La France et l'Algérie', in Maurice Thorez, Jacques Duclos and François Billoux, *La France et l'Afrique du Nord* (Paris: Editions de France Nouvelle, n.d. [1955]), pp. 3–32.
Léon Feix, *Un Impérieux Devoir national! Imposer la paix en Algérie*, Report to information meeting of Parisian communists, 17 January 1957 (Paris: 1957).
Le Drame algérien: Sept ans de malheurs (Paris: PCF, December 1961).

Secondary sources

Ageron, Charles-Robert, *Modern Algeria: A History from 1830 to the Present* (London: Hurst, 1991).
Ageron, Charles-Robert, 'Le Parti communiste algérien de 1939 à 1943', *Vingtième Siècle* (October–December 1986), 39–50.
Ageron, Charles-Robert, 'Emigration et politique: L'Etoile nord-africaine et le Parti du peuple algérien', in Messali Hadj, *Les Mémoires de Messali Hadj* (Paris: Jean-Claude Lattès, 1982), pp. 273–97.
Ageron, Charles-Robert, *Histoire de l'Algérie contemporaine*, vol. 2 (Paris: Presses Universitaires de France, 1979).
Ageron, Charles-Robert, 'Une émeute anti-juive à Constantine: (août 1934)', *Revue de l'Occident musulman et de la Méditerranée*, 13:14 (1973), 23–40.
Ageron, Charles-Robert, 'Les Communistes français devant la question algérienne de 1921 à 1924', *Mouvement social* (January–March 1972), 7–37.
Ageron, Charles-Robert, 'Jaurès et les socialistes français devant la question algérienne (de 1895 à 1914), *Mouvement social*, 42 (January–March 1963), 3–27.
Aissaoui, Rabah, 'From Colonial Dispossession to Exile: Algerian Migration to

France from the Early Twentieth Century to the Eve of the Second World War', *Socialist History*, 39 (2011), 1–23.
Aissaoui, Rabah, 'Algerian Nationalists in the French Political Arena and Beyond: The *Etoile nord-africaine* and the *Parti du peuple algérien* in Interwar France, *Journal of North African Studies*, 15:1 (March 2010), 1–12.
Alexander, Neville, *An Ordinary Country: Issues in the Transition from Apartheid to Democracy in South Africa* (Pietermaritzburg: University of Natal, 2002).
Alleg, Henri, *Mémoire algérienne: Souvenirs de luttes et d'espérances* (Paris: Stock, 2005).
Alleg, Henri, 'Le torrent souterrain', in Henri Alleg (ed.) *La Guerre d'Algérie*, vol. 1, (Paris: Editions Messidor, 1981), pp. 13–283.
Alleg, Henri, *Prisonniers de guerre* (Paris: Minuit, 1961).
Alleg, Henri, *La Question* (Paris: Minuit, 1958).
Alleg, Henri (ed.), *La Guerre d'Algérie*, 3 vols (Paris: Editions Messidor, 1981).
Allouache, Merzak, *Bab el-Oued* (Boulder, CO: Lynne Rienner, 1998).
Ameyar, Hafida, *La Moudjahida Annie Fiorio-Steiner: Une vie pour l'Algérie* (Algiers: Association les amis de Abdelhamid Benzine, 2011).
Amrane-Minne, Danièle Djamila, 'Women at War: The Representation of Women in the Battle of Algiers', *Interventions*, 9:3 (2007), 340–9.
Amrane-Minne, Danièle Djamila, *Des femmes dans la guerre d'Algérie* (n.p.: Edik, n.d.).
Anderson, Benedict, *Imagined Communities: Reflections on the Origin and Spread of Nationalism* (London: Verso, 1983).
Ayache, Albert 'Essai sur la vie syndicale en Algérie, l'année du centenaire (1930)', *Mouvement social*, 78 (January–March, 1972), 95–114.
Barea, Arturo, *The Track* (London: Flamingo, n.d.).
Ben Badis, Abdelhamid, *Textes choisis* (Editions ANEP, 2006).
Benachour-Tebbouche, Nedjma, *Constantine et ses romanciers: Essai* (Constantine: Media-Plus, 2008).
Bendiab, Abderrahim Taleb, 'La pénétration des idées et l'implantation communiste en Algérie dans les années 1920', in René Gallissot (ed.), *Mouvement ouvrier, communisme et nationalisme dans le monde arabe*, Cahiers du 'Mouvement social' 3 (Paris: Editions ouvrières, 1978), pp. 127–46.
Benhassine, Mohamed Lakhdar, 'Le Séjour de Karl Marx à Alger ... du 20 février au 2 mai 1882', in *Alger: Lumières sur la ville, Actes du colloque* (Algiers, 4–6 May 2002), pp. 713–29.
Bennoune, Mahfoud, 'The Introduction of Nationalism into Rural Algeria: 1919–1954', *Maghreb Review*, 2:3 (1977), 1–12.
Bennoune, Mahfoud, 'Algerian Peasants and National Politics', *MERIP Reports*, 48 (June 1976), 3–24.
Bennoune, Mahfoud, 'Socioeconomic Changes in Rural Algeria 1830–1954: A Diachronic Analysis of a Peasantry under Colonialism', *Peasant Studies Newsletter*, 11:2 (1973), 11–18.
Benôt, Yves, *Massacres coloniaux, 1944–1950: La IVe République et la mise au pas des colonies françaises* (Paris: La Découverte, 1994).
Benzine, Abdelhamid, *Lambèse* (n.p.: Dar el Idjtihad, 1989).

Benzine, Abdelhamid, *Le Camp* (Paris: Editions Sociales, 1962).
Betts, Raymond F., *France and Decolonisation, 1900–1960* (Basingstoke and London: Macmillan, 1991).
Boittin, Jennifer Anne, *Colonial Metropolis: The Urban Grounds of Anti-Imperialism and Feminism in Interwar Paris* (Lincoln, NE: University of Nebraska, 2010).
Bouayed, Mahmoud, *Histoire par la bande* (Algiers: SNED, 1974).
Boukort, Benali, *Le Souffle du Dahra* (Alger: Enterprise nationale du livre, 1986).
Bourderon, Roger, 'Un journal clandestin pour les appelés: « La voix du soldat »: Entretien avec Alfred Gerson, Lucien Hanoun, André Moine', *Cahiers d'histoire de l'Institut de recherches marxistes*, 8 (1982), 89–111.
Bourgeois, Guillaume, 'French Communism and the Communist International', in Tim Rees and Andrew Thorpe (eds), *International Communism and the Communist International* (Manchester and New York: Manchester University, 1998), pp. 95–102.
Bourouiba, Boualem, *Les Syndicalistes algériens: Leur combat de l'éveil à la libération, 1936–1962* (Paris: Harmattan, 1998; Algiers: ENAG/DAHLAB, 2001).
Brower, Benjamin Claude, *A Desert Named Peace: The Violence of France's Empire in the Algerian Sahara, 1844–1902* (New York: Columbia, 2009).
Bunting, Brian (ed.), *South African Communists Speak, 1915–1980* (London: Inkululeko, 1981).
Buono, Christian, 'J'ai assisté à la naissance de « La Question » de Henri Alleg', *Realités algériennes et Marxisme*, 7 (16 September 1961), 42–5.
Busky, Donald F., *Communism in History and Theory: Asia, Africa, and the Americas*, (Westport, CT, and London: Praeger, 2002).
Byrne, Jeffrey James, 'Our Own Special Brand of Socialism: Algeria and the Contest of Modernity in the 1960s', *Diplomatic History*, 33:3 (June 2009), 427–47.
Camus, Albert, *Notebooks, 1951–1959* (Chicago, IL: Ivan R. Dee, 2008).
Camus, Albert, *Œuvres complètes, III, 1949–1956* (Paris: Gallimard, 2008).
Camus, Albert, 'Reflections on the Guillotine', in Albert Camus, *The Plague, The Fall, Exile and the Kingdom, and Selected Essays* (New York, etc: Alfred A. Knopf, 2004), pp. 607–56.
Camus, Albert, *The First Man* (London: Penguin, 1996).
Camus, Albert, 'The New Mediterranean Culture', in Philip Thody (ed.), *Albert Camus, Lyrical and Critical Essays* (New York: Alfred A Knopf, 1969).
Camus, Albert, *Resistance, Rebellion, and Death* (New York: Modern Library, 1960).
Camus, Albert, 'Appeal for a Civilian Truce', in Albert Camus, *Resistance, Rebellion, and Death* (New York: Modern Library, 1960), pp. 97–106.
Camus, Albert, 'Letter to an Algerian Militant' [1 October 1955], in Albert Camus, *Resistance, Rebellion, and Death* (New York: Modern Library, 1960), pp. 93–7.
Camus, Albert, *Actuelles, III: Chroniques algériennes, 1939–1958* (Paris: Gallimard, 1958).

BIBLIOGRAPHY

Camus, Albert, 'Misère de la Kabylie', in *Actuelles, III: Chroniques algériennes, 1939–1958* (Paris: Gallimard, 1958), pp. 31–90.
Cantier, Jacques, *L'Algérie sous le régime de Vichy* (Paris: Odile Jacob, 2002).
Cantier, Jacques, '8 Novembre 1942: Des résistants français lors du débarquement allié – Entretien avec José Aboulker, compagnon de la Libération', in Jean-Jacques Jordi and Guy Pervillé (eds), *Alger 1940–1962: Une ville en guerres* (Paris: Autrement, 1999), pp. 70–5.
Carlier, Omar, *Entre nation et Jihad: Histoire sociale des radicalismes algériens* (Paris: Presses de la Fondation nationale des sciences politiques, 1995).
Carr, E. H. *The Twilight of Comintern, 1930–1935* (London and Basingstoke: Macmillan, 1982).
Carroll, David, 'Foreword', in Jacqueline Lévi-Valensi (ed.), *Camus at Combat: Writing 1944–1947* (Princeton, NJ, and Oxford: Princeton University, 2006), pp. vii–xxvi.
Carter, Ian, 'Positive and Negative Liberty', in Edward N. Zalta (ed.), *The Stanford Encyclopedia of Philosophy* (Fall 2008 edition), http://goo.gl/cDsTMX (accessed 14 August 2011).
Castro, Fidel, with Ignacio Ramonet, *My Life*, trans. by Andrew Hurley (London: Allen Lane, 2007).
Chaintron, Jean, *Le Vent soufflait devant ma porte*, ed. Patrick Rotman (Paris: Editions du Seuil, 1993).
Cherki, Alice, *Frantz Fanon: Portrait* (Paris: Seuil, 2000).
Choukroun, Jacques, 'L'Internationale Communiste, le P. C. français et l'Algérie (1920–1925)', *Cahiers d'histoire de l'Institut Maurice Thorez*, 25:26 (1978), 133–59.
Clancy-Smith, Julia A., *Rebel and Saint: Muslim Notables, Populist Protests, Colonial Encounters (Algeria and Tunisia, 1800–1904)* (Berkeley, Los Angeles, CA, and London: University of California, 1994).
Claudin, Fernando, *The Communist Movement: From Comintern to Cominform*, Part One (New York and London: Monthly Review, 1975).
Cole, Joshua, 'Anti-Semitism and the Colonial Situation in Interwar Algeria: The Anti-Jewish Riots in Constantine, August 1934', in Martin Thomas (ed.), *The French Colonial Mind: Violence, Military Encounters and Colonialism*, vol. 2 (Lincoln, NE, and London: University of Nebraska, 2011), pp. 77–111.
Collot, Claude, and Jean-Robert Henry (eds), *Le Mouvement national algerién: Textes, 1912–1954* (Paris: L'Harmattan).
Colonna, Fanny, 'The Nation's "Unknowing Other": Three Intellectuals and the Culture(s) of Being Algerian, or the Impossibility of Subaltern Studies in Algeria', *Journal of North African Studies*, 8:1 (2003), 155–70.
Connelly, Matthew, *A Diplomatic Revolution: Algeria's Fight for Independence and the Origins of the Post-Cold War Era* (Oxford and New York: Oxford, 2002).
Courrière, Yves, *La Guerre d'Algérie*, 4 vols. (Paris: Fayard, 1968–71).
Courrière, Yves, *La Guerre d'Algérie: Les Feux du désespoir*, vol. 4 (Paris: Fayard, 1971).
Courrière, Yves, *La Guerre d'Algérie: Le Temps des léopards*, vol. 2 (Paris:

BIBLIOGRAPHY

Fayard, 1969).
Crémieux, R. A., *A.B.C. du syndicalisme* (Algiers: Imprimerie du prolétariat, 1924).
Crenshaw, Martha (ed.), *Terrorism in Context* (University Park, PA: Pennsylvania State University, 1995).
Crenshaw, Martha, 'The Effectiveness of Terrorism in the Algerian War', in Martha Crenshaw (ed.), *Terrorism in Context* (University Park, PA: Pennsylvania State University, 1995), pp. 473–513.
Daoud, Zakya, *Abdelkrim: Une épopée d'or et de sang* (Paris: Séguier, 1999).
Davidson, Basil, *Modern Africa: A Social and Political History*, 2nd edn (London and New York: Longman, 1989).
De Beauvoir, Simone, and Gisèle Halimi (eds), *Djamila Boupacha* (Paris: Gallimard, 1962).
De Bonis, Jacques, 'A la recherche du dernier quart d'heure', in Henri Alleg (ed.) *La Guerre d'Algérie*, vol. 2 (Paris: Editions Messidor, 1981), pp. 299–591.
De Gaulle, Charles, 'Que vienne la paix des braves', Vidéo Ina, http://goo.gl/c48sVv (accessed 17 February 2010)
Derrick, Jonathan, *Africa's 'Agitators': Militant Anti-Colonialism in Africa and the West, 1918–1939* (New York: Columbia University, 2008).
Dib, Mohammed, *La Grande Maison* (Paris: Editions du Seuil, 1952, 1996).
Djabi, Nasser, *Kaïdi Lakhdar: Une histoire du syndicalisme algérien* (n.p.: Chihab, 2005).
Djerbal, Daho, 'Les effets des manifestations de Décembre 1960 sur les maquis algériens', in *11 décembre 1960: Le Diên Biên Phú politique de la guerre d'Algérie* (Algiers: NAQD, 2010), pp. 63–92.
Donnat, Gaston, *Afin que nul n'oublie: L'Itinéraire d'un anti-colonialiste, Algérie–Cameroun–Afrique* (Paris: Harmattan, n.d.).
Dore-Audibert, Andrée, *Des Françaises d'Algérie dans la guerre de libération* (Paris: Karthala, 1995).
Douzon, Henri J., 'Les Occasions perdues', in Henri Alleg (ed.) *La Guerre d'Algérie*, vol. 1, (Paris: Editions Messidor, 1981), pp. 284–595.
Drew, Allison, 'Communism in Africa', in Stephen A. Smith (ed.), *Oxford Handbook of the History of Communism* (Oxford: Oxford University Press, 2013), pp. 285–302.
Drew, Allison, 'Communists, State and Civil Society in Colonial Algeria, 1945–1954, *Orient-Institut Studies* 1 (2012) – Rethinking Totalitarianism and its Arab Readings, special issue edited by Manfred Sing, http://goo.gl/8IxCNJ.
Drew, Allison, 'An Interview with Henri Alleg', *Socialist History*, 39 (2011), 42–59.
Drew, Allison, 'Urban Activists and Rural Struggles: Communists in Algeria and South Africa, 1920s–1930s,' *African Studies*, 66:2–3 (2007), 295–319.
Drew, Allison, 'Bolshevizing Communist Parties – the Algerian and South African Experiences', *International Review of Social History*, 48 (2003), 167–202.
Drew, Allison, *Discordant Comrades: Identities and Loyalties on the South African Left* (Aldershot: Ashgate, 2000; Pretoria: Unisa, 2002).

BIBLIOGRAPHY

Drew, Allison (ed.), Special issue: 'Wretched of the Earth', *Socialist History*, 39 (2011).
Drew, Allison (ed.), Special issue: 'The Abyssinia Crisis – Seventy Years On', *Socialist History*, 28 (2005).
Driver, C. J., *Patrick Duncan: South African and Pan-African* [1980] (Cape Town: David Philip, and Oxford: James Currey, 2000).
Durand, Pierre, *Cette mystérieuse section coloniale: Le PCF et les colonies (1920–1962)* (Paris: Messidor, 1986).
Einaudi, Jean-Luc, *Un rêve algérien: Histoire de Lisette Vincent, une femme d'Algérie* (Paris: Presses Universitaires de France, 2001).
Einaudi, Jean-Luc, *Un Algérien: Maurice Laban* (Paris: Cherche midi, 1999).
Einaudi, Jean-Luc, *La Ferme améziane: Enquête sur un centre de torture pendant la guerre d'Algérie* (Constantine: Media-Plus, 1993, and Paris: Harmattan, 1991).
Einaudi, Jean-Luc, *Pour l'exemple: L'Affaire Fernand, enquête* (Paris: Harmattan, 1986).
El Maghreb, 'Le Centenaire de l'occupation de l'Algérie', *Cahiers du Bolchévisme*, 4 (April 1930), pp. 363–9.
Evans, Martin, *Algeria: France's Undeclared War* (Oxford: Oxford University, 2012).
Evans, Martin, *The Memory of Resistance: French Opposition to the Algerian War (1954–1962)* (Oxford and New York: Berg, 1997).
Evans, Martin and John Phillips, *Algeria: Anger of the Dispossessed* (New Haven, CT, and London: Yale, 2007).
Fanon, Frantz, *The Wretched of the Earth* (New York: Grove, 1968).
Fanon, Frantz, *A Dying Colonialism* (New York: Grove, 1967).
Feraoun, Mouloud, *Journal, 1955–1962: Reflections on the French–Algerian War* [1962] (Lincoln, NE, and London: University of Nebraska, 2000).
Ferrat, André, 'Que signifient les évènements de Constantine?', *Cahiers du Bolchévisme*, 16 (15 August 1934), 940–7.
First, Ruth, *The Barrel of a Gun: Political Power in Africa and the Coup d'Etat* (Harmondsworth: Penguin, 1970).
Flanner, Janet (Genêt), *Paris Journal, 1944–1965*, ed. William Shawn (New York: Atheneum, 1965).
Fletcher, Yaël Simpson, 'The Politics of Solidarity: Radical French and Algerian Journalists and the 1954 Orléansville Earthquake', in Patricia M. E. Lorcin (ed.), *Algeria and France, 1800–2000: Identity, Memory, Nostalgia* (Syracuse: Syracuse University, 2006), pp. 84–98.
FLN, *Projet de programme pour la réalisation de la révolution démocratique populaire (adopté à l'unanimité par le CNRA à Tripoli en juin 1962*, in *Les Textes fondamentaux de la ré*volution (Editions ANEP, n.d.), pp. 69–134.
Francis, Claude, and Fernande Gontier, *Simone de Beauvoir: A Life … a Love Story* (New York: St Martin's, 1987).
Funès, Nathalie, 'Lodi, le camp des oubliés', *Nouvel Observateur* (18 March 2010), http://goo.gl/nkJqzm (accessed 2 October 2013).
Gallissot, René, *La République française et les indigènes: Algérie colonisée, Algérie algérienne (1870–1962)* (Paris: Editions de l'Atelier/Editions

ouvrières, 2006).
Gallissot, René, 'Marx et l'Algérie', *Mouvement social*, 71 (April–June 1970), 39–63.
Gallissot, René (ed.), *Algérie: Engagements sociaux et question nationale de la colonisation à l'indépendance, de 1830 à 1962 – Dictionnaire biographique du mouvement ouvrier: Maghreb* (Ivry-sur-Seine and Paris: Editions de l'Atelier/Editions ouvrières, 2006).
Gallissot, René (ed.), *Mouvement ouvrier, communisme et nationalisme dans le monde arabe* (Paris: Editions ouvrières, 1978).
Gallissot, René with Gilbert Badia (eds), *Marx, Marxisme et Algérie* (Paris: Union générales d'Editions, 1976).
Geiss, Imanuel, *The Pan-African Movement: A History of Pan-Africanism in America, Europe, and Africa* (New York: Africana, 1974).
Gleijeses, Piero, 'Cuba's First Venture in Africa: Algeria, 1961–1965', *Journal of Latin American Studies*, 28 (1996), 159–95.
Gosnell, Jonathan K., *The Politics of Frenchness in Colonial Algeria, 1930–1954* (Rochester, NY: University of Rochester, 2002).
Grzymala-Busse, Anna M., *Redeeming the Communist Past: The Regeneration of Communist Parties in East Central Europe* (Cambridge: Cambridge University, 2002).
Guerroudj, Jacqueline, *Des douars et des prisons* (n.p.: Bouchene, n.d.).
Guevara, Ernesto Che, 'Lessons of the Cuban Revolution', in William J. Pomeroy (ed.), *Guerrilla Warfare and Marxism* (London: Lawrence and Wishart, 1969), pp. 287–8.
Hadj Ali, Bashir [sic] 'Lessons of the Algerian Struggle,' in William J. Pomery (ed.), *Guerrilla Warfare and Marxism* (London: Lawrence and Wishart, 1969), pp. 254–60.
Hadjerès, Sadek, 'La Pensée de Fanon: Quelques uns de ses impacts dans la sphère socio-politique algérienne', paper presented at colloquium of ACB (9 May 2009), http://goo.gl/7C2I0U (accessed 24 June 2011).
Hadjerès, Sadek, 'Réflexions d'un témoin-acteur communiste', paper presented at forum on 'Quelques conceptions et pratiques de pouvoir en Algérie', Delphi (27–30 October 1995), http://goo.gl/JisYUA (accessed 4 July 2011).
Hadjerès, Sadek, *Essai sur les problèmes de la démocratie dans l'Algérie indépendante* (Algiers: Al Houryya, May 1962), http://goo.gl/U7IOKS (accessed 4 October 2013).
Hamouma, Hocine, *Les Enfants de décembre*, vol. 2 (Reghaia: ENAG, 2007).
Harbi, Mohammed, 'Je pense qu'il faut défendre ce film, mais en mettant en garde contre les possibilités de son utilisation', http://goo.gl/IARhah [accessed 23 November 2008].
Harbi, Mohammed, *Une vie debout: Mémoires politiques*, vol. 1, 1945–1962 (Paris: La Découverte, 2001).
Harbi, Mohammed and Gilbert Meynier (eds), *Le FLN: Documents et histoire, 1954–1962* (n.p.: Fayard, 2004).
Harbi, Mohammed and Benjamin Stora (eds) *La Guerre d'Algérie* (Paris: Pluriel, 2010).

BIBLIOGRAPHY

Hart, B. H. Liddell, *History of the Second World War* (New York: G. P. Putnam's Sons, 1971).
Hartog, François, Pauline Schmitt-Pantel and Alain Schnapp (eds), *Pierre Vidal-Naquet: Un historien dans la cité* (Paris: La Découverte, 2007).
Haudiquet, Pierre, 'L'Incendie', in Henri Alleg (ed.) *La Guerre d'Algérie*, vol. 2, (Paris: Editions Messidor, 1981), pp. 7–297.
Heggoy, Alf Andrew, *Insurgency and Counterinsurgency in Algeria* (Bloomington, IN, and London: Indiana University Press, 1972).
Hirson, Baruch, 'Not Pro-War, and not Anti-War: Just Indifferent. South African Blacks in the Second World War', *Critique*, 20–21 (1987), 39–56.
Hoisington, Jr., William A., *Lyautey and the French Conquest of Morocco* (New York: St Martin's, 1995).
Hopkins, Stephen, 'French Communism, the Comintern and Class Against Class: Interpretations and Rationales', in Matthew Worley (ed.), *In Search of Revolution: International Communist Parties in the Third Period* (London and New York: I.B. Tauris, 2004), pp. 106–28.
Horne, Alistair, *Seven Ages of Paris* (New York: Alfred A. Knopf, 2002).
Horne, Alistair, *A Savage War of Peace: Algeria 1954–1962* (London: Macmillan, 1977).
House, Jim, 'The Displacements of Colonialism: Migration, Re-housing and Nationalism in Algiers, 1945–1962 (unpublished paper, 2012).
Howell, David, *British Workers and the Independent Labour Party, 1886–1906* (Manchester: Manchester University Press, 1983).
Hughes, Edward J., 'La Prélude d'une sorte de fin de l'histoire: Underpinning Assimilation in Camus's *Chroniques algériennes*', *L'Esprit créateur*, 47:1 (2007), 7–18.
Ighilahriz, Louisette, *Algérienne* (Algiers: Casbah, 2006).
Jackson, Julian, *The Fall of France: The Nazi Invasion of 1940* (Oxford: Oxford University Press, 2003).
Joly, Danièle, *The French Communist Party and the Algerian War* (Basingstoke and London: Macmillan, 1991).
Jordi, Jean-Jacques and Guy Pervillé (eds), *Alger 1940–1962: Une ville en guerres* (Paris: Autrement, 1999).
Jordi, Jean-Jacques and Jean-Louis Planche (eds), *Alger, 1860–1939: Le Modèle ambigu du triomphe colonial* (Paris: Autrement, 1999).
Julien, Charles-André, *L'Afrique du Nord en marche: Algérie–Tunisie–Maroc, 1880–1952* (Omnibus, 2002).
Julien, Charles-André, *Histoire de l'Algérie contemporaine*, vol. 1, 3rd edn (Paris: Presses Universitaires de France, 1986).
Julien, Charles-André, H. Carrère d'Encausse and M. Rebérioux, 'Les Communistes et l'Orient en 1921', *Mouvement social*, 82 (January–March 1973), pp. 106–13.
Jurquet, Jacques, *La Révolution nationale algérienne et le Parti communiste français*, 4 vols. (Marseille: Monde en marche, and Paris: Editions du Centenaire, 1973–84).
Juving, Alexandre, *Le Socialisme en Algérie* (Alger: Jules Carbonel, 1924).
Kaddache, Mahfoud, *La Vie politique à Alger de 1919 à 1939* (Algiers: ENAG,

2009).
Kaddache, Mahfoud, *Histoire du nationalisme algérien: Question nationale et politique algérienne, 1919–1951*, 2nd edn, vol. 1 (Algiers: Société nationale d'édition et de diffusion, 1981).
Kalman, Samuel, 'Fascism and *Algérianité*: The *Croix de Feu* and the indigenous question in 1930s Algeria', in Martin Thomas (ed.), *The French Colonial Mind: Violence, Military Encounters and Colonialism*, vol. 2 (Lincoln, NE, and London: University of Nebraska, 2011), pp. 112–39.
Khalfa, Boualem, Henri Alleg and Abdelhamid Benzine, *La Grande Aventure d'« Alger républicain »* (Paris: Messidor, 1987).
Khatib, Hafid, *Le 1er juillet 1956: L'Accord FLN–PCA et l'intégration des « combattants de la libération » dans l'armée de libération nationale en Algérie* (Alger: Office des Publications Universitaires, 1991).
Koulakssis, Ahmed, *Le Parti socialiste et l'Afrique du Nord de Jaurès à Blum* (Paris: Armand Colin, 1991).
Koulakssis, Ahmed and Gilbert Meynier, 'Sur le mouvement ouvrier et les communistes d'Algérie au lendemain de la première guerre mondiale', *Mouvement social*, 130 (January–March 1985), 3–32.
Kriegel, Annie, 'Structures d'organisation et mouvement des effectifs du Parti communiste français entre les deux guerres', *International Review of Social History*, 11, 2 (December 1966), 335–61.
Kuhlken, Robert, 'Settin' the woods on fire: Rural incendiarism as protest', *Geographical Review*, 89:3 (July 1999), 343–63.
Lacheraf, Mostefa, *L'Algérie: Nation et société* (Algiers: Casbah, 2006).
Lacouture, Jean, *André Malraux* (London: André Deutsch, 1975).
Larribère Hadj Ali, Lucette, *Itinéraire d'une militante algérienne* (Blida: Editions du Tell, 2011).
Launay, Michel, *Paysans algériens: La Terre, la vigne, et les hommes* (Paris: Editions du Seuil, 1963).
Lazreg, Marnia, *Torture and the Twilight of Empire: From Algiers to Baghdad* (Princeton, NJ, and Oxford: Princeton University, 2008).
Lazreg, Marnia, *The Eloquence of Silence: Algerian Women in Question* (New York and London: Routledge, 1994).
Le Foll-Luciani, Pierre-Jean, 'Un microcosme de l'Algérie nouvelle? Le Parti communiste algérien en clandestin à Constantine pendant la guerre d'indépendance (1954-1962)', *Atala*, 16 (2013), 245–58.
Le Guennec, Nicole, 'Le Parti communiste français et la guerre du Rif', *Mouvement social*, 78 (January–March 1972), 39–64.
Lenzini, José, *Albert Camus* (Toulouse: Editions Milan, n.d.).
Lévi-Valensi, Jacqueline (ed.), *Camus at Combat: Writing 1944–1947* (Princeton, NJ, and Oxford: Princeton University, 2006).
Lewis, William H., 'The Decline of Algeria's FLN', *Middle East Journal*, 20:2 (Spring 1966), 61–72.
Lottman, Herbert R., *Albert Camus: A Biography* (London Axis, 1997).
Macey, David, *Frantz Fanon: A Life* (London: Granta, 2000).
MacMaster, Neil, *Burning the Veil: The Algerian War and the 'Emancipation' of Muslim Women, 1954–62* (Manchester and New York: Manchester Uni-

versity, 2009).
Maitron, J. (ed.), *Dictionnaire biographique du mouvement ouvrier français*, vols 18, 20, 27, 35, 41 (Paris: Editions ouvrières, 1982–3, 1986, 1989, 1992).
Mamdani, Mahmood, 'Political Identity, Citizenship and Ethnicity in Postcolonial Africa', keynote address, Arusha Conference, 'New Frontiers of Social Policy', (12–15 December 2005), http://goo.gl/i1eWZU (accessed 16 December 2013).
Mamdani, Mahmood, *Citizen and Subject: Contemporary Africa and the Legacy of Late Colonialism* (Princeton, NJ: Princeton University, 1996).
Mandela, Nelson, *Long Walk to Freedom: The Autobiography of Nelson Mandela* (London: Little, Brown, 1994).
Martin, Andy, *The Boxer and the Goalkeeper: Sartre vs Camus* (London, etc: Simon and Schuster, 2012).
McDermott, Kevin and Jeremy Agnew, *The Comintern: A History of International Communism from Lenin to Stalin* (Basingstoke and London: Macmillan, 1996).
McDougall, James, *History and the Culture of Nationalism in Algeria* (Cambridge: Cambridge University Press, 2006).
Messali Hadj, [Ahmed] *Les Mémoires de Messali Hadj* (Paris: Jean-Claude Lattès, 1982).
Meynier, Gilbert, 'Le PPA–MTLD et le FLN–ALN, étude comparée', in Mohammed Harbi and Benjamin Stora (eds) *La Guerre d'Algérie* (Paris: Pluriel, 2010), pp. 602–53.
Meynier, Gilbert, *L'Algérie révélée: La Guerre de 1914–1918 et le premier quart du XXe siècle* (Geneva: Librarie Droz, 1981).
Mirza, Bakar Ali, 'The Congress Against Imperialism', *Modern Review* (1927), 555–66.
Moine, André, *Ma guerre d'Algérie* (Paris: Editions Sociales, 1979).
Moore, Jr., Barrington, *Social Origins of Dictatorship and Democracy: Lord and Peasant in the Making of the Modern World* (Boston, MA: Beacon, 1966).
Moussaoui, Rosa, 'An Insubordinate Named Francis Jeanson', *L'Humanité in English*, http://goo.gl/CwV6Km (accessed 14 March 2010).
Nagy, Laszlo, 'Les « événements » du premier novembre et les premières réactions', 2 May 2012, p. 2, http://goo.gl/8Jw9yp (accessed 17 May 2013).
Narinsky, Mikhail and Jürgen Rojahn (eds), *Centre and Periphery: The History of the Comintern in the Light of New Documents* (Amsterdam: Internationaal Instituut voor Sociale Geschiedenis, 1996).
Orwell, George, 'Not Counting Niggers', in Sonia Orwell and Ian Angus (eds), *The Collected Essays, Journalism and Letters of George Orwell*, vol. 1 (Harmondsworth: Penguin, 1970), pp. 434–8.
Ottaway, David and Marina Ottaway, *Algeria: The Politics of a Socialist Revolution* (Berkeley and Los Angeles, CA: University of California, 1970).
Ouzegane, Amar, *Le Meilleur Combat* (Paris: Julliard, 1962).
Pattieu, Sylvain, *Les Camarades des frères: Trotskistes et libertaires dans la guerre d'Algérie* (Paris: Syllepse, 2002).
Pelling, Henry, *The British Communist Party: A Historical Profile* (London:

Adam and Charles Black, 1958).

Perinbam, B. Marie, 'Fanon and the Revolutionary Peasantry – the Algerian Case', *Journal of Modern African Studies*, 11:3 (1973), 427–45.

Peterson, Charles F., *Dubois, Fanon, Cabral: The Margins of Elite Anti-Colonial Leadership* (Lanham, MD, and Plymouth: Lexington, 2007).

Peyroulou, Jean-Pierre, 'Sétif and Guelma (May 1945)', *Online Encyclopedia of Mass Violence*, 26 March 2008, pp. 1–13, Stable URL: http://goo.gl/5yWszl, (accessed 11 August 2011).

Pike, David Wingeate, *In the Service of Stalin: The Spanish Communists in Exile, 1939–1945* (Oxford: Clarendon, 1993).

Planche, Jean-Louis, *Sétif 1945: Histoire d'un massacre annoncé* (Paris: Perrin, 2006).

Planche, Jean-Louis, 'Alger: Urbanisation et contrôle ethnique, 1930–1962', *Alger: Lumières sur la ville, Actes du colloque* (Algiers, 4–6 May 2002), vol. 1, pp. 231–45.

Planche, Jean-Louis, 'De la solidarité militante à l'affrontement armé: M.N.A. et F.L.N. à Alger, 1954–1955', in J.-Ch. Jeauffret and M. Vaïsse (eds), *Militaires et guérilla dans la guerre d'Algérie* (Editions Complexe, 2001), pp. 219–36.

Planche, Jean-Louis, 'Les Lieux de l'Algérianité,' in Jean-Jacques Jordi and Jean-Louis Planche (eds), *Alger, 1860–1939: Le Modèle ambigu du triomphe colonial* (Paris: Editions Autrement, 1999), pp. 180–203.

Planche, Jean-Louis, 'L'Internationalisme au feu des nationalismes: Les Communistes en Algérie (1920–1945)', in Abdeljelil Temimi (ed), *Mélanges Charles-Robert Ageron*, vol. 2 (Zaghouan: Fondation Temimi pour la recherche scientifique et l'information, 1996), pp. 661–88.

Prochaska, David, *Making Algeria French: Colonialism in Bône, 1870–1920* (Cambridge: Cambridge University Press, and Paris: Editions de la Maison des sciences de l'homme, 1990).

Prochaska, David, 'Fire on the Mountain: Resisting Colonialism in Algeria', in Donald Crummey (ed.), *Banditry, Rebellion and Social Protest in Africa* (London: James Currey, and Portsmouth, NH: Heinemann, 1986), pp. 229–52.

Quandt, William B., *Revolution and Political Leadership: Algeria, 1954–1968* (Cambridge, MA, and London: MIT, 1969).

Radiquet, Paul, 'Les paysans d'Algérie en lutte contre les expropriations', *Cahiers du Bolchévisme*, 8 (15 April 1933), 576–82.

Rebah, Mohamed, *Des chemins et des hommes* (Algiers: Mille-Feuilles, 2010).

Rees, Tim and Andrew Thorpe (eds), *International Communism and the Communist International, 1919–43* (Manchester: Manchester University, 1998).

Reid, Donald, 'Review Article: The Question of Henri Alleg', *International History Review*, 29:3 (September 2007), 573–86.

République algérienne, Ministère de l'information, *A Travers les Wilayas d'Algérie* (November 1960).

Revel, Gaston, *Un instituteur communiste en Algérie: L'Engagement et le combat (1936–1965)*, ed. Alexis Sempé (Cahors: La Louve, 2013).

Rey-Goldzeiguer, Annie, *Aux origines de la guerre d'Algérie, 1940–1945* (Paris:

La Découverte, 2002).
Riegler, Thomas, 'The State as a Terrorist: France and the Red Hand', *Perspectives on Terrorism*, 6:6, (2012), http://goo.gl/tNBASq (accessed 4 October 2013).
Righi, Abdellah, *Hadj-Ali Abdelkader: Pionnier du mouvement révolutionnaire Algérien* (Alger: Casbah, 2006).
Rodinson, Maxime, *Marxism and the Muslim World* (London: Zed, 1979).
Rotman, Patrick, *L'Ennemi intime* (Paris: Editions du Seuil, 2007).
Ruedy, John, *Modern Algeria: The Origins and Development of a Nation*, 2nd edn (Bloomington and Indianapolis, IN: Indiana University, 2005).
Ruedy, John, *Land Policy in Colonial Algeria: The Origins of the Rural Public Domain* (Berkeley and Los Angeles, CA: University of California, 1967).
Rueschemeyer, Dietrich, Evelyne Huber Stephens and John D. Stephens, *Capitalist Development and Democracy* (Cambridge: Polity, 1992).
Ruscio, Alain, 'Les communistes et les massacres du Constantinois (mai–juin 1945)', *Vingtième Siècle. Revue d'histoire*, 94 (2/2007), 217–29, http://goo.gl/YfhvaR (accessed 16 August 2011).
Saarela, Tauno, 'International and National in the Communist Movement', in Tauno Saarela and Kimmo Rentola (eds), *Communism: National and International* (Helsinki: Suomen Historiallinen Seura, 1998), pp. 15–40.
Saarela, Tauno, and Kimmo Rentola (eds), *Communism: National and International* (Helsinki: Helsinki: Suomen Historiallinen Seura, 1998).
Sandle, Mark, *Communism* (Harlow: Pearson, 2012).
Schwartz, Laurent, 'L'Engagement de Pierre Vidal-Naquet dans la guerre d'Algérie', in François Hartog, Pauline Schmitt-Pantel and Alain Schnapp (eds), *Pierre Vidal-Naquet: Un historien dans la cité* (Paris: La Découverte, 2007), pp. 24–41.
Schweitzer, Thomas-Adrian, 'Le Parti communiste français, le Comintern et l'Algérie dans les années 1930', *Mouvement social*, 78 (January–March 1972), pp. 115–36.
Seferdjeli, Ryme, 'Rethinking the History of the *Mujahidat* during the Algerian War: Competing Voices, Reconstructed Memories and Contrasting Historiographies', *Interventions*, 14:2 (2012), 238–55.
Seferdjeli, Ryme, 'French "Reforms" and Muslim Women's Emancipation during the Algerian War', *Journal of North African Studies*, 9:4 (Winter 2004), 19–61.
Shepard, Todd, *The Invention of Decolonization: The Algerian War and the Remaking of France* (Ithaca, NY, and London: Cornell, 2006).
Shipway, Martin, *Decolonization and its Impact: A Comparative Approach to the End of the Colonial Empires* (Oxford: Blackwell, 2008).
Simons, H. J., and R. E. Simons, *Class and Colour in South Africa 1850–1950* (Harmondsworth: Penguin, 1969).
Sivan, Emmanuel, 'Colonialism and Popular Culture in Algeria', *Journal of Contemporary History*, 14:1 (January 1979), 21–53.
Sivan, Emmanuel, *Communisme et nationalisme en Algérie, 1920–1962* (Paris: Fondation Nationale des Sciences Politiques, 1976).
Sowerwine, Charles, *France since 1870: Culture, Society and the Making of*

the Republic, 2nd edn (Basingstoke: Palgrave Macmillan, 2009).

Spielmann, Victor, *Colonisation et question indigène en Algérie en 1922* (Algiers: Imprimerie du prolétariat, [1922]).

Sportisse, William, Entretiens avec Pierre-Jean le Foll-Luciani, *Le Camp des oliviers: Parcours d'un communiste algérien* (Rennes: Presses Universitaires de Rennes, 2012).

Stora, Benjamin, *Algeria, 1830–2000: A Short History* (Ithaca, NY, and London: Cornell, 2001).

Stora, Benjamin, *La Gangrène et l'oubli: La Mémoire de la guerre d'Algérie* (Paris: La Découverte, 1991, 1998).

Stora, Benjamin, *Histoire de la guerre d'Algérie (1954–1962)* (Paris: La Découverte, 1993).

Stora, Benjamin, *Histoire de l'Algérie coloniale (1830–1954)* (Paris: La Découverte, 1991).

Stora, Benjamin, 'Commentaire', in Pierre Journoud and Hugues Tertrais (eds), *1954–2004: La Bataille de Dien Bien Phu, entre histoire et mémoire* (Paris, Société française de l'histoire d'outre-mer, 2004), pp. 251–3.

Stora, Benjamin, *Nationalistes algériens et révolutionnaires français au temps du Front populaire* (Paris: L'Harmattan, 1987).

Stora, Benjamin, 'Faiblesse paysanne du mouvement nationaliste algérien avant 1954', *Vingtieme Siècle: Revue d'histoire*, 12 (October–December 1986), 59–72.

Stora, Benjamin, *Dictionnaire biographique des militants nationalistes algériens, 1926–1954* (Paris: Harmattan, 1985).

Stora, Benjamin, *Messali Hadj (1898–1974): Pionnier du nationalisme algérien* (Paris: Harmattan, 1982).

Sutton, K. and R. I. Lawless, 'Population Regroupement in Algeria – Traumatic Change and the Rural Settlement Pattern', paper presented at the symposium on 'Settlement and Conflict in the Mediterranean World', I.B.G., Newcastle (6 January 1977).

Thomas, Benjamin E., 'Motoring in the Sahara: The French Raids of 1951–1953', *Economic Geography*, 29:4 (October 1953), 327–39.

Thomas, Benjamin E., 'The Railways of French North Africa', *Economic Geography*, 29:2 (April 1953), 95–106.

Thomas, Martin, 'Colonial Violence in Algeria and the Distorted Logic of State Retribution: The Sétif Uprising of 1945', *Journal of Military History*, 75:1 (2011), 125–58.

Thomas, Martin, 'Colonial Minds and Colonial Violence: The Sétif Uprising and the Savage Economics of Colonialism', in Martin Thomas (ed.), *The French Colonial Mind: Violence, Military Encounters and Colonialism*, vol. 2 (Lincoln, NE, and London: University of Nebraska, 2011), pp. 140–73.

Thomas, Martin, *The French Empire between the Wars: Imperialism, Politics and Society* (Manchester: Manchester University Press, 2005).

Thomas, Martin, *The French Empire at War, 1940–45* (Manchester: Manchester University, 1998).

Thomas, Martin (ed.), *The French Colonial Mind: Mental Maps of Empire and Colonial Encounters*, vol. 1 (Lincoln, NE, and London: University of

Nebraska, 2011).
Martin Thomas (ed.), *The French Colonial Mind: Violence, Military Encounters and Colonialism*, vol. 2 (Lincoln, NE, and London: University of Nebraska, 2011).
Thorez, Maurice, *Fils du peuple* (Paris: Editions Sociales, 1960).
Todd, Olivier, *Albert Camus: A life* (London: Vintage, 1998).
Todd, Olivier, *Albert Camus: Une vie* (Paris: Gallimard, 1996).
Trotsky, Leon, 'Resolution of the Fourth World Congress on the French Question', *The First Five Years of the Communist International*, 2nd edn, vol. 2 (New York: Monad, 1972), pp. 275–84.
Vallaud, Pierre, *La Guerre d'Algérie: De la conquête à l'indépendance, 1830–1962* (Paris: Acropole, 2006).
Viallaneix, Paul, 'The First Camus', in Albert Camus, *Cahiers II: Youthful Writings* (New York, Alfred A. Knopf, 1976), pp. 3–104.
Vernadsky, George, *A History of Russia*, [1929] (New Haven, CT: Yale, 6th revised edn, 1969).
Vidal-Naquet, Pierre, *L'Affaire Audin* (Paris: Editions de Minuit, 1958).
Vince, Natalya, 'Transgressing Boundaries: Gender, Race, Religion, and "Françaises musulmanes" during the Algerian War of Independence', *French Historical Studies*, 33:3 (Summer 2010), 445–74.
Wall, Irwin M., 'The French Communists and the Algerian War', *Journal of Contemporary History*, 12 (1977), 521–43.
Williams, Philip M., *Crisis and Compromise: Politics in the Fourth Republic*, 3rd edn (London: Longman, 1964).
Wolf, Eric R., *Peasant Wars of the Twentieth Century* [1969] (Norman, OK: University of Oklahoma, 1999).
Wood, Nancy, 'Remembering the Jews of Algeria', in Tyler Stovall and Georges van den Abbeele (eds), *French Civilization and its Discontents: Nationalism, Colonialism, Race* (Lanham, MD, etc: Lexington, 2003), pp. 251–70.
Zaretsky, Robert, *Albert Camus: Elements of a Life* (Ithaca, NY, and London: Cornell University, 2010).

Unpublished theses

Laisne, Guillaume, 'Engagements d'un quotidien en société coloniale: le cas d'Alger républicain (1938–1955)', (Mémoire présenté pour le Master recherche, Institut d'Etudes Politiques de Paris, 2007).
Planche, Jean-Louis, 'Antifascisme et anticolonialisme à Alger à l'époque du Front populaire et Congrès musulman, 1935–1939' (3rd cycle thesis, Université de Paris VII, 1979).
Zagoria, Janet Dorsch, 'The Rise and Fall of the Movement of Messali Hadj in Algeria, 1924–1954' (PhD, Columbia University, 1973).

INDEX

Abbas, Ferhat 92–3, 103, 111, 123–8, 130–1, 135–7, 146, 151–2, 155, 160, 194, 196–7, 234, 244, 255, 262
Abdallah 130
Abdelmoumène, Noureddine 134, 162, 171–2, 187, 197, 253, 259, 271
Abdelouahad, Taïeb 71–4
Aboulker, José 120, 122
Abrial, Jean-Marie Charles 115
Abyssinia 91, 98, 103
Acampora, Georges 200–1, 220
Achiary, André 147–8, 152
Africa 8, 235–7, 267
Agence France–Afrique 129
Ageron, Charles-Robert 104
Aït Ahmed, Hocine 162, 184, 190, 208, 262, 273
Aït Hamouda, Amirouche (Colonel Amirouche) 227, 237, 269
Akkache, Ahmed 168–9, 190–1, 199, 220, 222, 241
Akrour, Djoher 223, 228
Algeria (general)
  agricultural production 18–19; cities social divide 12, 20–2, 163–4, 174; class stratification 3, 20–2, 23; commercial bourgeoisie 3; departments (Algérois, Constantinois and Oranie) 14, 15, 21, 34; French conquest 11–25; land division and stratification 11–25, 153–4, 267–8; migration to France 21; Muslim landed elite 3–4, 19–20, 22, 31, 153, 267–8; peasantry and land hunger 3, 12, 19–21, 23; proletarianisation 6; religious cleavages 4, 13; urbanisation 20–1, 23, 262; *see also* Algeria (politics; war of independence)
Algeria (politics)
  Algeria as 'another country not France' 92, 234; Algerian Statute 161, 170; Algiers Charter (1964) 276–7; Anglo-American landing 122–6; Berber crisis 162; citizenship post-independence 276; Constantinois massacre (1945) 171; Constituent Assembly (1946) 155; elections 27, 37–40, 64, 71–4, 87, 93, 99, 102, 146, 150, 152, 155, 160–2, 167–8, 190–1, 194, 234, 260, 272; European exodus 268; imagining an Algerian nation 7–9, 23, 49–50, 105, 120, 252–66; May Day (1945) demonstrations 136–8, 146; National Assembly 145, 160–1, 166, 195, 220, 235; National Constituent Assembly 269; nationalist–communist unity talks 155–7, 166–71; Nawadi intellectual circles 81; political assassinations 257, 259; post-war reconstruction and nationalisation 262–4, 276–7; Vichy Algeria 113–20, 125–6, 129, 133; *see also* France
Algeria (war of independence, 1954–62) 180–266; *Algérie francaise* 233–4; All Saints' Day launch 180, 199–200; ALN–GPRA rivalry 255; CNRA 207; 'Declaration of the Sixty-One' 192; de Gaulle on Algerian self-determination 240–5; Evian Accords 254–5, 258–9, 262; FLN abstention from French self-determination bill (1961) 245; forced resettlement 187–8; French army 219, 230; French opposition 185, 187–8, 192, 221, 230–3; French political reforms 194–7, 219, 231; hunt commandos 237; independence referendum (1962) 260; MNA 193; moves to cities 244–5, 252; negotiations to end war 194–6, 207, 229, 234, 240–5, 252–8, 260–4; PCA

[298]

INDEX

181, 183–4, 194, 226, 229–30, 232, 235, 239–45, 252–66, 273; PCF calling for French–FLN negotiations 183–4, 194, 229–30; peasant support 181–3; Section administrative spécialisée 187, 197; shifting political allegiances 192–8; special powers bill 195–6; *see also* ALN; FLN
Algerian Assembly 160–6, 196–7
Algerian Communist Party *see* Parti communiste algérien (PCA)
Algerian Front for the Defence and Respect of Liberties 167–8, 170–2
Algerian Muslim Congress (1936) 92–7, 99, 102–3, 119; *see also* Islam; *'ulama*
Algerian reform movements *see* assimilation with France; Jeunes algériens
Algérie nouvelle 126
Alger républicain 94, 105, 111–13, 122, 124, 126, 137–8, 150–1, 154, 156, 181, 191, 200–1, 202–3, 205, 219, 233, 256, 259, 270–3, 275, 277–8
Ali, Zraibi 62
Ali La Pointe (Ammar, Ali) 217–18
All Africa People's Conference (1958) 235–6, 241
Allaouchiche, Baya Bouhoune 122, 129, 166, 202, 218; *see also* Union des femmes d'Algérie
Alleg, Henri 68, 147, 191, 223–4, 230, 236, 240, 257, 259, 272, 276–7; *La Question* 230–1, 257; military tribunal 241; prison escape 256; relaunching *Alger républicain* 259, 270–2; *see also* Salem, Harry
Allouache, Hamid 225
All Saints' Day (Algerian war of independence) 180, 199–200
ALN *see* Armée de libération nationale
Amara, Ahmed 125
Amara, Ferchouk 96
Amirouche (Colonel) *see* Aït Hamouda, Amirouche
Amis de la démocratie (Friends of Democracy) 133, 136
Amis du manifeste et de la liberté (Friends of the Manifesto and Freedom, AML) 131, 134–8, 146, 152, 186
Amnesty International 277

Amsterdam International 29
Anglo-American landing (1942) 122–7
anti-Semitism 16, 21–2, 35, 62, 83–5, 94, 115–16, 120, 125, 129, 134, 169, 227, 276; *see also* Crémieux decree
Arab League 134, 136
Arab workers' congress (1930) 48–9
Arbib, Georgeo 222
Armée de libération nationale (ALN) 180–216, 236, 241, 258–60; access to military equipment 240; arrests and detentions 220–8; battle for the countryside 185–8; CDL integration 201, 203–6, 209, 217, 225, 240, 257; fear of infiltration 226–7; GPRA 251, 255; guerrillas, female (*mujahidat–musabilat–fida'iyyat*) 186, 197–8, 217–19, 226–7, 238; guerrillas, male (*mujahidin–musabilin–fida'iyyin*) 185, 197; health services 197, 238–9; legal representation 182; Main rouge (Red Hand) 220, 233, 253; Melouza massacre 220; Morice Line 228–9; peasant support and organisation of 185–6; restructuring, post-independence 268; restructuring (Soummam) 207; sabotage and terrorism 218–21; underground political network 186, 217, 220, 225–6; youth–student support 186, 197, 226–7; *see also* Algeria (war of independence); FLN
Arrighi, Victor-Noël 39
assimilation with France 27–8, 42, 44, 82–3, 86, 92–3, 99, 103–4, 111, 131, 152, 174
Association des amis du théâtre Arabe 193
Association des étudiants musulmans d'Afrique du Nord 162–4
Association des 'Ulama musulmans algériens (AUMA) 60; *see also* Blida–Mitidja peasant protests; *'ulama*
Attouche, Louise 227
Aucouterier, Jean-Baptiste 39
Audin, Maurice 223, 224, 241, 255
AUMA *see* Association des 'Ulama musulmans algériens
Aurès 12, 27, 118, 159, 164–5, 168, 180, 182–4, 190–1, 201, 206, 209, 233, 239
autogestion 276–7

[299]

INDEX

Babou, Abdelkader 200, 202, 206, 240–1, 273
Bachir, Abdelouahab 72–3, 96
Badsi, Mohamed 89, 93, 96–8, 159
Badsi, Sid Ahmed 89, 96–8, 159
Bandung Conference (1955) 189
Barberousse *see* Serkadji prison
Barbour, Nevill 197
Barbusse, Henri 45
Barthel, Jean 89–91, 95, 97–8, 103
Batista, Fulgencio 259
Behghezal 132
Beijing Asian Women's Congress 166
Bekaddour, Zoulikha 197, 220, 223
Belkaïm, Kaddour 102, 111–12, 120, 125
Bellarbi, Sid Ahmed *see* Boualem (pseud)
Bellissant, Roger 164
Belouchrani, Omar 136
Ben, Myriam 181
Benaïch, Maurice 62, 64–5
Ben Allal, Mebarek 93
Ben Badis Circle 172
Ben Badis, Shaykh Abdelhamid 42–3, 60, 69, 82, 84–5, 92, 99, 130, 276; 'only one race – the human race' 85–6, 232
Ben Bella, Ahmed 160, 162, 165, 184, 208, 255–6, 260, 263, 268, 271–3, 276–8; Algerian constitution (1963) 276; conservative religious leaders 275; FLN independence programme (1962) 262–3; overthrow of 278; PCA autonomy 271–3; support of Boumediène 268–9
Ben Boulaïd, Mostefa 180, 182
Bendib, Omar 111, 132
Bendjelloul, Mohamed-Salah 60, 82, 84–5, 93, 96–7, 102–3, 112, 130–1, 102
Ben Hadj 97
Benhamou, Rabah 201–2
Ben Khedda, Benyoussef 205, 219, 255, 268, 275
Ben Lekhal, Mahmoud 38, 42
Ben M'Hidi, Larbi 206, 217
Bentami, Belqacem 35, 72, 74
Bentobbal, Lakhdar 237
Benzine, Abdelhamid 200–1, 224–5, 233, 256, 270, 272, 277
Berhail, Hocine 190
Berlioz, Joanny 132–3
Berque 152
Berrahil 182
Berrahou, Abdelkader 159, 198

Berrahou, Mejdoub 159, 165, 182, 191, 198
Berrahou, Yamina 182
Biboulet, Pierre 37, 39–41
Billoux, François 127–8, 130
Blech, René 100–1
Blida–Mitidja peasant protests 56–80; agricultural workers 59, 61, 72–6; anti-expropriation struggles 59, 62–3, 65–72, 75; AUMA and *El Hidaia* 60–2, 68–9; city–countryside–mountain political triangle 59, 76; communists and peasant protests 58, 61–7, 76; elections (1933) 71–6; Islamic organisations 68–9; JC influence 61–2, 65–6, 68–9; reforestation 62–3, 66–9, 72; markets and communists activity 65–7, 69; Muslim demonstrations (February–March 1933) 69; PCF 61, 63–4, 68–76; peasant djemâa (self-government) 67; protests underground–above ground 64–7; railway workers 65; refusal to pay taxes 63–4; repression 67, 71, 75; rural political space 65–7, 69, 75–6; urban activists–rural movements 75–6
Blum, Léon 92–3, 99–101
Blum-Viollette bill 99, 103–4
Boillat, Fernand 241
Boiziz, Paul and Simone 256
Bossus 70–1
Boualem (pseud) 46, 48–9, 56, 59, 62, 64–5, 68, 70, 73, 85–6
Boualem, Bachaga 205
Boualem, Mohamed 205, 256
Bouaza, Djamila 228
Bouchakdji, Ali 72
Bouchama, Abderrahmane 61, 89, 271
Boudia, Mohamed 184
Boudiaf, Abdelhamid 190, 254, 256–7
Boudiaf, Mohamed 208
Boudida 161
Boudjenah, Fafa 197
Boudjenah, Sliman (pen-name El-Ferkad) 57–8, 70, 73, 135, 170, 197
Bouhali, Larbi 82, 91, 94, 102, 114, 125, 128, 132, 154, 161, 163, 169, 173, 190, 221, 225–6, 239, 242, 252, 254, 256, 271
Boukémiat, Hamed 63–4, 71–2
Boukort, Ben Ali (pseud El Mounadi) 39, 57–8, 82, 85–6, 88–90, 93, 98, 102,

INDEX

112, 114, 133, 150–1, 155, 160; Islam and communism 90–1, 133; *Peuple d'Algérie, quels sont tes amis?* 90; *Quand le peuple d'Algérie parle* 97
Bouhired, Djamila 218, 228
Boulahrouz, Ali 201
Boumediène, Houari (Colonel) 229, 241, 255, 258–9, 262, 264, 268–9, 272, 278
Boumendjel, Ahmed 235
Boupacha, Djamila 241
Bourguiba, Habib 241
Bourneton, Charles 49
Boussouf, Abdelhafid 229, 237
Boye, A. 33
Brahim, Touami el Hadj 72–3
Briki, David Yusuf 201
Briki, Jean Yahia 201, 227–8
British consul-general 33, 69, 135–8, 146–9, 164–5, 173, 183, 213, 225, 236, 240, 257
British Embassy 273, 275, 277
Bukharin, Nikolai 46–7
Buono, Christian 224, 241
Busquant, Emilie 94

Caballero, Paul 119, 133, 149, 154, 161, 169, 182, 190–1, 241
Cachin, Marcel 26, 29
Camp Morand 256
Camus, Albert 15, 16, 23, 87–92, 99–102, 105, 113–15, 125, 133, 137; Communists 87, 100–1, 194; executions and torture 222; famine 111, 137, 150–1; *Manifesto of Algerian Intellectuals* 101; Mediterranean culture 100–1, 104–5; non-violence 137, 193–4, 230; punishment of collaborators 132, 137; war of independence 194–5, 230
Cantara rouge, La 56
Caracéna 201
Carde, Governor-General 69
Carlier, Omar 59
Casanova, Laurent 111
Castel, André 200–1
Castro, Fidel 259
Catogni, Georges 241
Cattoir, Jean 117
Cazala, René 101
Celor, Pierre 42, 44
Cercle franco-indigène nord-africain 35
CGT *see* Confédération générale du travail
CGTU *see* Confédération générale du travail unitaire
Chabila, Djilali 46, 61
Chaintron, Jean *see* Barthel, Jean
Challe, Maurice 235, 237, 254
Chaoui, Ahmed 204–5
Chataigneau, Yves 132, 146–7
Chatain, Jocelyne 227–8
Châtel, Yves-Charles 122–3
Chaulet, Pierre 218
Chemouilli, Gilberte *see* Taleb, Gilberte Chemouilli
Chevallier, Jacques 174
China 166, 200, 243, 261–2, 270
Chouadria, Mohamed 152, 154, 157
Christofol, Jean 132
Circle of Progress 60, 81, 89, 194
cities and political resistance 8, 208, 217, 221, 226–7, 244–5
Cold War 8, 145, 163, 183, 193, 195, 235–6, 267, 273
Combat 125, 133
Combat social 47
Combattants de la libération (Liberation soldiers, CDL) 191, 198–206, 240; *see also* PCA; ALN
Comintern *see* Communist International
Comité algérien de secours aux indigènes (Algerian committee for aid to natives) 35
Comité de coordination et d'exécution (CCE) *see* Front de libération nationale (FLN)
Comité d'études coloniales (Committee of colonial studies) 31–2, 34, 37–8; *see also* PCF
Comité français de libération nationale (CFLN) 126–7, 132
Comité national français (CNF) 122–3
Comité révolutionnaire pour l'unité et l'action (CRUA) 172, 184, 207; *see also* MTLD; FLN
Committee of North African Union and Action 169
Communauté algérienne 193
Communist Information Bureau (Cominform) 163
Communist International (Comintern) 5–7, 33–4, 45, 56–9, 76, 86; anti-colonialism 5, 28, 33–4, 45, 56–7, 59; Bolshevisation 31, 35–40, 46;

call for Algerian independence 5, 32–3; congresses *see* Communist International Congresses; dissolution (1943) 127–31; ENA 70; new line (class against class) 6, 30–1, 46–50, 68, 103; PCA formation 89, 96; PCF 30, 33–4, 46–7, 58, 86; Popular Front 6, 86–8, 103, 110; Second World War 112–15, 119; Soviet Communist Party influence within 36; Twenty-One Points (1920) 29–31, 33, 50n11; *see also* PCA; PCF

Communist International Congresses 2nd (1920) 28–9; 3rd (1921) 31; 4th (1922) 33–4; 5th (1924) 35–6; 6th (1928) 47, 49, 56–7, 62; 7th (1935) 88–9

Communist parties of North Africa 2nd Conference (1944) 132

Confédération générale du travail (CGT) 28, 33–4, 38, 88, 92, 97, 130, 136–7, 159, 162, 164, 186, 192, 202, 205, 220; *see also* CGTU; UGSA; UGTA

Confédération générale du travail unitaire (CGTU) 33, 41, 43–4, 46, 48, 57–8, 62, 70, 88

Congrès interfédéral communiste de l'Afrique du Nord (Blida, 1922) 61

Congress of Oppressed Nations (1927) 45, 57–8

Conseil national de la révolution algérienne (CNRA) 207, 229, 255, 262–4, 268, 273; *see also* FLN

Constantine républicain 94

Constantine's war of religion (1934) 83–6

Constantinois massacre (1945) 7, 146–53, 163, 180, 192; electoral reforms 160–6; anti-corruption politics 147; interpretations 149–53; *jihad* against occupying Christians 149–50; numbers killed 148–9; PCA ambiguous initial reaction 180

Cornavin, Gaston 58

Counillon, Georges 204, 239

Cremadès, Alice *see* Sportisse, Alice Cremadès

Crémieux, R. A. 35

Crémieux decree 16, 115–16, 120, 125, 128, 232; *Statut des juifs* 115, 125; *see also* anti-Semitism

Croix de feu (Cross of Fire) 83

Cuba 259, 271, 267, 277

Dadoo, Yusuf 271
Daladier, Edouard 110
Dalibey, Rachid 154, 164, 190, 199, 226
Danelius, Ditmar 121
Debabèche, Alidin 91, 98, 102, 111, 118–19
De Beauvoir, Simone 132, 188, 228, 230
'Declaration of the Sixty-One' *see* Algeria (war of independence)
Défense, La 86, 93
De Fréminville, Claude de la Poix 87–8
de Gaulle, Charles 114–15, 130–2, 135, 138, 147, 232–5, 239–45, 254–7, 264, 272; Algerian electoral reform (1958) 234; Algeria visit 244–5, 252; army mutiny and 'Barricades Week' 241, 243; CFLN 126; CNF 122–3; Constantine Development Plan 234; Constantinois massacre 147; Fifth Republic 234–5; Free France 114–15, 123, 126; Giraud–de Gaulle accord 126; GPRA 242–3, 252; OAS putsch 254; PCF 123, 127, 234–5; self-determination referendum (1961) 245, 252; year of Algerian independence (1962) 257; *see also* France; FLN
Dei, Odette Rossignol 118, 121
Deloche, Robert 91, 102–3
Deloison, Maurice 121
Deluca, Edouard 147
Demain 30
Demusois, Antoine 132
Denier, Albert 147
Dépêche algérienne, La 90, 155
Destour Party 45, 121
Dib, Mohamed 20, 164
Disque rouge, Le 56
Djilani, Mohamed 44
Domenech, Henri 98
Donnat, Gaston 66, 201–2
Doriot, Jacques 37, 115
Drif, Zohra 218
Droit du people, Le 30
Duclos, Jacques 195–6
Duncan, Patrick 277
Durand 63–4
Duval, General 152

East Germany 221, 229
L'Echo d'Alger 119, 155
Egalité 134
Egypt 43, 68, 165, 190, 194, 218, 261, 273

INDEX

Einstein, Albert 45
El Amel 82
Electricité et gaz d'Algérie (EGA) 201, 220
El Hourriya (Liberté) 153–4, 156–7, 254, 270–3 *see also Liberté*
El-Krim, Abd 34, 38
El-Mokrani, Mohamed 16, 98
El Moudjahid 220, 278
El-Okbi, Shaykh Taïeb 60–1, 68–9
El Ouma (Nation) 70, 83, 86, 99
Emir Abdelkader 14, 28
Emir Khaled 28, 33, 43–4, 58, 86, 98
ENA *see* Etoile nord-africain
Engels, Friedrich 26
L'Esclave du rail 56
Esplaas, Roger 150
Estorges, Paul 84, 97, 130, 132, 184
Etoile nord-africain (North African Star, ENA) 6, 44–6, 57, 61, 86, 94, 97–9; independence 44–5, 83, 94–5; PCF 44–6, 49, 88; rejection of communist label 83; *see also* Hadj Ali, Abdelkader; Messali, Ahmed
Evian Accords 254–5, 258–9, 262
L'Express 230

Fajon, Etienne 127–9, 135, 151
Fanon, Frantz 22–3, 63, 75, 188, 195, 219–20, 229, 235–9, 253–4, 256, 262; ALN Melouza attack 220; *Black Skin, White Masks* 188; female guerrillas 238; FLN post-independence 253; PCA differences with 253–4; peasantry 254; silences 238–9; *Wretched of the Earth* 241, 253, 256; *Year V of the Algerian Revolution* 237–8
Fanon, Josie 253
Farrugia, Jean 201, 203, 227–8, 233–4
fascism *see* Comintern; France; PCA; PCF
Fayet, Pierre 137
Fédération de France du FLN (FFFLN) 221, 253, 262–3, 268, 271
Fédération de France du PCA (FFPCA) 221, 254, 256
Fédération des élus indigènes (FEI) 42, 82–3, 86, 92–3, 95–9
Fédération socialiste algérienne 26
Federation of Mayors of Algeria 218
Feix, Léon 132, 168, 194
Feraoun, Mouloud 193, 196, 206, 208, 218–21, 225–6, 230–1, 233, 236–8, 241, 244, 255, 257–8

Fernandez, Ramón Via 114, 118–19, 121
Ferrat, André (pseud André Mourad) 57–9, 70, 76, 82, 85, 88–91
Figaro, Le 244
Fiorio-Steiner, Annie 199–200, 222
Flanner, Janet 138, 244, 260
FLN *see* Front de libération nationale
Fodil, Mustapha 209
Force ouvrière 171–2
France
 aid workers 268; Algerian independence referendum (1962) 260; Algerian war opposition 241–3, 255; anti-fascism 86–9; banning of PCF, PCA, PPA 113–14 118–19; Blum-Viollette bill 99, 103–4; centenary of conquest (1930) 6, 48; CFLN 126, 132; *Combat* resistance movement 125, 132; Constituent Assembly (1945) 152, 155; Fifth Republic 234; Fighting France 125–6, 148, 152, 185; FLN attacks in France 234; Fourth Republic 232; Free France 114, 126; French new left 242–3, 255; French Revolution 26, 31, 34, 110–11, 120; French Union 145, 161, 163, 202; German occupation and liberation 114–15, 117, 132; Michels circular (1933) 86; mutiny of Algerian soldiers 119; Paris Commune 15, 26; police brutality 256–7; Popular Front (1936) 6, 92–5, 97–100, 102–5, 110, 117, 120, 162, 269–70; Régnier Decree (1935) 86, 90, 101; Rif War 34–5, 38–9; Ruhr occupation 34–8; Second Republic 15; special powers 196; Third Republic 15, 16, 115, 152; Vichy regime 114–19, 122, 125, 145; *see also* de Gaulle, Charles; FLN
France combattante, La 125–6, 148, 152, 185
France observateur 254
Franco, Francisco 93, 115
Fraternité algérienne 33; *see also* Emir Khaled
Fraternité musulmane 43
Free France *see* de Gaulle, Charles; France
French Chamber of Deputies 69
French Communist Party *see* Parti Communiste Français (PCF)
French–Muslim Union 100
Friends of the Soviet Union 93, 100, 113
Froger, Amédée 218

[303]

INDEX

Front de libération nationale (FLN) 180–280; Alcohol and tobacco boycott 193, 199; Bandung Conference 189; battle for the countryside 185–8; CNRA 229; Europeans 192, 255; external FLN 207, 228–36, 253; FFFLN 221, 253, 262–3, 268, 271; First Congress (1964) 276–8; France, attacks in 234; Frantz Fanon 237–9; GPRA 234, 236, 240, 245, 252–64; health care 238–9; imagined Algerian nation 184–5; intellectuals, killing of 220, 227; internal–external tensions 196, 206–8, 226; internal organisation destruction of 206, 219, 226, 252, 255; internal power struggles 258–60, 264; Jeanson network 242; military–political tensions 8, 207–8, 217, 229, 239, 242; Moroccan and Tunisian bases 196, 228; neutralising opponents 185, 188–91; origins 184–5; PCA 8–9, 182–4, 189–92, 199, 204–9, 225, 239–40, 243–5, 252, 259–63, 269; PCA and softening of FLN attitude 207, 242; peasant and rural support 181–3, 185–6, 189, 207–8, 263; power struggles 239, 268–9, 271–2, 276–8; punishing collaborators 198, 208, 236, 256; Soummam Congress (1956) 206–9, 239–40, 263; Soviet assistance 226; strike (1958) 234; student boycotts and strikes 197–8; Tripoli conference (1962) 262–4, 268, 273; underground networks 186, 208–9, 217, 226; village resettlement 187–8; 'Voice of Free Algeria' 238; see also Algeria (war of independence); ALN

Frossard, Ludovic-Oscar 29

Gandhi, M. K. 45
Garaudy, Roger 128, 132
Geromini, Charles 194
Ghana 235–8
Gherab, Abdelhamid 202, 204–5
Ghomri, Halima 182, 199
Ghomri, Tahar 159, 161, 165, 182, 191, 198, 209
Gide, André 91, 100–1
Gimenez, Gabrielle 117–18, 121, 219
Girard, Maurice 101–2
Giraud, Henri 123, 125–6
Gitton, Marcel 96–8

Goloubieva, Seraphima ('Suzanne') 57
Gouvernement provisoire de la République algérienne (GPRA) 234–45, 252, 255, 262–4, 268–9, 271–2; see also FLN
Great War (First World War) see World wars
Guerab, Abdelhamid 256
Guerroudj, Abdelkader 165, 182, 190–1, 198, 201, 206, 222, 227–8, 240, 273
Guerroudj, Jacqueline Minne 165, 191, 198, 201, 203, 205, 222–3, 227–8
Guerrouf, Mohammed 159, 182, 184 190–1
Guessoum, Abdelhamid 101
Guillon, Maxime 34

Hadj Ali, Abdelkader 37, 43–5, 68, 89, 98
Hadj Ali, Bachir 163, 168–9, 182, 190, 198, 200–1, 203, 205, 225, 242–3, 244, 254, 273
Hadjerès, Sadek 127–8, 134, 162–4, 169, 200, 205, 222, 225, 239, 243–5, 273; Berber crisis 162–3; CDL 200, 205; PPA-MTLD 163; *Our people will overcome* 243–5
Hamida, Benthami Ould 42
Hamou, Hadj 273
Hamouda, Mohammedia 200
Hamouda, Néfissa 227
Hamoun, Belkacem 205
Harbi (Captain) 259
Harbi, Mohammed 160–1, 269
Harkis 198, 256, 272
Harmel, Michael 271
Henriet, Paul 39–40
Hitler, Adolf and *Mein Kampf* 86, 102, 110, 117, 137, 149
Ho Chi Minh 38, 173
Hocine, Baya 223, 228
Hocine, Sfari 186
L'Humanité 29, 32, 57, 95, 101, 150–1, 183, 230
Humbert-Droz, Jules 46

Ibanez, Thomas 117–19, 121
Idir, Aissat 136
Ighilahriz, Louisette 181, 197–8, 226
Ighilahriz, Malika 226
L'Ikdam (Courage) 28, 39, 45–6, 87
L'Ikdam nord-africain 45
L'Ikdam de Paris 45

INDEX

Inal, Ahmed 165
Inal, Djaafar 271
India 261
Indigénat 16, 26, 35, 41–2 44, 72, 86, 131, 145
Industrial and Commercial Workers' Union 6
International Brigade 101, 114–15, 128, 181; *see also* Spanish Civil War
International Confederation of Free Trade Unions (ICFTU) 195, 275
International Federation of Trade Unions 29
International Red Aid (Secours populaire) 93–4
Islam 11, 14, 42–3, 69, 90–1, 133, 276; Algerian Muslim Congress (1936) 93, 95–7, 102–3; anti-colonialism 4, 42–3, 60, 169; anti-Semitism 62, 83; attacks on Muslims in Algiers 257–8; Communist–Muslim alliances 96, 104, 132; Constantine's war of religion 83–6; Ibadi Islam 14, 43; Islamic reformists 81–3, 92–3; Jonnart Law reform 27–8; Muslims and French citizenship 130–1; *Nahda* Muslim cultural–political renaissance 81; Salifiyya movement 42; state repression of 81–3; Sunni Islam 11, 42; Wahabite movement 69; *see also* AUMA; '*ulama*
Issad, Hassan 44
Iveton, Fernand 201, 203, 220, 222–3, 227

Jaurès, Jean 27
Jeanson, Francis 242
Jeune Algérie, La 129
Jeune Méditerranée 101; *see also* Camus, Albert
Jeunes algériens 27–8, 49, 134
Jeunes filles communistes d'Algérie (Communist Girls of Algeria) 129
Jeunesse communiste (JC) 36, 38–40, 42, 46, 58, 59, 61, 65–6, 82, 95, 101, 113, 117, 120, 129–30, 159, 203
Joannès, Victor 149
Jonnart, Charles 27
Jonnart Law (1919) 27, 28, 71
Julien, Charles-André 29, 31, 34, 94; *see also* Socialist Party
Justrabo, René 182, 190–1

Kabylia 12, 16, 21, 82–4, 101, 111, 118, 134, 148, 162, 164, 184, 189, 193, 196, 200, 203, 206–9, 220–1, 236, 257, 268, 276
Kaïdi, Lakhdar 195
Kateb, Mohamed 118
Keddar, Ahmed 203
Kessous, Aziz 193
Kessous, Mohammed el Aziz 94, 124
Khaidallah, Chedly 45
Khalfa, Boualem 138, 151, 200, 219, 256, 270–2
Khalid, Abdelaziz 194
Khidder, Abbas 271
Khider, Mohammed 208
Khrushchev, Nikita 196, 273
Kolaroff (Comrade) 37
Kraba, Hamou 166
Krim, Belkacem 187, 237, 256

Laban, Maurice 101, 114, 117–18, 121, 128, 132, 159, 181–2, 201–3, 209
Lacheref, Mostefa 23, 208
Lacoste 219, 232
Lagaillarde (General) 252
Lakhdar, Kaïdi 271, 275
Lakhdar, Si 186
Lakhdari, Samia 218
Lakhnèche, Mohamed 222
Lambert, Pierre 201
Lambèse prison 121, 124, 224, 233, 236–7, 256; *see also* prison struggles
Lamrani, Laïd 169, 181–2, 190–1, 201, 209
Lansbury, George 45
Larribère, Camille 200
Larribère, Lucette *see* Manaranche, Lucette Larribère
Launay, Michel 60
Laurens, Louis 31, 34
League against Imperialism *see* Congress of Oppressed Nations
Le Beau, Georges 94
Lellouche, Henri 85
Lenin, Vladimir 28–9, 31, 36
Lenoir, Paulette 113
Lenoir, Roland 114, 117
Lestrade-Carbonnel 148, 152
Lévy, Simon 116
Liberté 113, 126, 129, 131, 133, 135–6, 150, 152–4, 156, 160, 162, 166–70, 173, 184, 190–1, 200, 219, 225, 254; *see also El Hourriya*

[305]

INDEX

Ligue française pour la défense des droits de l'homme et du citoyen 26–7, 29, 42
Lledo, Jean-Pierre 203
Lledo, Noël 203
Lodi camp 223, 232–4, 242; see also prison struggles
Loriot, Fernand 29
Loup, Elyette 199, 222
Loup, Jean 199
Lozeray, Henri 39, 43, 91, 132
Lutte sociale 26, 29–30, 33–5, 38–9, 42, 47–8, 56–8, 68, 71, 82, 87, 91, 93, 95–6, 102, 113–14, 118, 122, 124–6

Mahmoudi, Ahmed 61, 72, 76, 91, 102
Maillot, Henri 203–5
Main rouge (Red Hand) 220, 233, 253
Maison Carrée prison 223
Mallet, Théodore 163
Malraux, André 91, 95, 230
Mamdani, Mahmood 14
Manaranche, Lucette Larribère, 129, 157, 200, 225
Mandela, Nelson 258–60
Manifeste du peuple algérien 124–8, 130–1
Manifesto of the 121 241–2, 254
Marcelli, Georges 227–8
Marouf, Mohammed 44, 91, 94, 102, 125, 186, 202, 219–20
Martin, Maurice 102
Martinez, Antoine 200
Martini 202, 219
Marty, André 128, 130–3, 168
Marx, Karl 26, 163
Marxism 1, 4, 34, 116, 133, 155, 159, 161, 202, 221, 225, 253, 274
Masseboeuf, Jean 202, 219
Massu (General) 201, 219, 221, 232–3, 241
Matarasso, Léo 224
Mau Mau uprising 180
Mazoyer, Étienne 34–5, 39, 48
Mazri, Azzedine 190
Mboya, Tom 236
Mekki, Chebba 181
Mella 135
Melouza massacre 220
Menouer, Abdelaziz (Ali) 34–8
Merdaci, Mahmoud 199
Messali, Ahmed 45–6, 94–5, 98–102, 105, 111, 113, 116, 119, 121, 131, 136–7, 149–52, 160, 162, 167, 172, 189; see also ENA; MNA; MTLD; PPA
Mestoul, Mohammed 70
Michel, Fernand-Jules 68–9
Mignot, Elie 102
Minne, Danielle 227
Minne, Jacqueline see Guerroudj, Jacqueline Minne
Minne, Pierrre 165
Mira, Ali 61, 76
Mira, Mohamed 61
Mitidja see Blida–Mitidja peasant protests
Mitterand, François 174
MNA see Mouvement national algérien
Moine, André 133, 169, 181, 190, 199, 222, 241
Moine, Blanche 181, 222
Mollet, Guy 194–6, 229
Monde, Le 219, 230
Monjauvis, Lucien 64, 73, 85
Montagné, Marcel 204
Moore, Barrington Jr 3–4
Morice Line 228–9; see also ALN
Morinaud, Emile 83
Morocco 8, 34–5, 38–40, 43, 122–6, 166–7, 169, 238, 227, 241, 256–60, 263, 269
Moscow 34, 37, 47, 56, 61, 70, 82, 86, 89, 94–5, 113–14, 128, 169, 201, 226, 255, 273, 277
Mostefaï, Chawki 116, 123–4, 136–7, 235, 258, 264
Mostefaï–Susini Agreement 264
Moussa, Hilali 198
Moussaoui, Djillali 205
Mouvement national algérien (MNA) 189, 193, 220, 240, 243, 252; against terrorism 189; attacked by FLN 189; attacks FLN leaders 272; independence negotiations 252; *La Voix du peuple* 189; PCA denounces as counter-revolutionary 243; see also Ahmed Messali; MTLD; USTA
Mouvement pour le triomphe des libertés démocratiques (MTLD) 160–6, 169–72, 181, 184–5, 189, 191, 201, 207; *Algérie libre* 170; factionalism 162–3, 172; see also Abbas, Ferhat; ENA; Messali, Ahmed; MNA; PPA
Mozabites and Mzab Valley 14, 57–8, 73, 135, 169–70, 173–4
MTLD see Mouvement pour le triomphe des libertés démocratiques
Muslims see Algerian Muslim Congress;

[306]

INDEX

Islam; *'ulama*

Naceur, Rafa 62–3, 67, 71
Nahon, Emma 222
Namia, Robert 87, 101
National Federation of Democratic Youth 166
National Revolutionary Party 47
Nehru, Jawaharlal 45
Nekkache, Mohamed Seghir 197
Neplaz, Étienne 237
Neveu, Henriette 133, 149–50, 163
Neveu, Raymond 163
Nkrumah, Kwame 235
North African communist parties 128, 132, 135, 171, 226, 254
North African interfederal congress (1922) 33
North African workers in France 43–5, 57

Oculi, Lise 129
Oran républicain 94, 271, 273
Ordinance of 1 July 1943 126
Organisation armée secrète (OAS) 252–8, 264, 267, 272
Organisation de la résistance populaire 278
Organisation spéciale (OS) 162, 165–6, 168, 172, 184
Orwell, George 104
Ouennouri, Mohamed 222
Oussidhoum, Rabah 101
L'Ouvrier algérien 275
Ouzegane, Amar 82, 88, 91, 95, 97–8, 101–2, 114, 125–8, 130, 132–3, 147, 149–57, 161, 193, 198, 207
Ouzegane, Fattouma 198, 253

Padmore, George 235
Padula, Émile 88, 101
Pan Africanist Congress 277
Papeau, Jean 163
Parisien, Le 233
Parrès, Joseph 124, 151
Parti communiste algérien (PCA) 133; Algerian–European ethnic tensions 162, 172–3; Algerianisation 9, 97, 145, 152–60, 169; Algerians climb party hierarchy 157–9, 161; amnesty and anti-repression campaigns 7, 146, 151–4, 164, 167–8, 170, 172; anti-colonialism 6, 7, 97, 145, 153, 161; anti-fascism 7, 97–8, 101, 104, 120, 152; Arabic radio broadcasts 171, 189–90, 202; Arabic usage 96–8, 153, 156–7, 161; as Algerian not French party 161; as French not Algerian party 168; Caballero affair 191; Charter of union and action 166–7; clandestinity and repression 7–9, 18, 20–1, 23, 113–22, 124–5, 170, 200, 206, 270; congresses and conferences *see* PCA congresses; Constantinois massacre 153, 155, 160; Constituent Assembly 155; demise of 2, 9n4, 267–80; *El Djezaïr el Djedida (New Algeria)* 156, 191, 200; ethnic profile 129–30; *Etudes et documents* 225; external wing 221, 229, 252, 256–7; FFPCA 221, 254, 256; French Union 145, 161, 163; Friends of Democracy 133, 136; generational change 7, 152–3, 157–60; Guerrouf affair 190–1; imagining the Algerian nation 7–9, 120, 261; independence 6, 7, 98, 104, 117, 120, 124, 126–9, 133, 153, 166, 168; international–national dynamic 4–6, 166, 171; Jewish member concerns 169; join armed struggle 190–1, 198–207; launch 6, 49, 95–8; May Day (1945) 136–8; membership 2, 96–7, 102–4, 129, 133, 145–6, 152–3, 155, 159–60, 163–4; military tribunals 113, 121, 241; Morocco–Tunisia–Vietnam 166–9; MTLD discord and PCA expansion 163; Muslim organisations 98, 102, 104, 112, 120; national democratic front 160–1; nationalism 6–9, 102, 128, 157, 164, 167; national question 7–8, 156, 231–2, 270; 'nation in formation' thesis 7, 9, 111–12, 120, 127, 130, 155–6, 168–9, 257; organising in urban shantytowns 163–4; *Our people will overcome* 243–5; patriotic union 128; PCF influence on 2, 7, 9n4, 97, 102, 104, 127–8, 131–4, 145, 152, 161, 163, 168, 270, 274; political–paramilitary networks destroyed 219–20; political pluralism 261, 263; political principles (1954) 172; Popular Front 92, 95, 97–9, 102–4, 120, 171, 270; propaganda war 252–7; proportional representation 172; 270–1; refuse to disband 259–60, 274; right of peoples

[307]

to self-determination 172; rural recruitment 159, 164–5; Second World War 119–22, 128; sovereign national assembly 168–9, 172; structure of 96–7; underground and mass work 7, 114, 120–1, 206, 225, 243; 'Union for Democracy' 155; Yvanez affair 191; *see also* Comintern; North African communist parties; PCF

Parti communiste français (PCF) 5, 10n8, 37, 44, 57, 61–2, 65, 87–9, 92, 113, 122, 138, 145, 242; agrarian revolution 70; *Al-Alam-Al-Ahmar* (The Red Flag) 44; Algeria as 'nation in fact' 194; Algeria as 'nation in formation' 7, 110–11, 120, 149, 168, 183, 232; Algerian communist party 88–9, 95–8; *Al-Raïat-Al-hamra* 46; anti-fascism 5–7, 68, 76, 86, 89–95, 101–3, 110, 125; anti-war campaigns, 34, 39, 40, 119–22; Arabisation 58, 73, 82; banning and repression 7, 48, 56, 113; Barthel circular 90–2; Blida–Mitidja 56–80; Bolshevisation 35–40; *La Caserne/El Kazirna* 34–5; Cold War 145, 163, 183, 193; colonial commission 37–8, 47, 56; colonial question 37, 57, 89–95; congresses and conferences *see* PCF congresses; Constantinois massacre 7, 149–50; demoralised and fragmented (1930) 56–8, 82, 89; departmental-municipal elections 37–8, 40, 87–8, 93; independence call 69, 82–3, 92, 95, 102–3, 117; international-national dynamic 4–6, 103–4; joins Second World War 119–20; launch 5, 30; membership 41, 47–8, 58, 87, 91, 95, 103; Muslim support 35–7, 40, 44, 88, 90, 94; new line purges 6, 46–8; Popular Front 6–7, 89–95; Sidi bel Abbès thesis 30–5; trade unions 30, 41, 48, 56, 91; 'We are no longer in France' 5, 40; *see also* Comintern; PCA

Parti d'avant-garde socialiste 278
Parti de l'union populaire de l'oued-M'zab (PUPOM) 170, 197; *see also* Boudjenah, Sliman
Parti du peuple algérien (PPA) 99, 101–4, 116, 119, 123–4, 128, 133–8, 152, 155–7, 160, 162–3, 191; banning 113, 116; boycott Constituent Assembly elections 155; Constantinois massacre 146–9, 186; derided PCA as PCF region 134; independence 133–4, 146, 162; *L'Action algérienne* 134; May Day (1945) 136–8; social base 99, 103–4, 116; University of Algiers 116, 123, 134

Parti national révolutionnaire (PNR) 47, 70, 72, 75–6
Parti populaire française 115
Patriote, Le 225
Paysan algérien, Le 64–5
PCA *see* Parti communiste algérien (PCA)
PCA congresses
  1st (1936) 96–8; 2nd (1937) 102; 3rd (1946) 154; 4th (1947) 161; 5th (1949) 163; 6th (1952) 168; conferences (1940) 117–18, (1941) 120, (1943) 128, (1944) 133, (1961) 25th anniversary 257
PCF *see* Parti communiste français (PCF)
PCF congresses
  Tours (1920) 29–30; 4th (1925) 37; 5th (1926) 41, 47–8; 7th (1932) 57; 8th (1936) 91; 9th (1937) 102; 13th (1954) 183; 16th (1961) 254; Algerian region congresses and conferences (1925) 37, (1929) 48, (1932) 58, (1933) 70, (1934) 82

peasant struggles *see* Blida–Mitidja peasant protests
Peschard, Raymonde 165–6, 201, 227–8
Pétain, Philippe 113–15, 119, 125, 138
Peuple, Le 278
Peyrouton, Marcel 124–5
Pia, Pascal 105, 113
Planés, Marcel 112
Poincaré, Raymond 33, 44
political space 2, 3, 6–8, 10n5, 81, 92, 103–4, 8, 167, 188, 191, 227–8, 240–1
PPA *see* Parti du peuple algérien
Prague 166, 169, 201, 221, 252, 256–7, 259
Pravda 273
prisons and prison struggles 217–51; campaign for better conditions 233–4; communists organise in 217; execution of FLN activists and FLN retaliations 218, 227–8, 236; politicising criminals 233; literacy classes 236; political prisoners 186, 222–3, 232–3; public and gendered political space 218; reforms 236–7, 256; strikes 50, 233, 236, 240; torture

INDEX

chambers 221–5; underground networks 233; *see also* Camp Morand; Lambèse prison; Maison Carrée prison; Serkadji prison

Radiquet, Paul 58, 62–8, 70–1, 82
Raffini, Georges 101, 114, 117–18, 121, 182, 209
railway workers 26, 31, 43, 41, 48–9, 56, 60, 65, 70–1, 97, 118, 152, 165
Ramdane, Abane 167, 189, 192, 205–6, 208, 217–19, 229, 257
Rassemblement franco-musulman 112
Réalités algériennes et Marxisme 221, 225, 231
Rebah, Nour Eddine 201, 225
Red Crescent (Algeria) 227
Red International of Labour Unions (RILU) 29, 48
Resha, Robert 258–9
Reynaud, Paul 114
Rezkallah, Maître 219
Ricci, Gaston 59–62
Rolland, Romain 45, 95
Rosenberg, Ethel and Julius 172
Rouzé, Michel 94, 124, 151
Roy, M. N. 28
Rueschemeyer, Dietrich 3
Russell, Bertrand 45
Russian Revolution (1917) 1, 5, 6, 28, 30, 56

Saâdane, Chérif 146, 151
Saadoun, Mustapha 203–5, 256–7
Safir, Abdelkader 124
Saharan oil discoveries 255
Sahraoui, Larbi 76
Sahraoui, Mustapha 76
Saïl, Mohamed 101
Saillen, Yvonne 121
Salan, Raoul 219, 235, 252, 254, 260
Salem, Gilberte Serfaty 129, 224
Salem, Harry (pseud Henri Alleg) 120, 129–30, 147; *see also* Alleg, Henri
Salmeron, Antoine 200
Salort, Jacques 121, 200–1, 227–8, 270
Sartre, Jean-Paul 132, 230–1
Schiavo, Henri 40–1, 47–8, 61
Schmitt, Paul 124
Secours populaire (Popular or Red Aid) 93–4, 113, 182, 190
Secteur postal Algérie 254

Section française de l'internationale communiste (SFIC) *see* Parti communiste français
Section française de l'internationale ouvrière (SFIO) *see* Socialist Party
Sen, Sun Yat 45
Serfaty, Gilberte *see* Salem, Gilberte Serfaty
Serkadji (Barberousse) prison 39, 42, 67, 73, 85, 117, 121, 191, 217–18, 220–4, 226–8, 231–4, 236, 240; Barberousse républicain newsletter 233; *Nidham* clandestine network 222; *see also* prison struggles
Serrano, François 71, 119, 125
Sétif massacre *see* Constantinois massacre
Sfaxi 132
Sfindja, Djamal 125
Shaykh Mohamed 236
Sicard, Jeanne 100
Sidi bel Abbès (Red Mecca) 5, 30–5, 37, 48–9, 62, 70, 87, 95–6, 98, 157, 172, 182, 244
Sino-Soviet split 270
Sivan, Emmanuel 2, 75, 104, 159, 269
Slimane, Si 182
Smadja, Albert 223
Smaïli, Ahmed 66, 101, 114, 117, 119, 121, 124–5, 132
Socialist International 1
Socialist Party (SFIO) 26–9, 34, 38, 41–2, 116, 193–4
Soir républicain 113
Soustelle, Jacques 187, 192
South Africa 2–6, 10n7, 48, 104, 128, 162, 235, 258–60, 267, 277; Nelson Mandela and Robert Resha 258–60; OAS 'apartheid for Algeria' 254; Patrick Duncan and Pan Africanist Congress 277; Rand Revolt 33; Second World War 120–1
Souvarine, Boris 29
Soviet Communist Party 36, 273
Soviet Union Great Terror 95, 110
Spanish Civil War 93–4, 99–101, 114; Algerians in International Brigade 101; Britain–France–USSR 101, 112, 114–15; Franco attempts to seize power 93; Spanish Popular Front 92
Spanish in Algeria 16, 21, 92–4, 115, 137–8

[309]

INDEX

Spielmann, Victor 33, 35, 47, 58
Sportisse, Alice Cremadès 97, 129, 155, 166, 172, 184, 190, 225
Sportisse, Bernard 83, 125, 157, 225
Sportisse, Lucien 83–5, 97, 157, 225
Sportisse, William 117, 125, 157, 171, 203, 206, 225, 270
Stalin, Joseph 36, 124, 127–8, 153, 163, 169, 182, 196, 231–2, 257
Stephens, Evelyne Huber 3
Stephens, John 3
strikes 30, 50, 59, 61, 70, 86, 92, 94, 159, 168, 219, 233, 236
Suez crisis 218–19
Susini (General) 252, 264
Syria 40

Taleb, Abderramane 227–8
Taleb, Bouali 122, 137, 209, 227, 256
Taleb, Dji 35
Taleb, Gilberte Chemouilli 113–14, 122, 151, 157, 221, 256, 271
Tamzali, Abdennour 35
Targe, Père 39
Tell, Le 73
Temps modernes, Les 132, 241–2
terror and terrorism 13–14, 95, 110, 113–14, 181, 183, 189, 193, 196, 206, 208, 218, 220, 222, 226, 229–31, 234, 238, 242, 252, 254–5, 258, 260, 271
Thorez, Maurice 7, 68, 69–71, 86, 102, 150; Algeria as 'nation in formation' 7, 110–11, 120, 149, 168, 183, 232; Algerian independence 69, 120; Algerian oil 239; anti-racism 70; revolutionary unity 102, 111; 'we communists, we do not know races' 110–11; *see also* PCF
Tiffou, Constant 241
Tillion, Germaine 114, 200
Timset, Héléne 222
Timsit, Daniel 129–30, 164, 201, 218
Tixier, Adrien 149
Torrecillas, Jean 117, 125
torture 113, 118, 121, 167, 197–8, 219, 221–4, 226, 229–31, 238, 241–2, 256, 272, 278
Touati, Emile 121
Toumi, Abdallah 160
Tripoli conference (1962) 262–4, 268, 273
Trotsky, Leon 5, 34–6, 52n46
Trotskyism 48, 98, 189

Tunisia 8, 45, 89, 166–7, 169, 227, 229, 238, 241, 263, 269

UGSA *see* Union générale des syndicats algériens
UGTA *see* Union générale des travailleurs algériens
'ulama 42, 60, 68, 81, 83, 89, 96, 130–2, 134, 156, 159, 167, 170, 186, 207; *see also* Algerian Muslim Congress; AUMA; Islam
Union démocratique du manifeste algérien (UDMA) 155, 160, 163, 166, 169, 173, 185, 190–1, 196–7, 207
Union des femmes d'Algérie (Union of Women of Algeria, UFA) 129, 157, 165–7, 172, 200, 202, 234, 275–6
Union des jeunes filles d'Algérie (Union of Young Women of Algeria) 113
Union des jeunesses démocratiques d'Algérie (Union of Democratic Youth of Algeria, UJDA) 122, 129, 158, 166, 201, 200–1, 203
Union française (French Union) 145, 161, 163, 202
Union générale des étudiants musulmans algériens (UGEMA) 197, 242, 264
Union générale des syndicats algériens (UGSA) 195, 201, 220, 274; *see also* CGT; UGTA
Union générale des travailleurs algériens (UGTA) 195, 198, 242, 264, 272, 274–6, 277; *see also* CGT; UGSA
Union intercoloniale 38, 43
Union nationale des femmes algériennes (National Union of Algerian Women, UNFA) 275–6
Union syndicale des travailleurs algériens (USTA) 195
United Nations Organisation 134, 136–7, 145, 195, 219
United States 8, 34, 122–6, 132–3, 135, 148, 183, 273; anti-communism 191; perceptions of 153, 163, 183, 253, 273
University of Toilers of the East (KUTV) 34, 61–2, 82, 89
USTA *see* Union syndicale des travailleurs algériens

Vaillant-Couturier, Paul 31–2
Valle 71
Vergès, Jacques 241

INDEX

Vial, Isabel 121
Vichy Algeria 113–20, 125–6, 129, 133,
Vichy regime 114–19, 122, 145
Vidal-Naquet, Pierre 241, 255
Vietnam (Indochina) 8, 38, 57, 130, 166–7, 171, 173, 181, 183–5, 188, 240, 243, 258, 261
Vincent, Lisette 117–18, 121, 132
violence 185–7, 192–8, 208, 218–19
Viollette, Maurice 92–3, 99–100
Voirin, Odet 200
Voix des humbles, La 86, 127, 131
Voix du prisonnier, La 256
Voix du soldat, La 199, 205, 222
Voix indigène, La 82

Weygand, Maxime 114
Wilayas 180, 184, 207, 227, 229, 234, 240, 242, 258, 263, 268–9, 272, 276
Wolf, Eric 17, 19
women 12, 13, 81, 96–7, 122, 128–9, 134, 137, 155, 160, 165–6, 172, 182, 186, 188, 197–200, 217–19, 226–8, 232–4, 244, 275–7; *see also* ALN; Jeunes filles communistes d'Algérie; UFA; UNFA
World Congress of the International Union of Students 166
World Congress of Women against War and Fascism 97
World Federation of Trade Unions (WFTU) 195, 275
World wars
 Anglo-American operation 122–6; Atlantic Charter 123; Battle of Stalingrad (1943) 124; conscription of Algerians 123; First World War 6, 21, 28, 30, 38, 81; German invasion of USSR 119–20; German occupation of France 114–15, 117, 132; Molotov-Ribbentrop Non-aggression Pact (1939) 7, 112, 114, 118; Munich Pact 110; Poland partition of 112; Second World War 7, 110–45, 159, 166, 181, 185, 199–200, 204, 231, 270

144, 149, 166, 181, 186, 197–8, 201, 226–7, 239, 242, 269
Yvanez, Roland 191

Zakaria, Moufdi 58
Zalmaï, Abdelkader 205
Zannettacci, Nicolas 97, 102, 111, 128, 130, 270
Zedong, Mao 166

Yacef, Saâdi 209, 217, 219, 221, 226, 228
Yacine, Kateb 271
Younes 132
Young Algerians *see* Jeunes algériens
Young Communists *see* Jeunesse communiste
youth 33–4, 73, 81, 91, 115, 120, 122, 134,

EU authorised representative for GPSR:
Easy Access System Europe, Mustamäe tee 50,
10621 Tallinn, Estonia
gpsr.requests@easproject.com

www.ingramcontent.com/pod-product-compliance
Lightning Source LLC
Chambersburg PA
CBHW030117240426
43673CB00041B/1309